BEYOND THE VISIBLE ...

Beyond the Visible and the Material

The Amerindianization of Society in the Work of Peter Rivière

Edited by
LAURA RIVAL
and
NEIL WHITEHEAD

OXFORD
UNIVERSITY PRESS

OXFORD
UNIVERSITY PRESS

Great Clarendon Street, Oxford OX2 6DP

Oxford University Press is a department of the University of Oxford.
It furthers the University's objective of excellence in research, scholarship,
and education by publishing worldwide in

Oxford New York

Athens Auckland Bangkok Bogotá Buenos Aires Cape Town
Chennai Dar es Salaam Delhi Florence Hong Kong Istanbul Karachi
Kolkata Kuala Lumpur Madrid Melbourne Mexico City Mumbai Nairobi
Paris São Paulo Shanghai Singapore Taipei Tokyo Toronto Warsaw
and associated companies in Berlin Ibadan

Oxford is a registered trade mark of Oxford University Press
in the UK and in certain other countries

Published in the United States
by Oxford University Press Inc., New York

British Library Cataloguing in Publication Data

Data available

Library of Congress Cataloging in Publication Data

Beyond the visible and the material: the amerindianization of society in the work of
Peter Rivière/edited by Laura Rival and Neil Whitehead.
p. cm.
A collection of 14 papers contributed by worldwide colleagues in honor of Rivière's
work as he nears retirement from the Oxford Institute of Social and Cultural Anthropology.
Includes bibliographical references and index.
1. Indians of South America—Amazon River Region. 2. Ethnology. 3. Rivière, Peter.
I. Rivière, Peter. II. Rival. Laura M. III. Whitehead, Neil L.
F2519.1.A6 B48 2001
981'.100498—dc21   2001036816
ISBN 0–19–924475–8
ISBN 0–19–924476–6 (Pbk.)

1 3 5 7 9 10 8 6 4 2

Typeset in Ehrhardt by
Cambrian Typesetters, Frimley, Surrey
Printed in Great Britain
on acid-free paper by
Biddles Ltd., Guildford & King's Lynn

This book is dedicated to the memory of
Andrew Gray, 1955–1999

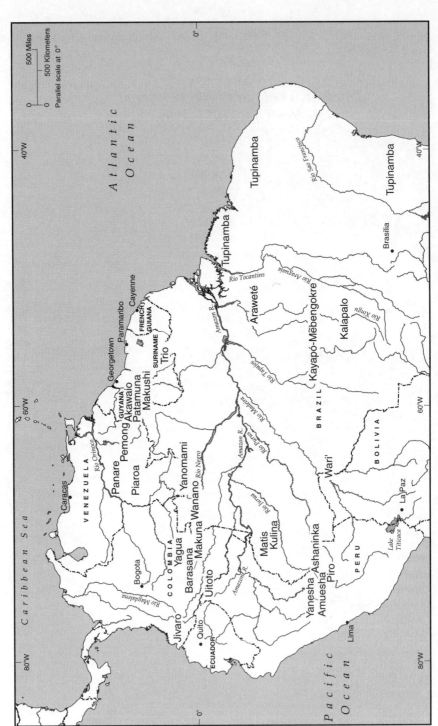

Map 1. General map of South America with the principal groups mentioned in the book

PETER RIVIÈRE

David Parkin, University of Oxford

IT gives me great pleasure as head of the Oxford Institute of Social and Cultural Anthropology (ISCA) to be asked to say a few words prefacing this book on the Amerindianization of society in the work of Peter Rivière, which draws in his current and former colleagues and students who have worked in South America and who can therefore speak to his considerable regional expertise through their own written tributes. But, as well as appreciating his regional work, which is read for its clarity and ethnographic interest by anthropologists working in other regions, we should also acknowledge his considerable theoretical and methodological contributions. In rethinking basic concepts in the understanding of marriage and kinship in his early book *Marriage among the Trio* (1969) and in articles (see for example Rivière 1971) he was doing what was later called deconstruction in anthropology, and although this is hardly a term he would embrace, it illustrates the pioneering nature of his early writings.

Of particular importance was his demonstration of the remarkable Amazonian kinship system, where for instance the local group is often the primary endogamous and politically autonomous unit, yet able discreetly to build up extra alliances, a finding that forced kinship analysts working elsewhere in the world to interrogate long-held assumptions concerning their regions. His reconsideration of marriage and kinship also enabled him to foresee some cultural implications of new reproductive technologies, as instanced in his response to the Warnock Report in 1985 (in *Anthropology Today*), in which he showed how the social consequences and new ideas of relatedness created by test-tube births, artificial insemination, and embryo transplantation and donorship already had parallels in the societies documented by anthropologists. In his book *Individual and Society in Guiana* he was also one of the first to produce a study locating the analysis of individuals within dynamic regional structures, and, as part of this, among the first in the subject to provide systematic studies of regional comparison, through his comparative work on lowland South America, which of course continues.

His scholarly publications are numerous, beginning in 1966 and continuing. The list comprises six monographs, including the recent one entitled *Absent-Minded Imperalism* (1995), and the shorter, popular but important one on Colombus (1998), with a forthcoming full-length biography of Sir Robert Schomburgk, the nineteenth-century scientific traveller. There have also been two major translations of Lévy-Bruhl's work, two editions of McLennan and Lubbock, and countless articles, chapters, and reviews. Nor must we forget the several major public lectures he has given, including the much-cited famous Malinowski Memorial

Lecture on 'The Couvade Reborn', to which some of the chapters of this edited collection return, nor the fact that for five long years, 1974–7, Peter Rivière edited *Man* (as the *Journal of the Royal Anthropological Institute* was then called).

Throughout all this he has been a modest but effective pillar of political and administrative strength in ISCA. He has been teaching at ISCA since 1971, having spent 1962–5 as an anthropology student at the institute, completing his D.Phil. within a year or so after returning from fieldwork in Surinam, having had earlier experiences in Guyana and Central Brazil. His international reputation is long established, but nationally as well he has been a powerful political force for the subject. He was a member of the old SSRC social anthropology committee throughout the 1970s, becoming a chairman in 1979, and managing among other things to get the ESRC to recognize the need by anthropology students to learn the languages of the regions of study and to be allocated extra grants for this (sadly now long since withdrawn). As chairman of the ASA at a time (mid- to late 1980s) when this body was central to the professional and academic activities of British anthropology, he fought to save threatened anthropology posts in universities by protesting directly to vice-chancellors, and often succeeded. Even recently, as chairman of the Faculty of Anthropology and Geography at the University of Oxford, he has helped put in place a number of changes likely to benefit anthropology in the future, often after prolonged, creative encounters with the university administration, which he evidently enjoys. Although he may be within sight of formal retirement, it is clear that he has a long list of projects that will fill up his time thereafter. This volume is, then, a stock-taking by scholars who have been nurtured by Peter Rivière's contributions over the years, and who will continue thus. It also is an opportunity for the subject and for the ethnographic study of lowland South America.

February 2001

CONTENTS

NOTES ON CONTRIBUTORS

KAJ ÅRHEM is Professor of Social Anthropology at Göteborg University (Sweden). He has carried out fieldwork in the Colombian Amazon and in Tanzania. The subjects of his publications range from social organization and human ecology to indigenous religion and cosmology. His most recent books are *Makuna: Portrait of an Amazonian People* (1998, Smithsonian Institution Press) and *Ethnographic Puzzles: Essays on Social Organization, Symbolism and Change* (2000, Athlone Press).

AUDREY BUTT COLSON studied History at London University and Social Anthropology at Oxford. She was University Lecturer in Ethnology at Oxford between 1955 and 1982, and a Fellow of St Hugh's College. She has worked amongst, and published extensively on, the Akawaio (Kapong) of the upper Mazaruni basin, Guyana. She has also worked with the Maroni river Wayana Indians of Suriname and Guyane, the upper Cuyuni river Akawaio and the Pemong of the Gran Sabana, Venezuela. She has been a Research Scholar and Visiting Lecturer at the Instituto Venezolano de Investigaciones Cientificas (IVIC), Caracas, Venezuela. Her publications concentrate on Akawaio and Pemong conceptual systems and syncretisms. They also include joint works in collaboration with the late Revd Fr. Cesáreo de Armellada, Capuchin missionary among the Pemong and an eminent linguist, writer, and scholar.

JEAN-PIERRE CHAUMEIL is Directeur de recherche at the Centre National de la Recherche Scientifique (CNRS), and Deputy-Director of a CNRS research team in Paris (EREA, Équipe de Recherche en Ethnologie Amérindienne). His numerous publications on Amazonian Anthropology include the monograph *Voir, savoir, pouvoir* (1983, Paris: EHESS), and *La Politique des esprits: Chamanismes et religions universalistes* (2000, Nanterre: Société d'Ethnologie, co-edited with D. Aigle and B. de la Perrière).

JANET CHERNELA received her Ph.D. at Columbia University in 1983. She is Professor of Anthropology at Florida International University and Visiting Adjunct Professor in the Center for Latin American Studies at Georgetown University. Her publications include *The Wanano Indians of the Brazilian Amazon: A Sense of Space* (1993, University of Texas Press) and numerous articles, including 'Ideal Speech Moments: A Woman's Narrative Performance in the Northwest Amazon' in *Feminist Studies*, 1995.

PHILIPPE ERIKSON is Lecturer in Anthropology at the University of Paris X-Nanterre (France). His numerous publications on western Amazonian (especially

Panoan) social organization and cosmology include *La Griffe des Aïeux: Marquage du corps et démarquages ethniques chez les Matis d'Amazonie brésilienne* (1996, Spanish translation, Abya Yala, 1999) and *Les Dialogues du rituel: Promenades ethnolinguistiques en terres amérindiennes* (2000, Nanterre: Société d'Ethnologie, co-edited with A. Monod Becquelin).

THOMAS GRIFFITHS is a freelance anthropologist and social development consultant specializing in community mapping and indigenous self-development in Latin America. He is currently working as policy adviser to the Forest Peoples Programme. He is soon to publish a phonological sketch and lexicon of the Nɨpode-Uitoto Amerindian language with the Oxford University Phonetics Laboratory.

PAUL HENLEY is Director of the Granada Centre for Visual Anthropology, Department of Social Anthropology, University of Manchester. In addition to making films on various Venezuelan indigenous groups (Panare, Arawak and Pemon, Warao), he is the author of *The Panare: Tradition and Change on the Amazonian Frontier* (1982, Yale University Press) as well as numerous other articles and monographs, including *South Indian Models in the Amazonian Lowlands*, which was awarded the Curl Essay Prize of the Royal Anthropological Institute in 1994, and later published in an expanded version in the Manchester Papers series by the Department of Social Anthropology, University of Manchester.

VANESSA LEA is a Lecturer in Social Anthropology at UNICAMP University, São Paulo, Brazil. She began studying anthropology with Peter Rivière in the 1970s, and has done fieldwork in Central Brazil since 1977. She is the author of numerous articles on social organization, kinship, and gender. She is presently preparing a book on her research with the Mẽbengokre, entitled *Intangible Wealth and Partiple Persons*.

CLAIRE LORRAIN is Adjunct Professor of Anthropology at McGill University in Montreal. She received her Ph.D. from the University of Cambridge (King's College), and has done fieldwork among the Kulina of south-west Amazonia in Brazil. Her research interests include the nature of Amazonian politics with relation to symbolism and economics, on which she has published in the *Journal of the Royal Anthropological Institute* (2000).

LAURA RIVAL is University Lecturer in Anthropology and Development at the University of Oxford. Her doctoral research was among the Huaorani Indians, on whom she has published numerous articles and two books (*Hijos del Sol, Padres del Jaguar: Los Huaorani de Ayer y Hoy* (1996, Abya-Yala) and *Trekking Through History: The Huaorani of Amazonian Ecuador* (2001, Columbia University Press). She has also carried out research among the Makushi Indians of southern Guyana, and is about to start a new research programme on the political economy of logging in Esmeraldas, Ecuador.

ANNE-CHRISTINE TAYLOR is a Senior Research Fellow of the Centre National de la Recherche Scientifique (CNRS), and Director of a CNRS research team in Paris (EREA, Équipe de Recherche en Ethnologie Amérindienne). She has done extensive fieldwork among the Jivaroan Achuar of Ecuador, and has published numerous articles on various aspects of Jivaroan culture, most recently on the politics of memory. Her current research focuses on indigenous notions of selfhood and mental states.

EDUARDO VIVEIROS DE CASTRO teaches anthropology at the Museu Nacional of Rio de Janeiro. He was Simon Bolívar Professor of Latin American Studies at the University of Cambridge (1997–8), and is currently Directeur de Recherche at the CNRS in Paris. His publications include *From the Enemy's Point of View: Humanity and Divinity in an Amazonian Society* (1992, University of Chicago Press). The chapter here presented is part of a book in preparation, to be published under the title *Conceptual Imagination in Indigenous Amazonia*.

NEIL WHITEHEAD is Professor of Anthropology at the University of Wisconsin-Madison and was supervised by Peter Rivière for his doctoral study of the Caribs in Venezuela and Guyana. He has since written numerous works on the anthropology and history of north-eastern Amazonia and the Caribbean, including *Lords of the Tiger Spirit* (1988, Foris Publications) and *Ralegh's Discoverie of Guiana* (1998, Manchester University Press and Oklahoma University Press). He was the editor of *Wolves from the Sea* (1995, KITLV Press) and the co-editor of *War in the Tribal Zone* (with R. B. Ferguson, 1999, 2nd edition, School of American Research Press) and *Wild Majesty* (with P. Hulme, 1992, Oxford University Press). He is currently writing a book on the Kanaimà (Duke University Press), as well as editing two collected volumes, *Dark Shamans, the Anthropology of Assault Sorcery*, and *History and Historicity in Amazonia*. He is also preparing a new edition of Hans Staden's sixteenth-century account of his captivity among the Tupi. He is Editor of the journal *Ethnohistory*.

LIST OF FIGURES

LIST OF MAPS

LIST OF TABLES

1

Forty Years of Amazonian Anthropology: The Contribution of Peter Rivière

Laura Rival, *University of Oxford,*
and
Neil Whitehead, *University of Wisconsin, Madison*

Amazonian anthropology has always, from the time of the first European encroachments into the Americas, been a highly contested intellectual field. The 'new' world that was encountered in intellect and imagination by the first Europeans provoked fundamental debates about the nature of humanity—whether it was the formal disputation of Las Casas and Sepúlveda in Seville as to the intellectual capacities and spiritual origins of the peoples of America, or Jean de Léry and Antoine Thevet disputing the meaning of the Christian Eucharist within Protestant and Catholic liturgical tradition by reference to the anthropophagic rituals of the Tupinamba. The burdensome heirloom is still with us, in the form of a cultural category characterized by salient naturalistic and idealistic features. Contrary to what happened to native peoples in other 'orientalized' regions of the world, the Amazon Indian became a generic category (the original Human) several centuries before the start of modern anthropology, that is, long before the first fieldwork-based, ethnographic studies were written and published. To this day, Amazonia, understood as the region comprising the river basins of the Amazon and Orinoco and the Atlantic Coast, is the last and favoured refuge of explorers, naturalists, and adventurers of all guises in search of the last savages, and the ultimate wilderness.

Because of the ambiguous way in which the 'Amazon' exists as a cultural category of colonialism defined long before the nineteenth-century wave of European colonial expansion, and also because of the kaleidoscopic variations in indigenous society and culture that can be traced across the last five centuries of encounter, Amazonian anthropology has never provided an ethnological context for easy consensus. The metaphor of the kaleidoscope is apt for it is one that Peter Rivière (1984: 102; 1987*b*: 472) has used himself; it expresses that Malinowskian interest in the 'imponderabilia of everyday life', coupled with a clear appreciation of the way in which such variety may yet be structured, patterned, and limited despite its expressive and performative complexity.

Forty years ago, Amazonian anthropology was no less an intellectually fractured and fissioned field. On the one hand, American cultural ecology proffered a synthesis of the archeological, historical, and ethnological through the *Handbook of South American Indians*, under the editorship of Julian Steward, while, on the other, French structuralism, evinced in the works of Claude Lévi-Strauss, suggested nothing less than a new vision of anthropology, deriving principally from his examination of Amazonian materials. Whatever the strengths and weaknesses that have subsequently emerged in these approaches, they both share, as with their sixteenth-century counterparts, an intellectual interest in Amazonian peoples as exemplars of broad social and cultural process.

In this context Peter was a leading member of the first generation to set new, professional standards of ethnography in Amazonia that stood in counterpoint to generalized uses of indigenous cultural and social materials that largely had been collected second-hand, or by naturalists and explorers whose descriptions of Amazonian Indians were based on a combination of observation and recording techniques inspired by museum and botanical inventories, and whose typologies were cast in strong assumptions deriving from cultural diffusionism and environmental determinism.

The close engagement with living peoples that ethnographic projects require in turn meant that broad theoretical explanation was insufficient, and often quite mistaken, as to the intricacy and persistence of the 'tropical forest cultures' that the *Handbook of South American Indians* had tended to dismiss as derivative of, or, lacking the capacity of the kinds of socio-cultural development apparent from the Andean and circum-Caribbean regions. In particular, this new ethnography has largely opposed the general framework of cultural materialism that remained significant for other scholars, especially in the United States, and certainly shows the inadequacies of explanatory models that present autochthonous Amazonians as environmentally determined through a failure to recognize endogenous development as possible. It is the purpose of this introductory essay to reflect on the emergence of Amazonian ethnography in the last forty years, to try and discern in retrospect what the prospect for future studies, their methodology and problematic, could and should be. To this end, and as was the case in the original conference at Linacre College, University of Oxford, which was the occasion for many of the papers to be first drafted, we will take stock of the specific contributions made by an emphatically *social* anthropology to the field of Amazonian studies.

For example, Peter Rivière, a leading figure in British social anthropology, has made key contributions to the debate opposing 'materialists' and 'mentalists' (see in particular Rivière 1969*a*, 1984, 1987*a*, and, more recently, 1997). This commitment to and interest in the particularities of Amazonian social processes, is not an abstract interest in the 'particular', understood as a theoretical commitment in the manner of the Boasians. Rather, the particular is important as a means to connect theory, methodology, and context. Lowland South American groups are not bearers of distinctive traits to be inventoried and classified, but organized totalities responding to specific social rules, laws, and constraints. Interest in the particular, therefore, results from an appreciation of the necessity of accurate scholarship, no less than brave new worlds of theory, as Rivière's work on the dialectical relationship between cosmological schemas and forms of social organization demonstrates, work that has inspired Erikson's and Chaumeil's analyses of blowpipe symbolism (this volume).

THE DIALECTICS OF AMAZONIAN SOCIAL CLASSIFICATIONS

This kind of scholarly practice has been fundamental in both establishing the intellectual outlines for anthropology in the Guianas (see chapters by Butt Colson and Whitehead), and demonstrating the importance of this region to the overall anthropology of Amazonia. Discussion of social classifications in Amazonia, for instance, of the meaning and practice of affinity and consanguinity, could hardly begin without Rivière's seminal contribution on the Trio, or Overing Kaplan's discussion of the Piaroa. Subsequent debates on the nature of Amazonian kinship derive much of their force from the way in which they relate to Rivière's (1984: 42) insights into the constructed and manipulated categories of Amazonian kinship and have served to allow illuminating distinctions to be drawn between the northeastern, western, and south central Amazonian societies with regard to the politics of marriage exchange (see also Thomas 1972 and Kaplan Overing 1975). We now understand that the ideal settlement is composed of a set of siblings co-residing with their spouses and children, who do not differentiate, terminologically or otherwise, between the fact of consanguinity and the fact of co-residency, and this endogamous nature is often based on a peculiar combination of polygyny and brother–sister relationship. The challenge is to develop conceptual tools for the positive characterization of societies which are intrinsically amorphous and highly individualistic (Rivière 1984: 4), and lack formal social groupings such as clan, moiety, lineage, or age-set. Rivière's solution was to identify a fundamental and invariant social structure, to which he most often gave the name of 'settlement', and which he morphologically described as being constituted according to five principles. A settlement core is constituted through cognatic descent; kinship is expressed by a two-line prescriptive relationship terminology; there is an emphasis on co-residence in ordering relationships, and uxorilocality is the preferred residence rule; finally, settlements are endogamous, small, and impermanent. Moreover, this social structure is reinforced by indigenous ideals regarding who should live with whom, and why. For instance, the value of the nuclear family in relation to the extended kindred is stressed in most systems, and so is the strength of mother–daughter solidarity, and the salience of sibling relationships as structural links between the nuclear families composing a settlement. Today, as he has indicated in his contribution to Carsten and S. Hugh-Jones (Rivière 1995*b*), he would reformulate these principles around the concept of the 'house', and develop an analysis of Amazonian social organization germane to those proposed by Lea and Århem in this volume.

Thus, prescriptive marriage rules are carefully distinguished from descriptive ones in *Marriage among the Trio*, whose author insists that expressing these rules in genealogical terms is misleading, because such expression does not correspond to the indigenous point of view, which expresses relationships in categorical, rather than genealogical, terms. Trio social philosophy works at conceptually blurring genealogy and co-residence. The extent to which these rules are followed in practice is therefore crucial, for if most marriages seem to occur between individual members of the prescribed categories, the actual proportion of marriages between individuals in the correct genealogical relationship is nowhere very high (Rivière 1984: 53; 1969*a*: 143–8). Yalman (1962, 1971) also tried to show that prescriptive alliance does not necessarily operate between enduring groups. While debating the nature of a highly affinal prescriptive terminology, Rivière was acutely aware that affinity as politics means that marriage includes replication as well as reciprocation, a point further elaborated by Viveiros de Castro (this volume). *Marriage among the Trio* was the first extensive and rigorous ethnographic work entirely dedicated to Amazonian kinship systems, and exploring all aspects of post-marital residence arrangements, a crucial social institution throughout Amazonia. If it is less read today than *Individual and Society in Guiana*, it is almost certainly because the elucidation of marriage with the sister's daughter is no longer considered an important theoretical question. It is a question which, as Rivière readily admits himself (in an interview conducted by Laura Rival on 15 November 1999), can today be settled in two pages, rather than in a full-length monograph.

From *Marriage among the Trio* to his most recent exposition of Amazonian kinship (1993), Rivière has shown a determination to forestall the import of exogenous models to conceptualize Amazonian social forms by carefully avoiding the mention of 'Dravidian', or 'Dravidianate', systems. Indeed, 'Dravidian' does not appear in the index of *Individual and Society in Guiana*, where, building upon his previous attempt to formalize kinship structures and marriage rules, he gives a characterization of kinship system and social organization in the Guianas, and, in a cross-cultural perspective, Amazonia, based on a simple, economical, and highly effective choice of terms.[1] The analytical discussion, always limpid and perspicuous, is invariably supported by a remarkable knowledge of empirical facts, as well as by an eagerness to engage with the regional ethnography. The argument, in the purest British style of social anthropology, goes from the most concrete to the most ideal, from kinship terminologies and associated behaviour patterns to underlying principles of social classification, and this, without ignoring exceptions, so that data can be reinterpreted (Rivière 1969*a*: xi).

In retrospect, after years of zealous efforts by a number of specialists to prove or disprove the existence of Dravidian systems in Amazonia, the suspicion[2] that Dumont's theory creates a false problem for the region is being proved right. No one will question the fact that Henley's (1996) recent discussion of Dravidian systems, although partly contradicting Rivière's rejection of the 'invented intellectual puzzle', is directly inspired by Rivière's apparently banal remark that 'in larger villages there tends to be a predominance of affinal links and in smaller settlements consanguineal ties' (Rivière 1984: 35). And exactly the same can be said about Viveiros de Castro's and Fausto's (1993) discussion of potential affinity, which detaches the notion of affinity, not only from the genealogical referent of cross-cousin, but also from kinship altogether. Although Rivière has never talked about potential affinity as a metaphysical principle, he was the first author to note that not all affinal relations are the same and to differentiate affines from potential affines, and to contrast affinability (i.e. the potential for becoming an affine) from affinity, as well as related from unrelated affines (Rivière 1984: 56).

Rivière's stress on the fact that 'throughout the region it is the affinal relationships that are politically important because they contain the potential for expressing hierarchy' (Rivière 1984: 73) stimulated Joanna Overing and her students to spend much time arguing that consanguineal relationships too are political, albeit expressing politics, not of difference and hierarchy, but of egalitarianism and identity. The discussion of the genealogical nature of cross-ness is pursued by Dieter Heinen (forthcoming), while the debate about the politics of alterity and affinity is continued by Viveiros de Castro, Henley, and Chernela (this volume). Lorrain discusses hierarchy and egalitarianism in the context of gender relations, and Taylor, Århem, and Rival take up the issue of consanguineality and conjugality.

Rivière's examination of Amazonian social categories has also led to the formulation of another influential principle, that of 'political economy of people', and contributed centrally to the debate on the Amazonian notion of personhood. By political economy of people, is meant that wealth in people (and not in material goods) constitutes the basis for exchange, distribution, and their regulation. The dynamics of village leadership reflect the fact that 'scarcity in the region is not of natural resources but of the labour with which to exploit them' (Rivière 1984: 90). The social and political consequences of the fact that it is people who are in short supply are unravelled in a number of publications that try to elucidate the basis of political authority in societies lacking coercion and control over scarce resources. This is also one of the issues examined by Lea and Århem in this volume.

The ethnographic observation that the Guiana village 'is a single-cell political unit that cannot survive internal division and competition' (Rivière 1984: 80) constitutes the basis of Rivière's analytical reflection on political processes in Amazonia, where any dissension in a settlement immediately leads to some insiders turning into new outsiders. Internal dissensions, like contact with outsiders, are often articulated in terms of sickness and witchcraft: 'any community contains the seeds of its own dispersion [as] there are not only few means for mediating disputes but there are mechanisms that actively encourage them' (Rivière 1984: 74).

Cosmological ideas relating to the causation of death and sickness often lead to dispute, and are part and parcel of political processes. Sorcery accusations and the aetiology of sickness also contribute to rendering the population scarce; 'they reflect worries about the total or partial disablement of human resources' (Rivière 1984: 91). The original inspiration for this idea is unmistakably Evans-Pritchard's work on Azande witchcraft,[3] and although the idea that sickness represents a failure in social relationships as well as the malfunctioning of human organisms as such may appear rather functionalist today, this idea nevertheless represented a real insight into Amazonian sociocultural systems. It allowed a move away from the prevalent negative characterization of Guianese societies (absence of any enduring social groupings, impermanence of settlements, high mobility of the population, and so forth), in order to explore politics as these societies understand it (that is, as based on personal autonomy, egalitarian structures, and the dispersion of power), and, finally, to discuss for the first time the indigenous concept of power—political or otherwise (see also Butt Colson and Whitehead in this volume).

A different analytical framework might apply today, centred on the fundamental discontinuity between the body and the soul (Rivière 1974*a*). All Amazonianists share the intuition, which none feels confident enough to articulate into a theory yet, that it is this placing of the human body at the very core of politics (see Whitehead in this volume) that renders the management of social distance extremely difficult in the region, and mediation, or some form of solidarity with outsiders, hardly possible at all. This intuition is developed in several of the book's contributions, particularly those of Henley and Chernela, who discuss the mediating role of ceremonial dialogue, hospitality, and political asylum. Århem, Chaumeil, and Erikson, for their part, show the intricate links between trade, life-cycle rituals, and continuity, while exploring the issue that despite extreme isolationism and radical dichotomization of the settlement from other settlements and/or from the forest, social relationships with the 'outside' do exist, and non-hostile social spaces beyond the community level are created. Not all Amazonian societies use trade to break settlement isolation, or trade partnerships to offer social and mystical protection from outsiders. Solidarity between settlements and the existence of intermediary positions between total insiders and absolute outsiders, that is, the establishment of social relationships with people with whom there is no known kinship or affinal ties, are often precarious. This is why Viveiros de Castro and Taylor, in contrast with Henley and Chernela, stress the role of warfare in creating links of exchange and interdependency between communities. Whitehead and Butt Colson, who focus on mystical predation which instantly transforms male insiders (fellow villagers, kin) into outsiders (complete others, cannibal killers), show that the problem that remains to be solved is not so much whether trade or warfare is the dominant source of inter-community social linkages, but to find ways of speaking about Amazonian sociality which do not reduce the analysis to the antinomies of hypo-sociality founded on the morality of consanguinity between insiders, that is those who share a common residence, and hyper-alterity based on outside predation. What needs theorizing is what makes someone an insider as opposed to an outsider, and, as Rivière has long realized, this requires a genuine understanding of gender relations.

Women, and their economic exploitation by men, play a central role in Rivière's model of Amazonia's political economy, which was seen as being primarily concerned with the management of scarce human resources among slash-and-burn cultivators, mainly of bitter manioc, for whom the conjugal pair represents a unit of economic self-sufficiency, but in a political context which binds leadership with generosity and increased food production. In *Marriage among the Trio*, Rivière examined the politics of marriage, and in his famous article 'Of Women, Men and Manioc' (see also Rivière 1984: 90 ff.) it is the general question of the relationship between men and women which, through the varying political and economic position of women in several north-west Amazonian societies, he set out to explain. The argument that the processing of manioc products and the time invested in the task highlight the political manipulation of women's work by men is too well known to be rehearsed in any great length here.[4]

The validity, if not the originality of this proposition, stems from his use of Claude Meillassoux and Terry Turner (Rivière 1984: 41) to wedge new arguments against Marvin Harris's cultural ecology: it is not proteins, but the agents of production and reproduction, that is, women, who are scarce resources. Settlements are in competition with each other for the recruitment of such scarce resources, and the natal family achieves political status and autonomy by retaining control over the productive and reproductive capacities of its young women. Like a number of Melanesianists (most notably Godelier 1982, Josephides 1985, and Strathern 1987), Rivière and others found some validity and inspiration in neo-Marxist and feminist explanations of the exploitative nature of conjugal economic relations. His conclusion that whereas the relationship between those of the same sex is egalitarian, that between those of the opposite sex is asymmetrical, with women in the subordinate position, is very similar to the one put forward by Collier and Rosaldo (1981), who are not mentioned in his work (for example in chapter 7 of *Individual and Society*), almost certainly because Collier's and Rosaldo's bride-service model is itself derivative from Turner's work on uxorilocality among the Kayapó. Discussion of gender politics stands also in marked contrast to the psychoanalytical versions of feminism proposed by a number of North American cultural anthropologists (in particular Murphy and Murphy 1974, and Gregor 1985; for a brief overview, see Rival, Slater, and Miller 1998: 320), who proposed a Freudian interpretation of masculine sexual frustrations, anxieties, and defensive reactions as expressed in Amazonian myths, rituals, and other cultural practices.

The originality of his position was also reflected in a pragmatic recognition of the limits to the exploitation of women's labour; women do not appear to see themselves as inferior to men, and, more to the point, people are not just scarce resources, they are individuals, who can at any time reassess the competence and power of their leaders, and decide to cease to be their followers and to support their personal influence. Individual freedom of action cannot be entirely controlled. This is why he has always been keen to stress that it is the nature of the individualism so often noted by Amazonian ethnographers that needs further analysis. And although Rivière has not thought about individualism in terms of the postmodern notion of body politics and performativity,[5] he has, before anyone, recognized and extensively discussed the dialectics between individualism and gender politics in Amazonia.

In this volume, Lea, Lorrain, and Griffiths, and to some extent, Rival and Taylor, continue the debate on gender politics in Amazonia, in a way that stresses the contribution of Peter Rivière, as all these authors adopt an approach that he would characterize as political economy, and examine the constitution of gender relations in the context of other relationships such as kinship, politics, and ritual. Lorrain, in particular, discusses the epistemological limits of analysing lowland South American institutions and social arrangements in terms of sexual antagonism, hierarchy, and power asymmetry, while Lea shows the limits of analysing uxorilocality as the expression of the means by which men can exercise a more effective control over women. Lea finds that, ironically, Terry Turner's thesis that married daughters with husbands and children who continue to live with their parents make it possible for older men to control people, particularly younger men, applies more to Guianese societies than it does to Kayapó society, for which the model was originally intended.

Whereas in *Individual and Society* Rivière seems to have let the question rest with the conclusion that individualism is an attribute of the atomistic social systems that the individuals constitute, he has clearly brought elements that have allowed others to develop a more satisfactory theory of the created person in Amazonia. For example, throughout his career, he has stressed, first the detachability (Rivière 1974*a*, 1987*b*), then the 'unconfinability', of the Amazonian soul (Rivière 1999). He has also insisted on the importance of indigenous ideas about shared substance as a constraint on individual freedom. Rivière's idea that 'individualism', for lack of a better sociological term, resulted in the Guianas from the fact that 'societal and individual relationships remain[ed] at the same order of complexity' (Rivière 1984: 98), anticipated Seeger, Da Matta, and Viveiros de Castro's (1979) thesis that Amazonian societies are not structured by sociological units, but in terms of the circulation of symbols and substances which guarantee social continuity and reproduction more effectively than the lineal transmission of physical substances. And when new ethnographic work on the central Gê and Tukanos became available in the late 1970s to 1980s, he was then able to confirm his intuition that no distinction can be made in Amazonia between the reproduction of society and the reproduction of the person, for social structures relate to the construction of the individual and the fabrication of the body, rather than to the definition of groups and the transmission of goods, as, for instance, in Africa.

Rivière has also repeatedly stressed that there is considerable variation within the region as to the extent to which the reproduction of the individual (as a social being) and the production of society (as sets of social formations) are aspects of one and the same process. Several contributions to this volume illustrate this point, in particular those of Lea, Henley, Chaumeil, and Erikson. Rival stresses the need to elucidate individual capacity through the dynamics of multiplication as distinctively and specifically Amazonian. Rethinking the articulation between the generative powers of individuals and society as a relational system, as well as the role of the nuclear family and domestic units in linking up individual bodies into relational chains, should allow us to propose an updated version of individual and society in Amazonia.

WRITING HISTORY AND COMPARING CULTURES

The question of history has been prominent in anthropology for the last two decades and it seems appropriate to try and delineate how this might affect the search for the invariant principles of social construction that were so much the substance of early professional ethnography of the region. Peter Rivière started his career with the study of the Trio, a Carib group which he would to this day describe as a self-contained, bounded culture unscarred by contact with non-Amerindians; and he is presently writing important historical books, such as his splendid volume on Robert Schomburgk and the Pirara incident, *Absent-Minded Imperialism*, which was published in 1995, and a forthcoming biography of the nineteenth-century scientific traveller Sir Robert Schomburgk. This should not be interpreted as a shift from an ahistorical, monographic approach taking the isolated community as a microcosm of society to a focus on the ways in which 'isolation' has erased or masked the complex and diversified historical trajectories of native societies.

Ethnographic understanding cannot be achieved without a sense of history, which Amazonianists have so often been chided for lacking. As a result, it could never be convincing to hear the suggestions of the cultural ecologists as to the inherently limited nature of native Amazonian cultural opportunity for economic development, nor that an apparent intellectual disinterest in history, as structuralist readings of myth often seemed to imply, would be an adequate point at which to let the matter rest. Appreciation of the historical nature of indigenous sociocultural development means that ethnographic interests need to be wider than Amerindian village life and to encompass the larger national society in which indigenous people are ultimately embedded. Despite his claim that he ended up doing fieldwork among a Brazilian ranching community purely to please the Director of the University of London's newly founded Institute of Latin American Studies, who had appointed him in 1966 as the first Senior Research Fellow, 'had no enthusiasm for Amerindians', and wanted the Institute to research Latin, not native, people (Rivière 2000*a*: 34), Rivière's work *The Forgotten Frontier: Ranchers of North Brazil*, like Charles Wagley's *Welcome of Tears*, underlines the need both to situate social and cultural facts historically, and, in anticipation of much current work on 'cultural flows' and 'world systems', to define societies and cultures as inherently connected to larger political and economic systems.

Furthermore, like Audrey Butt Colson, who had already begun her important work on the Akawaio, Rivière displayed in his early work a fine appreciation of the way in which earlier materials, such as the somewhat scattered work of William Curtis Farabee, Niels Fock, and Walter Roth dealing with various aspects of the society and material culture of the Guiana highland peoples, though not ethnographies of professionals, could none the less be mined for the basic elements of a historiographical understanding. Together they have given an example of the integration of history and ethnography that was inspirational then and still highly relevant now. A whole generation of Amazonianists has therefore learnt the names of Humboldt, Schomburgk, Crevaux and Coudreau, or Brett and Im Thurn, Brown and Hilhouse, Kappler and Koch-Grünberg, Stedman, Spruce, Bates, and so forth. All these nineteenth-century materials were precursors for the professional anthropology of the twentieth century and, as we step into the twenty-first, this integration of historical materials into ethnographic interpretation clearly emerges as a key aspect of anthropological endeavour, and Rivière clearly emerges as a key figure in the transmission of that sense of history even more strongly, both with regard to highland Guiana in *Absent-Minded Imperialism*, and with regard to the history of anthropology itself in his work on William R. Smith and John F. McLennan and the Aberdeen roots of British social anthropology.[6]

We need to establish a clear separation between Western historiography and indigenous historicity. Names of tribes are not purely objective historiographic data, and European history is not native history. At the same time anthropologically informed readings of European texts has been shown to be a viable source of historical ethnographic data (Whitehead 1998), just as an interest in historicity has alerted us to the forms of historical consciousness that proliferate amongst these stereotypical 'peoples without history'. In this way there are a number of inter-linked tasks that ethnography must take seriously. We will need to reflect on Amazonian notions of time, in particular the ways in which 'time is embedded in and represented by space' (Rivière 1984: 99), and how notions of time may relate to the construction of histories and senses of historicity. Amazonian historicity may thus be conceived as the diversity of these societies or the degree to which they incorporate the notions of time, change, and space. There is possibly in all these cultures, as in European folk cultures, a continuous, non-linear time, which is always there, and is indistinguishable from the cosmos of which it forms a part.

This continuous time is just like space; temporal discontinuities are located in continuous time in the same way as settlements are dispersed throughout the forest, for these rather amorphous societies exist within a narrow time scale, often imposed by the ferocity of colonial occupation that effectively erased, through displacement, dispersion, and disease, the earlier landscapes of memory. The contemporary settlement is not only formed by co-ordinates of time and space, but it is also constituted by a network of social relationships which are ordered by a system of classification that is self-perpetuating. It is a system that not only allocates people in this generation but ensures appropriate reallocation in the next. It is the combination of these factors that gives meaning to the present and assurance of continuity. There is in the present proof of the past and promise of the future, as Whitehead's analysis of the shamanic warfare of prophets and death-shamans illustrates. Similarly, Århem's contribution, which focuses on the time–space dimension in which Tukanoan societies develop, makes this point in a different way. Århem follows Rivière's (1984) careful consideration of history as a factor of change in interpreting ethnographic facts collected in the present, such as, for instance, the size of settlements. Lea's paper also stresses the importance of the development process and of family cycles within Kayapó society. It is because many Amazonian societies exist in a narrow time scale that minimal differences exist between synchronic and diachronic perspectives (Rivière 1984: 102), and that the settlement (or the house) as a process becomes the relevant level of social analysis. This also explains why social determinants and historical factors are more important than ecological ones in explaining size of settlements, and why village history is political history (Rivière 1984: 31).

Differing approaches to native historicity may thus lead to an attempt to understand the historical experience of those who have undergone domination and colonization, or what these historical events mean today, or even temporality from a native perspective. For example, Rivière (1993) reminds us that generational continuity is often articulated with reference to the principles of substitution and replication (see Århem's, Lea's, and Taylor's contributions), and expressed in botanical metaphors, a point developed in Rival's discussion of Makushi use and representation of manioc seed and clone. Rather than a substantive engagement with the particularities of actual history, some theorists prefer, like Lévi-Strauss and all Amazonianists influenced by French structuralism, to explore indigenous understandings of time and space, though it is not always clear how this study of historicity can be divorced from the actual uses and construction of indigenous histories. Rivière both takes a historical perspective on ethnographic materials, and treats historical materials anthropologically.

A similar hesitation exists for many anthropologists with regard to comparative projects and Amazonia has not generated such attempts with any regularity. This has possibly resulted from an understanding of comparative studies as intensive investigations limited to a particular region or a homogeneous group of societies, and offering new hypotheses on a solid basis of reams of ethnographic facts (Evans-Pritchard 1951; Radcliffe-Brown 1952; Rivière 1984: 6–9; 1995*d*: 301). But such exercises would allow Amazonianists to avoid the shortcomings of idealist sociologism (for example, Clastres), and empiricist sociologism (for example, Chagnon), two forms of sociologism that mirror naturalism, and fail to identify and explain the cross-cultural variability of Amazonian social systems.[7]

The ways in which Peter Rivière has pioneered cross-cultural comparisons in

north-eastern Amazonia, and then Amazonia, have been many and varied, starting
with his activities as a teacher. In 1967 he taught the first full-fledged course on the
indigenous societies of lowland South America to be taught in a British university,
and each of his courses, which have been enormously popular with students, has
been designed and taught as an exercise in comparative analysis.[8] That Peter
Rivière's next big writing project after completing Schomburgk's biography should
be, in his own words 'a comparative study of lowland South American native
culture based on the notions of essence and process' is hardly surprising. He has
throughout his career demonstrated what could well be described as a passionate
curiosity for Amazonian ethnographic facts, as well as an unremitting eagerness to
examine the local theories through which these facts are ordered and acquire meaning. In his use of the comparative approach, new insights are achieved by asking
the right question, even if the answer he gives is not always the correct one. A good
illustration of this is his comparative work on the correlation between manioc
processing and the political status of women, in which he tried to find a sociological explanation by comparing differences in social morphology (in the Maussian
sense), and then checking for its cross-cultural validity. A cultural construction
(women are in short supply, and safe, marriageable women even more so), the
endogamous rule, and an aetiology of sickness based on sorcery accusations, which
reflect worries about the total or partial disablement of human resources (Rivière
1984: 91), all combine in his explanation, thus highlighting that a few comparable
principles underlying social action and social thought generate the infinitely variable forms of observable behaviour.

   It is important to stress that many consider the comparative method to be of
prime validity first and foremost within Amazonia (for example, compare the ways
in which the different groups studied by Butt Colson and Whitehead interpret
cannibal rites and construct the veracity of Kanaimà* accusations), and would be
reluctant to engage in the comparative analysis of, for instance, gender and sexuality in Amazonia and Melanesia (see the forthcoming volume edited by Don Tuzin
and Thomas Gregor, to be published by Cambridge University Press). Such
comparative efforts are doomed, if the fundamental difference that exists between
these two ethnographic universes, in particular the gulf separating their distinctive
symbolico-religious classifications, is not recognized. What makes Amazonia
absolutely unique and yet little understood, apart from the failure to properly
historicize and compare our understanding of ethnographic practice, is its
shamanic world-view; that is, the deep-seated belief in the dual nature of reality,
which is both visible and invisible, and in constant transformation. In the highly
transformable shamanic world, in which identities are constantly recycled, relations to the phenomenological world are shaped in a way that grants maximal sociological impact to religion. Peter strongly holds that before comparing the meanings
of social order and of the person (particularly the gendering of persons) in
Amazonia and Melanesia, we need to have a clearer view of cultural regularities by
comparing differences within Amazonia itself.

The design of cross-cultural comparative models is an intellectual endeavour properly questioned today, but which may yet be regarded as a valid intellectual pursuit, indeed one that remains the main task of anthropology.[9] All the contributors to this volume share the view that cross-cultural comparative research within Amazonia is an essential step towards the successful contribution of Amazonian anthropology to the general theoretical development of social anthropology. Because fieldwork-based research started comparatively late in this region of the world, and because it has been preceded, and is still paralleled, by so much non-ethnographic Western thinking and writing, the immense task of discussing comparatively the now substantial and growing Amazonian ethnography is still largely ahead of us. It is in great part thanks to Peter's relentless effort to develop cross-cultural analyses of Amazonia's unique social structures and cosmological systems that the way ahead for future research is clearly signposted. His ability to sustain a two-way dialogue between Amazonian thought categories and social meanings, on the one hand, and key anthropological concepts such as descent, affinity, marriage, hierarchy, gender, body, soul and spirit, on the other, is an inspiration to all Amazonianists.

Together the thirteen essays collected in this volume contribute to the advancement of Amazonian anthropology in a number of ways. Most importantly through the way in which they question the basis of consanguinity and affinity, two fundamental categories commonly regarded as constitutive of Amazonian social formations, and often used to mark the dialectical relationship between 'insiders' and 'outsiders'. As such, they attempt to go beyond the received view that insiders or consanguineal (i.e. real) kin form the ideal society of true humans against, but also with the aid of, outsiders (affines, enemies, and non-humans), whose creative and generative powers which must be tamed and gradually incorporated play a vital role in the making and sustaining of society. Taken as a whole, these contributions explore the notions of consanguinity, affinity, insiders, and outsiders in all their complexity in four different ways.

The first proposition comes from Viveiros de Castro (and to some extent from Taylor as well), who examines what is 'given' and what is 'constructed' in both consanguinity and affinity, thus modifying his recent thesis that whereas consanguinity in Amazonian kinship systems is achieved and constructed, affinity is 'natural' and 'given'. Viveiros de Castro now formulates the problem in a way which aspires to reconcile Lévi-Strauss with Dumont. With his 'grand unified theory of Amazonian sociality', he proposes that if Amazonian consanguinity, which he now defines as a mode of affinity, needs affinity to be defined, the reverse is not true, for affinity is 'axiomatically primitive'. This leads him to contend that the soul is 'affinal' and the body 'consanguineal', and that relations between kin are not culturally derived from naturally given corporeal connections.

The second proposition, which argues that there exists a wide range of positions mediating between total insiders (consanguineal kin) and absolute outsiders (enemies, captors, and cannibal predators), is mainly concerned, in Chernela's own words, with 'boundary permeability'. Chernela, Henley, Butt Colson, and Whitehead all use Rivière's work, in particular his 1970 essay 'Factions and Exclusions in Two South American Village Systems', and his 1971 essay 'The Political Structure of the Trio Indians as Manifested in a System of Ceremonial Dialogue', to understand the ways in which the non-closure of settlements is obtained through ceremonial dialogues (Henley), the ways in which groupness is created through speech acts, including verbal hostility (Chernela), or how and why insiders may become cannibal killers (Butt Colson and Whitehead). Chernela discusses the means by which the Wanano avert the social and mystical dangers posed by outsiders through the expression of solidarity in the context of fragmentation. Their boundary-related behaviour stems from the necessity of establishing political unity beyond the settlement level. Henley further shows that ritual functions as one of the main institutional mechanisms through which settlement isolation is broken. Despite their ideological stress on autonomy and self-sufficiency, Panare communities are dependent on others, and integrated into wider social worlds, not through hostility, warfare, and predation, but through rites of passage that mark the individual life cycle. More generally, relationships with people with whom there are no known kinship or affinal ties are established in an effort to overcome the dual opposition of hyper-sociality and hyper-alterity.

Århem, Lea, Chaumeil, and Erikson offer a third way of questioning insider/outsider dualism by focusing on generational continuity, descent, and consanguinity. Their contributions follow Rivière in demonstrating the existence of mechanisms and institutions that counter the extreme isolationism of settlements, and the fragmentation of the social field. One strategy to counter such fragmentation is to stress the importance of generational contiguity and genealogical connections over time, a strategy clearly at work in the lineal ideologies discussed by these four authors. Århem, following Hugh-Jones (1995), exposes in the clearest and most synthetic fashion the fact that Makuna consanguinity covers an ambiguous structure open to two alternative gendered readings. In the male and, in this society, ideologically dominant, reading, consanguinity becomes agnation (Descent House stressing consanguineal ties between Father–Son and Brother–Brother), as it emerges in the Yurupari male initiation rituals. In the female reading, consanguinity, which is procreative, commensal, and endogamous (Consanguineal House), corresponds to uterine kinship, as it is experienced through daily life and shared residence, as well as through ritual exchanges of food between hosts and guests, and kin and affines. With social change and modernization, larger and more stable communities constituted on the supersedence of exogamic, agnatic groups by village-wide uterine kinship, replace the *maloca* as the House Society model.

Chaumeil and Erikson similarly stress the symbolic and ritual construction of male lines of descent among the Yagua and the Matis, while Chernela shows that among the Wanano group identity, 'descent', and 'genealogy' are forged in the present through a ritual reconstruction of the past. Butt Colson's analysis of Itoto

(Kanaimà) also confirms Århem's double understanding of consanguinity in various ways. She explains that not only are Kanaimà killing techniques understood to be passed on from Father to Son and from Brother to Brother, but also that 'where several brothers live with their father and form an operative group, they tend to attract Itoto (Kanaimà) accusations'. In other words, Kanaimà assassinations both create and destroy agnation, seen as the antithesis of endogamous consanguinity based on the incorporation of affinity through residence, collaboration between in-laws, and, more importantly, the solidarity and continuity of Mother–Daughter and Sister–Sister female relationships, seen by the Pemong and Akawaio as the real source of stability and continuity down the generations.

Once we take into account that Lea may be underestimating the role of Kayapó men's houses (emphasized by Turner, and now on the wane), her thesis that the Mother-in-law grounded in matrifocal residential units where she lives with her daughters and sisters and where she reigns over transient men, is at the centre of Kayapó society may also be understood according to the model proposed by Århem. Lea's decision to focus solely on the continuity of uterine lines may be interpreted in two alternative ways; either she neglects the male, ritualistic ideology of agnatic descent embodied in the men's house (and underplays the fact that with modernization and change the female reading of the matri-house has been extended to encompass the whole village), or she faithfully portrays the Kayapó's structure, which would then merge the two types of consanguinity recognized as discontinuous by the Makuna, that is, the underlying uterine kinship form, and a dominant utero-cognatic descent form of kinship symbolically represented by plant metaphors. Whereas the second alternative implies that consanguinity encompasses affinity, the first one insists that the two are fundamentally dissociated.

Finally, Århem's thesis of one structure and two alternative perspectives, that is, a male reading and a female reading, may go a long way to solve the analytical dilemma of hierarchical versus egalitarian readings of Amazonian gender relationships underlined by Lorrain. This entails the recognition that alternative readings do not necessarily reflect ethnocentric Euro-American philosophical traditions, but are rooted in indigenous systems. Interestingly, if both Lorrain and Lea question gender inequality and power differentials between men and women, as well as the analyses proposed by feminist and non-feminist anthropologists, they do so very differently. While Lorrain gets inspiration from Rivière's (1984) model of the political economy of people, Lea reinterprets questions of gender on the basis of Rivière's later work (1993, 1995*b*) on house-based societies and botanic idioms, work which gives her arguments to privilege the house as moral person. As a result, whereas Lorrain recasts the individual versus society tension in terms of gendered individual power relations, Lea argues for the empirical existence of jural, corporate units which become the source of individual embodiment, personhood, and moral/political rights.

The fourth type of problematization addresses another major theme of Amazonian anthropology, embodiment and personhood, a theme which is treated

in virtually all the contributions, especially in Griffiths's analysis of Uitoto conceptions of human work as the source from which not only the human body (which 'is
always work in progress', human identity never being achieved for long, and never
given) and society, but also the world and the cosmos, are continuously recreated.
Henley, Århem, Chaumeil, and Erikson focus on bodies (particularly male bodies) as
they are made and remade in ritual, through painting, tattooing, or adorning. Henley
stresses that *bodily* change of initiated boys (and not change in soul or mind) becomes
the symbol of transgenerational continuity, as well as a cause for celebrating Panare
cultural identity. Such celebrations of the individual life cycle are not only marked
by the intensified production and distribution of food, but are also organized around
the human body as a central metaphor, and so are the ritual killings of the Pemong,
Akawaio, and Patamuna discussed by Butt Colson and Whitehead. And if the
construction of the body simultaneously involves the construction of personhood
and groupness, its destruction similarly entails the liquidation of village leaders, and
the dismantling of village communities. A number of contributions (in particular
Lorrain, Århem, Taylor, Rival, Viveiros de Castro, and Erikson) discuss embodiment
in relation to kinship and gender. Århem makes it clear that the two readings of
consanguinity discussed above are gender-based, and that, consequently, female and
male bodies may be conceived of as differentially constituted, which would explain
why, for instance, only men can usually become Itoto/Kanaimà (Butt Colson, but see
also Whitehead) or jaguars (Erikson), or why the procreative power predicated on
plant vegetative reproduction is more commonly associated with the female body.
For Lea, the House as moral person whose continuity depends on Mother–Daughter
and Sister–Sister solidarity and as matrifocal residential unit to which men are
weakly attached embodies 'given consanguinity' in contrast with the constructed
affinity and consanguinity of the men's house.

The challenge we are left with, for we do not pretend that this book alone will
suffice to arm a final and synthetic theory, is to come up with a model that will
account for the created person within a highly transformable world in which identities are constantly recycled, or, in other words, a model that will include all that
we know about the soul/body split, the difference it makes (or does not make) to
have a female or a male body, or an animal or a human body, to belong or not belong
to a particular residential unit, or to be an affine or a consanguine, and so forth. In
the end, this collection raises more questions than it answers, but we have written
it as a first step in the direction that Amazonian anthropology needs to take, which
is a bolder and more ambitious type of cross-cultural analysis.

ACKNOWLEDGEMENTS

We warmly thank Peter Rivière for his kind assistance while writing this Introduction,
through patient answers to a flow of questions, and loan of private materials. Many thanks
go to Audrey Butt Colson as well, for very helpful critical comments on a first version of this

chapter. Special thanks are due to David Parkin. We of course accept entire responsibility for any error or misinterpretations which remain.

* The spelling 'Kanaimà' is the rendering given by literate Patamuna. The spelling of 'Kanaima' in the chapter by Colson follows current orthography in non-Amerindian languages, such as Brazilian Portuguese, Venezuelan Spanish, and Guyanese English where the Pemon and Akawaio live, and which has been adopted by them (see also note, p. 232).

NOTES

1. See for example: 'The relationship terminologies, and kinship is the idiom of social inter-action, are in every case two-line and articulated by prescriptive exchange. The prescribed category everywhere includes the bilateral cross-cousin, although it may also include other genealogically defined individuals . . .' (Rivière 1984: 12), or '[T]here does not exist in the region identifiable and enduring groups that can be labeled as kin and affines and that stand in a relationship of spouse exchangers . . . an invariant feature of the social organisation is the principle of prescriptive direct exchange, and the existence of a prescriptive direct-exchange kinship terminology' (1984: 42); or even 'Affinity as politics means that marriage includes replication as well as reciprocation' (1984: 45).
2. This is expressed for the first time in writing in n. 6 of a recent paper: 'I am not convinced that the question of how Dravidian are Amazonian relationship terminologies is more than an "invented" intellectual puzzle. Even if there is an answer to it, I am not certain that it will tell us anything useful' (Rivière 2000a: 31).
3. Rivière says that, when a young undergraduate in Cambridge, Evans-Pritchard's work on the Azande caught his imagination to the point of driving his decision to give up archae-ology for anthropology. His work on sorcery accusations was also influenced by the work of Audrey Butt Colson (herself a former student of Evans-Pritchard), which Rivière discovered after coming back from a nine-month botanical and film expedition which took him, among other places, to the Guianas and the upper Xingú. The renowned film-maker Adrian Cowell was also on this expedition, which was to have a lasting impact on the lives and careers of the two young men. Peter remembers it as an unforgettable and fascinating moment, during which he and Adrian met two anthropologists in the field, Audrey Butt Colson and David Maybury-Lewis, as well as the Villas-Boas brothers.
4. The model, summarized, is as follows: (1) the conjugal pair is a self-sufficient productive and reproductive unit; (2) the division of labour is organized along sexual lines; (3) the activities of man and woman are complementary; (4) women work harder than men, therefore, interdependence is not based on equality; and, finally, (5) men turn products processed by women to their political advantage.
5. See for example his unremarkable, but nevertheless 'careful and honest', as Shapiro (1971: 852) so accurately put it, ethnographic observation that the leader's death is the death of the group, or that a leader is expected to 'lead from in front, by example and by initiating activities, and not by issuing orders from behind' (Rivière 1984: 73).
6. However, Peter does not himself stress the theoretical continuity between his graduate work on historical sources and, for instance, his current work on Schomburgk, except for the fact that he is using the same historical material in both. In his opinion, *Absent-Minded Imperialism* is more like a novel narrating historical facts; as for his current work

on Schomburgk, he calls it an intellectual biography. Both are inspired by very much the same drive to document the lives and ideas of half-forgotten but formative figures of anthropology as the one that led him to edit the works of McLennan (1970) and Lubbock (1978).

7. Peter Rivière has contributed to the development of Amazonian anthropology through his indefatigable commitment to (and talent for) comparative analysis. In the last forty years, he has reviewed more than 124 books relating to South America, including a large number of Amazonian ethnographies, and has examined at least 25 theses on Amazonia. This keen reading of Amazonian ethnographies and doctoral dissertations reveals an intense interest in the empirical data and ethnographic facts that constitute the *materia prima* of comparative analysis.

8. It is important to note here that Audrey Butt Colson started lecturing in 1956 on South American societies, mainly the Guianas, and with a particular emphasis on the Akawaio, from the Department of Ethnology and Prehistory at Oxford University. Francis Huxley, who was at Oxford for his anthropology training before he subsequently followed Meyer Fortes to Cambridge, and who came back to Oxford on a three-year Junior Research Fellowship at St Catherine's College, also taught on lowland South America. Before them, Miss Béatrice Blackwood (from the Department of Ethnology and Prehistory at Oxford University) gave a few lectures every year on Lowland South America as part of her 'Lands and Peoples' two-term course for Geography and Anthropology students. This course was followed in the third term by a course on the archaeology and prehistory of Latin America, which was mainly dedicated to the study of highland civilizations.

9. This leads Rivière to criticize Gregor's (1977) account of Mehinaku daily life on the ground that he chooses to focus on performance and behaviour instead of structures and principles: 'Forms of behaviour will always appear more variable than the principles which give rise to them. Indeed, the concentration on behaviour, because of the infinite forms it can take, *almost inevitably excludes the possibility of any comparative approach*. There exist detailed studies, focusing on principles, which demonstrate how these principles generate the variable forms of observable behaviour' (Rivière 1978*b*: 329).

2

GUT Feelings about Amazonia: Potential Affinity and the Construction of Sociality

Eduardo Viveiros de Castro, *Museu Nacional, Rio de Janeiro*

This chapter draws the barest outline of what might be a 'grand unified theory' of Amazonian sociality—a GUT, as physicists say. The acronym is meant to be (self) ironic, and here doubly so. What follows is a clumsily packed excerpt of an essay in preparation, which was supposed to be my contribution for the present volume, but which became unmanageably long. The purpose of that essay is to account for some recent arguments about the socially constructed (in the phenomenal sense of the term) character of Amazonian modes of kinship relatedness. My point, in a nutshell, is that no province of human experience is (given as) entirely constructed; something must be (construed as) given. I take as my example a dichotomy central to Western kinship theory and practice, namely, the consanguinity/affinity distinction of Morganian fame, and argue that in Amazonia, it is affinity that stands as the given dimension of the cosmic relational matrix, while consanguinity falls within the scope of human action and intention. This, of course, implies that 'affinity' and 'consanguinity' mean very different things in Amazonian and modern Western kinship ideologies: it is not only *who* is a consanguine or an affine that changes from here to there, but, first and foremost, *what* is a consanguine and an affine.[1]

My understanding of Amazonian kinship owes much to the trailbreaking work of Peter Rivière among the Trio (1969*a*), as well as to his masterful synthesis of Guianese social organization (1984). Most of what I have written on the subject is essentially a rejoinder to his query about the meaning of affinal categories in Guianese socialities. The present contribution intends to carry this dialogue on, being a further step towards what Rivière (1993) has aptly called the 'amerindian-ization' of traditional concerns of kinship theory. Such dialogical origin and purpose may explain, if not really forgive, the somewhat bizarre self-referential tone of this homage.

POTENTIAL AFFINITY

We have been long aware of the wider resonances of affinal idioms in lowland South America, at least since an early article by Lévi-Strauss on the sixteenth-century Tupinamba, in which he argued that 'a certain kinship tie, the brother-in-law relationship, once possessed a meaning among many South American tribes far transcending a simple expression of relationship' (Lévi-Strauss 1943b: 398). Or perhaps I should have said the wider dissonances of such idioms? For Lévi-Strauss's assertion makes a striking contrast, for example, with Rivière's (1984: 69) wary remark about 'whether the notion of affinity, as the term is generally under-stood, is applicable within the Guiana region'. Lévi-Strauss is saying that Amerindian affinity means *more* than what it means to us; Rivière is suggesting that it means *less*, since in the Guianese context the notion applies only when marriage takes place with a stranger. In the strongly endogamous societies of that region, a proper marriage involves no affinity, since it reasserts previous cognatic connec-tions and does not entail attitudinal changes. Thus affinity not only means less but the concept itself may be meaningless, at least for some South American tribes.

How are we to reconcile these two opinions? Their apparent disagreement is not related, I believe, to any major ethnographic differences (of which there are many, to be sure) among the groups concerned. In truth, I think that both authors are expressing the same situation. The similarity can be seen if we extend Rivière's point about affinity as applying only to marriage between strangers. Affinity in Amazonia may actually apply to relations with strangers *even if* no marriage takes place. In fact, it applies to strangers *especially if* marriage cannot take place or is not really an issue, which thus brings us back to Lévi-Strauss's remark on the extra-kinship usages of the brother-in-law idiom. Let us remember that *tovajar*, the Tupinamba word for 'brother-in-law', implies not only friendly alliance within and deadly enmity without, but also the reverse; it means at once 'close' and 'opposed'.

In my previous essays on Amazonian kinship (Viveiros de Castro 1993, 1998b; Viveiros de Castro and Fausto 1993), I argued that the Dravidianate relationship terminologies common in that region diverge in some important ways from the eponymous South Indian scheme as described by Louis Dumont. The main differ-ence is that the categories of consanguinity and affinity in Amazonia do not stand in what Dumont called a 'distinctive' or 'equistatutory' opposition, as they did in his Tamil model. The concentric pattern of Amazonian socio-political classifica-tions and of the cognatic idiom in which they are usually expressed inflects the diametric arrangement of the terminology, creating a pragmatic and ideological—sometimes terminological as well—imbalance between the two categories. As one goes from the proximal to the distal ranges of the relational field, affinity increas-ingly prevails over consanguinity, becoming the generic mode of relatedness. Instead of the Dravidian box diagram with its symmetrically deployed categories, the Amazonian structure rather evokes a Chinese box, with consanguinity nested within affinity. In brief, affinity hierarchically encompasses consanguinity.

This Amazonian(ist) twist given to the classical Dravidian model was produced by playing, as it were, Dumont against himself, allowing his concepts of hierarchy and encompassment of the contrary to infiltrate the Dravidian equipollent structure. Dumont, however, was quite aware of the possibility of having affinity and consanguinity related in this fashion. Indeed, he maintained that what distinguishes South Indian from North Indian kinship configurations is the fact that the former are not organized by hierarchical opposition, while the latter are. In North India, he wrote,

the word bhai, 'brother', effectively bridges kinship and caste by taking increasingly wide meanings when we ascend from the immediate relationships to wider and wider circles. It thus repeatedly encompasses on the higher level what was its contrary on the lower level. (Dumont 1983*a*: 166)

In the Dravidian terminologies, on the other hand, 'we find nothing of the sort, the (main) categories . . . stand in neat distinctive opposition', which Dumont (1983*a*: 166) also calls 'equistatutory opposition'.

Dumont seems never to have considered the third logical possibility, which would be the converse of the North Indian case: affinity repeatedly encompassing consanguinity 'when we ascend from the immediate relationships to wider and wider circles'. This is what I thought was found in Amazonia, especially (but not exclusively) in those locally endogamous, cognatically organized societies in which 'prescriptive alliance' is not supported by any descent construct, a situation first described among the Trio (Rivière 1969*a*), and afterwards among the Piaroa (Overing Kaplan 1975), the Jivaro (Taylor 1983), the Yanomami (Albert 1985), and other peoples (Viveiros de Castro (ed.) 1995*b*).

My proposal was not entirely new. Albert, for example, although he did not use the concept of hierarchical opposition, had arrived at something very close to this conclusion in his monograph on the Yanomami. And before that, the idea had been tersely formulated by Joanna Overing in a remark concerning the Piaroa and similar societies:

[W]e must distinguish among those societies that emphasize descent, those that emphasize both descent and alliance, and finally those that stress only alliance as a basic organizing principle. (Overing Kaplan 1975: 2)

This tripartition was meant to point out the theoretical interest of a particular case—the Amazonian—uncovered by the two ethnographic prototypes of the day: the African systems of British social anthropology (descent only) and the Australian and South Asian elementary structures of French structuralism (descent plus alliance). One can read here a distinction phrased in Lévi-Straussian terms, among those post-elementary kinship systems in which alliance is ancillary to the perpetuation of descent groups (relations have a regulative role, being subordinated to their independently constituted 'terms'), those elementary structures where the method of classes prevails (terms and relations are mutually constitutive), and finally those pre-elementary structures where the method of relations is in force (relations subordinate and constitute terms). But the tripartition can also be rendered into the Dumontian terminology, and read as distinguishing among those societies in which consanguinity encompasses affinity, those in which the two principles stand in an equistatutory relation, and those in which affinity encompasses consanguinity. Such a reading requires that we interpret 'descent' and 'alliance' in Overing's formulation as no more than institutional elaborations of, respectively, consanguinity and affinity taken as the two basic modes of relatedness. This allowed, to say that a society stresses alliance over descent as an institutional principle is tantamount to saying that it stresses affinity over consanguinity as a relational principle.

In my comparative essays on kinship mentioned earlier, I tried to draw all the ethnographically possible consequences (and perhaps a few impossible ones, too) from the idea of affinity as a dominant principle. I decided to call this principle 'potential affinity', in order to distinguish affinity as a generic value from affinity as a particular type of kinship tie. This distinction implies that affinity as generic value is *not* a component or part of 'kinship'. It is, rather, its contrary, and, being the dimension of virtuality of which kinship is the process of actualization, its condition.[2]

The distinction was forced upon me by a number of considerations. The initial question was the simple one of knowing what happened when one moved from intra-village ('local') to inter-village ('global') interactional and conceptual registers. In the classic *Elementary Structures* model, descent was the principle answering for the internal composition of the exchange units, while alliance took care of the interconnections among them, thereby generating the form and continuity of the global social system. With her Piaroa-inspired model, Overing Kaplan took the decisive step of bringing alliance to the interior of the units themselves, thus making it the principle of constitution and perpetuation of particular groups (endogamous localized kindreds). This shift opened up a whole new way of looking at Amazonian kinship universes, besides permitting a general reconceptualization of 'restricted exchange' systems. It created, however, its own set of problems. Instead of descent-based groups related by a global formula of alliance, we now had alliance-based local groups, but related by what? If alliance works from within, then how are supra-local relations expressed, since it cannot be through—nonexistent or rudimentary—descent constructs, nor through simple 'consanguinity'—for the latter is also concentrated in the local group? Were we to accept the traditional anthropological view of primitive society as kinship-based, we would be forced to conclude that 'the society', in a great many Amazonian cases, is synonymous with the local community: the local group is a total group. This would apparently corroborate the xenophobic outlook of sundry Amerindian peoples, who take unrelated persons and members of other groups to be dangerous beings lying beyond the pale of humanity. The 'outside' is pure negativity, or absence of relation. Sociality ends where sociability stops.

One solution Amazonianists provided for the question of supra-locality was to show that no Amazonian alliance-based local group is an island. In spite of its will to autarky, each community is (or was) at the centre of a web of relations with like groups and other collectives; these relations are given full, even if ambivalent, recognition in native ideologies. This said, such analytical emphasis on the wider sociological frame (the 'tribe', the 'nexus', the 'agglomerate', the 'regional system', etc.) in which the local quasi-monads are embedded does not really solve the problem, insofar as it remains inspired by a traditional concern with social morphological totalization. Even a cursory acquaintance with Amazonian ethnography makes one realize that the 'wider sociological frames' of that area are wide indeed, including far more things than local groups of the same ethnic or linguistic family, and I do not mean here only other tribes, or the large, socio-politically heterogeneous multi-ethnic systems of pre-Columbian South America. The sociological frames go as far as the native sociologies go; and the latter muster a motley crowd of Others, non-human as well as human, which are neither sortable nor totalizable in any obvious way.

The implications of the above are not limited to social morphology. Consider, for instance, the notion of a political economy of persons, repeatedly advanced for Amazonian and similar modes of sociality. It is a very interesting conceit. It takes for granted, however, exactly what it should not: that we know who the persons are, that every people on earth has more or less the same ideas about what qualifies as 'people' (and what qualifies people). But since as a matter of course we do not, what might a political economy of persons mean in worlds like the Amazonian ones, in which there are more persons in heaven and earth than are dreamt of in our anthropologies? The question remains open.[3]

But let us get back to supra-local relations in Amazonia. They form a variable mix: statistically residual (in the endogamous regimes common in this region) but politically strategic intermarriage; formal friendship and trade-partnership links; inter-communal ritual and feasting; physical and spiritual, actual or latent, predatory warfare. In some cases, these different modes may correspond to different levels of supra-locality: inter-village, inter-regional, inter-tribal, inter-ethnic, and so forth. But in many other cases, they intermingle, cross-cut, or oscillate conjuncturally within the same range. Furthermore, this relational complex also straddles 'natural' boundaries: animals, plants, spirits, and divinities are equally engaged in such connective-cum-divisive relations with humans. All these relations, whatever their components, manifest the same general set of values and dispositions, as witness the common idiom in which they are expressed, that of affinity. Guests and friends as much as foreigners and enemies, political allies or clients as much as trade partners or ritual associates, animals as much as spirits, all these kinds of beings bathe, so to speak, in affinity. They are conceived either as generic affines or as marked versions—sometimes inversions—of affines.[4] The Other is first and foremost an affine.

It should be stressed that this affinization of 'others' occurs in spite of the fact that the vast majority of actual matrimonial alliances take place within the local group. And at any rate, such alliances cannot but accumulate in the local group, since their concentration defines what a 'local group' is. By this last remark I mean to imply that the situation does not change much when we consider those Amazonian regimes that feature village or descent group exogamy. Potential affinity and its cosmological attendants continue to mark the generic relations with non-allied groups, enemies, animals, and spirits.

Besides these generic, collective relations of 'symbolic' affinity with the outside, there may (or perhaps must) exist a few particularized affinal connections, like those taking place between trade partners, ritual friends, shamans and their animal/spirit associates, or killers and their victims. Such personalized affinal relations (still non-matrimonial, in the sense that they are not based on an actual, or at least intra-human, marriage link) are cosmo-politically strategic, since they serve both as evidence and instrument of the generic relation.

It is this overall configuration that I named potential affinity, or 'affinity without affines'. What is truly important, however, is that such 'symbolic' affinity seems to embody the distinctive qualities of this mode of relatedness more fully than the actual affinal ties that constitute 'the group'. In the context of local-cum-cognatic 'prescriptive endogamy' (the expression is Rivière's) prevailing in many societies of the region, affinity as a particular relationship is expurgated of most of the meanings Amazonians attribute to its generic version, being masked or neutralized by consanguinity. Within the community, then, the situation can be described as one of 'affines without affinity'. Terminological ('virtual') affines are seen as types of cognates (namely, close cross-kin), actual affines are attitudinally consanguinized, specifically affinal terms (where they exist) are avoided in favour of their cross-kin alternatives or of teknonyms expressing co-consanguinity, spouses are conceived as becoming consubstantial by way of sex and commensality, and so forth. We can then say that affinity as a particular relation is virtually eclipsed by consanguinity as part of the process of making kinship. As Rivière observed (1984: 70), 'within the ideal settlement affinity does not exist'.

Rivière's remark undoubtedly expresses an ideal of many Amazonian communities. But I take this as implying that if affinity does not exist within the ideal community, it must then exist somewhere else. Within real settlements, to be sure; but, above all, without the ideal settlement, that is, in the ideal outside of the settlement, as 'ideal' (pure) affinity. For as the perspective (the native's and the analyst's) shifts from local relationships to wider contexts—inter-community ritual and matrimonial relations, inter-group trade and warfare, inter-species hunting and shamanism—the value distribution is inverted, and affinity becomes the overall mode of sociality. Sociality begins where sociability stops.

We have thus seen what puts these Amazonian kin collectives (the so-called local groups) in relation. But this is not enough; we must probe more deeply. In relation *to what* are such collectives defined and constituted? What *makes* such communities 'local'? I suggest they are defined and constituted in relation, not to some global society, but to an infinite background of virtual sociality. And I think they are made local by the very process of extracting themselves from this background and making, in the most literal sense, their own bodies of kin. These would be the respective meanings of 'affinity' and 'consanguinity' in Amazonia.[5]

I have repeatedly mentioned the value shift that takes place when we 'move' from the proximal to the distal ranges of the relational field. Such phrasings are deeply misleading, however. They express our deep-seated extensionist prejudices, for they presuppose that the movement embodied in Amazonian sociality is from intimate, 'everyday' cognatic sociability (where consanguinity prevails) to wider spheres of a somewhat extra-ordinary nature (where affinity overwhelms). The real situation, I argue, is the opposite: rather than being a metaphorical extension, a semantic and pragmatic attenuation of matrimonial affinity, 'figurative' affinity is the *source* of both 'literal' affinity and the consanguinity the latter breeds. And this because particular relations must be made up of and against generic ones; they are results not starting points. 'Classificatory' kinship relations cannot be thought of as projections of 'real' ones; rather, the latter are special, that is, particularized, reductions of the former.[6] In Amazonia, a real or close consanguine (which does *not* mean a 'biological' consanguine, 'ethno-' or otherwise) is certainly 'more consanguineal' than a classificatory or distant one, but a classificatory affine is more affinal than a real one. This suggests that Amazonian consanguinity and affinity are not so much taxonomically discontinuous categories, but, rather, zones of intensity within a single scalar field. In this field, the movement is not from the proximal to the distal, the ordinary to the extraordinary, but quite the contrary. Something extra must be summoned to bring forth the ordinary.

The real significance of the conception of affinity as the given does not lie in its kinship-typological incidences (which may not necessarily obtain). This idea can be understood as a privileged instantiation of the general ontological premises underlying Amazonian worlds.[7] The first and foremost of such presuppositions is that difference precedes and encompasses identity; the latter is a special case of the former. Just as cold is relative 'absence' of heat but not vice versa (heat is a quantity which has no negative state), identity is relative absence of difference but not vice versa. This is the same as saying that there exists difference alone, in greater or smaller 'amount'; the nature of the value measured is difference. In kinship terms, taking 'kinship' as a shorthand for what, in Amazonia, would perhaps be more aptly described as a 'theory of general relationality', this means that consanguinity (identity) is a limit point of affinity (difference). A limit point in the strict sense of the term, since it is never attained. What kinship measures or calculates in Amazonia is the coefficient of affinity in relationships, which cannot reach a zero-state, for, as we shall see, there is no total consanguineal identity between any two persons.[8] In fact, not even individual persons are perfectly identical to themselves, since they are not individuals, at least while they are alive.

So the cardinal rule of this ontology is: no relation without differentiation. In socio-practical terms, this means that the parties to any relationship are related insofar as they are different from one another. They are related through their difference, and become different as they engage in their relationship. But is this not what affinity is precisely about? For affinity is a relationship the terms of which are *not* related in the same way to the linking term: my 'sister' is your 'wife', and so on. What unites two affines is what distinguishes them. This would explain why affinity is such a powerful symbol of relatedness in Amazonia. It is a symbol 'far transcending a simple expression of relationship', or, in other words, a symbol which 'transcends' kinship as such. While the Other in Western social cosmology is rescued from abstract indetermination when we pose him as a *brother*, that is, as someone related to me insofar as we are both identically related to a third, superior term (the parents, the nation, the church, etc.), the Amazonian Other must be determined as a brother-in-law (Keifenheim 1992: 91). Relation as identity, relation as alterity.

But then, how does consanguinity enter the picture? Well, it must, precisely, 'enter', for it is not already there as a *given*. Since affinity is the fundamental state of the relational field, then something must be *done*, a certain amount of energy must be spent to create pockets of consanguineal valence there. Consanguinity must purposefully be carved out of affinity, made to emerge from the affinal background as an 'inventional' (i.e. intentional) differentiation from universally given difference. But then it can only be the ever incomplete outcome of a process of de-potentialization of affinity, its reduction to and through marriage. And that is the meaning the expression 'potential affinity' is supposed to convey: affinity as the generic given, the virtual background out of which a particularized figure of consanguineally dominated kinship sociality must be made to appear. Kinship is constructed, not given, because what *is* given is (potential) affinity.

THE CONSTRUCTION OF KINSHIP

My reliance on the notion of hierarchical opposition was first and foremost a direct consequence of the nature of the materials I was initially concerned with, that is, kinship terminologies of the 'two-section' type canonically described by Dumont. Since Dumont proposed the concept of hierarchical opposition to account for other—in fact, all—aspects of Indian society, his denial of its applicability to Dravidian kinship is intriguing, the more so as he used the very same concept to mount a devastating attack on the 'equistatutory' interpretations of socio-cosmological dualisms by Needham and his associates.[9] Dumont's argument that classificatory oppositions always carry a value asymmetry is, to my mind, correct and undeniable. To apply this argument to the critic himself, at least with respect to the Amazonian version of the Dravidianate schema, was, therefore, an obvious step to take. Furthermore, I was attracted to the notion of hierarchical opposition, in which I saw an interesting sociological application of the Praguean-linguistic concept of markedness. The importance of this concept for anthropology cannot be overemphasized. My thesis that affinity is hierarchically superior to consanguinity essentially means that the former is the unmarked category in

Amazonia, standing for 'relatedness' in a generic context, while the latter is the marked category or relational quality. Consanguinity is *non-affinity* before being anything else.[10]

Hierarchical opposition, however, is not an easy concept to handle in the Amazonian context. The difficulty comes from the fact that the Dumontian approach has its roots in the problematics of totality. As I was trying to establish a somewhat paradoxical regime of 'anti-totalization' in which the outside encompassed the inside, but without thereby creating simply a greater inside, I had no other option but to apply the concept of hierarchy to Amazonian materials in a way that deliberately distorted the Dumontian meaning. The challenge was to avoid ending up with a figure that 'contained' both the inside and the outside as different levels of a single whole, for such an outcome would have been equivalent to positing the outside as a wider milieu of interiority.[11]

This is, I believe, an important issue. In the hands of Dumont, encompassment defines the characteristic of a Totality—the society as cosmos—in which differences are nested within a superordinate holistic unity. Indeed, such structure has no exterior, for hierarchical encompassment is an operation not unlike the notorious dialectical sublation: a movement of inclusive synthesis, of subsumption of difference by identity.[12] Difference not only occupies the inner space of the 'whole', but it is also inferior to the whole. The general emphasis of Amazonian ethnology on the cosmologically constitutive role of alterity, in contrast, refers to a regime in which encompassment does not produce or manifest a superior metaphysical unity. There is no higher-order identity between difference and identity, just difference all the way. The subsumption of the inside by the outside, characteristic of the Amazonian cosmological process, specifies a structure in which the inside is a mode of the outside. As such, it can only constitute itself by, as it were, stepping out of the outside. To be true to its encompassed condition of being 'inside' the outside, the inside must become the 'outside' of the outside, an achievement of precarious nature. The Amazonian hierarchical synthesis is disjunctive, not conjunctive. Accordingly, the argument that the enemy is 'included in society' does not so much imply that the Other is ultimately a kind of Self, but, rather, that the Self is initially a figure of the Other.[13]

Let me be clear about this internal or inclusive role played by alterity. Internality in an ontological sense (i.e. otherness as a constitutive relation) is not the same thing as internality in a mereological sense (i.e. the other as part of a social or cosmological whole). In some respects, the first means the very opposite of the second. It is because alterity is an internal relation that one can say, without really indulging in paradox, that some Amazonian societies have no interior (Viveiros de Castro 1992: 4). The point about the outside encompassing the inside is *not* about the latter being 'within' the former, but, rather, about the outside being *immanent* in the inside.[14] The corollary of such immanence is that any arbitrarily chosen point of the 'inside' is a boundary between an inside and an outside: there is no absolute milieu of interiority. Reciprocally, any region of the outside is a possible pole of interiority.[15] The Dumontian language of 'wholes' and 'encompassment' is somewhat awkward in that it allows for a confusion between the two meanings of internality, especially when the cosmic values under discussion have a topological expression, as is the case in Amazonia.

I am not suggesting that we should shun any notion of totality as hopelessly un-Amazonian, but simply that we should be wary of a possible fallacy of misplaced wholeness. Any cosmology is by definition total in the sense that it cannot but think everything that is, and think it (this everything that is not a Whole, or this whole that is not One) according to a limited number of fundamental presuppositions; holistic approaches are thus amply justified. But it does not follow that every cosmology thinks everything that is within the category of totality, or that it poses a totality as the 'objective correlative' of its own virtual exhaustiveness. Accordingly, I venture to suggest that in Amazonian cosmologies the whole is not (the) given, nor is it the sum of the given and the constructed. The 'whole' is, rather, the constructed, that which humans strive to bring forth by means of a reduction of the Given as the anti-whole or pure universal relation (difference).

What I have in mind is something like the following structure.[16] Once supposed (i.e. given 'by construction'), affinity immediately poses non-affinity, for the first, as a principle of difference, carries its own internal difference, rather than embodying a transcendent unitarian whole. Non-affinity is an indeterminate value, as its marked status testifies. As I stated above, consanguinity is non-affinity before being anything else. But in order for this non-affinal value to become 'something else' (i.e. a determinate quality), it must proceed by reciprocally and actively extruding affinity from itself, affinity being the only *positive* value available (that is, given). Non-affinity is thus internally differentiated into affinity and non-affinity. It is always possible, however, to extrude yet 'more' affinity from non-affinity so as to further determine the latter as consanguinity. In fact, it is necessary to do so, because the internal differentiation of non-affinity reproduces affinity by the very process of extruding it. It is through the reiterated exclusion of affinity at each level of contrast that consanguinity appears as including it at the next level; affinity is thus disseminated downwards to the inner reaches of the structure. This recursive process of 'obviation' (Wagner 1978) of affinity, otherwise known as *the construction of kinship*, must remain unfinished forever; pure consanguinity is not attainable, for it means the end of kinship. It is a sterile state of non-relationality, a state of pure indifference, by which the 'construction' deconstructs itself (see Fig. 2.1). Affinity is the principle of instability responsible for the continuity of the life-process of kinship, or, to put it differently, consanguinity cannot but be the continuation of affinity by other means.

Figure 2.1 represents a 'structuring' rather than a 'structural' model, in the sense that it sets the conditions for the constitution of a value (kinship), rather than describing a constituted organizational form. It is therefore quite different from the standard Dumontian hierarchy, which articulates well-determined values from the start.[17] It looks more like what Houseman (1984) calls anti-extensive hierarchy,

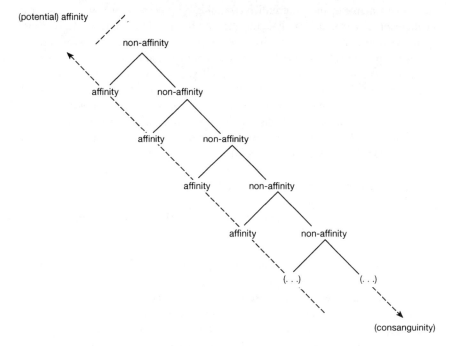

F<small>IG</small>. 2.1. The Amazonian construction of kinship

a configuration in which the marked 'anti-extension' (non-affinity) of the unmarked dominant principle (affinity) includes at a lower level the dominant principle as its own *marked* version. As the dominant principle is inherently *un*marked, such inclusion creates an irresolvable internal tension that simultaneously drives the subordinate principle towards ever further particularized actualizations and generates a counter-current of ever broader ascending generalizations directed to the dominant principle. Thus, every downward-branching triangle (originating in the right diagonal) separates two modes of the value embodied in the upper vertex, while the lower vertex of every upward-branching triangle (originating in the left diagonal) connects between the two opposed values lying above it. As the two diagonals are oriented, both the particularizing separations and the generalizing connections are asymmetric or hierarchic, but with inverse markedness: the way up is not the way down. In short, the dualism of affinity and consanguinity is in *perpetual disequilibrium*.

GETTING AMAZONIA IN THE GUT

I chose the phrase 'perpetual disequilibrium' to bring our discussion on firm Americanist ground. As is well known, Lévi-Strauss (1991) characterized the moving principle of the Amerindian cosmological process in precisely these terms: a dualism in perpetual or dynamic disequilibrium. The name of Lévi-Strauss usually evokes a strong partiality towards static, reversible, and symmetrically binary oppositions. This image, however, better fits some 'British' versions of the structuralist paradigm. Lévi-Strauss himself pointed very early on to the precarious nature of the symmetry exhibited by socio-cosmological dualities. It is hardly necessary to recall the points made in his famous article on dual organizations: the static quality of diametric dualism as a formal structure; the asymmetric values often attributed to diametric partitions as lived structures; the implicit or explicit combination of diametric and concentric forms of dualism; the derivability of the former from the latter; the triadic origin of concentric dualism, and its dynamic quality; finally and more generally, the derivative status of binary oppositions in relation to ternary structures.

One essential aspect of Lévi-Strauss's concentric model is its openness to the exterior. On the one hand, diametric dualisms define a self-contained whole cut off from the outside by an uncrossable boundary, a dimensional barrier heterogeneous to the internal meridian line. From the standpoint of the system, its exterior simply does not exist.[18] The exterior of the concentric model, on the other hand, is immanent in it: 'The system is not self-sufficient, and its frame of reference is always the environment' (Lévi-Strauss 1958: 168). The outside is therefore an internal, defining feature of the whole structure, or, to be more accurate, it is the feature that actively prevents the structure from becoming a whole. The 'concentric' outside is relative, and this makes the inside relative as well. Concentric dualism brings indetermination to the very core of the self (i.e. to the centre) rather than rejecting it towards the outer darkness of non-being. After all, geometrically speaking, the centre is but the inferior limit of the infinity of circles that can be drawn around it.[19]

The dependence of concentric dualism upon its own exterior is related to another famous openness: the 'opening to the Other' proper to the Amerindian bipartite ideology (Lévi-Strauss 1991: 16). The concept of this *ouverture à l'Autre* was directly derived from the dualism in perpetual disequilibrium displayed by the reference myth of *Histoire de Lynx*: the Tupinamba Genesis recorded by Thevet *circa* 1554. I trust Fig. 2.1 did not fail to bring to the reader's mind the diagram of the successive bipartitions that span the entire myth (Figure 2.2).

We are now in a position to see that the dynamic dualism of 1991 is simply a transformation of the concentric model of 1956. Note that *Histoire de Lynx*'s two-way splits start at the outermost reaches of the system, proceeding downwards, or, in the terminology used in the older concentric model, *inwards*. The further we move down the cascading proliferation of ever smaller distinctions in the dynamic schema, the nearer we are getting to the centre of the concentric model, the point where the 'Self' lies as an entity of infinite comprehension and null extension, or pure identity. But of course we never get there, for the centre's pure identity is purely imaginary. The centre is a limit of convergence, just like the 'consanguinity' of the kinship diagram in Fig. 2.1.

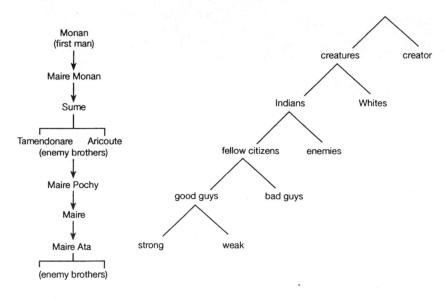

FIG. 2.2. Two-way splits in the Tupinamba myth (from Lévi-Strauss 1991: 76)

Figs. 2.1 and 2.2 not only carry exactly the same message in slightly different codes, but they represent the same structure. This will perhaps be made more evident if we attribute a specific interpretation to each level of the affinity/non-affinity diagram. The schema in Fig. 2.3, for example, models a syncretically 'ideal' Amazonian morphology of the type first described by Rivière.

Note, first of all, that Fig. 2.3 describes a single process encompassing inter-personal and intra-personal relations. The construction of the person is coexten-sive with the construction of sociality: both are based on the same dualism in perpetual disequilibrium between self-consanguineal and other-affinal poles. Intra-personal and inter-personal relations are also 'co-intensive', in the sense that the person cannot be conceived as a part of a social whole, but as its version on the individual scale, just as the *socius* is the person on a collective scale. In other words, this structure is fractal: a distinction between part and whole is meaningless.[20] It follows that the distance between the 'individualist' socialities of Guiana and the 'collectivist' socialities of Central Brazil may be shorter than we all used to imag-ine.

The upper half of the figure is self-explanatory; its lower part needs some elab-oration. The opposition of 'e/y sibling' and 'self' can be justified on the basis of the idea that Amazonian (same-sex) siblingship is almost always marked by a principle of relative age. It conveys a notion of diachronic and differential instantiation rather than total synchronic identification; it is also never free from a residuum of poten-tial affinity.[21] There is more to this, though. We could have added an intermediary

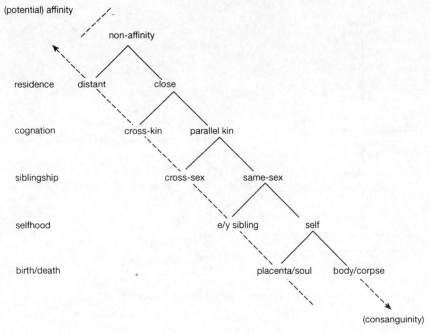

FIG. 2.3. Bipartitions of Amazonian kinship

step in the diagram, opposing a pole labelled 'twin' to the 'e/y sibling' pole, instead of having the latter confront directly the 'self' pole. With the 'twin' pole, we would have reached the lowest possible limit of inter-personal difference, since twinship is the extreme case of consanguineal identity: the absolute zero of affinal temperature, as it were. As Lévi-Strauss argued in *Histoire de Lynx*, however, twins are not conceived as identical in Amerindian thought, but rather as beings that *must* be differentiated. Either they are both killed at birth (which sets the score back to nil), or one of the twins is killed (which creates an absolute difference between the two), or both are spared, but in this case they are distinguished by their order of appearance (hence transformed into a e/y sibling pair). In indigenous mythologies, in which twins abound, two other strategies are envisaged: the twins have two different fathers, which makes them different from the start, or the narrative takes as its very theme their progressive differentiation. Therefore, even when they are indiscernible at birth, mythic twins always drift towards difference, thereby reproducing the self/other polarity. Twinship constitutes what we could call the *least common multiple* in Amerindian thought.[22]

Twinship and its internal 'oddness' allow us to proceed one step down in our diagram, and reach the intra-personal level, which I have sketchily divided in a 'placenta/soul' pole and a 'body/corpse' one. Let me start here by recalling that the placenta is often conceived as a double of the newborn, a kind of *dead twin*, or as the non-human Other of the child (Gow 1997: 48; Karadimas 1997: 81). In some mythological traditions, the placenta gives rise to an actual, and very antagonistic, twin (Guss 1989: 54). As to the opposition between 'placenta' and 'body/corpse', note that the placenta and the body are often opposed in terms of their spatio-temporal movements, the former going down (buried) and rotting, so that the latter can rise and thrive. It seems that the placenta is being conceived of as a kind of counter-corpse (C. Hugh-Jones 1979: 128–9), or as a body with its inside out (as the exteriorized entrails of the child; see Gow 1997).

The body/soul division manifests the same polarity. Like the placenta, the soul is a separable aspect of the person, or a double, that is, a twin. One's own soul is never really one's 'own'; being the other side of the person, it is also the side of the Other.[23] Placenta and soul, incidentally, are also temporally correlated: the separation of the first marks the beginning of humanization, that of the latter its end. The soul, like the placenta and the odd twins, is clearly located in the 'other-affinal' pole of the diagram. We touch here the relationally constituted core, or nuclear relation, of the person. The Amazonian construction of kinship concerns essentially the fabrication (and destruction) of *bodies*, while 'souls' are not made, but *given*: either absolutely during conception, or transmitted along with names and other pre-constituted principles, or captured ready-made from the outside. The soul is the eminently alienable, because eminently alien, part of the Amazonian person: it is 'given' and, thus, can be taken.

We have just seen that not even twins are perfectly consanguineal. Does this mean that an individual person becomes consanguineal reflexively, that is, for instance, once he/she is separated from his/her placentary Other? I do not think this is the case. A living person is 'dividual' (i.e. body *and* soul) and internally constituted by a self/other, or consanguine/affine polarity (Kelly 1999; Taylor 2000 and this volume). This composite entity is decomposed by death, which separates the principle of 'affinal' otherness, the soul, from the principle of 'consanguineal' sameness, the dead body. Unalloyed consanguinity can only be reached in death: it is the final result of the life-process of kinship, just as pure affinity is the cosmological precondition of the latter. Death splits the dividual person, or reveals its divided essence: as disembodied souls, the dead are paradigmatically affinal (as classically demonstrated by Carneiro da Cunha (1978)); as 'de-souled' bodies, however, they are supremely consanguineal. Therefore, death simultaneously undoes the tension (the difference of potential) between affinity and consanguinity that triggers the construction of kinship among the living, and completes the process of consanguinization, i.e. de-affinization, to which it corresponds.

Said differently, the oriented but cyclical structure schematized in Fig. 2.3 depicts the cosmological movement of transformation of affinity (alterity) into consanguinity (identity) and back again. The process of kinship requires the progressive particularization of general difference through the constitution of *bodies of kin* (the kin-fabricated singular body and the bodily instituted kin collective) as concretions of shared consanguineal identity within the universally given field of potential affinity. But the life-process of kinship ends each cycle with the production of a totally self-identical entity, the dead body, which is also completely different from everything else: it is pure substantive singularity. The 'other', relational rather than substantial, part of the person is represented by the soul, which may have a number of (alternative or sequential) posthumous affinal determinations: it may become an enemy of the living relatives of the deceased; it may take a non-human body as its dwelling; it may be passed on to non-consubstantial relatives; or it may become a generic principle of free subjecthood, a kind of universal ontological equivalent, the measure of all meaningful difference.[24]

There is of course another end-product of kinship at the close of each cycle: the procreated child, who completes the consanguinization process initiated by the marriage of its parents. This new body and soul dividual is never a consanguineal replica of its procreators, for its body mixes the bodies of its parents, hence of two male affines (see Taylor 2000 and this volume), and its soul/name must come from a non-parent: minimally, from an 'anti-parent', that is, the parent's parent or the parent's opposite-sex sibling.[25] Most importantly, this dividual child has to be *made* a relative by its parents, since Amazonian substantial identifications are a consequence of social relations rather than the other way around.[26] This means that the child has to be 'de-affinalized': it is a stranger-guest who must be turned into a consubstantial kin (Gow 1997; Rival 1998*b*). The construction of kinship is the deconstruction of potential affinity; but the reconstruction of kinship at the end of each life cycle through procreation must rely on the affinal givenness of human sociality.

EXAMPLES

All of the above would obviously benefit from a lot of fine-tuning. Meanwhile, it is not hard to find other ethnographic expressions of this general 'Amazonian' structure, which need not be directly coded in terms of kinship categories. The following examples come to my mind as I write:

1. The model of Kalapalo kinship terminology proposed by Basso (1973: 79), which could receive a Dumontian-hierarchical rather than ethnoscientific-taxonomical interpretation, especially if one considers the reversal of siblingship into cross-cousinship as the default relational idiom when one moves from intra-village everyday contexts to inter-village relations, and, in particular, to the great pan-village rituals, which, noteworthily, construct 'Xingú society' as a maximally inclusive unit.

2. The systematic gender associations carried by the right-downward and left-upward diagonal lines of the diagram when the latter is 'applied' to Achuar sociality. Pure consanguinity seems only to be attainable by and among women, just as pure affinity is a male condition. These divergent pulls generate an overall kinship dynamics excellently analysed by Taylor (1983, 2000, and this volume).

3. The trajectories described by the Barasana rituals of 'Fruit House' (left-upwards) and '*He* House' (right-downwards), which, incidentally, invert the distribution of gender values found in the Achuar case (S. Hugh-Jones 1993).[27]

4. The foregrounding of the consanguine/affine division (backgrounded in the life-process of kinship) effected in Wari' funerary endocannibalism (Vilaça 1992). It is tempting to speculate that the *affines* of the deceased are the ones who must eat the corpse precisely because this object represents the person in a state of pure consanguinity. The soul, in its turn, goes out on an affinally marked journey to the Beyond and finally becomes a wild pig that may be killed and eaten by the *consanguines* of the deceased.

5. The Piro construction of sociality as a deliberate 'mixing of blood' (Gow 1991). Starting from a state of pure potential affinity between different 'peoples', history unfolds as the very process of kinship. So we could also read our structure as describing the movement from myth (mythically given affinity) to history (historically constructed consanguinity), and back again. This macro-process is recursively reproduced in the micro-oscillations between identity and alterity which constitute the life cycle (Gow 1997).

6. The Araweté cosmological circulation between the *Maï* and the living. Fig. 2.4 combines two diagrams presented in my monograph (Viveiros de Castro 1992: 251, 253); they are the direct 'ancestors' of the structure proposed in this essay.[28]

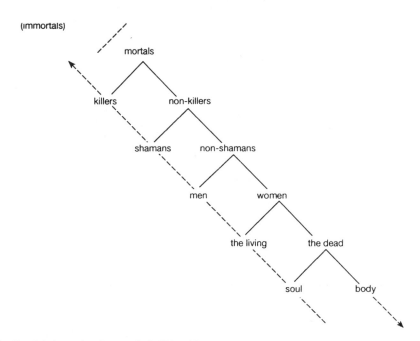

FIG. 2.4. Araweté socio-cosmological bipartitions

7. The Tupinamba and Jivaroan cannibalistic and *tsantsa* rituals, which involve a multiple splitting of the person into self-consanguineal and enemy-affinal 'halves' (Viveiros de Castro 1992: 287–92; Taylor 1993). More generally, the Amazonian processes of incorporation of the 'other' by the 'self', or, to be more accurate, the processes of determination of the 'self' by the 'other' that have been described by authors such as Taylor (1985, 1993), Vilaça (1992), Fausto (1997), or Kelly (1999), could be modelled along the lines of our structure. The latter can be made to represent the dynamics of predation as much as that of potential affinity, since they are one and the same, as I have often argued. Consider, for instance, Fig. 2.5. It is undoubtedly too schematic and needs substantial adjusting. However, its implications are clear.

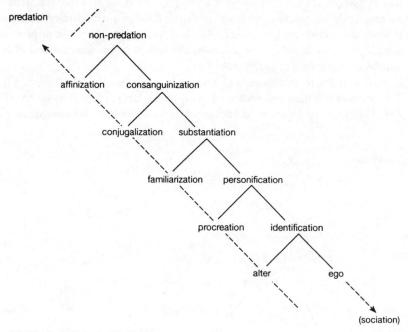

FIG. 2.5. The 'assimilation' of the Other

8. Last but not least, the model(s) of Kayapó social structure elaborated by Turner (1979*b*, 1984, 1992). Fig. 2.6 is a possible schematization of a far richer ethnographic analysis.[29]

If one accepts the schema displayed in Fig. 2.6, one might first wish to note that 'nature' encompasses 'society' (in the immanent sense discussed above) in Gê cosmology. Indeed, as Turner seems to be arguing in his more recent work, the ritual construction of society, that is, its determination 'against' its initially derived, marked condition of non-nature, must appeal to the powers of the

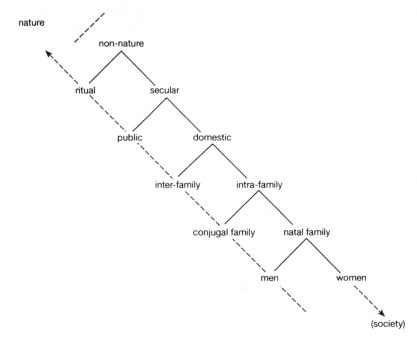

Fig. 2.6. Kayapó social structure (from T. Turner)

Outside. Consequently, and contrary to common belief, Gê social structure is not a closed system, after all. It is, instead, rather similar to the overall Amazonian socio-cosmological landscape (Ewart 2000). Furthermore, one might argue that in Gê cosmology women are not 'natural' in any simple sense of the term. What the diagram suggests, quite to the contrary, is that a pure, totally self-sufficient state of sociality would be synonymous to an exclusively female-constituted and reproduced world. This is what Gê uxorilocality is all about, I guess.

By way of conclusion, let me remark that whereas some Amazonian societies (and/or their ethnographers) seem to put great cultural stress on the downward diagonal of my meta-diagram (i.e. the consanguineally oriented vector of the process of kinship), others keep their eyes, so to speak, firmly set on the general source and condition of the process: potential affinity. Such differences in orientation within a single cosmological frame might account for the contrasts that are continuously surfacing in the ethnography of this region: peacefulness versus bellicosity, emphasis on sharing mutuality versus emphasis on predatory reciprocity, social introversion versus extroversion, this-worldly versus other-worldly speculative leanings, and so forth. These contrasts cannot but surface: they are, properly speaking, superficial. For all their 'gut feeling' salience, they are just partial readings of one and the same general structure that must needs have it *both ways*.

Still, the way up is not the way down.

ACKNOWLEDGEMENT

A modified version of this chapter has recently been published in Portuguese in the Brazilian journal ILHA.

NOTES

1. My argument comes directly from Wagner (1981), who states that in a semiotic regime in which human conventions are inscribed as primordial givens in the constitution of the universe, what lies outside convention is given over to invention, falling within the province of human creative intervention. The decisive step of the argument is the second one, for the first more or less echoes the received (though not necessarily false) anthropological wisdom about the naturalization of culture or society by pre-modern, 'animist' peoples. If culture is naturalized, then nature is culturalized, that is, its 'differentiation' becomes the responsibility of humans. An Amazonian version of this cosmological chiasmus was reinvented by myself, with a specific emphasis on the 'deictic' value of indigenous correlates of our nature and culture dualism (see Viveiros de Castro 1998*a*; the original version of that paper, published in Portuguese in 1996, was written in total oblivion of *The Invention of Culture*, which I had read fifteen years previously without understanding much of it).

2. See Viveiros de Castro 1993. The term I coined for this concept was not particularly felicitous. I contrasted 'potential affinity' not only to matrimonially created 'actual affinity' (brothers-in-law, for example), but also to 'virtual affinity' (e.g. cross-cousins, who are terminological affines in Dravidianate systems). The problem of course was that 'potential' and 'virtual' meant 'virtually' the same thing in the literature; the first term had often been used to designate what I called virtual affinity (potential affinity was not differentiated from it as a type of relationship in its own right). Perhaps a better choice would have been something like 'meta-affinity', by analogy with the *metagermanité* (meta-siblingship) proposed by Jamous (1991) to characterize the kinship matrix of the Meo of Northern India. The parallel is relevant, since Meo meta-siblingship (closely related to the *bhai* example evoked in the quotation from Dumont above) is the consanguineal (and cross-sex) analogue of the Amazonian hierarchical (and same-sex) meta-affinity. Taylor (2000: 312 n. 6) has recently proposed a cross-naming of the virtual/potential contrast, a suggestion I find quite defensible. However, as my distinction has made its way into the Amazonianist literature, I feel somehow obliged to honour it, or at least to stick to the adjective 'potential' (which I still find full of, how should I put it, potential), while dropping the word 'virtual' when referring to cognatically given affinity. I now prefer to use 'virtual' to designate the pre-cosmological background from which potential affinity derives (see below).

3. For the concept of a political economy of people, see, for instance Wagner (1981: 24–6), Meillassoux (1980 [1975]), Turner (1979*b*), Gregory (1982), and Rivière (1984: 87–100). These authors give different names to the concept and have somewhat different notions of what 'political economy' and 'person' mean. Their overall emphasis, however, is on the production and circulation of subjects in society, not of organisms in nature. There is thus no compelling reason to restrict the extension of 'people' or 'person' to our own species. Such restriction may be derived from an implicit reliance on the notion of biological reproduction, which is reproduced at a metabiological (if not metaphysical) level as the so-called 'social production of persons'.

4. As an example of inversion, see the Araweté spouse-swapping ritual friends, who are 'anti-affines' without being 'consanguines' (Viveiros de Castro 1992: 167-78).

5. The remainder of the chapter provides a very sketchy elaboration of this idea, which I hope to develop elsewhere. What I am calling the 'infinite background of virtual sociality' finds its fullest expression in Amerindian mythology, which describes the actualization of the present state of affairs as the break-up of a pre-cosmos endowed with *absolute transparency*, by which I mean a 'time' or condition in which the corporeal and spiritual dimensions of beings were still mutually and simultaneously accessible. In this pre-cosmological state, rather than an original indifferentiation between humans and non-humans, what prevails is *infinite* difference, but difference that is *internal* to every primordial character or agent (as opposed to the finite and external differences that make up the actualized, present-day world). This is expressed in the regime of 'metamorphosis', or qualitative multiplicity, characteristic of myth. It is impossible to decide whether the Jaguar of the myth, for example, is a bundle of human affections in feline shape, or a bundle of feline affections in human shape, since metamorphosis is an 'event' or a 'becoming' (i.e. an intensive superposition of states) rather than a 'process' of 'change' (i.e. an extensive transposition of states). Mythic narratives usually end with the separation of such pre-cosmological flows once the latter enter the cosmological process. Thenceforth, the human and the jaguar in/of the jaguar (and in/of the human) will alternately function as figure and ground to each other. The absolute *transparency* of mythic 'time' bifurcates into a dimension of relative *invisibility* (the 'soul') and one of relative *opacity* (the 'body'). Potential affinity goes back to this background of metamorphic sociality. The great Amerindian origin myths of culture always have their central *dramatis personae* related by trans-specific affinity: the 'human' hero and the 'vulture' father-in-law, the 'peccary' brothers-in-law, the 'manioc' daughter-in-law, and so forth. Human kinship 'originates' from these transnatural alliances, but must never let itself be sucked back into them, thence the effort embodied in rituals like the *couvade*, which strive to sever the potential connections between the newborn and pre-cosmological transparency. In this sense, the *couvade* is as much 'about' keeping body and soul *united* (as in the classic interpretation of Rivière 1974*a*) as about keeping body and soul *distinct*.

6. This is a general theoretical remark. Immediate or 'real' kinship ties are necessary for the fabrication of classificatory links and categories; they function as material and efficient causes. But reciprocally, so-called classificatory links are necessary for the institution of those same immediate kin-ties and of kinship in general; they are formal and final causes, and as such are presupposed by the first order of causality. The old quarrel between extensionists and categorialists boils down to this. The first believe that the (necessarily particular) fabrication also fabricates the (necessarily general) institution,

which is clearly false. The second make the opposite mistake, or rather, they do not see the distinction. These considerations will be developed in another context. Let me just note here that the distinction between fabrication and institution could be fruitfully applied to an apparently very different debate, that opposing 'projectionist' and 'immanentist' interpretations of animic cosmologies: the first posing that the anthropomorphization of non-human entities proceeds by the extension of human predicates to non-humans, the second refusing the notion of anthropomorphism and arguing that personhood is an immediate, substantial property of both human and non-human entities.

7. My point here is similar to Schrempp's (1992: 88–98) about Maori kinship as instantiating a more general and properly cosmological notion of form, rather than being a constitutive category in itself. What constitutes a particular kinship form must lie outside of kinship.

8. If one wishes to pursue the hot/cold image, one could say that affinity and consanguinity as expressed in kinship terminologies are conventional measures of relational 'temperature', but what is being measured is a certain relational 'heat' embodied in affinity. There is a conventionally negative affinal temperature, namely terminological consanguinity, but there is no negative affinal energy.

9. See Dumont (1983*b*) and Needham (1973). Needham's interest in dual symbolic classifications was related to his earlier work on two-section terminologies and their 'total structural' implications.

10. What I mean is that Amazonian consanguinity needs affinity to be defined, but the reverse is not true; consanguinity is a mode of affinity, while the latter is axiomatically primitive. It is important to note that this is *not* a semantic argument about the lexical structure of terminologies. It is in such limited sense that the concept of markedness entered the anthropology of kinship (Scheffler 1984). Dumont's remark about the Northern/Southern Indian difference is also couched in purely lexical terms, although he clearly means something of more general import. In the Amazonian case, I see no overwhelming signs of the unmarked status of affinal *terms*. If anything, it is the opposite that obtains, as in those terminologies showing a consanguineally biased neutralization of the consanguine/affine contrast in GØ. Otherwise, consanguineal and affinal terms are equally primary and non-neutralizable: an 'equistatutory' situation if we restrict ourselves to the lexical structure. So the Amazonian terminological landscape does not contradict the (debatable) thesis about the universally marked status of affinal and cross-collateral terms as against consanguineal and parallel ones (see Hage 1999). But, as I said, my point is not lexical. It concerns the pragmatics of kinship usages, the range of application of consanguineal and affinal terms, and the socio-cosmological values embodied in these two categories. Above all, it implies that the marked status of affinal terms within the domain of kinship is evidence that kinship as such is a marked (particular) mode of sociality as against the general, unmarked value of Otherness embodied in 'potential affinity'.

11. It is perhaps worth recalling that the spatial inscription of Amazonian socio-cosmological values, and the consequent emphasis on the distinction between the 'outside' and the 'inside', was first developed by Lévi-Strauss (1958) in the context of his discussion of concentric and diametric dualisms. But it was in Rivière's book on the Trio that the contrast received its first ethnographic elaboration (Rivière 1969*a*: ch. X, 'Inside and out').

12. I am aware that Dumont would disagree with this. He had often contrasted hierarchical encompassment to dialectical totalization (see the discussion in Houseman 1984: 305–6). But the distinction is not that easy to make (see for instance the deliberate conflation of the two figures by Turner (1984)), and in any case both modes of bringing in the whole fail to account for Amazonian cosmological operations.

13. See Viveiros de Castro (1992: 282–301). In my previous dealings with Dumontian matters, I occasionally slipped into a literal-minded application of the model and searched for 'the whole society'. This was certainly a mistake. Lost in between the everydayness of sociability and the everywhereness of sociality, 'society' is not very much of a concern for Amazonians; this makes it a problematic and fuzzy object. Where it does seem to emerge as a focal reification, such as among Central Brazilian peoples for instance, it can be accounted for as the output of a process of pre-emption of both intra-domestic sociability and trans-specific sociality. I am extending here the well-known argument of Terence Turner about the communal level of Jê societies being a transformation of domestic relations. Turner moves 'up' from the domestic to establish the communal; I am suggesting we should also move 'down' to that level. The public sphere is built up with the shreds and patches of the domestic and the cosmic. But since the 'domestic' is itself a particularized transformation of the 'cosmic', there is perhaps just one single basic movement.

14. If we consider the concentric topology of Amazonian socialities from an extensional point of view, it is quite obvious (even tautological) that the 'interior' is located in the 'exterior', since the inside sits inside the outside as naturally as, for example, a fish swims in the sea. But if we look at things from an intensional point of view, it is the other way around: the exterior lies within the interior, like the sea which dwells within the fish, making it a figure of (and not simply in) the sea. It is the sea 'within' which makes the sea 'without' a constitutive condition of the fish, or, to put it differently, it is the sea within which makes a fish die (i.e. cease to be a fish) once extracted from the sea without.

15. To pursue the image of the preceding note, this is the same as saying that in every drop of the sea there swims a virtual fish (which is one way of summarizing Amerindian 'perspectivism'; see Viveiros de Castro 1998a).

16. If the word 'structure' makes the reader wince, let him/her by all means put something else in its place—may I suggest 'process'? In the present case, it amounts to exactly the same, since what this structure structures is a process, and what this process processes is a structure.

17. In the standard or 'extensive' hierarchical model the dominant value includes its subordinate contrary as part of its own extension: 'Man' includes 'man' and 'woman', and so forth. As the standard Dumontian model operates upon well-determined values, it is not dynamic enough to account for Amazonian cosmological processes. The value reversal or bidimensionality of hierarchy is not sufficient here, for we need a principle of indetermination and recursiveness. Houseman (1988) provides a brilliant formulation of this argument in a different ethnographic context.

18. The line or frame separating the diametrically divided whole from its exterior belongs to the universe of the *observer*, not that of the observed.

19. A centre is obviously necessary for drawing a circle; but without a circle there is no centre, just a point. If the central point 'fabricates' the circle, the circle 'institutes' a point as a centre (see n. 6).

20. The inspiration here comes directly from Wagner (1991) and Strathern (1988, 1992), but also from the unpublished work of J. A. Kelly (1999), which stimulated me to write the present essay.

21. This, I would say, especially concerns brothers. Consider the Araweté usage of two married brothers calling each other *he rayin-hi pihã*, which can be translated either as 'my companion-of-mother-of-child' or as 'the companion of my mother-of-child'. In both cases, if my translation is correct, the expression means 'the husband of my (possible) wife'. So two brothers would 'see' themselves as related not through shared parentage but alternative conjugality, that is, through an opposite-sex 'relator'. Accordingly, Araweté married brothers should be defined as 'non-brothers-in-law' rather than vice versa: consanguinity is non-affinity.

22. Lévi-Strauss sees in the *clinamen* of imperfect twinship the key schematism of Amerindian asymmetric dualism. The contrast drawn in *Histoire de Lynx* between twin-ship in European mythologies (with their emphasis on similarity) and American ones (with their emphasis on difference) is strictly parallel to the contrast drawn in the *Elementary Structures* between the brother and brother-in-law relationship (Lévi-Strauss 1967: 554–5). This seems to point to the intrinsic continuity of the twin-centred mythol-ogy of *Histoire de Lynx* with the affinally centred *mythe unique* analysed at length in the *Mythologiques*.

23. In Amerindian cosmologies, the spiritual or 'invisible' dimension of reality is often referred to as 'the other side'. Such idiom, at first sight identical to our 'the beyond', may actually mean something else. The other side of the other side is *this* side: the invisible dimension of the invisible dimension is the visible one, the soul of the soul is the body, and so on. I suspect that the traditional 'Platonic' reading of indigenous body/soul dual-ities, which understands them to be synonymous with our 'appearance/essence' distinc-tion, is entirely wrong. It should be replaced with an interpretation of these two dimensions as constituting reciprocally the *figure* and the *ground* of each other, that is, a relation totally different from that between appearance and essence.

24. The body connects (and collects) kin, the soul separates them into singular persons, just as the soul connects non-kin (humans to non-humans, for instance) and the body sepa-rates them (Viveiros de Castro 1998*a*). 'Body' and 'soul' play inverse functions as we move up or down the diagram. The process of kinship continues the differentiation of bodies which began at the end of the pre-cosmological era; the soul is like the 'background noise' left by the cosmological Big Bang, the shadow of the primordial transparency among early beings. As the token of the infinite, internal difference of the virtual pre-cosmos (see n. 5), the soul prevents an ultimate and absolute differentiation of bodily exteriorities. The soul works at *connecting what is different*, and, in this sense, is like incest prohibition. This is another way of saying that the soul is 'affinal', while the body is 'consanguineal'.

25. Where souls (or their onomastic reifications so common in Amazonia) are thought to come from the interior of the *socius*, they must pass through channels systematically other than those through which corporeal substances circulate. It is possible to reach the neces-sary difference minimally by moving up one generation or one gender notch on the kinship grid, that is, by having the grandparents or the opposite-sex siblings of the parents as the soul/name givers. As far as I know, these relatives are never included in the circle of abstinence which is created when a kin falls ill, and which defines the body-sharing (and body-producing) unit of Amazonian sociality. In this sense, the celebrated *couvade* can be seen as an anti-naming ceremony.

26. Kin relationships do not 'culturally' express a 'naturally' given corporeal connection, because bodies are created by relations, not relations by bodies. If 'no relation without differentiation' is the first cardinal postulate of Amazonian ontology (see above), the idea that substances proceed from relations and not vice versa would be the second one, which I hope to develop elsewhere.

27. It is highly probable that some of the Barasana cosmological motives superbly diagramatized in C. Hugh-Jones (1979) could be translated into this figure as well.

28. As its present embedding in the first one makes clear, I wrongly interpreted the second diagram featuring the post-mortem transformations of the person (Viveiros de Castro 1992: 253).

29. I have left out the constitution of the person according to the same principles, which has been the subject of much elaboration by Turner (1980, 1995).

3

Wives, Pets, and Affines: Marriage among the Jivaro

Anne-Christine Taylor, *CNRS*

In his celebrated work on marriage among the Trio (1969*a*), Peter Rivière drew attention to an intriguing trait of this group's system of kin relations: the proximity between conjugal and brother–sister relations (Rivière 1969*a*: 190–1). This feature is also characteristic of the pattern of kin relations among the Jivaro,[1] a set of sub-tribes entirely distinct from the Trio, although they too—at least some of them—possess a 'two-section' or, to use the now more commonly used expression, Dravidian-type kinship terminology, coupled with a stated preference for close cross-cousin marriage. Like the Trio, the Jivaro assume that in some sense the conjugal and cross-sex sibling bond is interchangeable; and like the Trio, they contrast the two forms of a relation of necessary complementarity between a man and a woman in terms of normative behaviour. Among the Jivaro, however, the conventional attitudes proper to conjugal and sibling relations are quite distinct from those fostered by the Trio; moreover, whereas the Trio consider oblique marriage 'appetitive', the Jivaro find it highly improper.

In his book, Rivière focused on the economic and political implications of Trio marriage and the cross-sex sibling bond, rather than on the symbolic structure underlying the opposition between the two types of relationship. This is the issue I want to take up in my contribution. My concern is not with the structure and working of a kinship system, nor even with the stated values, norms, and ideas concerning the institution of marriage and the proper ways of living together as man and woman, a theme that has been particularly well covered by British anthropologists working in the Amazon (see Gow 1991; McCallum 1989*b*; Rival 1998*b*). Rather, my interest lies in uncovering indigenous representations of the relational forms that underlie lived kin relationships. Thus, my aim is to explore the premises informing Jivaroan conceptualizations of conjugal and cross-sex sibling ties, and thereby to shed some light on local understandings of social relations in general. My argument presupposes that relationships, that is to say, the forms of interaction between individuals as determined by what structuralist analysis calls the 'system of attitudes', are built on, and usually combine, more elemental schemes

of relating to non-selves according to their perceived identity or alterity in relation
to ego in a given context. I further hypothesize that these modes of 'relating to'
translate in indigenous conceptualizations as implicitly labelled affective stances.
'Seduction', understood as the eliciting of desire in another 'person', is an example of such a relational disposition, and it is, as we shall see, one of the components
of the conjugal relationship among the Jivaro. 'Predation', the killing and more or
less figurative consumption of the Other, offers, I believe, another illustration of
the kind of elemental stance I am referring to.[2]

The theme of predation has figured prominently in recent Amazonian ethnography, following Viveiros de Castro's brilliant exposition of the symbolic values
attached to kinship categories and their relative valency in the constitution of
sociality in lowland cultures (Viveiros de Castro 1992, 1993, 1995; Viveiros de
Castro and Fausto 1993). I will build on this work, particularly on the illuminating
distinction drawn therein between real, virtual, and potential affinity. The 'potential' refers to relations to entities—gods, enemies, animals, spirits—that escape the
process of consanguinization inherent to the actualization of the marriage relation.
Such beings remain by definition paradigmatic Others. As Viveiros de Castro
demonstrates, encompassing relations to these entities posited as being the ultimate source of human sociality are, in a great many lowland cultures, construed as
taking the form of predation. While I take due note of the caveats formulated by
some anthropologists (Fausto 1997; Rival 1998*b*) to the effect that too heavy an
emphasis on predation as the unique and somewhat transcendental scheme
governing all major aspects of social life tends to obscure the importance in
Amazonian world-views of processes of production or creation of life and of
'familiarization'—to borrow Fausto's term subsuming various modes of affiliating
others to self—it remains the case that Viveiros de Castro's concentric model
closely fits the general configuration of Jivaroan social organization, and that their
views of kin relationships are deeply permeated by the a priori categorization of
affines as enemies.

Among the Jivaro, entering into the state of matrimony is a very simple and
unritualized affair once a marriage is agreed on (and this is of course the long and
tricky part): the young man simply moves into the house of his father-in-law without further ado. There are, however, two features of Jivaroan marriage worthy of
attention. The first one is the element of coercion and antagonism that is built into
it. In-laws are expected to accept the marriage only reluctantly, and the girl herself,
even if she does not object to the marriage, is expected to be farouche and to shun
initially her husband's companionship and sexual overtures. What is latent among
the Shuar and Achuar becomes blatant among the closely related Candoshi, where
marriage takes the form of a stylized act of war, in which the woman is briefly
grabbed by the hair, thereby signalling that she has been taken (Surallès 1998).
Underlying Jivaroan marriage, in brief, we find a relation of violent capture.

A second notable feature is the role played by the young wife's celibate brother
closest in age: the boy is supposed to spend the first nights of a marriage lying

between husband and wife. This brother is the same one a young girl is paired with in early adolescence, in a kind of sexless, non-violent prefiguration of the conjugal relation. Thus, as soon as a boy gets his own bed in the 'male' part of the house (the *tankamash*),[13] at around 10 or 12 years of age, one of his sisters will start caring for him much as a wife would: she goes hunting with him, serves him food and manioc beer, and washes his clothes. It is also this brother who develops the most intimate relation with his sister's husband, and who ideally will eventually marry the latter's sibling, sister exchange being a highly valued arrangement among all Jivaroans. In fact, the spouse relation is largely overshadowed by this close male affinal bond, characterized by physical intimacy and often rowdy camaraderie.[4]

In contrast to this ostentatiously 'brotherly' tie between a man and one of his wife's bachelor siblings, relations between young spouses are widely acknowledged to be fraught with conflict. Recently married girls are much given to sulking, dragging their feet, and being generally wayward, and men expect to have at times to beat them into submission. The reason for this behaviour is quite readily stated by men: it is because women are inherently rebellious to, indeed ignorant of, real sociality and need to be taught it. At the same time, women are supposed to be sexually shy and indeed stingy with their favours, so they need to be constantly seduced by their husbands. In short, as the Achuar explicitly phrase it, women have to be both tamed and cajoled into sex. These considerations are frequently offered in justification for two typically Jivaroan cultural traits: on the one hand, conjugal 'pygmalionism', whereby grown men seek to marry very small girls (despite the sexual frustration this entails, since they won't have sex with them until puberty), in order to train them to be good wives through a kind of connubial imprinting, just as most animals have to be caught at a very young age in order to become real pets; on the other hand, the prestige linked to successfully 'domesticating' a woman captured in warfare and turning her into a loving spouse, a definite sign of masculine achievement since this is a feat that can only be carried off, it is thought, by mature and experienced men who know exactly how to dose seduction and coercion to achieve a proper taming.

The connection between conjugality and taming is particularly salient in the vast repertoire of magical 'thought-songs' called *anent* which spouses address to each other in the hope of modifying their partner's states of feeling. By means of these unspoken song rituals, both men and women seek to elicit sentiments of affectionate compassion in their partner by identifying themselves with a pet animal in search of 'forgiveness' or play, as in the following example:

wawàkuji asàna	being a little marmoset
tsankurchinia atéasu	slipping forgiveness between us
waitiau anénmaichi	pitiful little thing
kunchi kunchi winiaja	chirping 'kunchi, kunchi'
	I come to you
suira jiirsaipia	don't look at me resentfully.[5]

'Pet songs', however, by no means exhaust the register of conjugal *anent*, insofar as they do not usually play on tropes of sexual desire, a theme that is dealt with
in a distinct class of 'heart speech'. On the female side, seduction is expressed
mainly in terms of elusive prey to pursuing hunter; on the male side, seduction
songs play on images of desire-firing appearance, often associated with bird court-
ing display and/or certain qualities of light, as in the following short extract: 'soar-
ing like the onset of evening | the sun must be setting | you are perhaps thinking
| but it is I | radiantly I come | glowing yellow I come to you | look at me disdain-
fully . . .'.[6] But women may also, when angry with their spouses, use threatening
anent, meant to inspire fear and respect in brutal or uncaring husbands, in which
they identify themselves with fearsome predators, as in the following example: 'you
anger me so much | shaking the earth | disappearing underground | together with
my little children | shaking the earth I'll go . . .'.[7] In this case the implicit refer-
ence is to a class of cannibal forest spirits named *jurijri*, who live underground,
devour over-zealous hunters, and provoke earthquakes.

The themes alluded to in conjugal thought-magic, and the affective dispositions
they deal with, are entirely congruent with the behavioural patterns we mentioned
earlier, insofar as they combine the imputed feelings of a master for its pet in
certain stereotyped situations—namely a rush of pitying tenderness—of a hunter
faced with an angry predator—namely terror and avoidance—and, finally, of a
creature being either the object or the agent of a relation of courtship—namely a
suffusion of desire. The images evoked in these *anent* are thus both the cue and the
metaphor for the emotions they are supposed to elicit.

Looking carefully at these songs, some further points of interest can be made
concerning the relations they are predicated on. To begin with, these relations are
never reciprocal: for example, although the 'master' position is constantly being
imputed, the point of view espoused by the singer is invariably that of the pet and
not that of its master; thus, 'pet-position' songs are not meant to trigger 'master
songs' in return on the part of men, who actually use pet songs in exactly the same
way women do. In fact, the only *anent* in which the master's perspective is taken
are those sung by women to their real pets and domestic animals (dogs and
offspring of game animals), explicitly addressed as *tankuru*, 'my pet'. Similarly,
male and female-voiced tropes of seduction are not made to 'fit': whereas women
picture themselves as a game animal in flight, men, instead of adopting the
hunter's position attributed to them by women, identify with decidedly non-preda-
tory figures such as sunsets or toucans, while real stalked animals, addressed as
male affines, are given the feelings of a woman succumbing to desire. We must
therefore be careful to distinguish between, on the one hand, the terms of a social
relation—the 'persons' linked by a given tie—and, on the other hand, the implicitly labelled relational affect that is being set up between the terms of the relation,
such as the pitying tenderness elicited by pet imagery. Secondly, and closely related
to this point, we know that it is men who 'tame' women in marriage; nevertheless,
pet-position songs can be addressed by men to other men, namely brothers-in-law,

though in such cases pet and predator images are usually combined, the singer presenting himself as a 'compassion-awakening harpy eagle', for example. The latter kind of song can, in turn, be usefully compared to the *anent* addressed by hunter to game, in which the particular animal a man is pursuing is invariably treated, in the register of seduction, as a 'brother-in-law' (*saeru* or the diminutive *saichi*). This brings us to a crucial point, which is that *anent* in general, as opposed to other genres of 'ritual' or 'profane' songs, appear to be associated exclusively with affinal relationships: they can be sung by men to their brothers-in-law, by spouses to each other, by women to their sons-in-law, but they are never used between same sex or even opposite sex consanguines, except when these kin have just died, and then it is to deny that they are in fact kin[8] (see Taylor 1993). There is one significant exception to this rule, namely the class of *anent* used by women in their gardening magic. I will return to this point further on.

The features examined so far—the notion that women need to be tamed in and by matrimony, more generally the insistent connection between conjugality, taming, seducing, and hunting—strongly suggest that women are somehow related to game. Substantiating this claim adequately would require an extensive analysis of Jivaroan representations of selfhood and the experiences they stem from, a subject I cannot hope to deal with in this chapter.[9] Suffice it to say that, according to the Jivaro, personhood is invariably 'dividual' in the sense that it is based on an internalized relation to a figure of alterity. Thus, in the same way that men's subjecthood is predicated on the introjection of an agonistic, unstable face-to-face relation to an affinal 'enemy' (Jivaroan ceremonial dialogue is both a salient 'model of' and 'model for' precisely this relation), women's identity is based on an intimate, constitutive sibling relation to game animals. This notion of relational or split identity extends to, and is well illustrated by, the shrunken face trophies (*tsantsa*) used in Jivaroan war feasts. One of the ritual names given to the head is that of 'profile' (*misha*), an allusion to the bipartition of the face according to the chains of relations extending from either 'side' of the profile and the distinct perspectives they set up (Taylor 1994). In short, Jivaroan women are structurally 'half-animal' in the same way that Jivaroan men are 'half- enemy', insofar as both genders' sense of self is rooted in the memory of a series of culturally shaped experiences, of actual or virtual confrontation in the case of men, of 'compassionate familiarity' in the case of women. These premises account for the marked differences in the socialization of children according to sex, the assumption of partial animality imputed to girls justifying the strict training they receive (as opposed to boys who are very much left to their own devices) and the strong control exercised by men over their sexuality. The relatedness of women to game also helps to explain why women are assumed to be the natural caretakers of captured pets. And of course it ties in neatly with the affinal treatment of animals by men in their hunting *anent*, since their wives are in a sister position in relation to their prey.[10]

Adding these chains of 'invisible' relations to the triad formed by a male ego,[11] his wife, and his brother-in-law, each of the genealogical positions can then be divided according to the scheme of split identity alluded to above: thus a woman stands between two cross-sex 'siblings' (an animal and a human one) just as she is between two 'spouse' figures (her brother and her husband); likewise, a man is connected to two 'brothers-in-law', his wife's human and game brothers, as he is to a pair of women, his sister/'spouse' and his wife.[12]

This series of relations in turn folds over, in such a way that real brothers-in-law who give you their sister (and vice versa), and thereby allow you to have children, may be equated with game brothers-in-law you kill and take pets from, potential affines with game in general (i.e. animals that have not been particularized by the direct relation established between a killer and his victim), and 'true' or virtual enemy affines with predators.

If we accept the notion that affinity is coloured and indeed defined by its connection with a horizon of predatory enmity and, further, that relations to animals that are eaten or that eat humans are, in the Jivaroan order of things, exactly parallel to relations with male affines, the saliency of taming is self-evident: taming is the flip side of predation, the alternative to devouring or being devoured, that is, a positive relation to and between beings posited as inherently cannibal. And this would explain why the idiom of taming, eating, and seducing used in *anent* is restricted to affinal and conjugal relationships.

However, this leads us into another set of issues. To begin with, the conjugal process of taming wives is expected to produce children, who will in turn marry and have children of their own; and pets, of course, are not in fact tamed 'WB' affines, but rather the children of an animal brother-in-law that has been or will be killed. Furthermore, pets are raised by women in a quasi-maternal relation (although in her songs to them a woman never actually addresses them as 'children', *uchiru*), and 'pet-position' *anent*, by stressing dependency, seem to refer to this pseudo-maternal relation of 'grown', protective care-taker to helpless small creature. To this should be added the important fact that women consistently address the male (affinal) intended recipient of their *anent* in consanguineal terms, either as 'father' (*aparu, apachi*) in the case of a spouse or as 'son' (*uchiru*) in the case of a son-in-law.[13] The fact that the 'pet-position' seems to be modelled on a child-to-parent relation, and that women, in their songs, treat their male affinal addressees as Gen. + 1 or − 1 male consanguines, suggests that taming is viewed as a form of mothering or more generally of parenting. But what then is the status of taming in regard to parent–child relations and more broadly to consanguinity? Are taming relations simply consanguinity by another name? To answer these questions I now turn to the issue of local construals of parenthood and procreation, and switch the focus of my analysis from 'horizontal' links to relations between generations.

Let us return briefly to the assimilation (underscored earlier on) between conjugal and cross-sex sibling relations. In terms of 'vertical' connections, the temporal and conceptual overlap between the H/W and B/Z relations carries the implication that a man's child is also in some sense the child of his brother-in-law, insofar

as both men share the same 'wife', and are thus in a position of co-father in relation to her child; for a man, his sister's child is the deferred offspring of the
pseudo-conjugal pairing they experienced as adolescents, whereas his own child is
partly that of his brother-in-law. Such ideas might be seen as gratuitous extrapo-
lations with little grounding in ethnographic fact, until it is taken into account that
Jivaroan notions of conception and procreation do not posit a substantive link
between genitor and child. Rather than the transmission of substance imbued with
principles of identity, what makes 'father' and 'child' is the relation that develops
between them, both in and out of the mother's womb.[14] In light of this, the assimilation of MB/FZH to a 'father' position, by virtue of his quasi-conjugal relation
to M/FZ is by no means far-fetched; it merely stands as a somewhat unusual vari-
ant of the many forms of co-fatherhood posited by a number of indigenous
cultures throughout the Amazon (see, for example, Gregor 1985; Viveiros de
Castro 1992; Rival 1998*b*; Vilaça 1992, 1995). Given, furthermore, that a wife is
'sister' to two sorts of brother-in-law (co-fathers to ego), an 'intimate enemy' on
the one hand, a game animal on the other hand, ego's children will in fact be,
according to their sex, either half-affine or 'enemy' in the case of boys, and half-
animal or 'prey' in the case of girls. This configuration is precisely the source of
the dual selfhood that shapes male and female identities. Thus, even same-sex children (in relation to ego) are never fully and truly consanguineal.

The question then becomes, what exactly constitutes the other half of the
paternal relation, that is, that part of the vertical tie that is not imputed to the
ghostly 'enemy' or 'game' co-father? What, in short, is the non-affinal residue of
consanguinity? I would claim that it is simply identity, that is to say, a non-difference (and therefore a non-relation) seen as the outcome of a kind of cloning. In
other words, the fraction of ego's son that is not affinal is identical to his own position as father; likewise, for a mother, that part of her daughter that is not 'other' is
a clone of herself. The indigenous representation of engendered sameness is
modelled, unsurprisingly, on the mode of propagation of the major cultivated
plants, primarily of manioc, multiplied by the planting of cuttings taken from the
stem of a grown bush. This form of reproduction is hypostasized in a complex
figure called *nunkui*, who is both the 'mother' of garden plants as well as her own
children. In their gardening *anent*, women establish an identification with this
entity, and through this assimilation to a self-cloning (and also uni-gendered, i.e.
exclusively female) figure they ritually set up a fully consanguineal relation with
their own stock of plants. It must be stressed that *nunkui* songs are in fact self-
addressed. In these *anent*, women speak *as* '*nunkui* woman' and refer to their *own*
multiplication by evoking images of non-vegetal things flocking or proliferating, as
in the following example: 'being a nunkui woman | my children roll and grumble
| (like) river stones heaping | growing and thickening'. In this respect, gardening
anent stand in sharp contrast to the 'relational' invocations addressed by humans to
human or non-human affinal partners. At the same time, their self-referentiality is
entirely congruent with the self-replicating enunciator they are imputed to.

The idea that consanguinity is at the conceptual level rooted in the notion of identity allows one to make sense of several enigmatic aspects of Jivaroan relational patterns. For example, the strong and (given the Dravidian profile of their kinship system) unusual aversion of Jivaroans toward oblique (FZ or ZD) marriage is understandable in light of their notions of co-fatherhood: although terminologically affinal from the point of view of a male ego, these women are actually very close to being, potentially, either 'mother' (through F and FZ pre-conjugal pairing) or 'daughter' (through ego and Z pre-conjugal pairing). Conversely, the relative frequency, in the register of 'deviant marriages', of unions with a deceased father's wife (other than ego's real mother), a terminological 'mother' who is nevertheless far less 'close' to ego than his father's chosen sister, or with a wife's daughter by a former husband (i.e. a 'daughter', most often of a captured woman) points to the partial structural sameness between, on the one hand, father and son (insofar as a son can literally take his father's place in relation to the latter's wives), and, by the same token, on the other hand, between mother and daughter, henceforth treated as co-wives. On the subject of co-wives, it is worth noting that it is precisely the relation of full identity between uterine sisters that predisposes them to share the same husband, and justifies the Jivaroan high regard for sororal polygyny. As for male siblings, as soon as they grow out of, first, the real bond they have with their mother, and then, after weaning, the pseudo-maternal bond they have with the elder sibling (male or female) who takes charge of them in early childhood, they are, by contrast, singularized or 'decloned' by their pairing with a sister—and through her with a potential affine. Moroever, male siblings are separated both in spatial and social terms during the better part of their adult lives.

The 'fathering' role imputed to FZH (ideally ego's WF) also helps to explain the peculiar nature of, and strong contrast between, the F/S and WF/DH relationship among the Jivaro. Both relations are markedly asymmetric, but in very different ways. Whereas fathers-in-law are highly directive and bossy in their dealings with young resident sons-in-law, fathers relate to their bachelor sons, once these have reached early adolescence, in an embarrassed, wheedling, and ostensibly non-authoritarian way. And while the WF/DH tie is marked by a rigid and elaborate code of etiquette, adolescent sons are notably ill-behaved in their own households, and often rude to their fathers. Paradoxically, the WF/DH relationship thus comes to appear as a more truly social form of paternity than is the F/S relation. In effect, fathers are in a kind of functional double-bind vis-à-vis their sons: insofar as these boys are sons, they cannot treat them as affines or 'enemies'; but insofar as they are clones of themselves, they cannot relate to them at all. Indeed, it is only once a son has come under the direct control of a brother-in-law that he and his father are finally able to engage in a relationship that is conceived as social, that is, shaped by the norms of proper linguistic and behavioural interaction. The constrained (non-)relation of 'suspended paternity' between father and son gives way to a recognized form of relationship, now that the former's brother-in-law starts assuming the role of 'heavy father'. Likewise, mothers and daughters enter into a proper relationship—as opposed to a sort of clonal contiguity—only once the presence of a son-in-law has activated it. The same goes for same-sex siblings: thus brothers (who address each other by their names in childhood) become 'brothers' (who address each other as such, i.e. as *yatsuru*) through the mediation of their affines.

In sum, consanguineal ties are non-relations that are turned into proper relationships only when articulated to affinal ones. This does not mean, of course, that there is no affective interaction between an adolescent son and his father, or between two unmarried male siblings. I am claiming, rather, that such relationships, according to implicit Jivaroan evaluations, are not held to be truly social bonds, insofar as they are not governed by an elaborate set of codes relating to modes of bodily posture, ways of speaking and interacting, the giving and receiving of goods, food or drink, and so forth. They are viewed instead as a form of uncouth though friendly contiguity, seemingly modelled on the behaviour of species given to herding or flocking, such as bands of minnows or sparrows, an image recurring in *nunkui* songs, as stated earlier. This is a form of collective interaction which implies a measure of co-ordination and pleasurable gregariousness, possibly frolicking, but precisely not the kind of stern face-to-face tension between an 'I' and a 'you' that lies at the heart of subjecthood and true human society. According to the Jivaro, in other words, only affinal links are fully social. This is why, I suggest, *anent*, which are essentially representations of relations, are *addressed* exclusively to affinal Others. In this perspective, relations of procreation are, in the strict sense of the term, reproductive. What makes them dynamic and introduces differentiation in a process that would otherwise be replication *à l'identique*, is their combination with affinity. Structurally, a son would be his father were it not for the fact that he is also half-son to his father's brother-in-law, therefore half-affine to his father. Gender difference ties into this by adding a further dimension of alterity between parent and child, thus making it approximate more closely to a relationship. Relations between fathers and daughters or mothers and sons are thus construed as (and are in fact) more 'social' than relations between father and son or mother and daughter, as they appear to be among the Trio.

From the point of view of a Jivaroan man, conjugality supposes the combination of two distinct modes of relating to a 'different' being, namely taming and seducing. While the former is the practical metaphor of an abstract relation of filiation between non-identical beings, the latter corresponds to the transposition, in the sexual key, of a relation of carnal consumption. This composite bond between a man and a woman is both made possible and encompassed by 'marriage', that is to say, following the Jivaroans' impeccably Dumontian logic, the relationship established between brothers-in-law, the epitome of social bonds. Seduction and taming, in this context, clearly constitute processes of 'de-affinization' whereby potentially threatening others are turned into lovers and/or pets, that is, dependants. The juxtaposition of these kinds of relations in turn produces relations to children, who are, by virtue of the co-fatherhood imputed to FZH, only partly 'consanguineal' (i.e. identical) in relation to their care-giving genitors, and who will replicate their parents' split nature according to their sex. Hunting, by contrast, combines the seducing and killing of a male, affinal animal, a condensation of relational forms that also produces a kind of offspring, pets, that stand as adopted affinal 'children' in relation to their human masters (Bch in a female perspective, WBch from the male point of view). Unlike human children, however, game children-in-law are both sterile (they do not reproduce in captivity and no effort is made to pair them; indeed their sex seems to be largely indifferent to their masters) and orphans (their parent is the real or potential victim of a killing). In this respect, human relations to pets are clearly antithetical to game procreativity, since they imply the rupture of ascendant and descendant lines of succession in the game 'family', just as the reproduction of manioc plants is in turn antithetical to human procreation, insofar as manioc plants are thought to feed on the blood of human babies if allowed to be in contact with them. These brief notations evidently point to a series of questions, to be explored elsewhere, concerning the postulated mode of reproduction of game animals qua male affines, as well as the complex relation between male killing as a ritual form of procreation and female capacities for producing children out of their own bodies.

   In this chapter I have chosen to focus on the notions guiding Jivaroan conceptualizations of human conjugal and parental ties, the inner core of an elaborate web of relations binding humans on one side to self-reproducing and hence fully consanguineal female plants, and on the other to male affinal game animals and predators. These relations are played out between two opposite conceptual poles. One is that of predation, a 'hyper-relation' between entities posited as maximally different in which both terms are poised to annul or cannibalize each other; in this sense, the closest conceivable thing to a pure relation. The other is that of cloning, that is to say a non-relation predicated on a self-perpetuating unique term. This is of course the horizon of consanguinity, just as predation is that of affinity. But among humans bound by kinship there is no more room for 'pure' consanguinity than there is for pure affinity. Humans cannot attain the full consanguinity of auto-reproductive garden plants. The closest analogy might be the individuated mass of sibling puppies at play, or the 'vegetal' companionship of young sisters with their mothers. By contrast, the creation of proper social relationships represents the burden and destiny of fully accomplished persons— paradigmatically, adult males—engaged in confronting their many-guised affines, thereby forging their subjecthood as true Jivaroans.

ACKNOWLEDGEMENT

A highly modified version of this chapter has been published in French in the journal *l'Homme*.

NOTES

1. This large ethnic group forms an isolated linguistic family. The Jivaro presently number about 85,000 persons, spread over south-east Ecuador and north-east Peru. They share the same subsistence pattern (slash-and-burn horticulture, hunting, and fishing), although their territory is diversified in terms of environment, ranging from the high *montaña* to the swamps of the upper Amazon valley. It is generally agreed that in linguistic and cultural terms the Jivaro can be divided into two main branches: the so-called Candoa sub-family, including the Shapra and Candoshi, and the Jivaro proper, including the Shuar, Achuar, Aguaruna, Huambisa, and Shiwiar.

2. There is a good deal of confusion regarding the precise meaning of the notion of predation. In the work of Viveiros de Castro and of most anthropologists of structuralist bent, 'predation' is a purely analytic construct: it is the label for a highly abstract scheme predicated on the subsumption of one term of a relation ('other') by the other term ('self'). It does not refer as such to the empirical forms of killing and consuming 'others'. However, it is often understood as a category of actual practice. I think, therefore, that we need to distinguish between the three distinct levels lumped within the same category: predation in the abstract sense (perhaps best renamed 'incorporation', though this is admittedly an unsatisfactory term), predation as the symbolic form taken by 'incorporation' in a given cultural context, and finally the specific modes of killing and consuming 'living' others: hunting, exo- and endocannibalism, and so forth. In this chapter, I use the term 'predation' mainly in the second sense (except in my conclusion), to refer to the 'sensible form' taken by incorporation, its 'emic' manifestation in Jivaroan culture.

3. All vernacular terms belong, unless otherwise specified, to the Achuar dialect of Jivaro.

4. This is something that comes through very clearly in a set of Jivaroan myths that attribute the origin of women as sexual partners to the lust of a man for his pre-lapsarian 'brother-in-law', whom he transforms into a woman in order to have sex with him/her.

5. Taken from Taylor and Chau (1983: 104–5).

6. The full text in vernacular is in Taylor and Chau (1983: 108–9). Though it is not readily apparent in this extract, the song fuses two classic Jivaroan tropes: the setting sun and the toucan flight. Hence the reference to the 'soaring' evening and to the yellow colour of the toucan's neck feathers. Note also the call to 'look disdainful'; reticence on the part of a woman is considered highly erotic.

7. Vernacular text in Taylor and Chau (1983: 114).

8. Note that women insistently address all their male kin as 'brothers' (*umaru*) in only one case, that of the ritual collective war songs known as *ujaj* (a genre entirely distinct from *anent*) in a context where men themselves clearly identify themselves either with predators stalking their prey, or with the prey threatened by such predators.

9. See Taylor (1996) for a partial treatment of this subject.

10. This is equally true of a celibate man's 'quasi-wife' sister, since he is in a 'husband' position in relation to her, hence in an affinal position in relation to her animal 'siblings'. Consequently, men can invariably consider game animals as affines rather than siblings, regardless of their and their sisters' marital status.

11. For the sake of brevity, I will deal exclusively with a male ego's point of view in the rest of this chapter. However, it should be clear by now that men and women's perspectives on kin relationships are distinct, though complementary.

12. It is precisely these two women (or their classificatory equivalents) who are coupled with the head-taker throughout the *tsantsa* rituals. As I have shown elsewhere (Taylor 1994), these rituals can be interpreted as a spectacularly elaborate extension or 'blow-up' of the relational configuration constitutive of identity.

13. Men do not reciprocate, however, and simply use two personal singular pronouns when addressing women, whereas they emphatically use affinal kin terms when singing to their male human or animal in-laws.

14. For some development of this point, see Taylor (1996) and also Gow (1991).

4

Seed and Clone: The Symbolic and Social Significance of Bitter Manioc Cultivation

Laura Rival, *University of Oxford*

According to the thesis Peter Rivière formulated in 1984, the political economy prevalent in indigenous Amazonia is a political economy, not of goods, but of people, characterized by the management of the productive and reproductive capacities of individuals considered to be means of production and scarce resources, in particular women. In the well-known essay on the processing of bitter manioc and gender politics he subsequently wrote in 1987, he further supported this thesis by comparing various bodies of ethnographic data, and concluded that societies presenting a predominantly masculine version of social reproduction tend to control women by confining them to the repetitive, laborious task of detoxifying bitter manioc and processing it daily into culinary products that are central to group identity. In the societies of north-west Amazonia, which are characterized by a marked patrilocal ideology requiring the incorporation of foreign spouses within agnatic clan groups, women work longer hours, and more intensively, than Carib and Arawak women of the Guiana shield, where endogamous social reproduction depends as much on women as on men. This indicates that manioc processing among north-west Amazonians goes far beyond what is technically required to release the toxic Prussic acid (HCN). More generally, Rivière stresses that cultural preference for highly toxic cultivars of manioc over non-toxic (sweet) cultivars is largely independent of ecological constraints and other practical considerations, such as storability, high yields, or protection against predators, and is better interpreted as derivative of socio-political considerations which express the necessity to keep and submit female producers and reproducers within residential groups (see also Rivière 1984: 92).

The general model he proposes based on the observation that the division of labour is organized along sexual lines, that the apparent complementarity of male and female subsistence activities actually masks the inequality existing between the sexes, and that men turn products processed by women to their political advantage, is reminiscent of the gender analyses proposed in the early 1980s by a number of scholars (among others, Collier and Rosaldo 1981, Godelier 1982, and Josephides 1985), influenced by the seminal work of Meillassoux (1980). It is not my intention here to discuss the validity of the thesis that the length and complexity of manioc processing is directly related to gender politics and to male control exercised over women, a task undertaken by Lorrain and Griffiths in their contributions to this volume. Rather, I wish to reconsider the proposition that beyond the possible pragmatic reasons for cultivating such a deadly plant as bitter manioc, it may be possible to identify forms of conceptual thought and social practices that can inform us, not so much on the genderization of political control, but on Amazonian social categories and conceptions of social procreation. This is an important task, given that our understanding of consanguinity, and, more generally, the generative process in Amazonia remains comparatively poor. In their contributions to this volume Anne-Christine Taylor and Eduardo Viveiros de Castro similarly stress that, whereas substantial progress has been achieved in conceptualizing affinity in Amazonian societies, our understanding of consanguineal or cognatic ties remains comparatively undeveloped, especially for societies in which corporate groups are absent.

   In this essay based on ethnographic data collected[1] among three Makushi communities of the North Rupununi savannahs of Guyana, I draw on new genetic and botanical research on wild and cultivated manioc (*Manihot esculenta kr.* Euphorbiaceae), a main staple in most Amazonian societies (and the fourth most important food crop in the world), to show that the symbolic representation of wild and domesticated varieties of bitter manioc and the conceptual opposition of seed and clone in Makushi beliefs and cultivation practices reveal a great deal about the indigenous way of thinking about sexual reproduction, the generative process, consanguinity, and identity.

THE STRUCTURALIST POINT OF VIEW ON FILIATION
AND CONSANGUINITY

As first formulated by Descola (1986: chapter 5), the Achuar (and other Amazonian Indians) domesticate nature not only through transforming it physically by hunting and gardening, but also by maintaining social relationships with natural organisms and spiritual beings which are part of their forest environment. Whereas Achuar male hunters socially relate to game animals as affines, Achuar women sustain consanguineal relationships[2] with the plants they cultivate. The intervention of a female civilizing heroine, Nunkui, is crucial in the conceptualization of gardening as a form of technical knowledge expressing consanguinity. Nunkui, the equivalent of the Makushi Cassava Mother, is, like her, the mistress spirit of cultivated plants, manioc included. By this it is meant that she is their creator, their mother, as well as a fertility amplifying agent (Descola 1986: 239, 245). Nunkui's motherly authority, however, seems to derive more from the fact that she is an adoptive mother, than from the fact that she is their progenitor (Descola 1986: 249), and it is this particular mother–child relation that is transferred magically through chants from Nunkui to female horticultors.[3] Achuar cultivators see themselves as sharing with Nunkui, who is both a powerful friend and a close ally, as well as a kind of sister, the co-guardianship of plant children. All this seems to suggest that consanguinity is a relation of contiguity (and social proximity) between a female spirit, Achuar women, and cultivated plants, in which the condition of motherhood, both as an engendering principle and as a nurturing condition seems to predominate.

This thesis was slightly reformulated subsequently (Descola 1993: chapter 6), as the author put increasing emphasis on the fact that sweet manioc, the Achuar staple crop, has the vampiric power of sucking the blood from people, in particular from the female cultivators who mother them, and from their offspring.[4] All this makes sense, continues Descola, if we accept that blood exists in the world as a limited source of energy (Descola 1993: 113). With this conclusion, it seems to me, we have gone from a vague and particularly ill-defined notion of consanguinity as parenting in the female mode to a notion of reciprocal nurturing overdetermined by predation (as defined by Taylor and Viveiros de Castro in this volume).

Taylor (this volume) goes a step further when she defines consanguineal ties as 'non-relations that are turned into proper relationships only when articulated to affinal ones'. If true consanguinity can never exist, siblingship comes closer to represent consanguinuous ties than the genealogical link between a parent and a child does, for filiation automatically implies the coexistence of two identities within the child, one deriving from a tamed (affinal) other, and a residual one which in fact is an identical replica of the same-sex parent in his or her parental quality. For the Achuar, she also explains, consanguinity as non-difference corresponds to the exact similarity between an original and photocopies, replicas, or clones: 'the fraction of ego's son that is not affinal is identical to his own position as father; likewise, for a mother, that part of her daughter that is not "other" is a clone of herself.' Manioc cloning serves as a model to conceptualize engendered sameness as a form of a-sexual, uni-gendered reproduction. Nunkui is now understood to clone herself and abolish all differentiation between genitor/genetrix, child and sibling, as she is all of this at once. The Identity relation epitomized by Nunkui, who engenders the same, is the precise antithesis to the relation of predation by which the Other gets incorporated (Taylor 2000: 320). The structuralist thesis that gardens are female domains associated with consanguinity is now so formulated that all reference to the descent principle has been eliminated, and the role assigned to the biosocial production of life in the creation of social relations reduced to zero.

Such a view could not be further from the one expressed by, for example, Kaj Århem in this volume, a contrast which of course reflects deep-seated differences between Tukanoan and Jivaro conceptions of sociality. The Makuna, like the Barasana (Hugh-Jones 1995), like the Trio, and, indeed, like most societies of the

Guiana shield, equate consanguinity with co-residence, conviviality, and commensality. Århem talks of 'consanguineal sociality' and 'consanguineal consubstantiality', by which he means that co-residents of a longhouse, and today those of a modern village, think of themselves as undifferentiated kin partaking in the same common, everyday domestic existence. Consanguinity in this context amounts to a theory of relatedness and being alike, not through common origin, but through shared residence. In a similar fashion, while disagreeing on the political significance of the transformation of incoming, incorporated affines into consanguines characteristic of the Guiana shield endogamous cognatic systems, Rivière (1969*a*, 1984) and Overing (1983–4) have consistently opposed the view that consanguinity should be treated as a non-relation (Taylor) or, as a constructed sociality to be contrasted with affinity, a given and natural form of sociality (Viveiros de Castro this volume).

The interesting fact about the north-west Amazon/Guianese view of consanguinity as co-residence and shared domesticity is that it implies a model of alliance and affinity, as much as one of cognation/cognatic kinship. This is more clearly in evidence in the Barasana and Makuna contexts, where this type of consanguinity, which Hugh-Jones (1995) describes as a 'within-relationship' between members of a group contained in the same womb-house, coexists with an alternative view of consanguinity, that of an agnatic group replicating an ancestral group of brothers born of the same anaconda father. For Tukanoans, the agnatic group ideally comprises a father living with his sons (see Lea, this volume for a matrilineal-matrifocal version of consanguinity). What comes so clearly out of Hugh-Jones's (1979, 1993, 1995) ethnographic material is that whereas father–son relations and older brother–younger brother relations are consanguineal in the sense of marking genealogical contiguity, the relation between the contemporary agnatic group and the mythical (recreated) one is not, for they are not linked through unilinear continuity and transmission of shared lineage substance (i.e. descent). Rather, the contemporary group identifies ritually with the ancestral one, and comes spiritually into contact with it. This occurs during a ritual in which prepubescent boys are adopted by the proto-human, patrilineal ancestors, who bestow renewed fertility powers onto all men partaking in the ritual. Among Tukanoans, therefore, consanguinity results from the combination of an ideology of descent with processes of replication and incorporation, as well as ritual adoption, and male rebirth. This view of consanguinity agrees with the thesis put forward by Seeger, Da Matta, and Viveiros de Castro (1979), who argue that continuity in Amazonia is based on repeated short cycles rather than on linear progression, and that substitution rather than genealogical continuity structures relations between generations.

THE MAKUSHI MANIOC–FARMING SYSTEM

The Makushi, a Carib-speaking group, live in the Rio Branco–Rupununi region, a region politically divided between Brazil (Roraima State) and Guyana (Region 9).

There are approximately 20,000 Makushi today, of whom 7,000 live in Guyana (CIR 1993), an area subjected to intense colonial rivalry during the eighteenth century, and Portuguese military occupation. The Makushi, whose political role in the conflicts opposing Spanish, Portuguese, English, and Dutch occupiers was significant, resisted attempts by the Portuguese army to sedentarize them (Farage 1991, Santilli 1994). However, the development of a civil economy based on cattle ranching during the nineteenth century led to their partial sedentarization. With the expansion of cattle ranching at the turn of the century, they experienced increased land shortages and pressure to work as domestic servants or cowboys, and many of them left the Roraima hills in Brazil for the Rupununi savannahs of what is now Guyana (Farage 1991), where they can still be found, living in relatively small communities headed by a captain or 'toushau'.

Makushi families traded manioc and manioc derivatives, particularly *farine*, a meal made of dried granules of grated manioc (Diniz 1966, Farabee 1924, Farage 1991), for manufactured goods, and for the last two hundred years, at least, they have complemented their domestic economy with casual work and trade of garden or forest products. Non-subsistence economic activities, dictated by demand, have varied over time, and from place to place. White settlers have needed the Makushi for their agricultural products as much as for their labour, and there is little doubt that such demands have modified the indigenous agricultural system. For instance, outside influence has accentuated the importance of horticulture over hunting and gathering, and reinforced the tendency towards sedentarization in savannah-based nucleated villages, causing farm land shortages and shorter fallow periods. As farms must last longer, people tend to select varieties that can stay in the ground longer. Furthermore, the condemnation of native politico–ritual activities by missionaries, on the one hand, and new trade opportunities, on the other, have meant that manioc surpluses traditionally produced to prepare fermented drinks for festive occasions have been increasingly processed into *farine* and sold, a trend which has undoubtedly influenced the choice of cultivated landraces. However, Makushi slash-and-burn agriculture, which is mainly based on the cultivation of bitter manioc, of which they maintain a great number of varieties, is still predominantly directed toward subsistence. Bitter manioc is consumed daily as *farine* (*u'wi*), manioc bread (*kai*), fermented drinks (called *parakîrî*, *kasiri*, and *wo'*), casereep (*kumasi*), a black, thick paste used throughout Guyana to cook meat and fish, and starch tapioca (*imu yanasa*) or porridge.

Farming practices and the management of varietal diversity

Each year during the dry season households clear new farms in old fallows or secondary forest. Clearing a new farm (*mîî ya'tî*), an exclusively male activity, is considered hard work. It was traditionally performed by a man with the help of his relatives and friends (*mayu*), in exchange for food or drinks (*parakîrî* or *wo'*). Co-operation in forest clearing now tends to be restricted to immediate kin, and farm burning (*mîî po'tî*) and ground clearing are undertaken by the household, children included. The farmer hoes the field, and shapes the soil into mounds (locally known as 'banks') in which he plants cuttings ('manioc sticks' in colloquial English) prepared by his wife from long stems of freshly harvested manioc. Roots are usually harvested nine months after planting, when and as they are needed. As in most Amazonian societies, manioc processing is the responsibility of women. Although food is intimately connected with gender specialization, it is not uncommon to see a man helping his wife detoxifying the tuberous roots, or helping her preparing different foods. As predicted by Peter Rivière (1987*a*), despite having a sophisticated range of manioc-based foods and drinks, Makushi women seem to spend less time cultivating and processing manioc than north-west Amazon women do, and this is in part due to the fact that although there is a clear gender division of labour in Makushi society, this division is rather lax in practice, with men often performing 'women's' tasks. Moreover, both men and women farm together most of the time, and men's knowledge of manioc is as extensive as that of their wives.

Sweet manioc, which, like yam or sweet potatoes, occupies a secondary place in the Makushi diet, is not regarded as 'real', that is, bitter, manioc. 'Bitter' (*kîse*) and 'sweet' (*kana*) varieties are seen as two entirely different kinds of crop. *Kîse* refers here to a group of food plants that become edible only after elaborate processing. Marianne Elias collected four different names of sweet manioc landraces, and 87 different names of bitter manioc landraces, corresponding to 76 varieties.[5] Each household she surveyed owned on average 16 landraces. No informant had an accurate or exhaustive knowledge of the varietal diversity present in their village. While certain varieties were preferred for particular uses, she found much functional redundancy among varieties. The Makushi seem to enjoy diversity for its own sake, and more for aesthetic and recreational reasons than for security purposes (see also Carneiro 1983). They cannot explain why they have so many varieties. Like collectors, they just have them. It is also clear that they are driven to cultivate as many varieties as possible by a deep-seated curiosity that pushes them continuously to 'try out' new types.[6] If a number of utilitarian and aesthetic criteria can be shown to play a role in variety selection, it is nevertheless true that cultivators protect rare varieties for their own sake. Low-yielding rare varieties are kept at a low density, in one or two mounds per farm, which is considered to be enough to prevent their loss. Cultivators explain that they do not like losing varieties, for a 'bad' variety sometimes becomes 'good' under different conditions. As a result, conscious selection on manioc varieties acts primarily to preserve diversity; it is not aimed at maintaining or augmenting specific desired traits.

Because they continuously lose varieties (intentionally or unintentionally), Makushi cultivators have devised strategies to acquire new types and compensate for losses. In particular, they have learnt to adapt to severe droughts and floods, which represent important environmental selective factors and which often lead to the loss of varieties, especially those present in low densities, or those owned by a few cultivators only. Exceptionally dry weather such as that caused by El Niño from August 1997 to April 1998 not only affects root production, but also destroys propagation material. To protect the cuttings from drought, and, to a lesser extent, flood, cultivators have developed special planting strategies. For example, they are careful to protect planted cuttings which, at first sight, look dried-out, but which will almost certainly sprout again with the first showers. Mounds are reshaped with taller profiles, and replanted with six or eight (instead of four) cuttings to maximize the chances of having at least two well-developing plants in each. In drought conditions, rather than saving harvestable roots, cultivators try to preserve the stems as 'germplasm banks'. For this, they look for swampy areas, areas which are, under normal circumstances, flooded, and transport their best stems—sometimes over great distances—from their farms to the swamps, to stock them in large bunches there, until it rains. In short, the general strategy is to prioritize the long-term reproductive cycle (Rival 1998*a*).

The most common practice through which cultivators acquire new varieties or recover lost ones, a practice which greatly contributes to the maintenance of manioc diversity, is the exchange of cuttings between neighbours, relatives, and friends. Cultivators can recall the origin of all the varieties they have in their farms, no matter how far back they have to go. Couples who have been married for twenty-five years or more have on average at least three varieties in their farms which are clones of cuttings they planted in their first farm. In former times when the rule of uxorilocality and brideservice was more generally applied, a young husband was expected to cultivate with his wife the farm of his parents-in-law, until his father-in-law gave him permission to set up his own farm. The young husband would then receive a share of cuttings from his father-in-law, a stock which he complemented with cuttings brought from the farm of his own parents. The young wife would receive cuttings from her mother, sisters, mother-in-law, and sisters-in-law. The couples we interviewed always specified which varieties were brought into the conjugal farm by the husband, and which by the wife.

It is perhaps because the transfer of cuttings is initiated by a request from a farmer in need that cultivators so accurately remember the origin of the cuttings they cultivate. The most general term used to express the idea of transfer is 'borrowing'. A farmer short of planting material or willing to try a new variety asks another farmer to give him or her stems, which he or she will 'repay' at a later stage with stems of a different variety, or with *farine* or *parakîrî* made with roots from borrowed varieties. There is no specified rule on how long after having 'borrowed' a farmer must 'give back'. The only occasion when the transfer is not receiver-initiated and when there is no payback is when a farmer compensates damage (such as destroying part of a neighbour's crops through uncontrolled fire) by donating cuttings. The exchange of cuttings between closely related kin and neighbours whose farms are contiguous and who still practise a form of shared labour (*mayu*) is less formal and generalized—in the sense that strict reciprocity is not an issue. Only very occasionally will a farmer acquire cuttings of a rare variety by paying with cash, a cutlass, a bicycle, or any other trade item. This type of exchange is more likely to occur between unrelated cultivators, that is, those who have no family connection and who do not live in the same village. The general law, however, is that cuttings must be reciprocated with cuttings and nothing else, otherwise, it is believed, yields will be low.

The most common way of giving cuttings to another farmer is to invite him or her to one's farm at harvest time. As the farm owner digs out the roots, he or she prepares long stems stripped of all leafy material that he or she hands to the borrower. Alternatively, he or she may share the unused stems stored in large bundles placed along the shady edge of the farm. Two types of exchange, one 'massive' and the other 'occasional', can be distinguished. Cultivators who need large amounts of planting material for a new farm borrow cuttings from just a few varieties, which they usually already possess, but not in sufficient quantity. Those who want to try out a variety they do not have in their farm ask for a stem or two while visiting the farm of a neighbour, friend, or relative. Cultivators, who are always keen to acquire new varieties, multiply the trial cuttings carefully until the desired density is reached. The closer the locality from which a new variety originates, the more likely will its real name be remembered. In contrast, a variety coming from a distant locality may be called after a toponym. Given the nature of massive and occasional exchanges, the varieties most likely to be exchanged are neither the most common, which are always in sufficient quantities, nor the rarest, which are always in short supply.

In contrast with Chernela (1987), who has reported exchanges over an area 465 kilometres wide, most exchanges (and all massive exchanges) occur within the village community, in particular among immediate neighbours, who are usually related through descent and marriage.[7] In accordance with the general rule in Amazonia that social proximity is spatial proximity, close kin who do not live close or do not visit on a regular basis do not exchange cuttings either. This results in even distribution of varietal diversity within particular villages, and uneven distribution from village to village. Whereas bitter manioc varieties total up to 139 in the Rupununi (Forte 1999), the average number of varieties found in any single village is about half this figure (Elias, Rival, McKey 2001), as if varietal distribution mirrored village endogamy.

As a result, some families never interact, while others are continuously exchanging cuttings. Cuttings were not traded across ethnic boundaries in the past, and even inter-village exchanges were—and still are—restricted, which, of course, does not exclude acquisition through warfare, looting, and the taking over of another tribe's old farms. Some cultivators carefully avoid asking for cuttings, as they derive great prestige from relying on their own stocks, while lavishingly giving away to borrowers. Others, who keep their farms at a distance and never invite visitors and share only reluctantly are considered 'stingy'. Yet others do not dare asking for coveted cuttings, which they quietly pick from the farms of neighbours or hosts (this behaviour may lead to generalized theft in times of drought and starvation). To summarize, while some families always experience a deficit of planting material, others almost never borrow cuttings. And whereas some share their surpluses generously, others prefer to let their unused bundles of cuttings dry out. The examination of the social networks underlying massive exchanges reveals two contrastive groups, 'source' and 'sink' families. 'Source' families manage manioc production efficiently; they rarely experience shortages, and usually have a sufficient surplus of stems to give away as planting material. 'Sink' families, by contrast, manage their stocks poorly; they often run out of cuttings for their new farms, and depend heavily on borrowing. 'Source' cultivators are proud and respected community members, with a higher status than 'sink' cultivators. Key to the motivation of efficient cultivators is the sense of responsibility they feel to ensure that domesticated plants, especially bitter manioc, will not die. The life of bitter manioc must be maintained and propagated through replanting, and through encouraging and helping other cultivators in the community to plant and replant (see Griffiths in this volume for parallel beliefs among the Uitoto).

The incorporation of volunteer plants

The brief overview of Makushi manioc cultivation offered above illustrates the ways in which social relations between men and women, as well as between co-villagers and kin, are materially expressed through farming practices. It also illustrates the combined action of natural and human selection, and the role of indigenous botanical knowledge and indigenous social processes, in fostering bitter manioc varietal and genetic diversity. This approach, while taking us away from a focus on social and cultural activities conceived as direct responses to limiting ecological factors, invites us to address head on an issue that has always been of great interest to Peter Rivière: the symbolic and social meaningfulness of technical processes. Encouraging the growth of seedlings (*tepuru pîye*, from *tepuru*, seed) constitutes another common practice by which Makushi cultivators acquire new varieties and contribute to the maintenance of manioc diversity.

Cultivators pay special attention to volunteer plants grown from seedlings, which they have no difficulty identifying. Although they may compete with, and affect the growth of, planted cuttings, seedlings are only rarely weeded, and usually left to grow until they reach maturity.[8] Like common varieties, they are harvested and their roots processed. If the farmer is satisfied with the yield, the colour of the root, and any other characteristic, the stem is divided into cuttings which are soon replanted and multiplied in a specific location. If the tuberous roots are found unsatisfactory, the stem is generally discarded, although cultivators keen to experiment clone it, hoping that it will become more productive after one cultivation cycle. Spontaneous seedlings are thus multiplied over generations of planting, and, since they often present novel combinations of morphological characteristics, are usually treated as new varieties. Naming these new phenotypes is not easy, so most cultivators keep the non-specific denomination *tepuru pîye*, which they apply to different phenotypes. When the characteristics of a spontaneous seedling closely match those of a known variety (it is thought that all varieties are pre-existent, each with a fixed name), the seedling assumed to have grown from the seed of this particular variety is assimilated to and named after it by adding the term *perurupe*, such as in *paranakîrî pîye perurupe*, 'seed of white man stick'. Seedlings which are considered entirely identical to a known variety are treated exactly like any other member of this variety.

Cultivators tend to assimilate completely spontaneous seedlings to known varieties, especially if their morphological characteristics are not sufficiently distinctive. They often forget the seed origin of particular stems, and are actually aware of making mistakes in identifying varieties, as they accidently include the new phenotypes of seedlings within that of a known variety. However, the behaviour of *tepuru pîye*, which rarely reproduce the features characteristic of the particular varieties from which the seeds originate, but display instead novel or unusual combinations of traits, a property enhanced by allogamous reproduction,[9] puzzles them. It contradicts their understanding that cuttings produce individuals similar to those from which they originate. In their effort to explain such unusual trait combinations, they presume that a seed from any given variety, because of its small dimensions, will be influenced by other varieties after falling to the ground, and denatured. This perception may in turn explain why Makushi cultivators never plant manioc seeds, but propagate clones of *tepuru pîye*, despite their knowledge of seed planting, a technique they commonly use to grow crops such as papaya and corn. It may also explain why cultivators never give away cuttings from spontaneous seedlings, but only cuttings from third- or fourth-generation clones, which they have replanted in various types of soil, and observed.

Wild manioc: scientific versus indigenous knowledge

Despite having been cultivated and propagated vegetatively for more than 3,000 years, bitter manioc has retained its ancestral capacity for sexual reproduction (Renvoize 1972). Its ancestors, the wild forms of manioc *M. peruviana*, and *M. esculenta* subsp. *flabellifolia*, for example, are sexually propagated, and do not have a good aptitude for vegetative propagation.[10] In other words, whereas wild varieties reproduce sexually and cannot be reproduced vegetatively, domesticated varieties, which are mainly reproduced vegetatively, have not lost their capacity to reproduce sexually.

Makushi cultivators know that whereas wild varieties can only be seed-grown, domesticated varieties are both seed-grown and grown by cultivators who replant cuttings. They make full use of manioc seeding potential and of its surprisingly long seed dormancy, a phenomenon poorly documented and little understood by Western scientists (but see Silvestre and Arraudeau 1983). They also know that most varieties in their farms produce flowers, and that these produce fruit which dehisce at maturity, dispersing their seeds before the plants are harvested.

Therefore, if the Makushi seem to ignore the role of the male and female flowers in producing seeds, they recognize that seeds are projected by exploding capsules, and transported by birds or by the wind before falling on the ground and producing new *tepuru pîye* plants. They observe that seeds typically germinate when a new farm is cut in an old fallow, and seem to acknowledge that preserving a vegetation cover prevents seed germination. Spontaneous seedlings are commonly found in places which were cultivated as long as thirty-five years ago. One farmer even found a *tepuru pîye* plant in a new farm he had just cleared in a high forest location, which was, according to oral tradition, cultivated by a group of Caribs more than fifty years ago. Interviewed cultivators recalled a very severe drought they experienced in the early 1950s, and which lasted almost two years. Their crops dried out, and they soon ran out of planting material, which they recovered by clearing old farm locations, where seeds germinated, providing them with new stocks of cuttings. The surprisingly long dormancy suggested by these observations can be explained by the long survival of seeds in seed banks (see also Amuesha comments in Salick, Cellinese, and Knapp 1997).

Whereas scientists tend to think of wild manioc as representing varieties that are different from, and historically anterior to, *Manihot esculenta*, the Makushi consider *kwana* to be a feral and degenerate type of manioc that escaped from their gardens, and now grows in non-cultural spaces, such as hilltops in the savannah. It develops small, hard, and fibrous roots, which are difficult to harvest. In the past, during times of famine, roots of wild manioc were harvested and processed into bread and *farine*, as those of any variety of cultivated manioc. These roots were too bitter to be used alone, or to be used for *kasiri* (the drink made of grated pulp from which the poisonous juice is not squeezed out). Today, only some cultivators driven by curiosity pay attention to wild manioc and try to plant it. An old man told Marianne Elias that he tried to get new varieties out of wild manioc, which he thought to be highly drought resistant. Other people reported having tried to plant wild manioc in their farm to repel leafcutter ants. That all these attempts failed did not greatly surprise the cultivators, who know that wild manioc does not grow from cuttings, but from seeds. And it would never occur to a Makushi farmer, even the most curious and experiment-driven, to plant manioc seeds, as if for them seed propagation were the province of nature, and not of human action. In short, it is because its seeds have germinated outside of cultivated areas that wild manioc is represented as a degenerated cultivar which has stopped producing tuberous roots and has become permanently sterile, that is, incapable of producing tuberous roots.

SEED AND CLONE: THE DYNAMICS OF REPLICATION

My aim in the rest of this essay is to examine Makushi conceptualization of spontaneous seedlings as a source of regeneration. As is so often the case with indigenous technical and environmental knowledge systems, Makushi manioc cultivation cannot be fully understood without considering cultural representations of a more religious nature. As I shall discuss now in greater detail, the incorporation of plants grown from (sexually reproduced) seedlings that appear spontaneously in farms expresses a number of fundamental concepts regarding the issue of biosocial reproduction prevalent among the Makushi, and among other Amazonian cultures as well. My primary aim is to analyse the fact that farmers greatly appreciate cuttings from *tepuru pîye* for their 'vitality' and their 'youth'. A farmer once told me that normal cuttings (i.e. clones) get accustomed to the soil; 'they are too tamed', and end up producing less and less. Cuttings from spontaneous seedlings, by contrast, often produce increasingly better yields. They come from a plant which has occurred naturally (i.e. without human control), and this makes them vigorous. The plant from *tepuru pîye*, he added, has not been cultivated, and has not born children yet.

Like many other societies around the world (Leenhardt 1979, J. Fox 1967, Rival 1998*b*), the Makushi establish an identity of substance and structure between plants and humans. The linguistic association between body parts and parts of the manioc plant is summarized in Table 4.1. It is not my intention here to discuss whether the analogy between the vegetable kingdom and humanity is best understood semantically as a 'botanic idiom' (J. Fox 1967). I mention the association between the human body and the manioc plant because it has some influence on cultivation practices and on the social exchange of genetic material between cultivators. A number of farming practices clearly indicate that manioc plants are like persons, and should be treated as such. For example, several cultivators mentioned that they talk to their manioc plants to make them grow better. Another common practice aimed at encouraging growth and tuber production is to plant a magical plant (generically known as *bina* in Guyana) in the middle of the field, or to chew the root of such a plant, and spit it over the mounds. Similar plants are used to protect human health and enhance human potential. Finally, there seems to be a

TABLE 4.1. *The linguistic association of body parts with parts of the manioc plant*

Part of the plant	Makushi term	Makushi translation
sap	î'teku	(its) milk
fine roots	ikara	(its) vein
bark	pi'pî	(its) skin
root, tuber	imun	offspring, children
node	itenu	(its) eye
elongated root	tepî'ru	bony root (from tepî', bone)
fat root	mai'ponke	root like a bum
fibrous core of the tuber	tepî'	(its) bone
starchy part of the tuber	ipun	(its) flesh

connection between the planting of cuttings and the treatment of corpses. Three to five cuttings of the same variety are usually planted together in each mound, pointing to the west. Although most people are aware that cuttings planted eastward grow as well as those pointing westward, they still maintain that a westward orientation protects the plant from the sun and favours its growth. The burial of dead people feet to the east, head to the west, with the face looking to the rising sun, is linked to the belief that death brings the regeneration of life. In connection with this belief, cuttings that are given away, especially to distant relatives or non-kin, should be like dead sticks, absolutely devoid of signs of life. As one informant explained: 'I borrowed sticks from my brother. Before giving them to me, he pinched all the sticks to kill the eyes and kill the roots, so they could be mine.' Manioc leaves are thought to be the plant's hands, which explains why all leafy materials and knots left on cuttings should be removed before these are given away, to avoid bad harvests caused by the transfer of the yield potential from the donor's farm to the farm of the receiver.

Everything is done to stimulate and protect the growth of manioc plants, which are like people, and everything is done to protect and perpetuate life in them. This is why stems, the source of life, are particularly cared for. Ideally, as mentioned earlier, all stems with potential for survival and perpetuation should be cut and planted, and only a small proportion discarded. Cultivators who cannot use all their planting material, either by replanting it in new farms, or giving it away to neighbours, relatives, or friends, store the unused stems in tight bundles on farm edges, where they germinate, seed, and remain alive long after the fallows have turned into secondary forest. Some farmers say that their keenness to protect farm-grown varieties is due to the fact that, ultimately, manioc is owned by Cassava Mother (*kîserayan*), who demands from humans that they protect and nurture her children. Some Makushi women throw the fine (i.e. non tuberous) roots (*ikara* in Makushi, which means 'its veins') of the first harvest in the fire, as a thanksgiving to the mistress spirit. Others say that a farm is owned by a husband and a wife, but the cuttings they plant belong to Cassava Mother, in the sense that they originate from her body, as a number of myths make clear.

In one myth, a man spends his life looking for Cassava Mother. He finally finds her on top of mount Roraima, where she appears under the form of a giant manioc tree. Large quantities of manioc fruit, seeds, and branches are scattered on the ground underneath the giant plant. He collects branches and seeds, brings them back home, and shares them with neighbours and relatives, who plant the seeds and make cuttings from the branches. This is how the different types of manioc that the Makushi grow to this day, each with its own name, came into existence and were multiplied. After some time, it was discovered that seeds had flown from mount Roraima to the Mapari mountain (a goldmining place in the vicinity of Karanambo), where they grew by themselves into giant bananas, yams, and other cultivated crops. Although this myth is a complex cultural representation that cannot be reduced to one single dimension or message, it clearly conveys the idea that manioc exists first and foremost as a cultivated (that is a domesticated or cultural) plant, whose unalterable blueprint is Cassava Mother, the mistress spirit of all bitter manioc, and, by extension, of all cultivated crops. Another myth links the original manioc plant and Cassava Mother to a young girl menstruating for the first time. She was in ritual confinement away from the village. Tempted to eat a white and sweet fruit, she violated food prohibitions (she had been especially warned not to eat any fruit), and was bitten by a snake. Her parents who found her dead buried her on the spot. The first manioc plant grew on her grave, and from its stem came all the existing varieties.

This latter myth takes us to a different dimension of the analogy between plants and humans, the capacity for procreation as a model of biosocial reproduction. What captures the indigenous imagination is the fact that at some point during the life cycle the body becomes mature and capable, not so much of self-regeneration, but of engendering new beings, which are at once similar and different from their procreator. Planted cuttings regenerate stems (i.e. further cuttings) and generate tuberous roots, which are called 'children' (*imun*). *Imun*, a term which means tuberous roots, offspring, and children, as well as the five fingers attached to the palm of the hand (see also Hugh-Jones 1995: 238), is used to refer to the children of the manioc plants, of the farmer who has cared for the plants and harvested the roots, and of Cassava Mother, the mistress spirit that owns manioc, looks after its well-being and ensures good harvests. People say that manioc 'bears children like women do', and add, laughing, that selecting the more productive stems to replant, is to increase the farm's 'female population'. Therefore, cultivated manioc plants, like humans, are fertile and procreate. Plants that do not produce enough tuberous roots are said to be 'bony' or 'male'. Contrary to ideas held by Melanesian populations such as the Nakanai, who understand seeds and shoots to be 'children' in relation to the plants from which they come, and which the Nakanai call 'mothers' (Yamaji 1994: 13–46), the Makushi are adamant that only roots are 'children'. Moreover, they see absolutely no consanguineal relations (parent–child or sibling–sibling) between cuttings obtained from one (or more) stems cut from one plant. The only relation of consanguinity involved is that between the stem and the roots, the roots being the material manifestation of the stem's fertility. As the following myths indicate, plants that bear no roots are considered either temporarily infertile or sterile—hence male.

A popular myth among the Makushi, of which there are many different versions, links the existence of wild and cultivated manioc to the marriage of an older and a younger sister to, respectively, lazy Owl (*prototo*) and hard-working Duck (*maiwa*). Owl's garden contains less than ten mounds, but the roots are so big and abundant that his visiting mother-in-law can fill her *warishi* (plaited basket) with the roots dug out of a single mound. Duck's plantation, by contrast, is so vast that the mother-in-law, who has just found out that the manioc here has no tuberous roots, gets lost in the centre, where she turns into a ground pigeon, one of Cassava Mother's personifications. Duck's manioc ends up covering neighbouring hills and mountains, where it can still be found as the extremely bitter, poisonous wild variety whose leaves are used to protect farms from the leafcutter ant. The moral lesson Makushi informants draw from this mythic tale, is that a hard-working son-in-law is worthless if he is sterile, and cannot produce children.

The linking up of manioc cultivation with sexuality, reproduction, and marriage, and the parallel expression of cultural anxiety with fertility and sterility is also found in another myth, which relates the story of two young, unmarried sisters who throw away with anger the stem of a manioc plant in the farm they are harvesting, because this plant has no tuberous roots. The stem which has been cruelly discarded instead of being replanted cries: 'I don't have a big penis, this is why they are throwing me away, but I would have borne good if they had given me a second chance . . .'. It then appears briefly to the sisters as a young, handsome man, before leaving the farm for ever. The sisters, who long to see him again, bitterly regret having thrown away the stem. By relating this myth to those discussed earlier, it becomes possible to establish correspondences between the fact that bitter manioc takes its origin in the dead body of a girl who has her menstruation for the first time, hence becomes fertile, and eats prohibited fruit, a euphemism for engaging in illicit sex; the fact that two unmarried sisters discard a plant thought to be sterile, but which turns out to be a sexually attractive (and almost certainly fertile) potential husband; and the fact that a mother-in-law compares the horticultural production of her two daughters' husbands, one whose plantation is modest in size but highly productive, and one whose vast, but entirely unproductive plantation, puts an end to her line of descent, and causes her to vanish from the social sphere of humanity. Not only are rootless manioc plants incapable of producing something other than themselves, but they curtail all possibility of nurture and commensality, the basis of consanguineal relations (see Gow 1991 and Århem in this volume).

In order to understand this point fully, we need to examine the fertility status of two types of seed-grown manioc, *kwana* (wild manioc) and *tepuru pîye*, spontaneous seedling. *Tepuru pîye* too is naturally propagated through seeds, but these grow on cultivated ground, where the seedlings are surrounded by farm-grown varieties. Seedlings are opposed to clones, for they 'grow by themselves'; wind and birds propagate them, not Makushi cultivators. And they are differentiated from manioc that 'escaped' from the human domain of culture and cultivation, grows in the wild, and can no longer be cloned. Both are conceptualized as seed-grown cultivars, but with the difference that *tepuru pîye* 'joins in', and progressively comes under human control, is propagated vegetatively, and bears edible roots. Whereas *kwana* has lost the capacity to produce children and can only reproduce itself through seed germination, *tepuru pîye* originates from a seed, but then, if successfully cloned, starts a long line of plant mothers which produce abundant roots rich in starch that can be processed into food until losing all vitality. In other words, whereas *kwana* is absolutely and definitely sterile, *tepuru pîye* is sterile in the sense that, like a pre-pubescent youth, it has yet to become fertile.

The Makushi understand seed-grown and cutting-grown manioc plants to be productive in different ways. Seed-grown manioc, which only occurs in the wild is a good source of new planting material, but it does not produce food (i.e. edible tuberous roots). Manioc plants grown from cuttings, by contrast, are the products of domestication and intense cultivation which, after a while, need to be replaced with planting material from plants that have grown from seeds, and have never been cultivated before. The contrast between seed and clone, as well as their complementarity in reproduction can be further illustrated by comparing Makushi ethnographic data with data collected by Nicolas Journet (1995) among the Curripaco of Colombia. His monograph contains a rich interpretation of the mythic origin and cultural significance of manioc domestication, which highlights further the issue of male sterility and fertility.[11]

The Curripaco tell mythical stories about two blood-related cultural heroes, Iapirikuri and Kaaritairi. They compare Iapirikuri, the orphaned, unmarried, and childless hero who is at the origin of war and hunting to wild manioc, the rootless and sole survivor of an abandoned garden which has no tuberous roots. Both are sterile orphans. Iapirikuri, who has a small penis, is sexually impotent. He adopts the children of war victims, and copulates incestuously with his paternal aunt. For the Curripaco, Iapirikuri is a sterile hero who cannot reproduce. Similarly, they represent wild manioc as a seed-grown plant resulting from self-pollination and condemned to germinative reproduction, like all wild plants (trees in particular), which cannot multiply rapidly and massively as cultivated plants do. Kaaritairi, the garden hero, is, by contrast, married and the father of several children. Kaaritairi's eldest son, himself married and a father, resides with his family in Kaaritairi's longhouse. Kaaritairi has secretly stolen the knowledge of manioc cloning from Tapir, an animal well known throughout north-west Amazonia for its sizeable penis, and its sexual prowess. During a manioc beer ceremony, Kaaritairi makes sexual advances to his daughter-in-law. This outrages his eldest son, who attempts to murder his father. Kaaritairi escapes, and comes back some time later, to teach the art of manioc cultivation to his younger son and daughter, leaving his murderous eldest son and his family to subsist on wild fruit. In the end, the family, reunited, cultivates manioc on a large scale. Journet (1995: 108–18; 240–8) concludes that Curripaco myths illustrate the way in which these Arawak Indians associate gardening and human fecundity, and social reproduction and manioc cultivation. The Curripaco have two models of masculinity, hence of society and its reproduction. The orphan and infertile Iapirikuri, war and hunting hero, has no ascendants or descendants and lives with his younger brothers. Kaaritairi, garden and peace hero, is associated with the hypersexed tapir, and lives surrounded by his children and grandchildren.

In the Makushi context too manioc plants represent fertility and the relationship of procreation. Whereas manioc reproduced through seed is conceptualized as a source of planting material only, manioc reproduced by propagating cuttings is a source of edible roots. Both are needed for maintaining a healthy and varied stock of cultivars. Cultivators say that there is no point in replanting cuttings from wild manioc because it does not produce tuberous roots, that is, children. Wild manioc (and by extension spontaneous seedlings), which simply regenerates itself is male, while cultivated manioc propagated by cuttings, which reproduces not only the original plant, but multiplies it and produces small children, is linked to the regenerative figure of the mother. Reproduction from seed is conceptualized as male, while the vegetative and regenerative potential of cultivated manioc is regarded as essentially female. Moreover, seed, stem, and starch-rich root, all contain a bone-like, lasting, semen-like generative principle derived from sunlight (see Reichel-Dolmatoff 1971: 48, C. Hugh-Jones 1979, S. Hugh-Jones 1995). Although the stem is said to be mother-like in that it bears children roots, these are also the product of a father-like agency, sap, which is analogous to milk, and, like milk, derives from semen, the quintessential male substance. Starch obtained from the lengthy processing of bitter manioc roots constitutes the purest and most concentrated form of seminal substance. This conceptualization corroborates Carib beliefs about sexual reproduction, seen as the fusion of a male seed and female flesh or skin (Rivière 1974*a*).

CONCLUSION

By exploring the symbolic significance of Makushi bitter manioc farming arrange-ments, planting techniques, management of varietal diversity, and botanical know-ledge, I was able to highlight the ways in which seed and clone provide metaphors (as discussed by Lakoff 1984, 1987, Bloch 1993, and Rival 1998*b*) for the concep-tualization of replication and continuity. The homological treatment of plants and humans this implies has been noted by Rivière (1993), who has suggested that Amazonian indigenous representations of descent and genealogical ties are often expressed using a botanical idiom. This should be no surprise to anthropologists working in the Durkheimian tradition, who document the constitutive relationship between forms of conceptual thought and social practices in distinct cultural universes. Techniques to use and exploit nature form a privileged domain for analysing this fundamental relationship (see also Erikson, this volume). Makushi particular understandings of the nature of seed-grown manioc and of why culti-vators should protect and incorporate such plants in their farming system reveal a great deal about their way of thinking about sexual reproduction, the generative process, consanguinity, and identity. It also sheds new light on the structuralist thesis that gardens are female domains associated with filiation and consanguinity.

The use and perception of manioc seed dormancy, the analogy drawn between the manioc plant and the human body, the filial relation established between stem and roots, the conceptualization of wild manioc as a feral and degenerate cultivar, and, finally, associations between gender, fertility, and sexual reproduction, are all facts which have led me to contend that the process of manioc domestication should be studied in the context of both cultural representations and cultivation practices. The Makushi divide the species *Manihot esculenta* into two completely unrelated groups of crops, *kana* (sweet or non-poisonous varieties classified with sweet potato and mainly cultivated close to houses) and *kîse* or manioc proper (i.e. mono-cultivated bitter or poisonous varieties grown in separate plantations), of which the Makushi cultivate probably more than one hundred different varieties (Elias, Rival, McKey 2001). If it were not for the fact that it is considered a degenerate descendant of *kîse*, *kwana* (feral manioc growing naturally in wild areas far from houses and farms) should be considered a third, separate species. *Kîse* is further sub-categorized in numerous named and recognized cloned varieties which, taken together, are distinguished from *tepuru pîye* (unnamed, seed-grown manioc plants). Once they have reached maturity, individual *tepuru pîye* plants are either discarded or cloned, henceforth fully incorporated within the *kîse* varietal pool.

Whereas trained natural scientists stress the significance of seed-grown manioc for the maintenance of varietal diversity, the Makushi incorporate sexually produced individuals into the stock of material from vegetative propagation to maintain the crop's vitality. The two points of view are relatively close, and one is easily translatable into the other. By contrast, indigenous knowledge and scientific knowledge are miles apart when it comes to classifying sweet and bitter varieties of manioc. Whereas the scientific classification system places all varieties on a continuum of relative HCN concentration, the indigenous system dissociates 'sweet' and 'bitter' varieties as entirely different species. And whereas for the biologist wild manioc is the primal germ plasm, the ultimate source of diversity, in other words, the original ancestor, for the Makushi cultivator, wild manioc is the unproductive, infertile, kinless affine who has lost all potential for sociality and who can no longer be incorporated within socialized spaces. The equivalent of the biologist's original ancestor is Cassava Mother, the seed of life and mistress spirit, the mistress/owner, or matrix/womb, of the *kîse* species, who lives amongst her plant children to look after them and lead them (Butt Colson 1989).

The symbolism attached to Makushi planting techniques and management of bitter manioc cultivars is structured by underlying rules of homology and transformation between manioc, seminal substance, and offspring comparable to those extensively discussed by C. Hugh-Jones (1979) for the Barasana. In Makushi thought, productive bitter manioc plants, in the same way as a child is the product of the sexual union of her father and her mother while also being the fusion of her biological body and the spiritual life energy or soul that inhabits it, result from, and perpetuate, a range of consanguineal relations: the mother–child relation between the stem and the roots it produces; the nurturing and protective parent–child relation between cultivators and manioc plants; the relation of spiritual adoption, which is also a father–son and a master/owner–followers relation; the relation between Cassava Mother and manioc plants; and, finally, the largely unspecified relation of friendly co-operation between Cassava Mother and Makushi cultivators, which cannot be forced into a sister–sister or a co-mother consanguineal alliance without betraying the ethnography. Moreover, co-participation in parenthood involves three principles: the stem (semen/sap, womb/matrix, and children/roots) and its biological capacity for procreation; a more abstract principle, that is, the creator/protector of cultivated plants, the spirit/owner/mistress; and men and women cultivators in conjugal pairs who own the socialized space (the farm) in which plants grow, and who are the nurturing propagators of 'parents' (stems), as well as the consumers of 'children' (roots). There is little doubt that if the Makushi have not experimented with planting manioc seeds, or have not tried to hybridize wild and farm-grown varieties to augment further the number of varieties, as well as to obtain more performing ones, this is in part due to their symbolic representation of what makes wild manioc plants different from both volunteer plants grown from seedlings and plants grown from cuttings.

Let us now unravel the underlying social categories and principles embedded in Makushi farming practices, which, I have argued, form an integral part of the conceptual framework within which geneaological ties become culturally and socially meaningful. Unlike most tuber crops, manioc is propagated by stem cuttings, a material different from the edible part. The absence of use competition between propagation material and edible material enables cultivators to develop a farming system based on two modes of reproduction, with seed-grown plants producing 'parents' and cutting-grown ones producing 'children'. Furthermore, if cultural representations underlying this farming system establish some kind of genealogical link, it is between two different entities, stems and roots, with the result that 'children' never grow to become 'parents'. It is in the nature of properly socialized stems (i.e. clones) to produce roots, but roots never produce or reproduce anything; they are consumed.[12] And if non-cloned manioc that grows outside the human realm reproduces only itself (not in multiple copies, but just as one individual), it is because it has lost the capacity of being a parent and producing children. Ironically, therefore, wild seed-grown manioc, which for Western biology is sexually reproduced, is, for the Makushi, a self-cloned clone. Seed-grown manioc found in cultivated, thus social and conjugal spaces, may have no ascendant or descendant, but it can, with human help, generate plants with sets of children, as farmers who select for productivity while encouraging individuation and varietal diversity are in fact selecting to increase the parent/children ratio.

None of these relations results from sexual intercourse, but sexuality nevertheless marks their origin. As seeds are not understood to result from sexual reproduction, and as a plant grown from a seed replicates itself but does not multiply, the contrast between seed and clone does not correspond to a contrast between sexual and vegetative reproduction. Cultivators use the reproductive capacity of volunteer seed-grown plants to start new parent–child lines. Each line represents a two-generation 'interface', and lasts until it runs out of energy and its fecundity declines. What is actualized every time a plant produces roots, it seems, is the potential for a fecund sexual future, so that reproduction corresponds to the production of roots. Not only is the capacity to bear root children activated in the stem by the male principle (seed, semen, bone, sunlight) that it contains, but it is also linked to the fact that domesticated manioc originates from the body of a girl menstruating for the first time.

If none of this is entirely incompatible with Taylor's structuralist denial of consanguinity as filiation, it nevertheless challenges her adoption of cloning as the Achuar botanic idiom for expressing the nothingness of consanguinity, or, in her own words, the 'non-relation predicated on a self-perpetuating unique term'. Taylor's contribution to this volume does not mention what cloning is for the Achuar, and the reader is left with the impression that she uses the term to mean, as we commonly do in contemporary Western cultures, the propagation of a group of organisms produced asexually from one stock.[13] She also seems to suggest that the most important feature of this type of propagation is its potential to replicate and multiply ad infinitum identical copies of an original hard copy, for which the photocopy would serve as a better model, as it certainly does for Western intellectuals such as Jameson (1988) or Baudrillard (1989), who have written extensively about the lack of creativity, originality, or individuality, hence authenticity and difference (and, more generally, the cultural impoverishment) that such a technological development has supposedly brought to our contemporary cultural systems.

As I hope to have demonstrated in this chapter, the Makushi hold a rather different view of cloning. Rather than understanding cloning as a non-creative, repetitive replication, they use it within their horticultural system, which incorporates both vegetative and sexual reproduction, to increase difference and maintain high levels of diversity, as botanists are starting to recognize. Makushi artificial selection reinforces natural selection in a deliberate effort to encourage varietal diversity (Elias 2000). If it is true that human selection truly operates only on clones when cultivators choose after each harvest to replant cuttings or not, they also tolerate, protect, and even in some cases encourage the growth and multiplication of volunteer seed-grown plants which are the real source of new genotypes, that is, of original diversity. And whereas they do not seem to have the knowledge that seed-grown plants are the product of sexual reproduction, that is of genetic recombination following the fusion of gametes issued from male and female flowers, they none the less represent the difference between seed-grown plants and clones in symbolic terms that suggest an apprehension of sexuality and its potential to generate new life and create difference.

Makushi cultivators do not identify clones with replicas of an original living organism, nor do they attribute monstrous genealogical ties (for example, at once parent and sibling) to populations of clones, for they never separate multiplication from the capacity to procreate, the latter representing the real focus of cultural interest. Cultivators encourage diversity of phenotypes, and gardens are peopled not only with a wide range of manioc varieties, but also with plants that are not necessarily identical to their predecessors. What one finds under cultivation in

Makushi manioc gardens is not a single clone, but many different clones, in constant renewal. Varieties, despite attempts to freeze them into a well-defined and finite stock of named and classifiable types, do not grow in gardens as fixed entities with their specific names and strictly defined characteristics, but are, rather, subjected to a fluid and evolving process by which farmers continuously gain and lose them. Furthermore, plants are not conceptualized in relation to a common origin (i.e. the stem from which cuttings were prepared and planted), but to a common name (the name of the variety to which they belong), and in terms of their generative potential of bearing *imun* roots, that is, of reproducing more than themselves. Genealogical continuity between stems and roots is more important than the supposed identity of plants belonging to the same variety.

To Taylor's assertion that consanguinity is meaningless unless coupled with affinity, I would like to add that the reverse is as true. Affinity is meaningless, unless there are gendered and fertile social persons with procreative capabilities, who share substance on the basis of genealogical proximity, thus pre-empting the sharing of substance through common residence within the domestic sphere. If consanguinity is about making alike through life-sustaining and other nurturing relations, such relations are not divorced from co-parenthood or relations resulting from co-parenthood. This explains why women are vectors of maximal distance, as well as of maximal identity, and why the relationship between two female cross-cousins can never be consanguinized, whereas male affines are easily incorporated and turned into consanguineal kin. The ethnographic information I have presented in this chapter demonstrates the centrality of relations of procreation in at least one indigenous Amazonian social thought system. Procreative, engendering, or generative power, whatever one wants to call it, or fertility, that is, the power to create a new life rather than just replicating one's own life, is absolutely central to the construction of the person and the fabrication of the body among the Makushi, as it is among the Barasana, the Makuna, the Curripaco, and many other South American lowland societies. Many social institutions, in particular the universal social recognition of the nuclear family unit (Rivière 1984), the *couvade* (Rival, Slater, and Miller 1998), or the social stigma attached to orphanhood and sterility (see among others Menget 1982, Journet 1995, and Rival 1996*b*), would simply not be comprehensible without the recognition of this basic fact. And so would the lineage ideologies of the Makuna (Århem 2000), Barasana (S. Hugh-Jones 1995), Canela (Crocker and Crocker 1994), Kayapó (Lea 1995 and this volume), and other Amazonian societies politicizing the power to engender and to pass on some common property, quality, or power. As Makushi cultivators form conjugal pairs, they become dynamic transformative syntheses embracing more than one quality or attribute, and form consanguineal relations combining the procreative given with processual and achieved nurturing. And it is the capacity to procreate and breed, as well as to generate new parent–child units, that Makushi cultivators replicate in their bitter manioc farms.

ACKNOWLEDGEMENTS

Fieldwork among the Makushi was supported by APFT (see n. 1). I am very grateful to Audrey Naraine and Cecilia Jeffreys for their enthusiastic participation in this project, and to all the villagers of Massara and Rewa for their warm hospitality and willingness to share their passion for bitter manioc with us. Many thanks also to Audrey Butt Colson and Anne-Christine Taylor who commented on earlier drafts. Ultimate responsibility for the final product is, of course, mine.

NOTES

1. Data were collected in collaboration with plant geneticist Marianne Elias within the EC-funded research programme APFT, Avenir des Peuples des Forêts Tropicales. APFT is a major interdisciplinary project sponsored by the European Commission (DG VIII), which examines the long-term co-evolution of human groups and the rainforest, as well as the contemporary ecological, cultural, and socio-economic status of rainforest peoples in Central Africa, the South-West Pacific area, and the three Guianas.
2. 'Chaque jardin est le lieu d'une association presque charnelle avec la femme qui l'a créé et le fait vivre' (Descola 1986: 218). (Descola 1994a: 175, 'Each garden is almost physically associated with the woman who created and nurtures it.')
3. However, as Descola adds, women give birth in their manioc plantations, from which men are absolutely excluded, so that 'le droit de maternité putative s'exerçant sur les plantes cultivées s'enracine tres concrètement dans le lieu même où la maternité réelle s'inaugure' (Descola 1986: 267). (Descola 1994a: 217, 'The right of putative motherhood over cultivated plants is thus concretely rooted in the very place where real motherhood is realized.')
4. In his own words, 'L'horticulture procède d'un marchandage dialectique où le manioc se laisse manger par les hommes pourvu que ceux-ci prennent soin d'assurer la continuité de sa descendance' (Descola 1993: 111), and 'le jardinage présente un curieux paradoxe: d'une entreprise débonnaire et dépourvue d'aléas, les Achuar ont fait une sorte de guérilla consanguine réglée par un périlleux équilibre des saignées. La mère se nourrit de ses enfants végétaux, qui prélèvent à leur tour sur sa progéniture humaine le sang dont ils ont besoin pour leur croissance' (Descola 1993: 112). (English translation, p. 92: 'Horticulture thus proceeds on the basis of a dialectical deal according to which the manioc allows itself to be eaten by human beings, provided that they assume responsibility for ensuring its continued propagation'; and p. 94: 'The Achuar have turned a care-free, unthreatening occupation into a kind of internecine guerilla war ruled by the risky balance of a series of blood-lettings. The mother feeds on her plant-children, who in turn take from her human offspring the blood that they need for their own growth'.)
5. See Elias, Rival, and McKey (2001) for a thorough discussion of Makushi systemic classification of *Manihot esculenta*.
6. Cultivators who decide whether or not to keep a variety, thus exercising some control over the frequency of each landrace, do not seem to select consciously for resistance to pests, diseases, or climatic conditions. Like other Amazonian cultivators (Boster 1985; Chernela 1987; Emperaire, Pinton, and Second 1998; Salick, Cellinese, and Knapp

1997), they consciously select varieties primarily for their productivity. For instance, Marianne Elias found the variety called 'white man stick' (*paranakîrî pîye*), which culti- vators value for its high yields, in 71 per cent of the farms included in her census. But cultivators know that high yield is a relative notion. A variety may be very productive in a particular farm, and in the first crop, but give poor results the second time it is harvested, or in another farm. Similarly, a variety may produce much more in the second crop than it did in the first one. There is no directional selection on time to reach maturity either, since cultivators need to have both precocious and late-bearing varieties to minimize risks and have a continuous supply of roots to harvest, at all times. Root colour, processability, and other criteria for selection are further discussed in Elias, Rival, and McKey (2001).

7. We did not find any significant gendering of these relations of exchange. Men and women equally participate in the exchange of cuttings, both as receivers and donors.

8. Marianne Elias found up to 400 seedlings in one young crop of 425 m^2, which is the highest density ever reported in the literature. Emperaire, Pinton, and Second (1998), for example, report one or two seedlings per farm.

9. This is due to recombination in a genome that is very heterozygous (Colombo 1997, Lefèvre 1989).

10. Marianne Elias identified six populations of *M. esculenta* subsp. *flabellifolia* in the North Rupununi savannah.

11. The fact that the Curripaco are Arawak-speakers, while the Makushi are Carib-speak- ers does not alter the significance of the cultural parallels between the two systems of representation of wild and domesticated manioc.

12. One wonders how far this can be related to the puzzling and unsolved question raised by Peter Rivière (1987*a*) as to why people bother cultivating such a poisonous plant (or, if poisonless, bloodsucking and lethal as among the Jivaros), and spend so much time processing it, whereas everywhere else in the world humans seem to have domesticated plants to render them increasingly more productive and less poisonous, and, conse- quently, less resistant to pests, henceforth today's efforts to help them regain defences by, for example, engineering the accretion of scorpion genes.

13. Incidentally, the word clone was coined during the 20th century from the Greek word *klôn*, which means shoot or twig. However, a shoot for many Amazonian Indians, and indeed many indigenous people around the world, is considered a 'child' of the plant mother.

5

The Blowpipe Indians: Variations on the Theme of Blowpipe and Tube among the Yagua Indians of the Peruvian Amazon

Jean-Pierre Chaumeil, *EREA-CNRS*

Thirty years ago, Peter Rivière (1969*b*) published an essay comparing two special-ized objects, the blowpipe and the hair tube, found in several indigenous cultures of southern Guyana and northern Brazil, a region divided into savannah and forest. He observed that groups located in the north of this region possessed blow-pipes but no hair tubes, while those in the south had hair tubes but no blowpipes. He showed that the complementary distribution of these two tubular objects reflected not so much the history or the mode of subsistence of these groups, but, rather, a broader set of ideas contained in their myths. Moreover, he proposed that the hollow tubes found in this cultural area should be interpreted as energy 'trans-formers' (they transform untamed, dangerous energy into controlled, socialized energy). According to this interpretation, the hollow tube is one of the means imagined by southern Guyana and northern Brazil indigenous societies to concep-tualize dynamically the relationship between nature and culture.

More recently, Laura Rival (1996*a*) has studied the blowpipe among the Huaorani Indians of Amazonian Ecuador, this time to compare it with the spear. She argues that the Huaorani blowpipe, used to hunt birds and monkeys, stands for relations of close kinship that correspond to the endogamous ideal. The spear, by contrast, is used almost exclusively in peccary hunts (the Huaorani consider peccaries to be 'aggressive invaders'). As such, it expresses self-defence against outside predators, and corresponds to the autarkic ideal. She concludes that the choice of weapons, a social (rather than technical) act, regulates social relations of inclusion and exclusion between human and non-human protagonists. Using Rivière's model, however, it can be said that the Huaorani blowpipe functions as an internal energy regulator, while the spear is intended to control external energy. In a similar perspective, Erikson (this volume) develops a closely related argument based on a comparison between the blowpipe and the bow among the Matis of the Brazilian Amazon.

Let us also recall that much has been written on the association of pipes and hollow tubes with the control of body orifices (oral voracity, anal retention and incontinence). It is well known that this subject was fully treated by Claude Lévi-Strauss, first in his 1964–5 course (see Lévi-Strauss 1984: 109–11), and on various subsequent occasions (1966, 1985: 211–16). Lévi-Strauss's initial interest in this theme arose from his examination of the role played by the sloth in South Amerindian myths. The sloth has been compared to a kind of stoppled pipe.

Du point de vue de l'ethnologie.sud-américaine, il est remarquable et sans doute significatif qu'une philosophie morale préoccupée par certains usages immodérés du tube digestif—positivement ou négativement, par en haut ou par en bas—coïncide, quant à son aire de distribution, avec celle de la sarbacane qui est aussi un tube creux, technologiquement lié à l'autre puisque la flèche expulsée par le souffle buccal est le moyen de la viande qui sera absorbée par la bouche avant d'être expulsée sous forme d'excrément.   (Lévi-Strauss 1984: 111)

From the ethnographic point of view, it is notable and doubtless significant that a moral philosophy preoccupied with certain immoderate uses of the digestive tract—positive or negative, above or below—coincides in its area of distribution with that of the blowpipe, which is also a hollow conduit, technologically linked with the other, since the arrow expelled by oral means is the source of meat, which will be taken in by the mouth before being expelled in the form of excrement.   (Lévi-Strauss 1987: 87)

My aim in this essay on the Yagua blowpipe is to carry on the discussion by comparing the hunting weapon with, this time, another type of tube, the flute, and with, by extension, palm trees. Relative to other Amazonian cultures, the Yagua can be said to have carried the plant metaphor as a form of self-representation rather far. Their religious philosophy abounds with references to palms and palm derivatives such as blowpipes and flutes, all associated with long-lasting qualities and integral bonds with past generations. The perspective on the flute and the blowpipe offered by the tube and the 'winds' that blow through it helps us to understand why the Yagua have retained both instruments. In addition, this perspective allows for a more intimate connection between various areas of activity, such as hunting, war, shamanism, and initiation rituals. A word of caution, however, is in order. The relations suggested within this limited set of objects far from exhaust all the uses and representations of the tube in Yagua culture. Moreover, only ritual flutes are considered here. A study of the full set of wind instruments (panpipe, fipple pipe, transverse flute, ocarina, and so forth) would take us too far from our main concern, which is not to compare artefacts, but, rather, the ways in which they are used in representation. Let us then start with an examination of secular bonds between the Yagua and their blowpipes.

THE BLOWPIPE INDIANS

Borrowed from Wustmann (1960), this popular expression is illustrative of the kind of images today associated with the Yagua in a large public fascinated by the

FIG. 5.1. Yagua hunter with his blowpipe (Chaumeil 1994)

Amazon. This is especially true in Peru, where tourist agencies make much of the cynegetic prowess of the 'blowpipe people', these unrepentant hunters whose deadly and quiet weapons can bring down with a single dart and from a respectable distance all kinds of game, thanks to the diabolical and unequalled efficacy of curare poison. Such an overrated reputation, which would undoubtedly trigger the Yagua's laughter, is, however, not entirely unjustified. The reputation of the Yagua and of some of their neighbours as blowpipe and curare purveyors goes back to the seventeenth century, when they traded these goods over great distances along the Amazon river. Countless works from missionary accounts to scientific studies devote some good chapters to this topic (Vellard 1965). We know that Yagua blow-pipes were exported over thousands of kilometres to the Andean foothills and the Ucayali region. In the other direction (north-east), blowpipes travelled a long way up to the Guianas. The blowpipe featured in Farabee (1918: fig. XXXVI), which he attributes to the Wapishana, who obtained it through trade from the Guyanese Makushi, is incontestably Yagua. The extensive network of historical trade routes for Yagua curare is also known in sufficient detail (Vellard 1965). Curare trading, which has a very long history among the Yagua, has gone through various flour-ishing phases, the last one going back only a few decades, when the great trading companies of Iquitos sent river peddlers to buy cheap Yagua curare, which was then resold in towns or abroad, especially in the United States.

If the blowpipe's geographical distribution is now well established (to the north, north-west, and west of the Amazon basin, see Yde 1948, Métraux 1949, and Boglár 1950), its antiquity is less so. The use of this hunting weapon of pre-Colombian origin in Peru does not seem to be of great antiquity in Amazonia. Its introduction may even be as late as the fifteenth or sixteenth century, and even later among some groups (Métraux 1949: 249). In any case, historical facts and ancient cultural grounding among the Yagua rule out the idea of a recent import.

Blowpipes are prestigious items within Yagua culture. They are still praised as hunting weapons for small to average size game animals, and are even sometimes used for larger game (in which case darts are coated with a double dose of curare). Larger game, however, is normally hunted with palmwood spears (*ruwatu*), which make up, along with clubs (*muwë*), the traditional arsenal used equally in war and in hunting. Whereas the role of the spear is to wound at a distance, that of the club is above all to finish off the wounded victim by striking a final blow. In Yagua tradi-tion, killing large game and enemies implies close contact, or at least a degree of physical proximity between the killer and his victim. Like other Amazonian peoples, the Yagua assimilate large game to enemies, in particular herds of pecca-ries, which are compared to raiding parties on the war path. Dream interpretation confirms this association, as to dream of peccaries forewarns an impending attack by enemies. The difference between hunting and war is so subtle that it is not surprising that the method of killing should be the same in both cases. Bows are known, but never used in hunting (and even less so in war). If the introduction of shotguns (*dudu*, literally 'bone' or 'flute') about thirty years ago has considerably reduced the use of clubs and spears, it has had little effect on blowpipe use. Consequently, the blowpipe has remained the emblematic hunting weapon well beyond its technical performance or its obvious qualities as a silent arm.

It is possible, as a matter of fact and without much exaggeration, to classify the Yagua blowpipe, which requires much precision in its making and which is truly magnificent, with art objects. The weapon, 1.50 m. to more than 3 m. long for a 5 cm. diameter at the mouthpiece (reduced to 2.5 cm. at the opposite end), is carved out of the rectilinear bole of several carefully selected tree species or palms. To allow the wood to dry more easily, the trunk of the selected tree is notched deeply all around the girth months before felling actually takes place. Two species are commonly used, pucuna capsi (*Lucuma bifera*) and *Bactris gasipaes*, as well as Brazilian paxiúba (*Socratea exorrhiza*). When slender *Bactris* palms are selected, the whole trunk is used. Erikson (this volume) has rightly stressed the technical difficulty involved in making blowpipes from this extremely dense and fibrous wood. However, and despite the fact that they give preference to *Lucuma bifera*, the Yagua, like their Ticuna neighbours (Goulard 1998: 407) or the Jivaro (Descola 1986: 275), demonstrate great expertise in realizing this difficult operation.

Yagua blowpipes are made of two parts tied together with plant fibres which are coated with a layer of pitch over which a thin bark is carefully wrapped. The bark, called *mënasu* (i.e. clothing, from *mëna*, 'placenta'), strengthens, protects, and clothes the instrument. A mouthpiece made of hardwood carved in the shape of an hourglass is then fitted onto the weapon, a few centimetres below the sighting notch which is made of two agouti teeth glued with pitch (for a more detailed description of blowpipe manufacture, see Fejos 1943: 47–51). The fashioning of the bore, which gives the weapon its efficacy, is the most delicate operation. The bore must be as smooth as a gun barrel. It is polished with a 'stem-brush' made of *Oenocarpus* palm, and partially coated with *Bixa orellana* mixed with sand for abrasive. This operation requires several days, even weeks, of architectural and horological work, with the weapon horizontally placed to avoid warping. The darts, delicately shaped out of the veins of *Maximiliana maripa* palm leaves, and coated with *Strychnos*-based curare, are stored in quivers carried across the shoulder, to which little bags containing kapok (for plugs), and piranha jaws (to nick the poisoned heads) are attached. The effective range of a Yagua blowpipe held vertically is of approximately thirty metres for an experienced shooter.

Yagua hunters consider their blowpipes to be very personal and intimate possessions, which they lend only reluctantly. Blowpipes made for sale are not lent either, but kept untouched until they are traded. A blowpipe is an animated object endowed with a 'mother' (*hamwo*), the spirit or vital principle of the species from which it is made. To mishandle it or to lend it out excessively causes it to warp and lose its 'power', in which case it must be 'cured' (*ñënásëranaria dudase*) through a therapeutic ritual similar to those performed by shamans. To this effect, a stem-brush is coated with the fine powder of a special variety of Cyperaceae. The same ritual is performed for a brand new blowpipe, in this case to increase the weapon's range, as well as the force of the dart's propulsion. Yagua shamans use Cyperaceae widely in their magic cures both to heal and to enhance the power and courage of their patients (Cyperaceae powder was also used in war rituals). Far from being inert objects, blowpipes are treated as 'persons' identified with their owners, who name them, lavish attention on them as family members, and carry them into their graves.

The Yagua term for blowpipe (*dudase*, *rudase*, or *dudasi* according to dialectal variations) can be broken into two classifiers: *-du* (which derives from the noun *du*, 'bone') and *-dase* (which derives from the name of a type of palm tree). The classifier *-du* may be used for any tubular or cylindrical object, including a plant stem or stalk. For instance, whereas the word for maize is *didu*, the word for flute is *dudu* (for its derivatives, we have *dudumata* for panpipe, *rudidu* for slotted flute, and *duduvú* for horn or megaphone), which is also the word for shotgun. The verb *sa-du* denotes the act of blowing (with the mouth or through a tube), as in hunting with a blowpipe (the dart is blown through the weapon), or as in casting a spell, when the shaman blows a magical dart sent from its extended arm (*sadu rimara nihamwo*, 'the shaman sends a dart towards someone' (i.e. to kill or to cause sickness)). The classifier *-dase* is used for all rectilinear elements, particularly palm trunks (palms form a sub-category marked by the word-ending morpheme *-ase*). It is also found in the term for the blowpipe's body or the gun barrel (*du dudase*, literally 'bone-flute'—'rectilinear hollow tube'). From a linguistic point of view, therefore, the qualities associated with blowpipes, for instance rectilinearity, hardness, and hollowness, are also found in bones, palms, and flutes. In addition, and because of the breath that goes through it, the blowpipe is also associated with shamanism. In the rest of this essay, I focus on these associations, starting with an illuminating myth involving a pair of twins, a blowpipe, and a flute.

BLOWPIPE AND FLUTE

There is a myth about the acquisition of the blowpipe and the flute, given here in the abridged version from the twins cycle, first episode:

An old woman, busy weeding her garden, hears from afar the resonant voice of the sacred flutes announcing the hunters' return. Then, not a sound. Worried, she goes to the village and discovers that all the inhabitants have just been killed by a band of wild Indians. Wandering through the ruins, she finds two children (the twins, *ndanu* the older one and 'placenta', *mёna*, the younger) crying next to the inert body of their mother, and decides to give them a home. Several days after, the twins have already grown up; they now talk and converse with their grandmother, who tells them of the carnage. Eager to take vengeance, they leave immediately to look for the remains of their murdered parents. On the way they see a quantity of game, but do not know how to hunt. Their grandmother teaches them how to obtain a ready-made blowpipe by quickly taking hold of the instrument released by the blowpipe tree, which opens and closes like a vice. Finding the operation too hazardous, the mischievous twins prefer to cut the tree in two (henceforth, they must make their own blowpipes), as well as stealing the poison darts after having neutralized the scorpion care-takers. Arriving at the site of the massacre, they are greeted by a burst of thunder announc-ing the arrival on Earth of their dead father's soul (accompanied by that of their dead mother in some versions). Playing a bone flute with terrifying power, the soul begins to dance. The roguish twins succeed in seizing the flute, which is first tested on the grand-mother, who falls head over heels from the powerful blast. The twins learn to play the magi-cal instrument without being overcome by the terrifying energy of its blowing-sound. Equipped with this formidable weapon, they decide to form an army (the creation of the Yagua clans) and go off to war. Arriving close to the enemy's village, the older of the twins turns himself into a sparrowhawk (or an egret) and settles on the top of the highest dwelling in order to attract the enemy's attention. When all the savages gather to gaze at the bird, the elder twin fells them with a single blow of the flute, and the warriors finish them off with bludgeon strokes. While the twins organize a big party to celebrate their victory, the dead father's soul, who has taken advantage of the collective drunkenness to descend once more on Earth, successfully recovers his stolen flute.

In the myth the acquisition of the blowpipe (to shoot animals) and of the bone-flute (to paralyse enemies) occurs almost concomitantly. The twins obtain the blowpipe just before they cunningly acquire the flute of their late father. Their learning how to use the former as a hunting weapon anticipates in some ways the correct use of the latter as a war weapon. However, the privilege of 'spontaneous fabrication' is lost in both cases, and the twins are now forced to make their own artefacts, either from the same materials but after a long technical process (blow-pipe), or by using different materials (wood instead of bone), each time a great ritual is organized (flute). The blowpipe tree mentioned in the myth belongs to the *Lucuma bifera* species, whose dense wood contrasts with the hollowness of palms. I have already mentioned that Yagua blowpipe makers prefer to use *Lucuma bifera*. However, the mythical *Lucuma bifera* tree trunk containing the blowpipe opens and closes in a movement recalling the contractions of childbirth, as if it was hollow (hence a palm tree), and as if the contained weapon was a child to be pulled out at the right time. In fact, there are two blowpipes, one containing the other, whose spontaneous birth occurs as the trunk opens up; the closing up of the trunk (stopped-up tube) causes its retention in the 'womb'. In other words, *Lucuma bifera*, which is favoured over palms, is nevertheless treated in mythical imagery as a hollow trunk giving birth to a second hollow tube.

The same hollow trunk imagery is applied to the giant tree of the myth about the origin of the Amazon river. According to this myth, the tree of life (*Chorisia sp.*) retains in its gigantic trunk the waters which form the Amazon river once the twins have felled the tree (open trunk). For the Yagua, the Amazon river is a line, a path (*nú*) that crosses earth from east to west. How can one not see in the giant river the bore of the blowpipe, or even the blowpipe itself, contained in the *Chorisia* trunk which, in falling, delimits precisely the circumference of the earth? As a matter of fact, the Yagua also represent the earth in the form of a tapered tree (in contrast to the *Chorisia*'s dome-shaped foliage) whose 'mouth' corresponds to the felling spot, the place where the trunk separates from the stump, and this part

FIG. 5.2. Preparing darts with curare (Chaumeil 1976)

of the tree is where the first ancestors are still living (Chaumeil 1983: 161). The entire earth now becomes a blowpipe through which the Amazon river flows.

Blowpipe and flute are linked in the myth associating hunting and warfare. But the flute's resounding blow, which immobilizes enemies without killing them (enemies must be clubbed (*muwë*) to death), stands in contrast to the silent and lethal 'blow' of curare-coated blowpipe darts. As mentioned earlier, the blowpipe, ideal for smaller game, can also be used for larger game, equivalent to the enemy. Large curare-wounded mammals which lure hunters in breathless pursuits are killed off with the same clubs that are used against the enemy. There seems to be in this case a homology between blowpipe/club and flute/club, with the paralysing mediation of curare/blow. The sound (blow) coming from sacred flutes during the great rituals, which is harmless for male initiates (they are like the mythical twins), is extremely damaging for young children, women, and non-initiates. This raises the question as to whether curare is really innocuous for humans. It is true that curare makers (a task traditionally performed by Yagua shamans) test the strength of the poison on themselves, by pricking their forearms with the tip of poison darts. Anyhow, blowpipe and flute are somewhat equivalent, even if the former has never formally been a war weapon.

However, if we now leave the mythical universe to enter the sphere of objects, we find within the Yagua arsenal a singular instrument, the trophy flute. It is almost identical to the mythical flute, and, like its homologue, capable of bringing enemies down at a distance.

THE TROPHY FLUTE

The Yagua, who, like many Amazonian peoples, have traditionally been great warriors, were actively involved in warfare until the first decades of the twentieth century, mainly with the prime objective of obtaining three types of human trophies: teeth, finger bones, and humeri. Teeth were acquired from the decapitated heads of enemies, and mounted in necklaces worn by the victors as a sign of great prestige. Finger bones were worn in bracelets as a sign of distinction or military rank. And, finally, humeri were used in the making of flutes, whose sound was believed to have the power of bringing enemies down. These trophies, exclusively and personally owned by those who had slain enemy warriors, did not all have the same destiny upon their owners' deaths. Whereas flutes and finger bones were buried in graves alongside their owners' dead bodies, teeth necklaces were preciously guarded and handed down to the next generation, in the hope that they would bring the latter prosperity, force, and longevity. To draw a parallel between the bone flute mentioned here and the mythical one mentioned earlier is easy enough. The only difference between the two is that while the former comes from an enemy, the latter comes from an ancestor who gets it back at the end of the myth. Without dwelling on the subject, it should be recalled that the Yagua maintain complex and varied relationships with their dead, depending on the personal qualities of the deceased, and on the circumstances of his (or her) particular death (Chaumeil 1994: 285–9). The names of great warriors, perpetuated through epic narratives, served as focal points for their 'ancestralization'. In marked contrast with the treatment of enemy remains (teeth and bones), the Yagua avoid as a general rule all direct or prolonged contact with corpses, which are today buried directly in the ground, and which were in the past almost certainly buried in funerary urns. However, and as discussed below, the manipulation of ancestral relics in the form of sacred flutes forms the core of male initiation rituals. This is all the more interesting in that the ritual function of these flute relics is not significantly different from that of human teeth necklaces at the family level. Several families, to my knowledge, still possess such necklaces (see Tessmann 1930: fig. 56.5, which shows a belt made of human teeth worn by Yagua women).

If tribal wars have ended (and with them the trophy flutes), such is not the case for shamanism, a form of invisible warfare still thriving amongst the Yagua. As one might expect, the theme of the blowpipe is also found in shamanism, albeit in a somewhat unusual form.

THE SHAMAN'S BLOWPIPE BODY

Not very different from that of other upper Amazon groups, the classic Yagua shamanic technique of aggression consists in 'blowing' (*sa-du*) invisible darts onto victims. Illness penetrates with the projectiles. In contrast with the hunter's body or the warrior's body which gets only partially involved, the act of blowing mobilizes the entire body of the shaman. The shaman gets his supplies of magical darts from forest spirits after negotiation, and ingests them through the mouth. Once swallowed, the darts slide down the digestive tube (lubricated with phlegm) into the stomach (equivalent to the quiver), where they are kept and fed with tobacco smoke (regularly swallowed by the shaman), and where the 'digestive' process is stopped, given that the efficacy of the darts depends on their being expelled upward by going back along the digestive tube lining, and not downwards (as excrement). The darts, which are deviated towards the shaman's arms, are not equivalent to undigested, vomited food. The shaman's stretched-out arms become a kind of launching pad, or blowpipe (for a more extensive treatment of the identification of the shaman's body with hollow tubes, see Duvernay 1973: 82). This 'killing arm', a kind of magical pipe connected to the stomach by the digestive tract, is not unlike the ancient war flute made with the humerus of an enemy. In both cases we find a similar process activated by blowing through an organ. This tubular model of shamanic aggression prevails throughout Amazonia and does not presuppose the actual use of blowpipes in hunting. What matters here is the principle, that is, breath contained within a tube. The Yanomami, for example, ignore the existence of blowpipes, but nevertheless shoot magic darts at their enemies. Yanomami shamans, moreover, use scorching projectiles ejected from hollow tubes in their fights (Lizot 1984: 39). Therapeutic techniques essentially proceed in reverse mode, as the shaman uses his mouth to suck out and extract pathogenic projectiles lodged in the sick person's body. The difference between these two techniques confirms the contrasting and complementary use of blowing: aspiration for healing, and expiration for harming (shamanic witchcraft).

The shaman's body is thus assimilated to a mobile blowpipe fully armed with quiver and darts, not unlike the Matis *mariwin* spirits described by Erikson in this volume. But there is more to it. The Yagua shaman is typically Amazonian in the sense that he becomes a privileged target for his rivals, and that he defends himself against their attacks by girding his body with a protective shield made from his own projectiles, a device precisely known as 'belt of darts' (*rimíndaha*). Acting in this way the shaman does no more than reproduce in himself the mythic pattern of two blowpipes, one encased in the other. If when acting he happens to leave his defence open for too long, he gets 'caught', exactly like the blowpipe in the myth. To keep his defence closed (stopped-up tube) ensures his protection, but prevents him from acting, which corresponds to the blowpipe's 'intra-uterine' retention in the myth discussed above. Shamanic 'creation', therefore, takes place in the balanced movement between two opposite states.

The crushing effects of downward emission of intestinal gas are at times comparable to those of upward expulsion of breath characteristic of blowpipe and shamanic avatars. This is particularly true of anteaters. These animals release bursts of farts potent enough to bring down their pursuers, which explains why Yagua hunters avoid coming into close contact with them. In conclusion, whereas the breath gushing out of pipes, digested or not, is always potentially dangerous, the stopped-up tube in which breath is enclosed is protective. However, the latter prevents all 'birth', unlike the open tube and the breath blown through it, which has the ability to give, as well as to take, life. This pneumatic model of procreation depends above all on a process of transformation resulting from the passage of blown air (or its equivalent) in a tube. The very notion of creation conforms to this central idea in Yagua thought.

The theme of transformation through blowing as a creative and life-generating process evokes a final realization of the tube amongst the Yagua, this time in relation to male initiation rituals, during which sacred flutes, known in the anthropological literature as Yuruparí, are made. There is no doubt that Yagua male initiation rituals should be attached to the widespread north-western Amazon ceremonial complex.

THE SACRED FLUTES

In schematic terms, Yagua male initiation rituals belong to the category of great clanic ceremonies, which are traditionally held in February (a propitious coincidence as we shall see below), when the fruit of the *Bactris gasipaes* palm ripens. Five pairs of flutes are used during these rituals, which women and non-initiates are strictly forbidden to see, on pain of death or illness. In native thought, these instruments embody the 'voices' and 'bones' of five ancestral spirits (that is, of five long-dead Yagua) whose chief function is to regulate hunting and the abundance of game, a task they accomplish in connection with the master spirits of animals. In compensation for their help in obtaining game, the flutes are regularly 'fed' during the ritual with manioc beer poured from a full gourd into their 'mouths' (*útó*, 'mouthpiece'). It should be recalled at this stage that the sacred flutes make their appearance right at the beginning of the myth about the twins, who temporarily recover the flute of their late father in order to take revenge. As practised today, male initiation consists in revealing to the initiands (young boys between 5 and 8) the identity of the ancestral spirits embodied in the sacred flutes. But their initiation lasts in fact several years, during which they must, as in the myth, accustom themselves progressively to the terrifying blowing sound of the flutes. In addition to confirming their clan identity, such apprenticeship results in a number of benefits for the initiands, who acquire power, growth, skill, courage, and immunity from illness—hence long life. Moreover, they learn songs, wear their first ornaments and body paints, and each receive a clan name that becomes attached to their person, all signs of a complete social transformation, or, one might say, of a second 'birth'. It is not difficult to imagine, therefore, that what 'comes out' of the flutes is a fully transformed child, destined to a long life and a glorious future.

With all these details in mind, we can now return to the comparison between sacred flutes and blowpipes. First of all, it is significant that the age at which a boy receives his first blowpipe from his father (between 6 and 8) coincides with his initiation to the sacred flutes. Once again, the situation is congruent with that of the twin myth. Furthermore, at the organistic level, several types of wind instruments compose the musical ensemble: horns, pipes, and block-flutes played in pairs according to the opposition older/younger, male/female, long/short. In the myth, the flute of the twins' late mother is sometimes mentioned. The horn, which incarnates the dominant ancestral spirit (*rúnda*), is composed of a mouthpiece (*útó* or 'mouth') made of incorruptible palm wood, on which the supple bark of *Trema micrantha* is coiled all along its length (the instrument may be up to two metres long). The bark is held in place at the level of the mouthpiece by two wooden splinters. If it is not stored in a moist environment the bark becomes quickly unusable. The same bark, coiled in a spiral, is also used to protect the blowpipe's bole. In the horn, therefore, the important part is the mouthpiece, the only part kept from one ceremony to the next. This is also the part on which the prohibition to look weighs most heavily. The tube symbolizes the *wirisió* spirit. It is shaped from the hollow part of a *Socratea exhorriza* stem covered on one end with a lump of clay worked into an orifice through which one blows. Technically, the body of the tube and the mouthpiece of the horn are like a blowpipe. The block-flute representing the *wawitió*, *yurió*, and *sipató* spirits is shaped from the long stalk (about three metres long) of an *Astrocaryum chambira* palm and could be mistaken for a blowpipe. This association, often made by the Yagua themselves, is all the more significant, given that, for them, the two instruments are conceptually similar: just as the blowpipe transforms wild game into human sustenance, the sacred flutes transform a 'wild child' into a socialized being ready for marriage. Following Erikson (this volume), it can thus be inferred that the flute–blowpipe model constitutes a mode of identification and of transformative action typical of the ancestral entities that regulate hunting. *Rúnda*, the dominant spirit, is said to be in possession of an atrophied penis, but this defect is largely compensated by the remarkable length of his blowpipe.

Far from being limited to Yagua culture, the association between sacred flutes and blowpipes is common throughout western Amazonia, as attested by several authors. Among the Desana, for example, the same term is used both for the horn mouthpiece and the blowpipe (Reichel-Dolmatoff 1997: 300). The Ticuna, close neighbours of the Yagua, have a myth (cited in Goulard 1998: 242) in which the cultural hero *Joi* extracts colours from a blowpipe to paint the bark horn which is later used for his son's initiation. Not much further northwards the Miraña also link bark horns and blowpipes, although in their case the values attributed to the various components are reversed (Karadimas 1997: 467–8). It would not be difficult to multiply such examples relating the two types of instrument.

Taking the Yagua myth on flute and blowpipe acquisition as my starting point, I have been able to outline a definition of the indigenous pneumatic theory, which, centring on tube usage, underlies a wide range of activities. I now explore a domain in which the tube model finds its most natural expression, the domain of palms.

THE BLOWPIPE, THE FLUTE, AND THE PALM TREE

As mentioned earlier, the *dudase* blowpipe shares with palms the same classifier, *-dase*, which applies to any rectilinear trunk or stem. In Yagua botanical nomenclature, palms form a separate class identified by the word-ending morpheme *-ase*, a class within which different palm species are thought to be related through sibling or cousin ties, somewhat like clan members. According to this system, the degree of kinship varies according to the degree of morphological proximity. However, the model is not entirely endogamous, as some palms are related through use to trees which do not belong to the same class. For instance, *Lucuma bifera* and *Bactris gasipaes* are 'cousins', for both are used in the making of blowpipes (Chaumeil and Chaumeil 1992: 30–1). Moreover, some palms are distinguished by their capacity for communication. The *Phytelephas macrocarpa* (ivory) palm, for example, has the reputation of understanding and communicating with all plants and animals in the forest, almost like a switchboard permanently connected to a telephone network. Shamans who maintain continuous contact with the 'mother' of this palm get wind of whatever machination or plotting is going on in the forest.

Bactris gasipaes and *Mauritia flexuosa* are undoubtedly the most important palms of the Yagua cultural universe. *Mauritia* palm groves are exceptional places for hunting and gathering. The two palms are often subsumed under the same species in myths and ritual chanting, a proof of their perfect identity. Moreover, they both possess a *hamwo* spirit, much more powerful than that of all other palms. It is so powerful that *Bactris* and *Mauritia* fruit cannot be collected all at once on the same day, but on two consecutive days, in order not to offend the susceptibility of tutelary spirits. In addition, the *Mauritia* spirit used to be represented under the anthropomorphic form of wooden statues (extremely rare today), that were 'fed' with manioc beer (like sacred flutes, see above), in the hope of obtaining favours in return. On a symbolic level, palm fruit gathering is very similar to hunting, as both extractive activities are carried out with restraint and respect, a fact amply illustrated by food exchanges.

Mauritia flexuosa is a bounteous and generous tree, from which the Yagua reap maximum benefit. They use not only the fruit rich in proteins, but also the fibres, which they dry and fashion into skirts, jabots, bracelets, garters, and other items composing the traditional Yagua dress. Traditional clothes vary in length from region to region, sometimes covering the entire body, as illustrated in Farabee (1917: figs. 27 and 28).

(a) Yagua man, Pebas, Peru

FIG. 5.3. The palm man (from Farabee 1917)

(b) Yagua men in grass clothing, Pebas, Peru

Dressed in this fashion, the Yagua look like walking palms. And it is not too far-fetched to propose that such garments covering the entire body refer implicitly to the blowpipe, especially given the fact that *Mauritia* and *Bactris* are two identical species for the Yagua. Turning now to shamanism, it is equally tempting to compare the palm garment and the shaman's shield of magic darts. If we accept these associations as meaningful, we should do justice to the Yagua by adding the new nickname 'palm-people' to the nickname 'blowpipe people' mentioned earlier.

Bactris gasipaes is the only palm species cultivated by the Yagua near their dwellings. It grows very slowly and fruits for the first time five or six years after having been planted, that is, often after a change of residence, even if mobility, which is actively discouraged by the government, is today less common. Despite their present sedentarized state, the Yagua return periodically to their ancient clearings located near abandoned sites containing graves to harvest palm fruits and exploit palm wood. Erikson (1996*a*: 188–9) has stressed the significance of the continued exploitation of these ancient *Bactris* groves for understanding relations between the dead and the living in a number of north-western Amazon groups, as well as ancestrality more generally. The Matis he studies are exemplary in the sense that they consider the palms to be the receptacles, if not the transformed bodies, of their ancestors. Rival (1993) develops a similar argument with regard to the Ecuadorian Huaorani, for whom *Bactris gasipaes* groves represent slow growth, generational continuity, and memory of the dead. The Yagua, who call the *Bactris* palm 'our placentas' (*humënati*), largely share these conceptions. *Humënati* is applied generically to deceased great warriors whose enduring individual names are still remembered, as well as to mythical ancestors (in the myth extensively discussed above, the name of the younger twin is *mëna*, or placenta, for he was born directly from the placenta). In addition, it has already been noted that the horn mouthpiece (made of *Socratea* or *Bactris* wood), which is assimilated to an 'ancestral' bone and to a blowpipe, is kept from one initiation ritual to the next, thus ensuring the link between generations of initiates. Wrapped in bark, and buried after each ritual, the mouthpiece is reused in the making of new flutes for subsequent rituals (the same occurs among the Miraña, for example, see Karadimas 1997), a practice which, needless to say, recalls the double funeral principle (probably known by the Yagua in former times). Similarly, the 'feeding' of the horn by its mouthpiece could be interpreted as a way of reviving the bones of the ancestors, and so could the 'feeding' of anthropomorphic statues said to represent the spirit of *Mauritia* palm groves. If most Yagua have today abandoned the traditional palm garment for Western clothes, they can still be seen wearing the old dress, sometimes hastily slipped over a shirt and a pair of trousers, whenever they participate in a great ritual, especially when playing the sacred flutes symbolizing the ancestors.

I mentioned earlier that the calendar of great clan ceremonies and initiation rites coincides with the ripening of *Bactris* fruit, that is, from February to April (the palm produces twice a year, with the second and lesser production occurring between July and September). The first ripening season called *púrendanu* ('the

Bactris time') in fact inaugurates the year's ceremonial cycle, and orders the calendar of ritual activities among the Yagua, as it does in many other north-west Amazon societies. *Bactris* time is lived as a time of abundance associated with *Bactris* fruit (from which a much appreciated stout beer is brewed), as well as with big collective hunts, preludes to 'wartime' (*huwedandanu*). It is also a chronological guide, as the Yagua calculate people's ages in '*Bactris* time', that is, with reference to the periodicity of *Bactris* fruiting seasons. Furthermore, the palm and its thorny trunk are associated with shamanism. Shamans add palm heart leaves to their hallucinogenic preparations in order to acquire the art of extracting magical darts, and, more importantly, to increase their own stock of projectiles, thus consolidating their defences. The protection offered by *Bactris* thorns is symbolically transferred onto the shaman's body, itself a complete blowpipe contained within another tube.

The Yagua, like many other *Bactris*-cultivating groups, associate the palm with the self, ancestors, and intergenerational continuity. Given their seasonal periodicity, these palms mark and punctuate the time dimension linked to the reproductive cycles of natural and human resources, a role played by stars in other societies. This is why the repertoire of clan songs intoned at the great annual ceremonies always starts with chants for the *Bactris* palms. It can be said that as hollow trees, they correspond to protective closed tubes shielding the Yagua against the outside. These palms actually form a natural protective ring around the Yagua (mirror image of shamanic shields), a defensive device whose efficacy is reinforced by the constant communication that natural species maintain among themselves and with shamans. Finally, the *Bactris*, cultivated close to houses, offer a form of protection directly connected to local ancestors.

CONCLUSION

This brief comparative analysis of the flute and the blowpipe takes us back to Peter Rivière's (1969*b*) interpretation of the hollow tube as a transformer of energy. The mythical theme of the two blowpipes, one nested inside the other, constitutes the central model of a mechanism by which two movements corresponding to blown air passing through a pipe that opens and closes are related. Seen from this angle, the model contains the idea of birth or spontaneous creation. As it opens and closes itself, the object or being reproduces itself identically, without any exogenous intervention. The act of splitting or cutting the trunk (as in the blowpipe myth and the myth about the Amazon-tree) amounts to transforming self-reproductive energy (cloning principle) into externalized energy reproducible henceforth through apprenticeship or fabrication (heterosexual principle). Whereas the breath leaving a pipe perfectly illustrates Yagua ideas about creation (transformation), this very same breath can turn against whoever is exposed to its terrifying power without minimal precaution. No wonder then that they grant so much importance to breath control, for example in shamanic practices. In making blowpipes and flutes (open tubes) they produce breaths capable of transforming natural energy into controlled and socialized energy, transforming either an enemy into consumable 'game' (blowpipe, trophy flute, or shaman's arm), or a child into a young initiate (sacred flutes). In so doing, however, they expose themselves by excessive opening to harmful breaths from enemies. In cultivating palms and covering their bodies with palm clothing or invisible darts (i.e. turning themselves into closed tubes), they are doing nothing other than taking precautions against such aggressions. These few considerations lead me to suggest that the Yagua identify not with one, but two interlocked blowpipes, one contained inside the other, which opens and closes, a movement no longer presided over by the ancestors, but directly controlled by men.

The theme of two interlocked tubes applies to two other important ritual objects, bark horn mouthpieces and human teeth necklaces. These objects, which constitute the entire patrimony traditionally transmitted in Yagua society, stand in contrast to all other objects and personal possessions that are destroyed or placed in the graves of the deceased. Mouthpieces can be said to represent a form of 'self possession' (i.e. essential, inherent, and collective possessions), for, as it was argued earlier, bones of ancestral hunting spirits are likened to blowpipes. The necklaces represent a form of external property, which, although exogenous, is worn and transmitted to descendants in the hope that it will bring them prosperity, vitality, power, and longevity, a function quite similar to that of horn mouthpieces during male initiation rituals. All these elements lead me to suggest that the blowpipe-body synthesized in the mouthpiece may be thought of as being contained within a secondary protective tube symbolized by the teeth necklace. The teeth, therefore, play a protective role similar to that of *Bactris* thorns. The construction of the self among the Yagua would thus proceed through the union of two complementary principles (or two 'breaths') contained within horn mouthpieces and teeth necklaces according to the model of interlocked tubes. Teeth necklaces, ritually transformed into self possessions are treated as hollow tubes (palm tree) whose breath (human teeth are the abode of *wuí*, warrior force) frees itself when the artefact is bequeathed to descendants.

The opening/closing principle becomes crystallized in the blowpipe, a symbol of self-identity and ancestrality, which for centuries was an item with great exchange value within long-distance, inter-tribal trade. In trading blowpipes, the Yagua do not simply export 'protecting palms'; they export their self-identity as well, in the same way as the dart expelled from the bole, which transforms potential enemies into trading partners. It is true that today blowpipe production has been somewhat diverted from its initial objective to supply the flourishing tourist market. The means of exchange have undeniably changed, but the fundamental idea underlying the whole system has, in my view, remained identical. The same observation applies to Yagua shamanism, which is now widespread in the urban world, where it has been invested with enormous power by the mestizo population, while remaining an active force among the indigenous population.

In this sense, it would not be correct to contrast the blowpipe and the spear among the Yagua. Intended to neutralize all enemies, human and non-human (i.e. large game), the spear is equivalent to blowpipe darts, if one excepts the size difference, but taking into account that shamans' magical darts may be as long as spears, which makes their extraction particularly difficult. The only complementary weapon necessary to kill is, as mentioned earlier, the club. The gun, of recent introduction, could easily replace either the club or the spear, but not the blowpipe, for, in abandoning the latter, the Yagua would lose infinitely more than a weapon, they would lose their 'soul'. This must be the secret reason why the Yagua are so attached to their image as 'blowpipe Indians', an image which makes them so popular, albeit for very different reasons, with professional dealers in Amazon exotica.

ACKNOWLEDGEMENTS

This essay was translated from the French by Susan Keyes and Laura Rival. I would like to thank Philippe Erikson and Dimitri Karadimas for their comments on the first version of this text.

6

Myth and Material Culture: Matis Blowguns, Palm Trees, and Ancestor Spirits

Philippe Erikson, *Université Paris X-Nanterre*

In his stimulating paper 'Myth and Material Culture: Some Symbolic Interrelations', Peter Rivière (1969*b*) discusses the complementary distribution of blowguns and hair tubes among several Carib and Arawak peoples of southern Guyana and northern Brazil. His aim is 'to show that other aspects of the respective cultures can be correlated with the absence or presence of the blowgun' (p. 153), and to try 'to indicate that the acceptance or rejection of a particular item may reflect and be reflected in a wider set of ideas' (p. 163). Rivière's paper also stresses the symbolical link between body ornaments and weapons, especially blowguns and hair tubes, both of which are 'not simply technical or aesthetic objects but also some sort of energy transformers' (p. 157). In the following pages, besides providing some first-hand data regarding Matis ethnology, I wish to follow some of Rivière's leads in a discussion of the reasons why this Panoan group of western Brazil has retained the use of blowguns, while neighbouring groups such as the Matses or the Marubo have abandoned it.

Even if little mention of explicit mythology will be made throughout this chapter, I will argue, much in line with Rivière, that non-utilitarian considerations have a significant influence on Matis technological options, and that blowguns and body ornaments do indeed belong to closely interrelated conceptual categories. I will also discuss the symbolical links, mediated by palm trees, uniting blowguns and notions of ancestrality, a topic also touched upon by Chaumeil in his discussion of Yagua materials (this volume). All in all, I shall contend that if the concept of 'total social phenomenon' could be applied to items of material culture as it is to institutions, blowguns would be worthy of the highest Maussian distinction. This chapter implicitly pleads for the recognition of 'total social objects'.

In lowland South America, blowgun users and shamans obviously have much in common, if only because both operate by means of small (visible or invisible) darts propelled by their breath (when hunting or performing sorcery), or expelled from their patients' body (in curing). Among the Matis, this intimate connection between curare and sorcery shamanism is further highlighted by the fact that a unique mystical principle, *sho*, is thought to guarantee the efficacy of blowgun hunters as well as that of shamans. Both equally rely upon it, and must follow similar fasts to enhance their potency; associated with 'mystical bitterness' (*chimu*), *sho* is incompatible with sweet foods. A Matis informant, explaining what made *kampo* (*Phyllomedusa bicolor*) frog poison an efficient remedy, compared it to curare. And, indeed, *kampon ënë* ('frog juice/secretions') is one of the main ingredients ritually 'sung' into curare during its preparation to enhance its potency. People who take *kampo*, I was told, react very much like monkeys, which, once shot, fall, but do not die right away. They feel ill and sweat, their lips and faces swell, they suffer from headaches and feel a burning sensation in their anal mucous tissues, before finally vomiting out the *chaka* (garbage, weeds, dirt, and so forth) that was harming them. The difference is that whereas monkeys eventually die, people recover, which implies that the dose of mystical bitterness can be controlled. Curare kills, cures, and binds, as Scazzocchio (1979) elegantly phrased it. It should therefore come as no surprise that factors related to human health should have repercussions upon weaponry, as I shall argue below.

The Matis have a long history of epidemic outbursts. Most of the population was wiped out by epidemics long before the first 'official' contacts of the late 1970s (Erikson 1996*a*), which led to the drastic reduction of mystical practices held responsible for their tragic decimation. Shamanic practices and the use of hallucinogens, tobacco, pepper, emetics, and stimulants were almost totally abandoned from fear of their possible negative effects. Matses men use *kampo* on a regular basis as hunting magic (Milton 1994, Romanoff 1984). By contrast, among contemporary Matis, *kampo* is now handled by older women only, and is exclusively used as medication, especially for stomach aches. But even such innocuous usage of *kampo* is subject to much debate and controversy. Mothers often refuse to let grandmothers (especially their mothers-in-law) treat their child with *kampo*, whose bitterness, they fear, might do more harm than good. In this context, blowguns and curare, whose mystical danger is deemed tremendous by the Matis, might easily have been abandoned in favour of other weapons, as seems to have been the case among neighbouring related groups. The Mayoruna/Matses, for instance, have retained frog emetic, but have switched from blowguns to bows after a series of misfortunes (possibly epidemics) attributed to blowgun power turning against blowgun owners (Calixto Méndez 1987, Erikson 1995). Present-day Matis willingly acknowledge their fear that stocking too much curare might provoke an 'overdose' of *sho*. Unlike their immediate forebears who kept many pots of curare at any one time without worrying, they limit themselves to one pot each. Their retention of blowguns is therefore a deliberate choice, which requires explanation, especially considering that other technological options were available to them.

BOWS AND BLOWGUNS: TECHNICAL COMPLEMENTARITY

Long before contact with Western society and long before the introduction of shotguns, the Matis were already faced with a choice of arms. Traditionally, they used two main hunting weapons, bows and blowguns. A generation ago lanceolated spears (*wanin paca*) were still in use, and a popular story tells how an ancestor used one in mythical times to perforate the unpierced anus of a *maru* spirit. Nowadays, spears are totally obsolete, though the sharp end of a bow may occasionally be used to kill a stingray for instance.

Though not unique (it also occurs in the Guianas and in the north-west Amazon), the combination of weapons used by the Matis is fairly uncommon, at least in western Amazonia, where most other blowgun hunters (the Huaorani or the Jivaro for instance) tend to complement their hunting kit with clubs and/or spears, rather than with bows (Yost and Kelley 1983, Descola 1986: 282). The Matis' closest neighbours, the recently contacted Korubo, use only blowguns, spears, and clubs (which has earned them the nickname of *caceteiros*, 'head-smashers').[1] As was probably the case for most pre-nineteenth-century Northern Panoans, the Korubo totally ignore bows and arrows.

Technically speaking, Matis blowguns and bows are complementary. Whereas the former are essentially used to hunt canopy species, the latter are used exclusively for terrestrial game and for warfare. Although bows are better suited for such hunts, blowguns are occasionally used to shoot peccaries, with darts (called *isan katso*) made especially for this purpose, which are larger than ordinary ones. However, the reverse idea of shooting arrows upwards is simply unthinkable. My informants laughed heartily at the suggestion that bows could be used to hunt canopy species (as many other bow hunters do). In fact, the very design of Matis arrows seems to forbid usage for smaller, arboreal animals.

With the exception of recently introduced, plain and featherless arrows used in fishing,[2] the Matis have only one kind of lanceolate arrow point, a most impressive sharpened piece of bamboo nearly forty centimetres long called *paca*, not exactly what one uses to shoot small birds with! Unlike most other Amazonian bow hunters, the Matis have no specialized tips to kill birds or monkeys (Chiara 1987, Grenand 1994, Lyon 1987). Furthermore, they seldom hunt small terrestrial mammals, by contrast with other Amazonian peoples, for whom these make up the bulk of meat intake, especially in situations of increased hunting pressure on reduced territories (Hames 1980). Large rodents (paca, agouti, or capybara) can only be eaten by old people, but are occasionally killed for their teeth, used for tool making. Another large mammal, the anteater, was only hunted in ritual contexts related to war, and mostly for its fur, used in hunting charms (Erikson 1986). Deer are also a potential target for archers, but they are rarely shot, as the Matis do not consider venison palatable, citing what they consider to be its foul smell. Apart from peccary or tapir hunting, and warfare, Matis arrows, then, are seldom used; when they are, their enormous tips are perfectly suited for the uses they are put to.

Matis blowguns seem similarly oversized. They are usually more than four metres long, which is much above the Amazonian average. This exceptional length makes them difficult to handle for horizontal aiming, thus reinforcing their specialization as weapons meant for vertical aiming. Furthermore, Matis blowguns are built in such a way that the capybara tooth used as an eyepiece is only available for aerial shots. For horizontal aiming, the weapon, because of its oval section, must be turned ninety degrees to prevent the blowgun from bending, in which case the eyepiece then lies on the side, useless. The Achuar, who shoot both terrestrial and aerial targets, have blowguns with round sections (Descola, personal communication).

Instead of having specialized arrow tips, the Matis have specialized weapons, each meant for specific types of game. Men usually set out for a hunt individually, and with only one type of weapon, which suggests that they have a fairly clear idea of what they are going after, perhaps even of what they are actually going to catch. Matis hunting appears strikingly predictable, as I argued in a paper which shows how closely the actual baggings of Matis hunting expeditions correspond to the predictions each hunter ritually states by means of palm figures representing the game he expects to kill (Erikson 1988). In a similar vein, Grenand (1993: 433) published statistics showing that chance encounters account for only 25 per cent of the Wayãpi annual yield from hunting and fishing. Calavia Saez (1994: 41) similarly reports that Yaminahua hunters declare before the hunt which particular species they are going to chase. Such predictability, based on deep ecological knowledge, might be more common than proponents of optimal foraging theory would have us believe. Optimal foraging theories assume that the costs of searching are equally shared between prey species (Alvard 1995: 794). Yet, if human hunters know beforehand what they are most likely to find and base their decisions upon such knowledge, chance encounter should play no part in the equation.[3]

One important consequence of this technologically based, specialized division of killing is that most of the meat the Matis eat, in terms of weight, has been killed by mature hunters using a bow. This is largely because Matis territory abounds with peccaries and tapirs. This, however, does not mean that blowguns play only a secondary part in the overall provision of meat, because the species that provide the largest quantities of meat are only available from time to time. Blowguns are useful in providing species that are indispensable for guaranteeing a steady supply of meat over time. After an unsuccessful bow hunt, an informant once stated that blowguns were better because, though admittedly procuring less meat per outing, they allowed hunters to get at least something each time they went hunting. In any case, for the Matis, as for the Taruma, Makushi, Wapishana, or Arecuna, blowgun skills are definitely the means by which a hunter's prowess is judged, and, therefore, the ultimate sources of prestige. Trying to account for a similar paradox, Rivière (1969b: 154) suggested that blowguns might have been retained in some parts of The Guianas not despite of, but rather because of, their relative inefficacy, which leaves the hunter with no other option than to display extraordinary talent;

in note 7, he offers a complementary (though possibly tautological) clue: the most highly prized meat might be that of those animals shot with the blowgun.

Neither of these explanations applies to the Matis. From their point of view, blowguns are extremely efficient, and more so than guns when it comes to killing monkeys (shotguns are too noisy). Moreover, they are more economical than shotguns, since there is no need to buy ammunition. Furthermore, hunting with a blowgun is not considered particularly difficult: young boys begin at an early age and start killing arboreal prey long before they begin to hunt peccaries with bows. Unlike the Huaorani (Rival 1996*a*), the Matis generally display no gastronomic preference for arboreal—over terrestrial—species. The mystical qualities attached to the manipulation of blowguns are, in their case, the critical factor. Prestige here stems as much from the amount of *sho* involved, as it does from the amount or the qualities of the meat brought home, or from the skills displayed to do so.

However, if we now turn our attention to non-alimentary hunting, a hypothesis somewhat similar to Rivière's does indeed make very good sense. Much of the time the Matis devote to hunting is not for food but rather for the teeth of minute titi (*Callicebus molochcupreus*), tamarin (*Saguinus mystax*), and squirrel (*Saimiri sciureus*) monkeys. Sap plays a major role in the diet of these monkeys, which, despite their small size, have spectacular teeth. Hunters often do not even bother bringing back the meat of these tiny monkeys, since it is prohibited to bearers of recently pricked face tattoos, which is tantamount to saying that only the very young or the very old may eat it. Yet, much energy is invested in pursuing them, because their canines are used to make necklaces and armbands, which count among the most highly treasured goods a Matis can own. In addition to being hallmarks of hunting excellence, such collars also contain *sho* (as most teeth do). One informant told me that whereas monkey teeth had *sho*, human teeth did not, although most other body parts do. Some of the long necklaces worn by the best hunters and their families attest to the slaughter of dozens of monkeys, which is no small feat, given their reduced size and great mobility. I saw one collar with 256 teeth, which required sixty-four kills. Only outstanding hunters can accumulate great numbers of teeth collars for themselves, as well as for their wives and children. Blowguns are clearly the best-suited weapons for killing titi, tamarin, and squirrel monkeys. This suggests they might have been retained, at least in part, because they enhance status by providing prestigious tooth trophies.

WEAPONS AND THE DUAL CLASSIFICATION OF ANIMALS

In the tropical forest, where broadly opportunistic attitudes seem to be the most widespread hunting strategy, the Matis impose upon themselves a set of technically useless but culturally meaningful limitations. I have discussed constraints relating to the choice of weapon brought along. Let us now see when blowguns are being used how the status of the prey in terms of Matis dualism, combined with the relative age of the weapon, also affects the selection or rejection of a given animal as a target. In short, I shall argue that the range of species available to a Matis hunter depends not only on the type, but also on the age, of his weapon; not only on his prey's biotope (arboreal or terrestrial), but also on its classificatory status.

The Matis distinguish two kinds of game animals, called *ayakobo* and *tsasibo*, which are also the names of their former moieties, the first symbolically associated with females and the outside, and the second with males and the inside.[4] A hunter using an old blowgun may kill any of the animal species usually killed with such a weapon, in other words, just about any arboreal species. But when hunting with a new blowgun, he should kill only animals of the *tsasibo* (insider) type. Meat of the very first *ayakobo* (outsider) prey killed with a new blowgun must be cooked by menopausal women or by adolescent boys, that is, by people undergoing a life transition, thus living in what might be called a 'bloodless' state. The meat is then ceremonially eaten in the longhouse. Nubile women are ostensibly (sometimes even boisterously) excluded from this ritual meal, which marks the blowgun's transition from new to old, and which is followed by a long period of ritual early-morning bathing intended to rid the participants of foreign, hence dangerous, blood (Erikson 1986: 196). It seems therefore that bows are essentially meant to hunt *ayakobo* game (epitomized by white-lipped peccaries) and/or kill the enemy, while blowguns are preferentially destined to kill animals of the *tsasibo* type. Using blowguns against *ayakobo* animals requires elaborate ritual precautions.

TABLE 6.1. *Matis dual classification of animal species*

Ayakobo	Tsasibo
White-lipped peccary (*Chawa*) (*Tayassu pecari*)	Collared peccary (*Unkin*) (*Tajassu tajacu*)
Woolly monkey (*Chuna*) (*Lagothrix lagothricha*)	Spider monkey (*Choshe*) (*Ateles paniscus*)
Howler monkey (Du) (*Alouata seniculus*)	titi monkey (*Masoko*) (*Callicebus molochcupreus*)
Squirrel monkey (*Sipi Chot*) (*Saimiri sciureus*)	Tamarin (*Sipi Wiren*) (*Saguinus mystax*)
Nocturnal monkey (*Bushti*) (*Sciurus sp.*)	Squirrel (*Capa*) (*Aotus sp.*)
Spix's Guan (*Kubu*) (*Penelope jacquacu*)	Tinamou (*Kuma*) (*Tinamous (sp.*)
Curassow (*Wesnit*) (*Mitu mitu*)	Macaw (*Kwenat*) (*Ara sp*)
Ant eater (*Shaë*) (*Myrmecophaga sp.*)	Jaguar (*kamun*) (*Panthera onça* & *Felis spp.*)
Paca (*mapwa*) (?) (*Agouti paca*)	Agouti (*mare*) (?) (*Dasyprocta agouti*)
Capuchin (*Tsima*) (*Cebus appella*)	
Trompetero (*nea*) (*Psophia crepitans*)	

The classification of bow-hunted animals is less often taken into consideration than that of blowgun-hunted ones, and, as it has no practical implication, it is sometimes unknown altogether. No difference is made between old and new bows, and there is little need to know what moiety terrestrial mammals belong to, since they are seldom hunted with blowguns, especially now that the moiety system is declining. None of my informants was able, for instance, to ascribe deer or tapir to any of the two moieties. However, in other ritual contexts, they still recall the classification of many terrestrial animals, especially anteaters and jaguars. While the former are unambiguously *ayakobo* and feminine, the latter are masculine and *tsasibo*, an opposition which comes as no surprise in the Amazonian context (Zerries 1984). For reasons explained below, I also suspect that pacas (*Agouti paca*) are *ayakobo*, and agoutis (*Dasyprocta agouti*) *tsasibo*.

As already mentioned, bow hunting and blowgun hunting are opposed in terms of the species they are associated with, just as hunting *ayakobo* animals differs from hunting *tsasibo* ones. This, in many respects, confirms Rival (1996*a*), for whom technological choices concerning hunting equipment effectively monitor social distance, regulating social closeness and/or drawing social boundaries between hunters and their prey. Indeed, as it does among the Huaorani, Matis blowgun hunting appears to be a technology of inclusion, since the victims are granted *tsasibo* status. And, as spear hunting does among the Huaorani, Matis bow hunting stands out as a technology of exclusion, since it relegates prey animals to *ayakobo* status. Yet, as we shall now see, the Matis case requires further interpretation, because their choice of arms does not only reflect (or even induce) the quality of the relationship between humans and socially objectified animals. Here, the alleged ontological status of users is also affected by the choice of arms, which operates as a kind of perspectivist shifter, much as phone booths do for Clark Kent/Superman.

PERSPECTIVIST IMPLICATIONS OF BOW AND BLOWGUN USE

Quite surprisingly in an Amazonian context, Matis hunters do not surround their hunting practices with a tremendous amount of secrecy. They bluntly state what they are after, and instead of using some of the euphemistic expressions referring to hunting usually found throughout native South America, they have no qualms in crudely saying that they are out 'to fetch meat' (*nami berek*). This attitude is probably related to their previously mentioned palm frond 'announcing' ritual, as well as to the composite nature of their hunting tool kit. Choosing to bring along such or such a weapon is in itself a way of 'announcing' one's intentions. Even in a world of WYSINWYG, WYSWYG sometimes occurs (Rivière 1994*a*). But there is more to it.

Authors like S. Hugh-Jones (1996*a*), Rival (1996*a*), and Descola (1999) convincingly state that one of the major reasons why many lowland hunters cherish blowguns is the greater stealth it allows them. Keeping a low profile and remaining modest while hunting are usually deemed essential for success, and curare presents the great advantage of killing 'gently', without bloodshed. Blowgun hunting seems non-aggressive, an obvious bonus for people who often see hunting as a form of prey seduction. Yet, unlike what commonly occurs with other Amazonian hunters, Matis outspokenness paradoxically reaches its peak when using blowguns. It is then, and only then, that Matis hunters explicitly identify themselves with jaguars, the mightiest of all predators. A Matis hunting with a blowgun (a solitary affair) thinks of himself as imitating a jaguar (also a solo hunter), and behaves in a way that would be strictly forbidden to an archer (who usually hunts in a group). For example, to look like a jaguar, he may paint his body (as well as his wife's) with genipa (*Genipa americana*), covering the skin with dots, in imitation of the jaguar's coat, a pattern which is also that of the *tsasibo* (the *ayakobo* use diamond-shaped spots). The jaguar pattern can only be used when hunting with a blowgun. Its use in bow hunting would frighten the prey, causing chased animals to run off. In other words, what is a useful stratagem in blowgun hunting becomes useless when hunting with a bow.

Identification with jaguars, who stand for stealth rather than for bloodshed, is also obvious during the rituals accompanying the preparation of curare. As they leave the settlement to gather vines in the forest, or on their way back, men imitate jaguar calls. While the women hide inside the longhouse, the men shout 'i i i i i', which is supposed to mean 'I am going to eat raw howler monkey guts', both because this is what real jaguars commonly do, and because jaguars often eat animal guts discarded by hunters. Men on a blowgun hunt not only take on very public feline qualities, but they also claim that jaguars themselves benefit from their successful hunting: not exactly a modest stance.

The message conveyed after a successful bow hunt, during the ritual in which white-lipped peccary heads are ceremonially eaten in the longhouse, is exactly the opposite. While holding a cooked peccary head before him, the ritual leader warns 'beware of jaguars' (*wënë kurenek*), as he moves the head along an imaginary path passing him on both sides. He then shows to the head the path leading straight to him, and says 'I am your owner/master' (*eobi min igbo*). This combination of gestures and words is glossed as a way of explaining to peccaries that from now on they should only use people's paths, and avoid all others, in order to avoid meeting jaguars. The ritual leader then says 'do not be frightened, I am not a jaguar', before adding bluntly 'I am your master', just in case peccaries do not prove stupid enough to accept this hypocritical argument.

Further proof of the contradictory (maybe even schizophrenic) symbolical logic underlying the rules opposing bow and blowgun hunting may be found in the different statements concerning the relation of each with body ornaments. To make a long story short, the Matis acquire *tsasibo* insider cat-like qualities by pricking ornaments on their faces. Symbolically, these ornaments represent extra whiskers and extra teeth, as well as blowgun darts and several other things. To put it simply, the more ornaments you wear, the more powerful your curare is (Erikson 1996*a*). Significantly, *isan katso*, the larger darts made for hunting peccary, can also be used as upper lip plugs (*mananukit*).

Ornaments are closely associated with blowguns, but are, by contrast, totally unrelated—even antagonistic—to bows. When discussing the *ayakobo* versus *tsasibo* nature of neighbouring indigenous groups (many of which speak nearly the same language), the Matis only include among *tsasibo* (insiders) people who have blowguns and/or the same kind of facial ornaments as themselves. Unlike blowguns, bows certainly do not go hand in hand with ornaments. Men who hunt with a bow (especially white-lipped peccaries), or men on the war-path should take all their ornaments off.

Of course, such behaviour has a very practical function. When running through the forest, the large round shell earrings are particularly cumbersome, and the bead necklaces break off easily. By contrast, wearing ornaments is less troublesome when hunting with a blowgun, which is far less strenuous. Yet, the Matis pay very little—if any—attention to such straightforward, down-to-earth arguments. When discussing the matter, they only insist that by taking your ornaments off, you become 'invisible', hence identical to the asocial *maru* spirits, the symmetrical counterparts of the *mariwin* ancestral spirits, who function as positive role-models in all moral and aesthetic matters. *Maru* spirits live in natural clearings, whereas *mariwin* spirits haunt cultural clearings, especially the cultivated palm groves growing on ancient village sites. The *maru* have no ornaments, whereas the *mariwin* sport extraordinary ornaments, wearing more labrets than any living person; they want to look like ancestor spirits, as people say. In addition, *mariwin* have remarkable body piercings, whereas *maru* are, as suits them, underpierced; their faces are devoid of labrets and their feet are said to be thorn-proof. As we know, even their bottoms tragically lack piercing.

The Matis always wear their ornaments (true social emblems), even when asleep in their hammocks at night. Ornaments are only taken off for purposefully asocial activities, which, in the main, require the use of a bow. This is why Matis hunters using a bow must temporarily rid themselves of what marks them as full social beings, and what makes them efficient blowgun hunters. As they take their ornaments off, they set their *tsasibo* qualities to one side, and take on *ayakobo* characteristics. Such a theory reassures them with respect to a possible face-to-face encounter with enemies. They believe with optimism that traditional enemies crossing the path of fully adorned Matis are frightened at the sight of Matis earrings, just as peccaries are. Should they meet their enemies unadorned, that is, carrying no more than their bows, these would increase their chances of victory, as well as enhance their state of invisibility, an additional protection. Furthermore, the benefits of imitating *maru* spirits include diminishing chances for retaliation, since unadorned warriors are said to look more like spirits (*tsusi*) than like humans, thus preventing the deceived and bereaved kin of their victims from even thinking of trying to get even.

TABLE 6.2. *Matis dual classification of living beings*

Ayakobo	Tsasibo
Outside	Inside
Women	Men
Foreigners	Ancestors
Bows	Blowguns
Invisible *maru*	Adorned *mariwin*

When hunting with a blowgun, a Matis takes on maximal *tsasibo* status and ideally specializes in *tsasibo* prey. When hunting with his bow, he adopts an *ayakobo* mode of being, and ideally sets out to kill *ayakobo*. This might be where the Matis hunter's 'hypocrisy' lies. You dress to kill, but do so in a way that appears as similar as possible to your intended victim. Choosing a weapon determines not only what can be hunted, but also what status can (temporarily) be assumed. Such perspectivistic manipulations are quite in tune with the general logic of Amazonian hunting, but do beg one question. How are jaguars to be killed? Jaguars being quintessentially *tsasibo* should ideally be hunted with blowguns, but this is not practical, given their size and dangerous nature. Shotguns provide today's perfect self-defence solution, but in the past bows were used for such a purpose, or when a man burning with a desperate urge to kill decided to vent off his rage (*kunenek*) against a jaguar.[5] Jaguars, although *tsasibo*, were treated as if they were *ayakobo*.

The status of jaguar hunting remains unresolved. Yet, whatever information further investigation might bring, it seems very unlikely to undermine the thesis that the Matis contrast bows and blowguns with great consistency, imparting a different set of values to each. Although apparently very similar, even the sharpening tools used respectively for arrows and darts are distinct. Chisels used for sharpening blowgun darts or digging the grooves of blowguns are made of agouti (*mare*) teeth, whereas those for sharpening arrow points are made of paca (*mapwa*) teeth. There might be a good technical reason to account for this difference, but one cannot but notice that it establishes yet another distinction between the two weapons. Furthermore, it is in keeping with Panoan mythology. One Matis story focuses on a *maru* spirit who was tricked into being scalped with a piranha jaw before having his anus pierced with a lanceolated spear (*wanin paca*). The hero of a Shipibo myth reported by Bertrand-Ricover (1994: 466–8) similarly scalps, and later impales 'toothed spirit' (*yoshin shëtaya*), a local equivalent of the *maru*, whose alternative name, according to Loriot *et al.* (1993: 431), happens to be 'bald spirit' (*yoshin shatan*).

Other Panoan stories show that *yoshin shëtaya* are closely associated with pacas (Bertrand-Ricover 1994: 485–6). Furthermore, in one of the versions, the scalping tool is a pair of scissors made of agouti teeth. This clearly gives the impression that

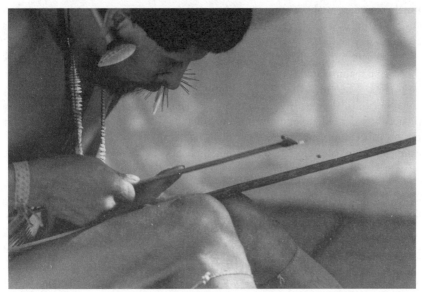

FIG. 6.1. Agouti tooth chisels are used to carve the groove of blowguns and to sharpen darts (photo © Philippe Erikson)

Panoan mythology plays on the opposition between the two rodents. Pacas are mates with asocial spirits, and agoutis are their enemies. In the Matis version of the myth mentioned above, the hero scalps the *maru* spirit, not with a 'blowgun chisel' (literally 'agouti stone', *maren mashash*) as in the Shipibo version, but with a piranha jaw. Yet, the Matis version clearly remains within the same paradigm, since piranha jaws are also tools associated with blowgun darts. They are used to nick the ends of darts just before shooting to ensure that the poisoned tips break into and remain within the wounded animal's flesh. Following Rivière (1969*b*), I am there-fore very tempted to link myth and material culture, and to contend that some technological choices, such as the selection of materials to make artefacts (agouti or paca teeth in this instance) may be greatly influenced by the symbolical message such a choice conveys (for a similar demonstration regarding the use of clay rather than calabash in the making of several Matis artefacts, see Erikson 1990 and 1996*b*).

It has been argued recently that it is the taking up of 'killer' status that defines a jaguar in a perspectivist universe. The Amazonian concept of 'jaguarness' could therefore be compared to a deictic device referring to whoever occupies the preda-tor slot in predator-prey predication (Århem 1996, Viveiros de Castro 1996*a*). Although fully accepting the force of this argument, I wish to stress that this thesis should not be taken too literally. Amazonian peoples clearly establish a distinction between 'taxonomic' and 'deictic' jaguars. Maybe more attention should be paid to what happens when humans hunt actual jaguars, this being a crucial test case.

Furthermore, as we have seen, the option of becoming a jaguar is not open to just anyone acting as a predator, but only to 'civilized', *tsasibo* ones. *Ayakobo* predators are in no way jaguars.

Matis data suggest that perspectivist transformations, although 'real', can none the less be manipulated (to fool peccaries, for instance), and their effects can only be partial. When shouting 'i i i i', Matis hunters are not imitating jaguars only metaphorically, they truly believe they are changing state, thus risking their lives (hence the strict obligation for women to hide; the shout both induces and indicates the transformation, warning others off). Yet, as my earlier comments about gut eating indicate, such imitation far from abolishes the distinction between animal jaguars and Matis hunters. When cooking curare, and despite an exacerbated feline state, Matis hunters are very cautious about warding off real jaguars. Pots left unattended, especially overnight, are carefully fenced with a kind of corral (*matokate*) which is explicitly meant to keep jaguars from messing around with the poison. The Matis willingly admit that nightly visits by jaguars are unlikely; the real risk comes rather from mice or grasshoppers. But this is a very good indication of what they think is happening when they are preparing curare. 'Jaguarness' is around, and it affects the hunters in their very being. However, such effect is more reminiscent of the familiarization process by which feline spirits are tamed, than it is of perspectivist switches or deep ontological transformations. In other words, even when shouting 'i i i i', preparing curare, or hunting with a blowgun, the hunter's particularly intimate relationship with 'jaguarness' does not abolish the distinction between himself and 'real-life' jaguars. 'Jaguarness' seems to be adding something to his human status, rather than abolishing it. As Rivière (1984) clearly argued on a sociological level, and as the following section clearly demonstrates, the inside/outside boundary usually tends to be quite ambiguous in lowland South America.

FOREIGNERS' BOWS AND ANCESTORS' BLOWGUNS

As we have seen, bows and blowguns stand in complementary opposition. Using a blowgun is seen as the quintessence of masculinity, and pregnant women commonly justify their preference for baby boys by stating that they will become blowgun hunters; they never say bow hunters. Cotton string, a product grown and spun exclusively by women, is used to shaft arrows. I have never seen—or heard of—cotton being used for anything else than the making of arrows, as if cotton string was solely produced to force arrow makers to incorporate a trace of female agency in their *ayakobo* craft. However, when it comes to making the palm fibre string to tie on the lids of their *tsasibo* curare pots, far from symbolically acknowledging dependency upon female agency, men do exactly the opposite. Instead of using an 'ordinary' woman-made string, they make their own, and do so in a way that is clearly meant to be inversely symmetrical, as they clumsily roll the string on their left thighs from bottom to top, a clear reversal of the female way of doing things.

Using a bow in many ways also means dropping off Matis identity, and acting as a forest spirit or as a foreigner. The close association of bows with the outside has undeniable factual grounding. Historical chronicles such as that of Figueiroa (1986 (1661)) report that, unlike most other Panoans (most of whom used bows rather than blowguns), the Mayoruna, ancestors of the Matis, Korubo, Matses, and many other Northern Panoans, used only blowguns and spears. As previously stated, this still seems to be the case with the Korubo, the Maia, and many other Northern Panoans (Melatti 1981). The Matses, who apparently adopted the bow only recently, claim to have learned its use from the Marubo, themselves neighbours of the Matis (Calixto Méndez 1987). The Matses, as previously stated, totally switched from blowgun to bow hunting shortly before permanent contact was established with mainstream Peruvian society. However, blowgun darts still appear in some of their myths, instead of the arrows found in comparable stories told among other Panoans, a fact which should guard us from establishing too literal connections between myth and material culture, a point also made by Rivière (1969*b*: 163).

Given its foreign origin, it is quite probable that the Matis consider the bow to be a foreign weapon. However, the existence of nineteenth-century Mayoruna language lexicons with an entry for bow (*tengatay*) (Castelnau 1859: 300) should not be overlooked. And a closer look at the Matis word for bow shows that it has undergone linguistic erosion over time. The Matis call their bows *pia*, which means 'arrow' in most other Panoan languages, in which bows are usually known as *kanati*, or *pia kanati*. Blowguns have undergone a similar linguistic erosion; they are called 'that which is held' (*trinte*), rather than *tépi*, as in the languages of other Panoan blowgun hunters (for instance, the Marubo and Shipibo-Conibo). In any case, blowguns are certainly considered much older than bows. Proof of this can be found in their close association with ancestor spirits, which is tantamount to stating their function as vectors of Matis identity.

Masked men representing Matis ancestor spirits (*mariwin*), who cannot speak but communicate through mimicry, often visit the living. Unsurprisingly, one of their favourite subjects of silent conversation is blowgun hunting. A close look at their ornaments reveals that the many labrets making 'beards' and 'teeth' around their mouths are in fact blowgun darts (see Fig. 6.2). To a certain extent, their faces are like quivers, which might explain why the masks are made of clay instead of calabash as among other groups. Curare stocked in clay pots traditionally has the reputation in the Upper Amazon of being more powerful than curare stocked in, for instance, bamboo tubes (Ordinaire 1887: 319).[6]

Matis ancestor spirits come to whip youngsters, allegedly to make them grow stronger and faster, and to rid them of their laziness. Whereas their presence is mandatory during the main tattooing ritual, they may also come whenever children have misbehaved. Parents never spank, but ancestors willingly take up that task.

FIG. 6.2. (a) Kapock ornaments on Matis masks (right) represent labrets, teeth, and beard, but display a striking resemblance to blowgun darts (left) (photos © Philippe Erikson)

Ritual whippings are not depicted as punishment, for the ancestor spirits act for the young's own good, by transmitting 'bitterness' (*chimu*), precisely the quality which is supposed to give curare its efficacy.

So it can be argued that the ancestor spirits act as weapons, more precisely, as blowguns. Significantly, the way they move their rods does not mimic whipping, but pricking, as if they were threatening to puncture the children's skin rather than

FIG. 6.2. (b)

slash it. And indeed, the *mariwin*'s whips are made of *daratsintuk* palm fronds covered with thousands of miniature needles. These are barely visible, but were shown to me by an informant who wished to explain why only whips made of such material should be used in ritual contexts.

Let us now get back to the actual weapon, and look at the blowgun itself. From a functional point of view, Matis blowguns are no different from those used in other parts of western Amazonia (Yde 1948). Yet, they seem to be more elaborately decorated than, for instance, their Yagua counterparts (Chaumeil 1987 and this volume). After wrapping the two halves of carved palm wood with a thin vine and then simply covering them with resin, as the Yagua do, the Matis go one step further. They add rings of eggshells called 'eyes' (*bëru*) at regular intervals, and glue a mixture composed of crushed bones on the bottom half of the stem, which makes it as rough as sandpaper. Although I have never heard anyone actually say so, this clearly makes them look like a palm tree, and, to be more precise, like a *Bactris gasipaes* palm (*pupunha* in Portuguese, *chontaduro* in Peruvian Spanish). The unique shape of the curved mouthpiece further increases this resemblance. It makes the blowgun's base look like the palm's adventitious roots, just as the eggshell 'eyes' evoke leaf scars on the trunk, or as the protruding pieces of bone evoke the palm's numerous needles, or even as the smoothness of the upper part evokes the palm's stipe. Inside the longhouse, maize leaves are inserted in the blowgun's end to prevent the intrusion of bugs and other bits. The resemblance is then even more striking, as the weapon now seems to have foliage as well. The reason the Matis should want their blowguns to look like *Bactris* palms is that these are very closely related to the *mariwin* ancestor spirits, who haunt palm groves and who are also known under the name of 'spirits of Bactris palm wood artefacts' (*winu winu tsusi*). Moreover, the idea that Matis masks are the bones of the ancestral spirits rather than their flesh,[7] seems to support the view that *mariwin*, just like palms, are hard on the outside and soft inside. For the Matses, the spirits of the dead live inside *Bactris* palms, which are called *kwenat* by the Korubo, a word used by the Matis to refer to macaws, a bird closely associated with *mariwin* spirits (Erikson 1996*a*: 223), and also frequently found in old gardens.

Having contended that the *mariwin* are like walking blowguns and/or walking palm trees, I can now propose the symmetrical argument that blowguns are palm trees, hence ancestor spirits. When I first discovered this symbolical connection, I was puzzled by the fact that Matis blowguns were made of *Iriartea ventricosa* (*takpan*) palm wood, or of the wood of a tree known as 'real tree' (*iwi kimo*), but never of *Bactris gasipaes*. To make matters worse, whereas Matis blowguns are not, Matis bows are indeed carved out of *Bactris* wood! This, of course, would ruin my beautiful structuralist construction, if it were not for two facts. First, that *Bactris* wood might be technically unsuitable for making blowguns, because it is probably too hard to carve a groove. Secondly, one might add that in order to use *Bactris* wood to make blowguns, palms would have to be sacrificed. Having recently accompanied Matis hunters in search of bow wood in ancient groves, I was impressed by their reluctance to cut trees down, and by their insisting that they should be preserved for future generations. One man apologized for his action by saying almost embarrassed that he was only cutting second-rate (i.e. crooked) trees. He then showed me three *wani* of different sizes, which, he claimed, had been planted by his maternal grandfather, and said he would cut just one (the biggest), leaving the medium-sized one for his son, and the smaller one for his (unborn)

FIG. 6.3. The silhouette of Matis blowguns (right) is strongly reminiscent of that of *Bactris* palms (left)

grandson. He then added the striking statement that the tree he had sacrificed was not all that big, only being 'like a person' (rather than like an ancestor?). Cutting palms obviously goes against the very essence of *tsasibo* continuity, for which the *mariwin* stand as a potent metaphor. Aggressive behaviour against palms suits the *ayakobo* better, and indeed, someone setting out to make a bow is precisely following *ayakobo* behaviour.

Logically then, blowguns are made to look like palms, but they are not made at their detriment. Bows, on the other hand, are made of palm wood, and to look as smooth as possible. Whereas decorative spines are added to blowguns, true spines are naturally scraped off palms used in bow making, and bows are further polished over and over again to the smoothest grain. This of course, is a response to technical constraints, just as is the fact that bows are made in such a way that the outside of the palm tree (the part that previously bore spines) becomes the inside of the bow (the part that faces the hunter when he holds his weapon to shoot). To be fully honest, I must also state that no attempt is made to hide the weapon's ligneous pedigree: in one of the most popular Matis hunting songs, bows are called 'peach-palm artefacts' (*wani winu*). Yet, I cannot help but be impressed by the fact that once transformed into bows, *Bactris* palms have become needle-less and necessarily face away from the archer.

SHOTGUNS

'Since hunters have taken up the use of firearms, anthropologists seem to have lost interest in weapons' (Govoroff 1993: 227). In an attempt to make up for this regrettable trend, let me state that the Matis have known (and feared) shotguns for many decades, even though they have only recently begun using them. 'Teachings of the elders' (*Darasibon chuyaket*) include stories of the days when the foreigners had to load their guns by the mouth, before they had barges (*lanchas*) and aircraft. This 'remote past' may in fact be more recent than generally believed, since muzzle-loaders were still in use in the Javari basin in the early part of the twentieth century (Lange 1912: 257).

Before contact, the Matis would just throw guns found in raided *seringuero* houses in the river, knowing enough to discard them, but too little to benefit from them directly. In 1985, when I did most of my fieldwork in Matis land, there were only three 16-gauge shotguns in use, and rarely ever any ammunition. Several older men were afraid to try them out, but most hunters enjoyed borrowing FUNAI guns, especially when tracks of white-lipped peccaries had been spotted. Back then, motivation for borrowing the shotguns was not to obtain more meat, since most of the kill was returned to FUNAI as a kind of 'rent' in return for the loan. If the situation has changed since then (there are now twice as many shotguns, all individually owned), introduced shotguns in the early days provided the Matis with an opportunity to display great generosity toward FUNAI. I have seen as recently as 1998 a young man, otherwise an excellent hunter, shooting at a bird without even bothering to aim at shoulder level, casually holding the gun upwards, at chest height, and missing his aim!

Another interesting aspect of the introduction of shotguns among the Matis is that many of the beliefs regarding traditional weapons do not apply to them. For instance, it is believed that if the guts of an animal killed with a bow or a blowgun are simply discarded and thrown away, instead of being carefully left in the forest, the weapon ceases to shoot straight, a fate that does not affect shotguns. This goes against the widespread Amazonian practice of restoring game stock fertility through the proper disposal of guts and other by-products of hunts (S. Hugh Jones 1996*a*), and may be related to the fact that Matis bows are surrounded with less ritual precaution than blowguns because they are used more pragmatically and to shoot at a much closer range. However, I am not entirely convinced by this spontaneous Malinowskian interpretation of the differential ritualization of weapons, because this principle also holds true when non-pragmatical considerations are considered. For example, only the jaws of animals killed using a bow (especially those of white-lipped peccaries, tapirs, and to a lesser extent, caimans) are collected and kept as trophies inside the longhouse. The jaws of animals killed with a shotgun are not collectables.[8] In a similar vein, I have seen women carrying their husbands' unloaded shotguns for them, which suggests that the prohibition forbidding women to touch traditional weapons does not extend to shotguns. The amount of ritual attention conferred on a weapon seems inversely proportional to its degree of proximity to *ayakobo* outsiders. Much care has to be taken in the case of *tsasibo* blowguns, little care in the case of *ayakobo* bows, and almost none for shotguns.

Another novelty is that the distinction between arboreal and terrestrial animals does not hold when hunting with shotguns, which are indifferently used for monkeys, tapirs, curassows, deer, marmosets, or peccaries. In 1985 guns were still marginal enough to be used without any regard for economic considerations. The idea of sparing ammunition was still unheard of. Yet, however polyvalent shotguns might be, it is quite obvious that the Matis tend to consider them as alternatives for bows, rather than as possible substitutes for blowguns. For obvious technical reasons, this seems to be a common occurrence throughout Amazonia, where introduced firearms have generally replaced bows long before they have supplanted blowguns (see Århem 1981: 63 on the Makuna). In the Matis case, however, the link between bows and shotguns is not merely technological, but also ideological, since both are perceived as intrinsically associated with 'outsiders'. It therefore comes as no surprise to find that the neologism coined by the Matis for guns, 'which causes to fall' (*tonkate*), should resemble so closely the word the ancient Mayoruna used for bows (*tengatay*) (see above quotation from Castelnau). Guns and bows both belong to the class of 'foreign' weapons used to kill *ayakobo* strangers in a violent, asocial manner. When the Matis explain that guns are much better than bows and arrows because they cause less bleeding, the totally bloodless action of blowguns immediately comes to mind. Blowguns obviously belong to a class of their own, and this certainly contributes to their survival.

CONCLUSION

To seek a simple explanation of why the Matis have retained their blowguns to this day would be vain. The complex set of reasons includes such varied factors as their obvious efficacy, incentives from FUNAI and the tourist market, and of course, the ideological motivations examined in this essay. As a means of killing without drawing much-feared blood, and as a link between ancestors and the present generation, blowguns appear to play a part that no other weapon, however efficient it might be, could ever play in the Matis' intellectual universe.

Debates over technological choices have tended to focus either on purely utilitarian, or on purely symbolical aspects. Both approaches are useful, and both equally deserve our consideration. Rival (1996*a*) convincingly argues that among the Huaorani, hunting technology monitors the social distance between animals and humans. This also holds for the Matis, but I would like to add that in their case, weapons are also a means of relating to other human beings, as well as to the self. Since cultures, especially in Amazonia, are far from being totally self-contained wholes, I wish to stress an additional dimension, well worth exploring. Technological choices, most of all regarding weapons, act as a means of relating with the outside, and, as such, partake in foreign policy. To choose to carry a particular weapon becomes a political statement. The depiction of decorated arrows as a kind of aposematic display certainly deserves more than a smiling acknowledgement (DeBoer 1990), especially given that Amazonian indigenous people are defined by their 'arms' more often than by anything else. To take but one example, that of the Makuna, 'different classes of beings are distinguished by specific traits referred to as "weapons" ' (Århem 1996: 188). Similarly, the choice of weapons by ancestors in myths often has very literal ontological implications (S. Hugh Jones 1988; Schoepf 1994). The weapon a man decides to carry, especially when it is 'interiorized' or incorporated', as with *sho*, defines not only his status, but also what he truly is. Such are the underlying factors that govern the technological options adopted by contemporary Matis.

ACKNOWLEDGEMENTS

This chapter is based on field research totalling 15 months and carried out at various times between 1985 and 1998. It was variously supported by the University of Paris X-Nanterre, the Centre National de la Recherche Scientifique (Legs Lelong), and the Fyssen Foundation. This support is gratefully acknowledged. Many thanks to Jean-Pierre Chaumeil and Laura Rival for comments on a preliminary version of this chapter.

NOTES

1. Despite speaking nearly the same language, the Matis know relatively little about the Korubo, with whom they have been enemies for the past fifty years, if not longer. Yet, interestingly enough, one of the few things they do know about them is the kind of wood (*kwama*) they use to make their blowguns. This they learnt over a year before they even knew they actually call themselves 'Witchombo', rather than 'Korubo'.

2. The Matis traditionally lived upstream, away from lakes and large rivers. One of their 'ethnonyms' is *deshan mikitbo* ('upstream people'). Most adults cannot swim, and fishing with bows seems to be a recently acquired technique, mostly favoured by Matis ascribed to the *ayakobo* moiety, whose link with the 'outside' world is discussed below.

3. The fact that human predators do not operate in an intellectual vacuum also invalidates Yost and Kelley's (1983) attempt to compare the efficiency of spears and blowguns. Theirs is in fact a comparison of *returns* for the *species* respectively hunted with each weapon. As Beckerman aptly states, technique and taxon are often a single dimension because 'many techniques are largely determined by the taxon of the intended prey' (1994: 181). Friday being pay day doesn't make work more 'productive' on Fridays than on ordinary days. In the same way, peccaries are bagged on spear days, but you still have to rely on blowguns the rest of the week.

4. Readers familiar with Panoan ethnology might be surprised to hear that the inside moiety is symbolically linked with males, whereas the outside moiety is linked with females. Other Panoans have it the other way around, but then, other Panoans are uxorilocal whereas the Matis are virilocal.

5. The Sharanahua also closely associated the killing of men and jaguars, since they had special spears exclusively destined for warfare and killing jaguars (Siskind 1973: 174). This is reminiscent of the Cashinahua, who used the same clubs against peccaries and enemies, although they used them differently: 'during warfare the concave side of the blade is held facing upwards; when killing peccaries, the convex side is faced up' (Kensinger 1975: 220). Killing a jaguar can have serious consequences, and one of my informants attributed his son's poor health to the fact that he had killed a jaguar many years ago. Moreover, 'powerful people' and good hunters sometimes reincarnate in jaguar form, a fate that Matis neighbours tend to attribute to shamans.

6. Blowguns and curare, being as they are vectors of social identity and emblems of *tsasibo* insideness, the Matis would probably find it very difficult to believe that these products anciently figured among the items that were most widely traded in native lowland South America (Mansutti 1986, Scazzocchio 1979).

7. I was recently told that unlike humans, whose cheeks alone are pierced, *mariwin* have labrets that go through their very bones. My informant then compared this to the holes that existed in peccary skulls. I have also recently learned that apart from the iconic dart ones that adorn the masks, the *mariwin* has true, ugly teeth 'deep inside', which are sometimes represented with peccary or caiman teeth. All this seems to confirm Dr Baer's interesting opinion that *mariwin* masks have much in common with some of their Piro counterparts (Baer n.d.).

8. This is not unlike the Matses' custom of keeping a separate set of trophies for animals killed by dogs. Needless to say, data such as this seriously impair Romanoff's (1984) functionalist hypothesis according to which such trophies are used as 'statistical devices' in game management.

7

From Longhouse to Village: Structure and Change in the Colombian Amazon

Kaj Århem, *Göteborg University*

Change has always been a recalcitrant topic to students of society. Constantly challenging, frequently puzzling, historical process—change, diachrony, transformation—refuses to be neatly conceptualized or easily explained. A review of some recent statements on the subject reveals three salient and recurrent themes. The first is the relationship between event and structure (Moore 1987, 1994; Ohnuki-Tierney 1990; Sahlins 1981, 1985, 1994); the second is the articulation between local social formations and external forces, or what Sahlins refers to as the 'structure of the conjuncture'. The third issue refers to the internal dynamics of social systems—the notion that discrepancies, incongruities, and disconformities within social systems constitute an important source of change (Leach 1964; Moore 1987: 735; Ohnuki-Tierney 1990: 24; cf. Hornborg 1988). In this essay I want to bring these themes to bear on a specific ethnographic case: the process of village formation among the Tukanoan groups, particularly the Makuna, in the Pirá-Paraná area of the Colombian Amazon. My central concern is to show how Pirá-Paraná Indians 'indigenize' (Sahlins 1994: 390) or culturally appropriate the 'village' as social category and settlement form by drawing on models and imagery from the pre-village longhouse community and local organization.[1]

In an earlier work (Århem 1981: 206) I suggested that the Makuna conceptualize society in terms of two complementary models: the descent (agnatic) model and the alliance model; one centring on patrilineal descent, birth-order hierarchy, and descent-group exogamy, the other on prescriptive, symmetric alliance, competitive equality, and local endogamy. I also proposed that the descent model was the dominant, hegemonic conception while the alliance model had a more elusive, implicit presence in Pirá-Paraná social organization, manifest notably in the settlement pattern and local politics.

Developing a parallel idea, Stephen Hugh-Jones (1995) has recently argued that Tukanoan society is best understood in terms of two alternative and coexisting indigenous models, which correspond to gendered readings of the traditional multifamily longhouse (the *maloca*) as metaphor and social category: the maloca as a fundamental agnatic unit in the descent system (male reading), and as a consanguineal group of men and women, that is, a node in the marriage network, a procreative unit, and reproductive social body (female reading). Both models are ritually underpinned. The Descent House as all-male agnatic reality is epitomized by the Yuruparí ritual in connection with male initiation, when women and children are excluded and the male participants are identified with the ancestors. Analogously, the Consanguineal House as procreative, female body and commensal community is given ritual expression in the Food-giving ritual, during which a highly formalized exchange of food between kin (hosts) and affines (guests) is progressively transformed into a joint feast with distinct sexual overtones (S. Hugh-Jones 1995, and Århem 1981: 199).

This essay examines the recent process of village formation among the Pirá-Paraná Indians in the light of these ideas. Traditionally, and well into the 1970s, the Tukanoan groups of the Pirá-Paraná area lived in scattered maloca settlements. The maloca was the social and political centre of their society. Over the past twenty-five years, however, the maloca-centred society has eroded, the longhouse has lost its pre-eminence as the paradigmatic residential unit and has been replaced by village communities consisting of concentrations of small, single-family houses. A new social and cultural order is developing, but one in which the past is conspicuously present. Traditional notions and values are both actively challenged and creatively adapted to changing conditions. In the process, the descent model as a dominant vision of society is receding into the background while the consanguineal model is coming to the fore, supplying a new basis for collective identity in the emerging, village-based society.

At the most general level, the essay addresses the classical question in historical anthropology: in what way does a society change, as it unfolds over time, and in what way does it remain the same? In trying to answer this question, the ensuing analysis starts from and progressively develops the now fairly established view that social systems are fundamentally ambiguous and inherently unstable, embracing alternative structures and contradictory models for living. This perspective, briefly explicated at the end of the essay, provides a provisional basis for mediating and eventually transcending the conceptual dichotomies between structure and event, internal and external, change and continuity, thus allowing for a more fine-grained understanding of historical process.

PIRÁ-PARANÁ SOCIETY: STRUCTURE AND INTERNAL DYNAMICS

Pirá-Paraná society forms an open-ended but closely integrated social universe of some five named, exogamous descent groups, each ideally constituting a distinct language unit associated with a bounded river territory and ancestral birthplace (House of Awakening). The various groups relate to each other as 'brothers', 'affines', and 'mother's children'.[2] The normative mode of marriage is the balanced exchange of women between groups of affinally related men. The norm is codified in a 'two-line' (Dravidian) relationship terminology. Dyadic sets of affines tend to develop close relations of intermarriage. The Makuna, inhabiting the lower part of the Pirá-Paraná river and a section of the Apaporis river, comprise one such pair of closely intermarrying exogamous groups. The two groups, referring to themselves as Ide masa (Water people) and Yiba masa (Earth people), share a contiguous territory and speak a common language, thus violating the Tukanoan ideal of linguistic exogamy.[3]

The maloca community

In the early 1970s the Makuna and other Pirá-Paraná groups lived in scattered malocas along rivers and streams. Set in a clearing and surrounded by gardens and palm groves, the longhouse was a world unto itself—a communal dwelling, workshop, meeting place, and temple. The traditional Pirá-Paraná malocas were majestic, wooden structures, covered by a thatched roof of palm fronds. Many still exist today in the village setting. Usually rectangular in shape, sometimes with a rounded rear, the building has two entrances—one at the front, called the 'men's door', and one at the rear, the 'women's door'. The interior space is likewise gendered and symbolically differentiated. The front and central part is male, public space, the focus of ritual and entertainment of guests. The rear and sides are the domain of women and domestic life. Here women processed the staple crop, manioc, and prepared meals. Along the side walls were the various family compartments where people slept, stored their private belongings, and took occasional meals. At the centre, the headman kept the collective sacred paraphernalia of the house: the gourds of shamanic substances—coca, tobacco, and beeswax—and the equipment for coca preparation. From a beam hung a finely woven palm-leaf box containing the ritual feather headdresses and other ornaments. The house was also the burial place of its inhabitants and, therefore, a dwelling for both the living and the dead.

Each maloca comprised a core of closely related male agnates—a father and his married sons, or a set of brothers and their wives and children. Marriage was virilocal and the adult male members of the maloca constituted, in effect, the lowest-order segment of the patrilineal descent system. The headman, or 'owner' (*ühü*) of the maloca was typically a senior member of the agnatic core: the eldest son or the most senior of a set of brothers. Authority was ephemeral and contingent upon the headman's ability to maintain peace and order in the maloca. His hold over junior kin in the maloca was, however, significant. In addition to the headman, ritual specialists—notably shamans (*kumua*) and chanters (*yoamara*)—wielded considerable authority. A resourceful headman, who was usually also a renowned ritual specialist, could occasionally extend his influence over a local cluster of malocas.

The agnatically related households of the maloca co-operated in communal tasks such as house repair and the regular re-thatching of the roof. Male agnates, joined by young kin and allies of other, neighbouring houses, also collaborated in the cutting and clearing of new garden land. However, it was as a commensal community that the maloca most clearly expressed its unity and collective identity. At least one meal a day, usually at daybreak, was communally shared in the domestic (female) part of the house. Ideally, each household contributed a share to this repast—a piece of manioc bread, a bowl of pepper sauce, or a pot of cooked fish or meat. Squatting around pots and trays, the men, women, and children of the various households would partake of the joint meal, thus manifesting and reaffirming the inclusive, commensal community of the maloca. In the evening the adult men gathered in a smaller, exclusive circle at the sacred (male) centre of the house, chewing coca, smoking and inhaling snuff—the spirit foods reserved for men. Thus, while the communal meal constituted the commensal, consanguineal community of men and women, the ritual consumption of spirit foods established and reproduced the essential, male, unity of the maloca as an agnatic group.

In spite of its congenial symbolic connotations, the maloca was far from a harmonious social unit. It was riddled with conflicts and submerged tensions. Strains were built into its very structure. Young men unwillingly submitted to the authority of their elder brothers, and senior, male household heads saw their younger, unmarried brothers as potential adulterers. Married men jealously watched over their wives, and quarrels among households over food allocation were endemic. In times of food shortage, the compulsion to share food was felt as a burden, a reluctant concession to the normative but fragile agnatic solidarity of the maloca. More than an expression of ideal unity, the communal meal and ritual consumption of spirit foods appear in this light as important tools for conviviality; as social and symbolic instruments for forging a precarious sense of community and common identity in a group continually seething with repressed tensions and thinly disguised dissonances.

Above and beyond the level of the maloca, solidarity and community were fostered by frequent public rituals, all of which took place in the maloca. Two pivotal occasions were the Yuruparí (in Makuna *He tire*) and Food-giving (*Wai büare*) rituals. The *He tire* was an exclusive male event, reinforcing and recreating the spiritual bond between men and their deified, patrilineal ancestors (*he büküra*), who were embodied in the sacred Yuruparí instruments, played at the height of the ritual. The prototypical *He* ritual was performed when adolescent boys were first brought into contact with the ancestors; the initiates were symbolically killed and reborn and thus incorporated as true members into the exogamous group. Significantly, only beer and specially blessed spirit food were consumed during the ritual.

The Food-giving ritual explicitly focused on the affinal relationship and symbolically elaborated the social significance of reciprocal exchange between intermarrying groups. Typically involving an exchange of complementary foods—roasted meat for smoked fish, or edible larvae for wild forest fruit—between hosts (kin) and guests (affines), the ritual underscored the necessary interdependence between affines and the close social bond created by intermarriage. This community of interest among allies was expressed through the communal meal that closed the ritual event, when men and women, kin and affines, hosts and guests together partook of the food exchanged. Jointly consuming the food at the rear of the house, the participants thus symbolically erased categorical distinctions and constructed a commensal community of consanguines. Significantly, the people who most frequently engaged in ritual food sharing were the close kin and affines inhabiting neighbouring malocas.

The commensal community fostered during the Food-giving ritual and the spiritual unity reaffirmed during the *He* ritual had close parallels in the discrete rhythm of daily life in the maloca—the alternation between the diurnal communal meal involving men, women, and children and the nocturnal sharing of spirit foods among adult men. The sacred inter-maloca rituals, like the everyday patterned activities of the maloca, continuously created and recreated two kinds of sociality: the consanguineal sociality of men and women (husband and wife, brother and sister) in the longhouse and local group, and the agnatic sociality among men at different levels of segmentation from maloca to exogamous group. The agnatic mode of sociality created an exclusive 'we', an essentialized identity asserting categorical boundaries between self and other, kin and affines. The consanguineal mode, by contrast, established an inclusive 'we', a corporeal, commensal identity dissolving essential distinctions and categorical boundaries. One corresponded to the male reading of the maloca as Descent House, the other to the female reading of the maloca as Consanguineal House (cf. S. Hugh-Jones 1995). The agnatic, male conception was represented as the privileged and dominant mode of sociality, while the female, consanguineal model was socially backgrounded and discursively downplayed, a pattern that reflected the institutionalized gender asymmetry in Pirá-Paraná society at large.

The local group

The systematic intermarriage between affinal houses tended to create loosely bounded, relatively stable, and highly endogamous local groupings of neighbouring malocas. Such localized settlement clusters were essentially composed of close kin and affines. Unnamed, without a linguistically fixed categorical identity, the local group formed, in effect, an alliance-ordered unit, the boundaries of which were contextually and situationally defined from the point of view of the different malocas constituting it. Held together by a local leader, or united in opposition to ambitious headmen in adjacent localities, the local cluster of malocas was politically and ritually constituted; its fluid boundaries were defined, maintained, and publicly expressed through joint political and ritual action.

Rituals, in the Pirá-Paraná view, were the supreme social activity, maintaining and recreating society and the entire socio-cosmic order. By sponsoring communal rituals, headmen and local leaders fulfilled their roles as exemplary persons and 'owners' of their following. But there was also an important agonistic element in Pirá-Paraná rituals, which turned them into instruments of power. Headmen used public rituals as a vehicle for gaining prestige and displaying and consolidating power. By repeatedly staging public rituals, ambitious headmen—who were often also ritual specialists—extended their authority and gathered a following as well as displayed their resistance to the political ambitions of other headmen. Some men sponsored communal rituals, while others did not, and some sponsored more frequently than others. Particular individuals and groups were invited while others were ignored, and some who were invited chose not to participate. In this way, participation in, or exclusion from, communal rituals displayed the state of political relations in the territory at any particular point in time.

The local group of kin and affines constituted the basic, effective political unit beyond the single maloca settlement. Strife among agnatic kin in different local groups invariably translated into conflicts between entire local groups. Analogously, conflicts between affines in different localities or territories generally mobilized whole local groups, thus pitching agnates of the same descent group in different localities against each other. Conflicts centred on flawed marriage exchanges, adultery or sexual abuse, or on death and disease among kin and ensuing accusations of sorcery. In former times, for instance, raiding for women between different territories appears to have been common. In all recorded cases (Århem 1987), the raiding party, or the group mobilized in defence against raiders, was composed of local affines (allies) rather than a set of agnates.

The upshot is that bonds of marriage alliance carried the obligation of political support and concerted action, even against agnates in different localities. The local group of allies functioned as a corporate group, defending its vested interests in local women against outside infringement. Affinally related men in the local group not only shared rights to each other's kinswomen as future wives, but also held the corresponding responsibility for providing wives for each other. From a male point of view, local women constituted the focal value of the alliance-ordered local group, affording it cohesion and a certain stability over time (Århem 1981: 209). The Food-giving ritual, which converted the affinal between-relationship into a consanguineal within-relationship, was particularly important for defining and consolidating the local group as an effective, political entity (cf. S. Hugh-Jones 1995: 237).

Komenya territory (1972)

The bulk of the Makuna-speaking population inhabits the Komenya (Metal) river, a left-hand (eastern) tributary of the lower Pirá-Paraná river. In 1972 the Komenya population amounted to some 250 people divided between twenty settlements (ten of which consisted of single-maloca settlements). The headmen (and core members) of the settlements belonged to three different exogamous groups: the Makuna-speaking Ide masa and Yiba masa groups and the Tuyuka-speaking

Rokahana. The Makuna-speaking groups accounted for the majority of the Komenya population. The principal Ide masa clan was the Saira (ten settlements), while the Yiba masa clans included the Yiba proper (one), the Roe (five), and the Emoa (two settlements). The Ide masa and Rokahana are related as 'mother's children' and rarely intermarry; both groups, however, are preferential marriage partners of the Yiba masa exogamous group. In effect, the Komenya river community as a whole formed a highly endogamous territorial unit.

The Komenya river is said to be the ancestral territory of the Yiba masa, who are closely (phratrically) related to the Barasana-speaking groups higher up the Pirá-Paraná river; in fact, the Yiba masa clans inhabiting the Komenya river originally spoke a Barasana dialect, but later adopted the language of their Ide masa affines. The ancestral territory of the latter is the Toaka river, a downstream affluent of the Pirá-Paraná river. This river is still inhabited by a handful of Ide masa settlements but, as a result of internal conflicts and the destabilizing impact of the Amazonian rubber boom at the turn of the twentieth century, the group was divided and dispersed. The Saira clan moved to Komenya, while a substantial portion of the Tabotihehea clan (another, senior, Ide masa group) moved downstream to the mouth of the Pirá-Paraná river where it remains today. The Tuyuka-speaking Rokahana, finally, properly belong to the upper Tiquié river territory. Their presence on the upper Komenya is due to their long-standing intermarriage with the Roe clan. Though the Komenya population formed a close-knit and fairly autonomous social unit, its component groups had important ties to other river communities in the Pirá-Paraná basin and upper Tiquié territory. Marriages outside the territorial group did take place, and descent ties connecting houses and local groups in different territories were maintained, and sporadically reaffirmed, through visits and joint participation in important ritual events.

In the early 1970s the Komenya river community was roughly divided into three loosely bounded local settlement clusters: the settlements of the lower and middle Komenya (the *Lower Komenya group*); those of the Nyikonya (Palm) stream, a tributary of the Komenya (the *Nyikonya group*); and those of the upper Komenya (the *Upper Komenya group*). Residents of different localities referred to one another in terms of the structure of the river system and the relative location of the settlements along the river. The inhabitants of the Komenya river thus spoke of the 'downstream people' (*roka gana*), 'Nyikonya people' (*Nyikonya gana*) and the 'upstream people' (*waiseka gana*).

The *Lower Komenya group* centred on a single political leader, the Saira headman Antonio (6), and his close agnates and affines. The Saira segment, including Antonio's younger brother Roberto (3) and patrilateral nephews was numerically and politically dominant in the group. By incessantly sponsoring public rituals, Antonio sought not only to consolidate his authority within the local group but also to extend his influence over the rest of the Komenya population (cf. Århem 1981: 84–7).

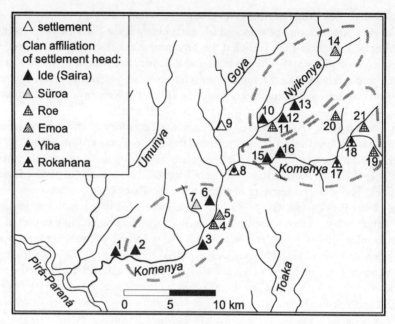

MAP 7.1. Makuna settlements on the Komenya river in the early 1970s

The *Nyikonya group* was similarly composed of a set of close agnatic and affinal relatives: three brothers (10, 12, 13) of the Saira clan, their married sons and
in-laws. The group formed a political unit in opposition to the Lower Komenya
group: though none of its headmen was recognized as a local leader, nor seemed to
aspire to such a position, they openly challenged the authority of the lower
Komenya leader, Antonio (who belonged to a 'junior' Saira segment). The
Nyikonya group also asserted its political autonomy by locally staging important,
public rituals. At the same time, a factional schism was building up within the

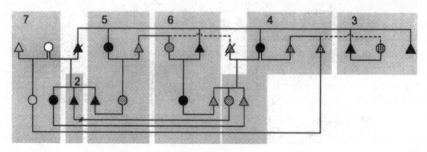

FIG. 7.1. The lower Komenya group Settlement (numbers correspond with Map 7.1)

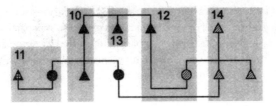

Fig. 7.2. The Nyikonya group

locality between the Emoa and Saira clan segments, threatening to split the group into two exogamous blocks; Ascencio (14), the ambitious Emoa headman in the headwaters of the Nyikonya stream, was actively seeking recognition as a local leader, but he was strongly opposed by the influential Saira faction.

Finally, the composition of the *Upper Komenya group* presented a more complex picture. In contrast to the other two local groups, the settlements forming the core of this group had no evident agnatic structure, and there was no dominant local clan segment in the group. Rather, the group centred around the close alliance between three intermarrying local segments of the Rokahana, the Yiba masa (Roe), and the Ide masa (Saira) exogamous groups. With no focused leadership or political coherence, the Upper Komenya group emerged as a residual group in Komenya political organization. Neither accepting the authority of the local leader of the Lower Komenya group, nor actively asserting political autonomy (like the Nyikonya group), it formed, as it were, a significant political non-entity—an antipolity. It was no 'group' at all in the strict sense of the term.

This pattern of socio-spatial segmentation, articulated by a fluid and discontinuous pattern of leadership is characteristic of what has been termed 'segmentary alliance systems' (Århem 1981: 262). The defining features of this type of social organization, distinctive of Pirá-Paraná society as a whole, are the progressive dispersal of kin and the concomitant concentration of affines, producing a spatial organization of small, localized, alliance-ordered groups or settlement clusters. Each local group, and the territorial unit constituted by the local groups occupying a single river or bounded river section, can be seen as a relatively autonomous,

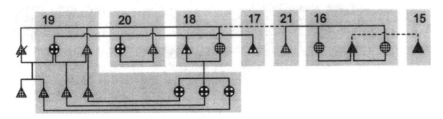

Fig. 7.3. The upper Komenya group

reproductive unit in the Pirá-Paraná social system, a large-scale Consanguineal House. The integrating force of systematic intermarriage was particularly evident in the Makuna case: here, close intermarriage had created a composite and largely endogamous identity which, in important respects, superseded the categorical identity of each of the component exogamous groups.

THE PROCESS OF VILLAGE FORMATION: EXTERNAL FORCES
AND LOCAL RESPONSES

The process of village formation in the Pirá-Paraná area must be understood in terms of a complex dialectic between the inner dynamics of the local society and the panoply of external forces acting upon it. Due to the relative inaccessibility of the area, Indian–White contact was until recently intermittent and largely indirect, mediated by indigenous communities closer to the colonial frontier along the Vaupés and Caquetá rivers, the principal waterways in the region. Although traders, missionaries, and explorers probably penetrated the Pirá-Paraná area as early as in the seventeenth century (S. Hugh-Jones 1981; Correa 1996), it was not until the great Amazonian rubber boom at the turn of the twentieth century that the Indians experienced a massive and direct confrontation with the outside world, which profoundly disrupted their society and severely reduced their numbers. Many Indians were forced to work in rubber camps, while others sought refuge in the inaccessible headwaters of small rivers and streams. The present distribution of indigenous groups in the Pirá-Paraná basin is largely a result of population movements during this turbulent period. More permanent and peaceful contact dates back only to the 1960s and early 1970s, when Catholic and Evangelical missionaries established themselves on the Pirá-Paraná river, and itinerant traders began to visit the area on a regular basis.

In the Vaupés region as a whole, the impulsion towards village formation was part of the 'civilizing' strategy of the miscellany of civil, military, and missionary authorities that had alternately or jointly governed the region since the conquest. The Catholic mission, in particular, had persistently worked for the sedentariza-tion and concentration of the dispersed indigenous population.[4] As a result of this active strategy, the indigenous populations along the Vaupés river and its major affluents—the Papurí and Tiquié rivers—had been effectively regrouped into villages from the 1920s and onward. Only remote parts, such as the Pirá-Paraná area, had remained outside missionary control and retained the maloca-centred settlement pattern until the 1970s. Even in these relatively isolated parts, however, the expanding frontier economy had had a powerful impact on the indigenous settlement pattern. Experiences from rubber camps, and visits to mission villages and trading towns had thus contributed to the establishment of the village as a conceptual category and community model long before it was actually adopted as a dominant form of settlement.[5]

In the late 1960s Evangelical Bible translators of the North American-based Sumner Institute of Linguistics (SIL) entered the Pirá-Paraná area, clearing small jungle airstrips and establishing mission posts among the major linguistic groups in the basin. At the same time, the Catholic mission founded an outpost and opened an airstrip at San Miguel on the middle Pirá-Paraná river. These early mission settlements became poles of attraction for the local population, supplying foreign goods and medical care. Over the following years, partly as a response to the ubiquitous presence of SIL, the Catholic mission intensified its pastoral and 'civilizing' labour in the area. A boarding school was opened at San Miguel in 1973, later moving to Sonenya on the upper Pirá-Paraná (1976). The mission redoubled its efforts to recruit local children to the new boarding school and offered continued education for those who had been trained at Mitú and Pedrera in the 1960s, when the Catholic prefecture had begun to extend its operations to the more remote parts of the region. Some of these pioneers now received further training as indigenous *catequistas* and *alfabetizadores* to champion development in their local communities. Time was ripe for village formation. Missionaries, government officials, and mission-educated Indians all propagated the vision of the village as a vehicle for progress and prosperity. In the late 1970s and early 1980s some ten villages were established in the Pirá-Paraná basin and its immediate surroundings. In the dominant missionary rhetoric, the village represented the progressive, 'civilized' community, based on Christian values and formal education—as opposed to the traditional, isolated and 'backward', maloca settlement. This village-based community model was, and continues to be, the guiding vision and motivating force of the missionary work in the region, a vision that has increasingly come to be adopted by the younger generations of Pirá-Paraná Indians themselves.[6]

The intensified missionary activity in the Pirá-Paraná area during the 1970s and 1980s coincided with a reorientation of the state's indigenist policy, which culminated in the new Constitution of 1991. Central to this new state policy was the legal recognition of the ethnic and cultural distinctiveness of the various indigenous groups in the country. In part, this progressive policy was a response to the resurgence of the Colombian Indian movement at the time. The Regional Indian Council of the Vaupés (CRIVA) was created in 1973 with the objective of defending and promoting the interests of the indigenous population.[7] In 1978 bilingual education was adopted as a general educational policy for indigenous communities in Colombia as a whole. The new, development-oriented indigenist policy, taking definite shape only in the early and mid-1980s, aimed to strengthen ethnic consciousness, local institutions, and communal land rights, and to provide public services and development resources to the indigenous communities. In accordance with this ambitious programme, the state took effective measures to extend indigenous control over land and territories. Old *resguardos*—protected Indian lands—were legally consolidated and new ones were created, granting indigenous communities full possession of titled land (Gros 1991). As part of this general development, the major part of the Vaupés region—almost 3.5 million hectares including the whole of the Pirá-Paraná river basin—was declared *resguardo* in 1982.

The village, as an administrative unit, was a basic building block in the new development policy. Implied in this policy—and somewhat at odds with its culture-sensitive orientation—was a view of development in terms of formal education, modern health services, and, in general, improved material living conditions through greater access to public services and increased participation in the national economy and society. The village instantiated this (essentially foreign) notion of progress.[8] Improved communication between local communities and frontier towns was another key feature of this development vision, shared by the State and the Church alike. The mission and the regional government jointly encouraged the establishment of new airstrips and trails to facilitate the flow of goods between regional centres and distant settlements, but also to extend control over these outlying communities.

The closer contact between Pirá-Paraná communities and the wider society over the past three decades has, furthermore, coincided with two dramatic economic upheavals in the region: the coca boom in the late 1970s and the gold rush in the late 1980s. When the illicit trade with coca leaves penetrated into the Pirá-Paraná area, it was embraced by the Indians as a new means of obtaining coveted merchandise. During its brief boom-period in the Pirá-Paraná (1980–3), the trade engaged almost all young men in the area and profoundly affected the local economy. Much of the traditional garden-land was converted into coca plantations, creating considerable profits for some. For a few years, shotguns, transistor radios, wrist watches, and outboard motors flooded the Pirá-Paraná communities. However, the boom declined as suddenly as it had arisen. In the early 1980s the white *coqueros* (coca entrepreneurs) left the area and the commerce ceased. Life in the Pirá-Paraná gradually reverted to the pre-boom rhythm of subsistence production and ritual feasting (Århem 1998*b*; S. Hugh-Jones 1992).

A few years later, in the mid-1980s, gold was discovered in the Traira hills along the Colombian–Brazilian frontier, only a couple of days' walking distance from the Pirá-Paraná basin. The gold rush that followed threw the entire Pirá-Paraná area once again into turmoil. Thousands of miners invaded the Traira river valley, and several mining towns grew up in the heart of the forest. In the late 1980s 'working gold' (*oro moare*) had replaced 'working coca' (*kahi moare*) as the main source of cash and manufactured goods in the Pirá-Paraná area. A considerable portion of the local Indian population was, in one way or another, involved in the gold economy. Most young men occasionally or periodically worked in the gold fields. While the men were away, the women and children were left for months at a time to sustain themselves as best they could. Economic differentiation accelerated and the demand for trade goods increased to a degree far beyond what most local people could possibly satisfy. Thus, while providing new economic opportunities, the gold economy, like the coca trade that preceded it, also created serious social problems. The process of village formation was to a considerable extent a local response to these social and economic challenges.

The village community

By the late 1980s the pattern of dispersed maloca settlements had largely shifted to one of nucleated villages (*comunidades*) composed of small, single-family houses of a variety of foreign and 'neo-Indian' styles and designs.[9] The typical Pirá-Paraná village features both a small school, where local children are taught elementary Spanish and how to read, write, and count, and a simple chapel in which mission-trained local *catequistas* give a rudimentary Sunday service. In the larger villages there are also a communal shop (usually sponsored by the mission), a dispensary served by a native health attendant, and a communal meeting hall (*casa comunal*) to host public gatherings and official visitors. These public buildings, which stand out from the ordinary family houses of the villagers, tend to be scattered around an open plaza, which forms the administrative (though rarely geographical) centre of the village. Adjacent to this official centre, there are invariably a rough soccer-field and a basket-ball ground. The larger and more important villages usually have an airstrip—a clearing cut on level ground in the surrounding forest. In most Pirá-Paraná villages there is also a traditional-style maloca serving as the ritual centre of the village. The presence of the maloca in the village setting is deeply significant, stressing the continuity between the past and the present. The 'traditional' cultural order, symbolized by the maloca, forms part of the emerging, 'modern' order that is epitomized by the village and the novel institutions it embodies.

The village has also brought a new authority structure to the local community. As an administrative unit, the village represents a new link between the local population and the State, and is perceived as such by the Pirá-Paraná people. For them, living in a village means participating in the wider social universe of the nation, which comprises both Indians and Whites. Each village is headed by a *capitan*, who is elected by the villagers and recognized by the regional authorities as the official head and spokesman of the village.[10] There is also a proliferation of other, new, civic and religious offices in the village setting, some salaried and all conferring prestige upon their holders: the schoolteacher, the catechist, the village secretary, the health attendant, and a variety of functionaries of local development committees and youth clubs. The *capitan* is often a senior man of traditional standing—a prestigious headman and ritual specialist. Increasingly, however, he is chosen from among the younger literate men, educated at mission school and experienced in dealing with outsiders. Indeed, the 'villagization' process in Pirá-Paraná has largely been propelled by these ambitious young men who are today taking over as village leaders. To them, the village with its manifold institutions and offices represents not only a potential source of income and material benefits, but also a new avenue to political influence.

The village has transformed the local political landscape in yet another way. Freezing the formerly fluid boundaries between local and linguistic groups, the village has emerged as a novel territorial entity, which defines political allegiances and regulates access to land and river resources. As a result, control over village territory has become a controversial issue in Pirá-Paraná politics, and boundary disputes, which were non-existent in the pre-village setting, are now becoming increasingly common.

Village formation on the Komenya (1975–1988)

An examination of village formation on the Komenya river exemplifies the process as it unfolded in the whole of the Pirá-Paraná area (see Map 7.1 and Figs. 7.1–3 above).

In 1975 the large maloca of the lower Komenya local leader, Antonio (6), broke up into several independent, single-family houses, clustered around the original maloca. This new settlement was baptized Villa Clara, signalling its change into a village community. Antonio became *capitan*, and his eldest, mission-educated son, Felicindo, became *alfabetizador* and the first government-paid local official on the Komenya river, as a school was opened in the new village. Attracted by the school, various adjacent settlements now also moved to Villa Clara. Antonio's political ambition was apparent: to concentrate the entire Komenya population into a single, large village under his leadership.

At the time, Roberto (3), Antonio's younger brother, lived in a small, separate maloca settlement on the lower Komenya. Also a renowned ritual specialist, Roberto was reluctant to submit to the authority of his elder brother and now actively encouraged various allies to join him and form an independent, nucleated settlement. Thus, in 1978, Roberto founded the village of Santa Isabel together with his (Roe) brother-in-law, Rafael (4) and the latter's Rokahana ally, Polo (17). The adult sons of these three men, all of whom had worked for white patrons and accumulated heavy debts, were instrumental in the process.[11] Ostensibly, the village was established on economic and political grounds, as a means of escaping the predicament of debt-bondage and to defend the villagers' interests against white traders and coca entrepreneurs. Roberto was appointed *capitan* and a village school was opened. As in the case of Villa Clara, its first paid teacher was the son of the village headman.

By 1981, Santa Isabel had grown into a village of some fifteen houses. A deep schism then developed between its two dominant, affinal factions—the Saira and Roe clan segments. The conflict, which later escalated into open violence, started when Rafael (4), the head of the Roe faction, requested one of Roberto's daughters as a second wife for his eldest son—a request that Roberto flatly rejected. As a result, the Roe faction decided to leave Santa Isabel for good and establish an independent settlement at the Nyi rapids on the Pirá-Paraná river. This settlement subsequently grew into Piedra Nyi village (see below).

In 1985 a series of deaths occurred in Villa Clara, causing its disintegration. The site was deemed inauspicious and abandoned, and the villagers gradually moved to Santa Isabel which was politically and numerically debilitated after the exodus of the Roe group. The decision to merge the two groups was strongly endorsed by the church and the civil authorities, who were in favour of an increased concentration of the dispersed Pirá-Paraná population. Thus reconstituted, the village of Santa Isabel, with school, shop, and a new airstrip, emerged as the political centre of the Komenya territory.

The rise and development—fission and fusion—of Komenya villages illustrate the interplay of internal and external factors in the process of village formation. The original establishment of Villa Clara was largely the result of the political ambitions of Antonio, the elderly traditional leader and ritual specialist of the lower Komenya group. Antonio wanted to consolidate his authority as a local leader by founding and heading a large and powerful community. The village here emerged as a new instrument in the traditional power game. However, by establishing the separate village of Santa Isabel, his younger but equally ambitious brother, Roberto, immediately frustrated Antonio's aspirations and affirmed his political independence. In this case, village formation was largely triggered by the hierarchical tension and dispute over rank inherent in the fraternal relationship. Eventually, the two villages fused, partly—and significantly—as a concession to the strong agnatic bond that nevertheless united their headmen, but also as a response to the affinal strife that divided Santa Isabel and caused the heaving-off of the Roe faction and the birth of Piedra Nyi village. In the process, Saira political control over the

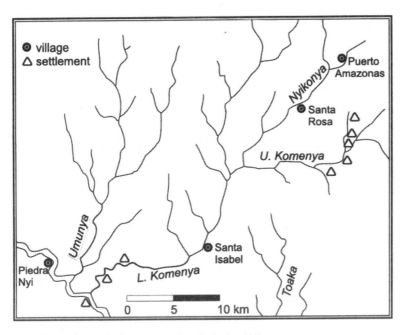

MAP 7.2. Village nucleations in Komenya territory in the late 1980s

Komenya territory was re-established. In sum, the case material suggests that tension and conflict within Pirá-Paraná society were important factors in village formation, along with external pressures and incentives.

By 1988, the major part of the Komenya population had regrouped into four nucleated villages: the relatively large Santa Isabel village on the middle–lower Komenya river, two smaller villages on the Nyikonya stream, and the village of Piedra Nyi on the Pirá-Paraná river, populated mainly by Makuna-speaking emigrants from the Komenya territory (Map 7.2). In addition, there was a handful of scattered settlements along the Komenya, most of them in the upper reaches of the river.

Santa Isabel village now consisted of seventeen houses (including two big malocas) forming five separate compounds or *barrios*. The population amounted to some 120 people, principally of the Saira, Emoa, Yiba, and Roe clans. A small creek divided the village into two halves: the downstream half, the original village site containing the administrative centre of the village, and the upstream half, referred to as the Villa Clara section after the now abandoned village from which most of its residents came. The downstream section contained two separate *barrios* situated on either side of a roughly cleared airstrip that also served as soccer-field; one was occupied by the Saira segment to which the village headman, Roberto, belonged (compound I), the other was dominated by a Yiba segment (two Yiba brothers and a Saira son-in-law; compound II). On one side of this field were also the chapel and the village school. The upstream, Villa Clara section consisted of three compounds centring on a Saira segment—the houses of Antonio and his adult sons (compounds III and V), and an Emoa segment—Antonio's brother-in-law, Pasico (4), and the latter's (patrilateral) nephew (5, compound IV; see Fig. 7.4).

In short, Santa Isabel was the result of the merging of two originally independent villages centred on the two Saira brothers, Antonio and Roberto. Significantly, the two brothers lived at opposite sides of the stream that divided the village; in fact, they lived very much at opposite extremes of the village. Antonio, the elder of the two, lived in a big maloca at the top of a hill overlooking the whole village. Next to him, at the foot of the hill, lived his close ally and brother-in-law, Pasico, also in a big maloca. By contrast, Roberto, the founder of the village and its present headman, lived in a modest, single-family house, next to the airstrip and the administrative centre of the village. The two brothers, living at opposite ends of the village, were thus associated with distinct but complementary aspects of the village: one (Antonio) with the traditional maloca community, the other (Roberto) with the novel social order symbolized by the school, the chapel, and the airstrip-cum-soccer-field. Though numerically dominated by the Saira clan, the village was significantly structured around affinal relations. Each section and compound was thus composed of intermarrying houses of different exogamous groups. Close ties of marriage and agnatic kinship cross-cut the spatial divisions and united the village as a whole. In effect, the village formed a highly endogamous, alliance-ordered unit analogous to the pre-village local group. Indeed, the Santa Isabel

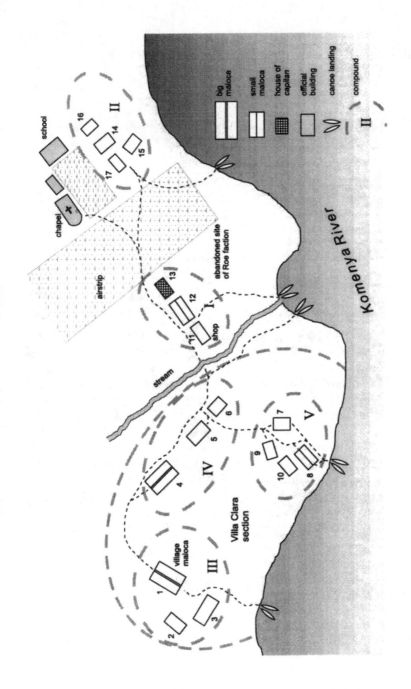

Komenya River

big
maloca

small
maloca

house of
capitán

official
building

canoe landing

compound

II

school

16

II

14

15

17

chapel

airstrip

abandoned site
of Roe faction

13

12

I

11

shop

stream

6

5

7

V

9

IV

10

8

4

village
maloca

III

Villa Clara
section

1

2

3

Fig. 7.4a. Plan of Santa Isabel village in 1988

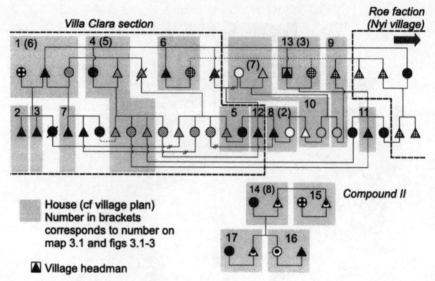

FIG. 7.4b. Composition of Santa Isabel village in 1988

village largely corresponded to, and effectively derived from, the lower Komenya group as it existed in the early 1970s (see Map 7.1 and Fig. 7.1).

The village of *Piedra Nyi* was founded in 1982 by its present Roe headman, Rafael, and his brothers and adult sons, as they broke away from the village of Santa Isabel and settled at the Nyi rapids on the Pirá-Paraná River. The move, as we saw, was the result of a conflict between Rafael's group and the dominant Saira segment in Santa Isabel. Soon after settling at Nyi, Rafael's group was joined by several close kin and affines from the Komenya territory, including segments of the Yiba, Josa, Saira, and Rokahana groups. This set of closely related kin and affines formed the core of the new village of Piedra Nyi (see Fig. 7.5). In 1988 it contained some thirteen houses. As distinct from Santa Isabel, the village of Piedra Nyi had a conspicuously modern layout and appearance. The headman's house commanded a small cluster of houses at the river front, separated by a spacious village square from the main body of the village, which stretched out in a line of houses, roughly parallel to the river. At one end of this line was the health post, at the other the chapel and the school. In the middle, facing the headman's house at the opposite side of the plaza, was the *casa comunal*. Beyond this line of houses, at the village margin, was the large, well-kept airstrip and the house of the SIL missionary-linguist who, with his family, had worked among the Makuna (initially on the Komenya) since 1970.

Situated on the Pirá-Paraná river just above the mouth of the Umunya river, the village of Piedra Nyi was established in Rasegana territory. The Nyi rapids are the

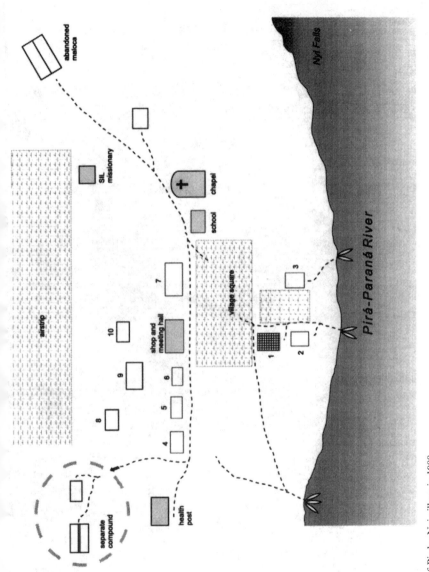

FIG. 7.5a. Plan of Piedra Nyi village in 1988

labels within image:
abandoned maloca
airstrip
SIL missionary
chapel
school
village square
shop and meeting hall
separate compound
health post
Pirá-Paraná River
Nyi Falls

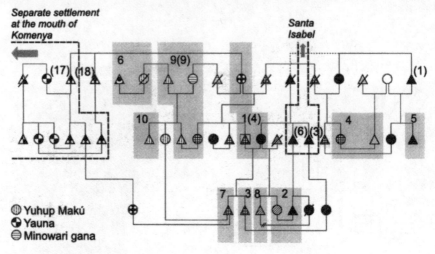

Fig. 7.5b. Composition of Piedra Nyi village in 1988

mythical birthplace of the Rasegana people, and Umunya is their ancestral territory. The Rasegana are classified as Yiba masa and, thus, 'brothers' of the Roe
people. The Roe faction in Piedra Nyi used this fact to justify their choice of site
for the new village and to claim the right to settle in Rasegana territory. From the
outset, Rafael had actively encouraged residents in the Umunya territory to settle
in the new village, so as to increase its size and political strength, as well as to reaffirm its legitimacy in terms of the traditional, descent-ordered pattern of territoriality. In 1988 there was thus a small compound of 'newcomers' from Umunya,
established some distance away from the main village. The compound consisted of
two houses headed by a Rasegana man and his Süroa affine. Significantly, the
Rasegana house was a big maloca. Just as in Santa Isabel, the ritual centre was
located away from the secular, official, village centre; the two principal symbolic
spaces of the village were thus located at opposite extremes.[12]

The two villages of *Santa Rosa* and *Puerto Amazonas* on the Nyikonya stream
were smaller and simpler in composition than those just described. Both had a
roughly linear spatial layout along the waterfront (most houses thus having direct
and separate access to the river). In 1989 Santa Rosa had ten houses, including one
large maloca inhabited by the Saira *capitan* Ricardo (1, Fig. 7.6); Puerto Amazonas
comprised five houses, the one inhabited by the Emoa *capitan* Ascencio (14, Fig.
7.2) slightly larger than the rest but still small by traditional maloca standards. Both
had a chapel and school building facing the central plaza of the village; neither had
a shop, dispensary, or airstrip. Each village was dominated by a single clan—Saira
in Santa Rosa, Emoa in Puerto Amazonas. These clans were in fact the two principal intermarrying segments constituting the pre-village Nyikonya local group.
Instead of consolidating into a single, alliance-ordered village, the local group thus

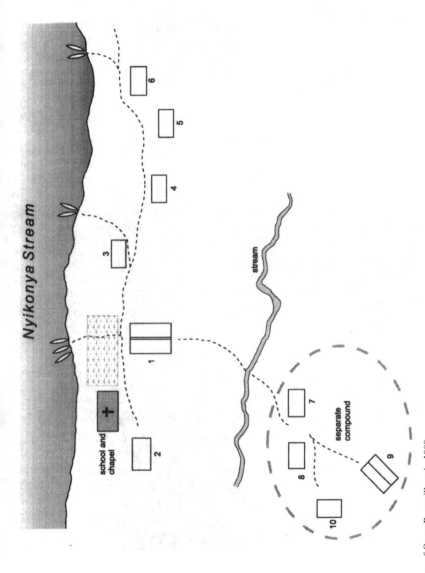

FIG. 7.6a. Plan of Santa Rosa village in 1989

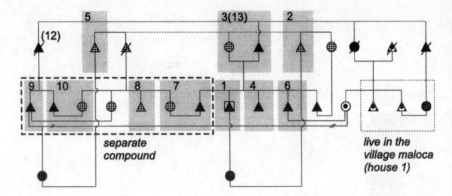

Fig. 7.6b. Composition of Santa Rosa village in 1989

split along the exogamous (Saira/Emoa) divide. However, in accordance with the general pattern of the segmentary alliance system, each village was in the process of developing a new, alliance-ordered structure—not, however, by re-establishing alliances between the two villages, but by forging new marriage links with local segments of the Roe and Rokahana clans on the upper Komenya river.

The two villages were officially established in 1983, several years after the formation of Santa Isabel village. The original idea was to establish a single, large village on the Nyikonya, on the model of Santa Isabel and, thus, to restore the political power balance in the Komenya territory. However, the Saira and Emoa headmen could not agree on who was to be the headman of the new village. They decided to form two separate villages, ostensibly on the grounds that they were 'different people' (belonging to distinct exogamous groups). In retrospect, it may be seen that this division was already prefigured in the factional strife between the same two power blocs which divided the Nyikonya group in the early 1970s. The dominant Saira faction in Santa Rosa was, in turn, subdivided into two segments, each inhabiting a separate compound, and each forming an incipient alliance unit organized around a series of marriage exchanges with segments of the Roe and Yiba clans (see Fig. 7.6). It was apparent that the Saira group in Santa Rosa was actively seeking to rebuild its political basis by substituting its original alliance with the Emoa clan for a set of new alliances with the Yiba and, above all, the Roe settlements of the upper Komenya territory. Similarly, the single Emoa segment that constituted the core of Puerto Amazonas village was clearly in the process of creating a separate alliance network with the local Rokahana group on the upper Komenya river.

The absence of any village in the upper Komenya in 1988 is significant in light of the data from the early 1970s. The dispersed settlements in this part of the territory, mainly composed of Tuyuka-speaking Rokahana and Makuna-speaking Roe, lacked then, as now, any form of political unity. In the late 1980s, more than fifteen years later, it remained a non-entity in Komenya politics. Rather than expressing a 'traditionalist' rejection of villagization, this lack of political cohesion among the upper Komenya settlements is, I believe, significantly related to the twin facts that the Rokahana are marginal 'immigrants' to the territory, and that the Roe are a junior clan in the Yiba clan hierarchy. It may also be significant that the upper Komenya is the home of a powerful line of Roe shamans, who contest the secular authority of the Saira headmen and local leaders on the lower Komenya. Whatever the reasons, the lack of unifying political leadership not only accounts for the absence of any nucleated village in this part of the territory, but also for the persistent attempts on the part of the headmen of the two Nyikonya villages to draw the upper Komenya population into their spheres of influence.

All in all, a remarkable continuity can be detected between the pre- and post-villagization social and political organization in the Komenya river territory. The pattern of village formation that emerged in the late 1970s and continued to develop during the next decade as a response to external pressures and new economic incentives, was largely prefigured in the pre-village settlement pattern and socio-political dynamics. In short, the unbounded, politically articulated, alliance-ordered local groups of the early 1970s were largely consolidated into the legally established and spatially demarcated village communities of the late 1980s.[13]

FROM MALOCA TO VILLAGE: THE FORGING OF A NEW SENSE OF COMMUNITY

The idea of the 'village' (*comunidad*) and the notion of 'progress' (*progreso*) had an immediate appeal for local, young men, who saw in the village a means of access to trade goods and other external resources. However, among senior men and women, the prospect of a local school was the principal incentive for village formation. In the village, parents, local elders, and ritual specialists could properly protect and spiritually supervise local children, and also provide them with a formal education that was increasingly considered necessary by all. The first local schools rapidly attracted families from outlying areas, and the nucleated communities so formed came to function as models for village formation in other localities.[14]

The village as a new form of settlement implied the break-up of the traditional longhouse community and the regrouping of its members in individual family houses within the village bounds. This revolutionary transition from communal maloca to single-family house had its precursor in the pre-village Tukanoan settlement pattern. In the early 1940s Goldman (1963: 37) observed how Cubeo maloca communities over time tended to segment as individual households progressively moved out to established satellite communities in the vicinity of the parent-maloca. Though still ritually dependent on the parent-maloca, these satellite communities represented the first step towards the establishment of a full-scale, independent maloca community (cf. Koch-Grünberg 1909: i. 58, 332; ii. 21). This cyclical pattern of growth, fission, and regrowth formed part of the development and reproduction of the traditional maloca settlement. The lines of cleavage in the maloca community typically occurred between older and younger brothers as the senior took over the headmanship after an ageing or deceased father.

The seeds of fission were inherent in the maloca community. The multifamily longhouse was fraught with tensions and suppressed conflicts between its agnatic members. When asked why they had abandoned the communal maloca in favour of the single-family house, several former headmen and maloca dwellers answered that they preferred living in a single-family house because it gave them more independence; they felt more at ease in their proper house and avoided the 'problems' and 'tensions' (oca, literally 'talk', 'strife') of the multifamily maloca. The single-family house was evidently associated with a greater sense of privacy and personal autonomy (see Goldman 1963: 38). It promised a release from the obligation of sharing and the intense sociality in the maloca community, and a consequent reduction of friction among close agnates.

Other, external factors were also significant in this process. The single-family house as a cultural model—an idealized unit of co-residence and consumption intimately associated with Christian values—was thus directly propagated by missionaries and implicitly communicated by the very notion of the village. The break-up of the maloca community was also a consequence of the historical development of the regional frontier economy, particularly the rubber boom at the turn of the twentieth century and the ensuing fragmentation and differentiation of traditional social and economic organization. The impact of the coca trade and mining economy in the 1970s and 1980s represents the culmination of this longer historical process. Some local men now succeeded in accumulating substantial wealth in trade goods, while others remained outside or at the margins of the extractive economy.

Material prosperity has today become an increasingly important source of power and prestige, and trade goods are an essential asset in the marriage market. There is also a clear correlation between trade wealth and subsistence efficiency; the possession of shotgun, ammunition, steel hooks and nylon line, torch and batteries considerably enhance the chances of fishing and hunting success, thus buttressing emergent economic cleavages. This new socio-economic dynamic has been instrumental in transforming the Pirá-Paraná settlement pattern. Economic differentiation propels the dissolution of the maloca community and encourages the creation of small, independent single-family households, each in control of its own resources and possessions. Concealment of wealth and selective constriction of food sharing, on the one hand, and theft of standing crops, on the other, have emerged as opposed but complementary coping strategies in the village setting, both equally erosive of social order.

Normative generosity and social transparency governed life in the pre-village maloca community. Conspicuous differences in wealth and consumption were rare and downplayed. The communal meal served to level out differences and reaffirm unity. In the differentiated village setting, by contrast, households tend to conceal subsistence yields and restrict sharing. 'You cannot share food with everyone', as one man put it, 'there are too many people in the village.' Disparities in food consumption are aggravated by the notable depletion of game and fish in the vicinity of the village. The successful hunter or fisherman, usually one with access to 'modern' hunting and fishing gear, takes pains to hide his bag on return to the village. If the yield allows, the hunter discreetly sends an invitation to a few close kin or affines to come and share the food with him, or he sends his children with carefully concealed pieces of meat or fish to selected, usually neighbouring, houses in the village. The less fortunate hunter or fisher is equally secretive for the opposite reason: to conceal his failure and keep what little he has for his own house.

With the atomization of the household economy and the constriction of the ordinary networks of food-sharing and mutual support, theft of standing manioc has become a serious problem in village life. While secrecy and concealment of food are strategies used both by the poor and the prosperous, crop theft is an extreme measure occasionally employed by impoverished women to cope with food scarcity. Theft is a coping strategy of the socially weak and marginalized. Of the handful of cases of manioc theft brought to my attention in Komenya (1988–9), all but one were perpetrated by single mothers (widows or women abandoned by their husbands). As such, theft and the social strain it engenders, are symptoms and consequences of the general socio-economic conditions in the village setting: as gardens are cut at ever greater distances from the village centre, women's workload increases proportionally. The situation is exacerbated by the fact that men, as a result of their increased participation in economic activities away from their home communities, have less time to attend to traditional subsistence tasks, including the clearing of new garden-land—especially for widowed or single kinswomen. Crop theft, then, calls attention to a developing gender asymmetry in Pirá-Paraná society. Stealing offers itself as a tempting possibility for destitute women to solve the dual problem of a growing labour burden and diminishing agricultural returns.[15]

An emerging village culture

Pirá-Paraná Indians are aware of these divisive tendencies in the village setting and seek to counter them by various means, thus actively constituting the village as a cohesive social unit. In the process, a village culture, blending old and new elements, is developing. The new institutions and offices, along with the 'village maloca' and the *casa comunal*, are key features of this emerging village culture. The name, the position of *capitan*, and the *personeria juridica* of the village—the authorized certificate or document obtained upon its founding—are the supreme insignia of the village's enduring identity beyond the transient existence of its members. Treated with reverence and invested with an almost sacred quality, the headman's diploma and the official village certificate are the direct counterparts of the sacred paraphernalia of the clan and exogamous group.

Despite contact with missionaries and traders for more than a century, and regardless of the presence of a school and a chapel in almost every village, indigenous cultural traditions are vital. The native cosmology has embraced and incorporated Christian notions rather than been replaced by them, and old rituals continue to be performed in the village setting. The village maloca now serves as a stage for public rituals rather than as a dwelling. As a ritual centre, the village maloca is either identified with the headman and his descent group or, more recently, with the entire village, having been collectively constructed by the villagers as a community project. The longhouse also functions as a spiritual sanctuary in the village setting, as men gather in the evening to chat, chew coca, smoke, and perform shamanic acts of curing and blessing. This traditional rhythm of life unfolds alongside the modern manifestations of the village world—the daily routines centred on the school, Western-style dress and hygienic practices, sports, games and songs learned at school and in mission villages, and the weekly church service, respectfully attended by most villagers but understood by few, except as a new kind of ritual event. The autochthonous and the alien reciprocally influence each other, generating a particular Pirá-Paraná blend of village culture. One young villager expressed this composite outlook thus: 'We like to have both maloca and *casa comunal* in the village; in the maloca we perform our own, ancestral dances, in the *casa comunal* we dance with the women the way the Whites do.'

In constructing the new village sociality, the Pirá-Paraná Indians actively draw on local models centring on the maloca as an agnatic and consanguineal social body. Ancient rituals take on a new significance in the village setting. Reasserting the connection with the past and committing the participants to common values, the rituals downplay social divisions and express unity in the face of growing material disparities. Now, as before, the Yuruparí ritual is the supreme religious expression articulating Pirá-Paraná cosmology and the descent-ordered vision of the world. Drawing together agnates from different villages, the Yuruparí ritual publicly manifests the unity and identity of the sponsoring exogamous group. However, celebrated in the village maloca and thus momentarily fusing maloca, village, and exogamous group, the ritual also confers agnatic meaning on the village as a whole. The Food-giving ritual, on the other hand, appears to be losing its earlier significance as a celebration of affinal solidarity and commensal unity. In the village setting it is increasingly replaced by secular, public events and new syncretic rituals—village meetings, work parties, *fiestas patronales*, and the weekly dominical feast—bringing kin and affines together and establishing the village as a corporate, commensal, and consanguineal community.

Formalized village meetings (*reuniones*) are arranged when important visitors arrive or before village representatives go on official visits to other villages. Such meetings, usually held in the school, chapel, or *casa comunal* rather than in the village maloca, draw together men and women, young and old. As with so many other elements of village culture, the formal character of these meetings bears the stamp of missionary influence. The village meeting is seen locally as an attribute of 'civilized' community life, and forms part of the new institutional set-up and cultural repertory that distinguish the village from the maloca. By contrast, communal work, such as clearing village-land, cutting grass on the soccer-field or airstrip, and repairing the school house or chapel, is modelled on the traditional work parties and is therefore always accompanied by beer drinking.[16]

In the 1980s a new, Christian form of festivity, promoted by missionaries and mission-educated Indians, surged in the Pirá-Paraná area and rapidly became part of local culture: the patron-saint festivals (*fiestas patronales*). Most villages are identified with a patron saint, which is the saint associated with the day the village was officially established. As in the case of Santa Isabel, the village is often named after this saint. Every year, on the day of its patron saint, one village organizes a great festival, inviting the members of all the other villages in the area. The next year another village sponsors the festival, and so on. In this way, the festival rotates among all the Pirá-Paraná villages. The festival involves inter-village sports competitions, a traditional dance ritual, and modern, secular dancing and feasting, usually accompanied by heavy drinking (*guarapiadas*).[17]

Of particular interest in this context is the Sunday ceremony or dominical feast. This weekly event begins with a communal meal in the headman's house (or *casa comunal*, school building, or chapel) and proceeds with a religious service and a public meeting at which important events are announced and disputes are aired and resolved. Each household brings a pot of food and a piece of manioc bread as a contribution to the communal meal. The joint eating, followed by the men's coca chewing, continue until the church bell calls the people to the religious service in the chapel. Alternatively, the ceremony starts with the mass followed by the public meeting, and ends with the communal meal. In either case, the event is a public expression and active affirmation of village unity, transposing values and practices of the maloca community into the village setting.

The religious service in the chapel typically consists of gospel reading, prefaced by hymns and prayers and followed by a commentary to the text. The service is given by the *catequista* or one of the younger, literate villagers considered knowledgeable in Christian liturgy and doctrine. The entire service is performed in the native tongue, but is heavily seasoned with Spanish terms and liturgical expressions. The commentary to the gospel serves, more or less explicitly, as an important ideological vehicle for social and cultural change. As the mission-educated *catequista* expounds his ideas about proper, Christian living, traditional views and values are creatively moulded, and new notions are introduced in a highly authoritative, ritualized context. The mass is, in effect, one of the principal agencies and propelling forces in the transition from a maloca-based to a village-centred society. The Sunday service and the ensuing gathering also present the young men with a new political stage where they may display non-traditional knowledge and skills, and thus exercise considerable influence in village affairs.

From this perspective, the Sunday ceremony takes on supreme social and cultural significance. Tirelessly promoted by the village headman, the dominical feast carries all the symbolic connotations of the daily communal meal in the maloca and the public Food-giving ritual, which united kin and affines in the pre-village local community. Like the communal meal in the maloca, the dominical village feast expresses consanguineal consubstantiality and commensal community, and like the Food-giving ritual it celebrates and reaffirms the relationship of mutuality, solidarity, and sharing between local affines-turned-consanguines. Indeed, the Sunday feast can be seen as a creative adaptation, a modernized, village version of the Food-giving ritual, transforming village members into residents of a metaphorical, or virtual, maloca. It turns the village into a Consanguineal House.

CONCLUSIONS

In its present form, the Pirá-Paraná village emerged in the 1970s and 1980s as a local response to a series of external forces: intensified missionary activities, the implementation of a new, development-oriented indigenist policy, and the creation and growth of the indigenous movement that roughly coincided with the coca boom and the subsequent gold rush. These recent events were only the latest manifestations of a long and turbulent history of contact, which had progressively debilitated the traditional maloca community and settlement pattern, while supplying alternative—Western, Christian—models for domestic and community organization. But the process of village formation was also significantly shaped by forces internal to Pirá-Paraná society itself. It developed according to an intrinsic logic grounded in the local social and cultural system. Two opposed but complementary features of Pirá-Paraná society were particularly important in this formative process: the internal stresses and divisive tendencies of the hierarchical descent system, and the integrative force of the symmetric marriage system.

Tensions between brothers were, as shown, a constant feature of life in the maloca community. Much of the strain centred on rank, jealousy, and the allocation of food among households. However, such tensions were continuously subdued. The task of the headman consisted to a large extent of preventing, repressing, and resolving conflicts within the maloca. The ritualized habits of the house—the daily communal meal, the evening gathering of men around the gourds of coca and tobacco, and the separation of the sexes in everyday household chores—all served to minimize and overcome these disruptive tendencies in the maloca. If a headman failed to reconcile disputing individuals, the maloca dissolved and its members dispersed, joining other malocas or forming new settlements that over time grew into new maloca communities. There was no real, long-term alternative to life in the maloca.

Against this background, the village emerged as an option, a new form of sociality and settlement organization, but one patterned on an old model—the consanguineal sociality of the endogamous local group. Propagated by missionaries and actively supported by government agencies and regional authorities, the process of village formation found deep resonance in local concepts and traditional Pirá-Paraná society. Not only did the village gradually become thinkable, but it also presented itself as an attractive alternative to the maloca community, a practicable means of escaping the rigours and tensions of maloca organization while at the same time offering the wider, inclusive sociality of the consanguineal community. The village emerged, in effect, as a novel form of the alliance-ordered local group of pre-village social organization. What was formerly a fluid and flexible socio-spatial arrangement expressing shifting political alignments to influential local headmen, now froze into a pattern of bounded and named political and administrative units. The process of village formation in the Pirá-Paraná area can thus be seen as a reification and congealment of the dynamic political and spatial order of the early 1970s. Structurally, the village of today is the endogamous local group of yesterday.

While reproducing the structure of the pre-village local group, the village is, in important respects, imagined and conceived of in terms of the traditional maloca community. As multivalent symbol and social category, the maloca supplies the conceptual basis and cultural underpinning of emergent village identity. The unifying principles of co-residence and generalized sharing are transferred from maloca to village, and the village comes to emulate the essential and commensal community of the maloca. The sacred *He* ritual performed in the village maloca, and the dominical feast celebrated in the *casa comunal* or village plaza, constitute the village as a grand maloca, an expanded—exploded—Descent House and Consanguineal House respectively. Indeed, as a focus of ritual celebrations in the village setting, the village maloca symbolically corresponds to the male, sacred centre of the maloca itself. By contrast, and by the same symbolic logic, the official, administrative centre—the school, the chapel, and the *casa comunal* surrounding the village plaza—have the commensal and consanguineal connotations of the female, secular spaces of the maloca where men and women, kin and affines, adults and children once mingled to eat, feast, and socialize. The village, then, incorporates and reproduces the gendered ambivalence of the maloca and its symbolic divisions.[18]

However, by turning to images and models of the pre-village maloca community to make sense of a new social reality, the Pirá-Paraná Indians not only confer meaning on the village in terms of traditional notions, but they also transform them and profoundly reshape reality. For as the exogamous, descent-ordered maloca loses its pre-eminence as the paradigmatic model for settlement organization, and as the alliance-ordered, endogamous village takes over as the tangible prototype for community formation, the entire Pirá-Paraná society subtly, but significantly, changes. Whereas in the maloca, the descent model and the agnatic identity of its male members hierarchically encompassed the consanguineal model, the situation in the village setting is reversed. Here, the endogamous, consanguineal identity of

the village—associated with a name and embodied in the official village 'paraphernalia'—encompasses and transcends the separate agnatic identities of its
constituent descent units. In effect, the process of village formation implies a shift
away from the descent model towards the consanguineal model as a new basis for
Pirá-Paraná social identity.

These provisional conclusions bear on wider issues in the study of change,
notably the problem of continuity in change—the relationship between the relatively invariant and the mutable dimensions of society.[19] With Hugh-Jones (1995)
I have argued that Pirá-Paraná Indians hold two alternative visions of society,
conceptualized as two complementary models of sociality: the agnatic (descent)
model and the consanguineal (alliance) model—expressed as gendered readings of
the traditional maloca. Elsewhere I have also suggested that the two models represent different structural possibilities inherent in the symmetric alliance structure—options that are empirically realized in the social systems of the Tukanoan
and the Guiana groups respectively, the former emphasizing the descent model,
the latter the consanguineal model (Århem 1989; see also Hornborg 1988 and
Rivière 1984). From this perspective, Pirá-Paraná society is transforming along a
trajectory, or activating a potentiality, inherent in its very structure. The shift of
emphasis from a descent-ordered to a consanguineal conception of society represents a perspectival shift, a different reading of the same structure, which eventually may lead to more radical change: the restructuring of the structure itself.

Seen in this light, the Pirá-Paraná case exemplifies a more general theoretical
perspective on social change. According to this increasingly accepted view, historical process is culturally ordered, mediated by structural patterns and cultural
schemes connecting past, present, and future social forms. At any particular historical conjuncture, change on one level of society implies continuity on another.
Every society encloses a set of alternative visions or models of sociality grounded
in the proclivities of the human mind and the ambiguities of social existence. For
every socially sanctioned model for living, there are alternative visions and counter-
models, variously represented as repressed possibilities, threatening absurdities, or
unattainable, utopian or other-worldly realities (see Aijmer 1997 and Århem 1989).

The presence of alternatives and counter-models is a constant and fundamental feature of social systems. However, it is also in the nature of culture to symbolically elaborate and socially stress one model at the exclusion of others; to present
one possibility as the right, sacred, and sanctioned order while backgrounding,
suppressing, or rejecting other options as wrong, sinful, or inhuman. The sanctioned vision is presented as the only possible, even thinkable way of life. Yet,
culture in the sense of a hegemonic, condoned view of society, always fails to
completely repress alternative models for the very reason that social existence is
inherently contradictory, ambiguous, and perspectival. Social life continuously
generates alternative visions and counter-models that are responsive to these inde-
terminacies, situated perspectives, and contrary tensions in human existence.

In this muted range of choices and partly subdued multiplicity of alternatives, present in all societies, there is a powerful mechanism for change. For as new circumstances arise and historical contingencies alter current conditions, suppressed alternatives and dormant possibilities come alive, become thinkable, and present themselves as viable solutions to new problems. Tensions erupt and call for readjustment and novel responses. Thus viewed, change dwells in structure. Always challenged, structure is continuously in the making, perpetually in the process of restructuring. Challenge and change are the empirical conditions of structure, just as structure is the condition of culture and, thus, of meaningful social existence.

ACKNOWLEDGEMENTS

This is a slightly edited version of a chapter with the same title in Århem (2000). I gratefully acknowledge the helpful comments on earlier drafts of this chapter from Sven Cederroth, Stephen Hugh-Jones, Jan Johansson, Alexandra Kent, and Laura Rival.

NOTES

1. Rival (1996*b*) provides a detailed case study of the process of village formation and its socio-cultural implications among the Huaorani of the Equadorian Amazon. On settlement nucleation among the Achuar, see also Descola (1981) and Taylor (1981).
2. 'Mother's children' represent an intermediary and ambiguous category in the Pirá-Paraná relationship system; intermarriage between exogamous groups related as 'mother's children' is infrequent but does occasionally occur.
3. Fieldwork among the Makuna-speaking groups in the Pirá-Paraná and Apaporis area was carried out during two sustained periods; 1971–3 and 1988–9 with shorter visits in 1990 and 1993.
4. In the process, early missionaries encouraged Indians to abandon their traditional settlements and even exhorted Christianized Indians to burn malocas (described as 'devils' houses') and ritual paraphernalia (cf. S. Hugh-Jones 1981).
5. S. Hugh-Jones (1995: 238–9, 251) notes that there existed a pre-contact Tukanoan notion of a concentric settlement, consisting of four malocas surrounding a fifth ritual centre. This ideal notion corresponded to the distribution of compartments in the primal, mythical House inhabited by the five sons of the Ancestral Anaconda of the exogamous group.
6. In both missionary and local development rhetoric, Indians were exhorted to 'wake up' (*despertar*), organize themselves (*organizarse*), and come together (*reunirse*) to live and work in community (*vivir en comunidad*). But there were also dissenting, actively 'traditionalist' voices (see n. 8).
7. Like most Indian Councils in Colombia, CRIVA was inspired by, and modelled on, the early and successful organization of the Indians of the Cauca highlands (CRIC). In the course of the 1970s and 1980s, CRIVA was subdivided into several local branches, including that of the Pirá-Paraná Indians (ACAIPI).

8. The notion of village-based community development clashed, to some extent, with the message promulgated by CRIVA, Indian Affairs officials, and various non-governmental agencies, which claimed that progress should build on local institutions and cultural traditions. Thus, along with the rhetoric of the village as a vehicle of progress there was an alternative discourse promoting the revitalization of the maloca community as the basis for local development. These conflicting notions caused considerable bewilderment among Pirá-Paraná Indians.

9. Dispersed malocas and isolated settlements continue to be prevalent in the area. A recent estimate suggests that as much as 40 per cent of the native population still (mid-1990s) live in dispersed settlements (S. Hugh-Jones, personal communication).

10. The office of *capitan* existed long before village formation. In the 1950s and 1960s certain local headmen were appointed as official intermediaries between the authorities and the local communities. Earning a small salary and enjoying considerable local prestige, the *capitanes* were expected to procure a labour force for government projects in the region.

11. Indebtedness was the paradoxical result of local involvement in the regional frontier economy, which still (in the 1970s) worked on the principle of debt-bondage (see S. Hugh-Jones 1992).

12. By 1988, the Rokahana segment (allies of the Roe and co-founders of the village) had splintered off from the parent village and established itself as an independent settlement just below the mouth of the Komenya river. Again the group was composed of two allies, the Rokahana headman of the maloca and his Yauna brother-in-law (WB).

13. This conclusion is corroborated by the scant comparative evidence on village formation from elsewhere in Vaupés (particularly Pinzón Sanchez 1979, Correa 1996).

14. One reason for the strong interest in the local school is the marked territoriality of Pirá-Paraná society and the metaphysical significance accorded to place and local belonging (see Århem 1998*a*). Staying in, and eating foods from, territories other than one's own is considered dangerous and believed to be conducive to sickness and misfortune. Parents are therefore reluctant to send their children to boarding schools outside their territory, even to schools in adjacent territories.

15. In none of the recorded cases was the accused woman punished although she was, in a sense, socially ostracized and suffered the consequences of being singled out not only as a thief but also as a 'lazy' woman and poor cultivator.

16. More ambitious village projects, requiring intensive labour and external resources, are referred to as *proyectos*. The notion of *proyecto* has become a key concept in current village discourse. The term refers to any project promoting the development of the village as a whole. The prosperity and political strength of a village is measured in terms of the scale and quantity of projects handled by the village headman. Indeed, the invention and realization of *proyectos* are seen as the main duty of the *capitan*, and his reputation is largely contingent upon his success in bringing goods, money, and other social and economic benefits to the village.

17. Increasingly, the feasting and drinking during the festival take place in the village maloca, thus assigning the longhouse a new role in the symbolic construction of village identity. Inter-village sports competitions are becoming an important boundary-maintaining force, instrumental in forging separate village identities (possibly playing a role analogous to inter-territorial violence—real and ritualized—in the past). For a parallel example, see Rival (1996*b*) on the Huaorani.

18. Correa (1996) has shown that, despite its modern appearance and heterogeneous composition, the multi-ethnic mission village of Acaricuara (central Vaupés) reproduces the idealized cultural scheme and internal divisions of the traditional maloca community (ibid. 70–1). For comparative evidence, see also Gasché (1972) on the Witoto.
19. See particularly Sahlins's writings on historical ethnography (e.g. 1981, 1985, 1994; see also Ohnuki-Tierney 1990).

8

The Composition of Mẽbengokre (Kayapó) Households in Central Brazil

Vanessa Lea, *Campinas University (UNICAMP), São Paulo*

INTRODUCTION

Rivière (1984) in his synthesis of the social structure of the Guianas uses Central Brazil as a kind of interlocutor with which to reflect on the contrast between these two areas. His analysis of the significance of houses in the Guianas (1995*b*) provides a striking contrast with my portrayal of Mẽbengokre houses in Central Brazil (Lea 1995), helping to highlight the wealth of social and cultural diversity which is gradually being appreciated in the ethnographies of lowland South America.

Some pertinent remarks about the Jê[1] have been made by Rivière although he has not undertaken fieldwork with them directly. Viveiros de Castro criticized him for reducing the societies of the Guianas to their individuals, remarking that: 'Despite his reference to the reproduction of the *person*, he seems to persist in working with an unanalysed concept of *individual*, as society's natural atom' (Viveiros de Castro 1985: 280; my translation). The direction of the criticism could be inverted because in 1980 Rivière had argued that:

Seeger and others [R. Da Matta and E. Viveiros de Castro] have recently stated that 'the societies of the continent are structured in terms of symbolic idioms that—and this is the difference from European and African symbols—have no concern with the definition of groups and the transfer of goods, but with the construction of the person and the fabrication of the body' (1979: 10). This point is well made, but *a two-way flow is involved, as the Gê material makes clear. The social persona results from recruitment in certain groups which thus maintain themselves with the enrolment of individuals.* (Rivière 1980: 537; my emphasis)

Da Matta opposes 'substitution', through name transmission, to descent evidenced 'through a continuum . . . ordered in temporal terms (closer to or more distant from a common ancestor . . .' (1979: 127). Rivière raises the important question that: 'It might be asked at this point if the Northern Gê do not in fact have unilineal descent disguised as name transmission' (1980: 538). In the light of data from Da Matta, Melatti, and Jean Lave, Rivière comments that name transmission does not appear to order short cycles: 'Rather it is a scheme of continuity, just as effective as unilineal descent, whereby social personae succeed one another in orderly linear progression' (1980: 539).[2] Thirteen years later, Rivière comments that despite the influence of the notion of the person 'the problem of descent and lineality has failed to go completely away—especially as far as the Gê are concerned' (1993: 509).[3] This is one of Rivière's insights into the Jê material to be taken up in this chapter.

There is not space here to analyse in detail the important role played by wives as the distributors of protein, handed over to them by their husbands. Rivière (1984: 89) noted the political importance accruing to those who distribute meat and fish as opposed to those who obtain it through hunting or fishing. This is a question that has been little explored in the ethnographies of the region, but which is vital for elucidating issues related to gender. In Mẽbengokre society, the fact that women take charge of the distribution of raw and cooked protein and garden produce is one of the factors that reinforces their pivotal role in the households, as I shall attempt to demonstrate in the remainder of this chapter.

One of the recurring questions that Rivière asks is why villages in the Guianas rarely attain populations of over fifty people (at least before the advent of missions and governmental Posts, which have resulted in larger concentrations of Amerindian populations) in comparison to the far larger villages found in Central Brazil. The motive given by Rivière was that a village tends to disintegrate when the leader father-in-law dies. Brothers-in-law only remain together after the death of their father or father-in-law if their children have intermarried. Otherwise they tend to split up to establish new settlements or to join already existing ones elsewhere.

Reflecting upon Rivière's question from the perspective of the Mẽbengokre, I argue that their villages attain relatively large-size populations due to the ceremonial interdependence of the matri-houses; added together they produce an organic whole. Name confirmation ceremonies not only produce beautiful people (*mẽmetx*), they also produce inter-personal harmony (*mẽdjumari metx*), and if they fail to do so they are not allowed to run their course, being cancelled before completion. Ceremonies can be rendered untenable in the absence of the owners of their constituent elements. In the Mẽbengokre village of Kretire, in the early 1980s, it was affirmed that there were not enough people to stage the major Bemp ceremony, despite there being nearly 200 inhabitants in the village. There was, however, no song and dance leader (*ngre nhõ djwoj*), the prerogative of one of the matri-houses. The owning House was in fact present but none of its inhabitants had inherited the role. This was eventually resolved by bringing a song and dance leader from the neighbouring Mẽtyktire village of Jarina. One may then ask how smaller villages which have occurred in post-contact times can be accounted for. The answer appears to be that either they team up with other villages for ceremonies, as in the example given here, or they desist from performing them. Nowadays it is not uncommon for people to refer to ceremonies as being opposed to 'work', it being problematic to stage major ceremonies whilst simultaneously engaging in large-scale work projects, such as Brazil nut collection or gold extraction (*garimpagem*), to obtain cash for purchasing Western goods. Although this was one of the reasons given to me for explaining the lack of ceremonies in certain periods, in others it was the resources generated through a monetary income that were channelled into the performance of major ceremonies, such as the Bemp held in Gorotire in 1983, east of the Xingú river (Lea 1984).

I wish to refute Turner's argument (1979*a*/*b*) that older men control younger men through uxorilocality, which ensures that their daughters remain living with them, along with their husbands and children. Rivière (1984) considers that this argument throws light on the social structure of the Guiana region, where a settlement is consolidated around its founding leader to the extent that he manages to maintain his sons-in-law residing within his community, along with married sons. Rivière (1984: 91, 93, and *passim*) was inspired by Turner (1979*a*/*b*) in formulating his characterization of the 'political economy of people' in the Guianas, where it is not land or protein which constitutes limiting factors but rather the people who can be impinged upon to hunt and to process garden produce, thereby helping to create and sustain viable settlements. It is my contention that Turner's model (1979*a*/*b*) may serve to elucidate the social organization of the Guianas more than it does for the Mẽbengokre, for whom the model was originally intended. For the Mẽbengokre, it is the eldest female uterine member of a matrihouse who is the key figure around whom a household is formed. Men come and go, through marriage, divorce, and death. When a woman is divorced, at her own instigation or that of the husband, her children remain with her, along with the in-marrying husbands of her daughters. The fact that widowed or divorced men always tend to remarry means that even those men who do attain the status of father-in-law are often obliged to leave the house of their daughters and sons-in-law, to move into the house of their latest wife. When they remarry, older men may become classificatory fathers-in-law in relation to the sons-in-law of their latest wife, but this may occasion their stepdaughters to move out of their mother's house, setting up a new house alongside that of the mother.

MATRI-UXORILOCALITY

This brings me to the object of this chapter, which is to examine Mẽbengokre residential patterns. I argue that Turner (1979*a*) is correct in designating the residential norm as matri-uxorilocality rather than merely as uxorilocality,[4] as is customary in the anthropological literature on the Jê, for the ideal is to live with the wife in the house of her mother and not merely in the wife's place. In other parts of lowland South America, uxorilocality refers to the fact that a husband should live in his wife's village, together with her parents, performing bride-service for a certain number of years. Most Mẽbengokre marry someone within the village where they reside and so matri-uxorilocality entails a man moving into the house of his wife's mother. If the latter is dead, then the husband, even if living neolocally, should live in that portion of the village circle traditionally allocated to his wife's matri-house. The fact that residential continuity between a mother and her daughters is more important than the role played by the father-in-law is compatible with the key institution of Mẽbengokre matri-houses (or Houses) that I have described in more detail elsewhere (1986, 1995).

There is a huge variation in Mẽbengokre household composition. The ideal household, in terms of quality of life, characterized by abundance of food, is constituted by a married couple with their daughters and unmarried sons, married daughters' husbands and daughters' children. In practice, households are frequently headed by divorced, widowed, or remarried women. Married sisters and their children ideally live together, and in fact frequently do so; alternatively, they live in neighbouring houses. If there is lack of space to accomplish this, or if there is animosity between sisters or matrilateral parallel cousins, then they may live temporarily or permanently in a different portion of the village circle. Nevertheless, they continue to regard themselves, and to be regarded by others, as belonging to the same matri-house. During the period studied, there were various cases of separated or widowed sisters, along with their children, living together with married ones. There were several cases of married brothers living with married sisters, usually when the brother's mother-in-law was dead, living in a distant village, or a foreigner.[5] There were a number of nuclear families (see Fig. 8.1), when a woman lacked a living mother or sister. Elderly widowed men sometimes remain living with their daughters temporarily, until they remarry or die. They tend to spend much time in the men's house, even sleeping there at night, due to the fact that once their wife is dead they are deprived of their *raison d'être* for continuing to live at that house. The matrilateral weighting of kin classification is attested to by calculations such as a woman residing with a classificatory mother who is her MMZD.

With the demise of residence in the men's house on the part of adolescent men, youths are now taking up residence with their wife before the birth of their first child, or between the death of the first child and the birth of a subsequent one. Turner (1966) mentions that at the time he began fieldwork, in the 1960s, such men only entered the wife's house surreptitiously after dark, being sure to leave by daybreak and thus being invisible to all but the wife. This is no longer the case. Given the high rate of both mortality and divorce, many men end up living with wives who have already had children by a previous marriage, though they may continue to have further children with the latest husband.

Together with the core members of the household there is frequently found a fringe of other relatives and visitors. This fringe includes adopted members, children fostered to an elder relative, putative members of the matri-house in question, the odd relative from the same House or from another House (such as the children of a dead sibling or other orphans), half or step-siblings, the elderly widowed men

TABLE 8.1. *Proportion of Mẽtyktire married men with and without children*

Year	Married men with children with present wife	Married men without children with present wife	Total of married men
1978	30	6	36
1979	32	7	39
1981–2	34	6	40
1987	56	17	73
1994–5	80	18	99 (including 1 case without information)

already mentioned, children of an in-marrying male whose mother has died, the occasional affine of this fringe, and grandchildren whose mother has died and father remarried.

Between 1978 and 1982 the number of Mẽbengokre houses in the village studied (Kretire) grew from 19 to 23. When the inhabitants of this village joined up with those of Jarina, the number of houses totalled 31 in 1987. In 1994, after a further village fission, there were 14 Mẽbengokre houses and two Tapayuna houses in the village of the von Martius waterfall with a population of 205 people, and 27 Mẽbengokre houses plus one Tapayuna house in the village of the Kapoto with a population of 337 people. The Mẽtyktire population has grown steadily since fieldwork was begun in the late 1970s, despite the precarious health situation provoked by malaria, tuberculosis, and sexually transmitted diseases.

In 1978 the population of Kretire was slightly larger than the population of the village of Jarina. These two villages totalled the whole of the Mẽtyktire subdivision of the Mẽbengokre, which merged together in a single village around the mid-1980s. The schism that later took place continues as registered in 1994–5. Totalling all the periods researched, the predominant household pattern was one covering

TABLE 8.2. *Population of Mẽtyktire villages*

Year	Village	Population
1978	Kretire	155
1979	Kretire	162
1981–2	Kretire	184 + Tapayuna
1987	Mẽtyktire	369 + Tapayuna
1994	cachoeira von Martius	205
1995	Kapoto	337
1994–5	cachoeira and Kapoto	542 (incl. approx. 40 Tapayuna)

three generations (66 houses). Not far behind were houses covering two generations (52 houses). Only a minority of houses attained the size of four generations
(17 houses). In 1978 there was one woman alive who had a great-great-grandchild,
entailing the coexistence of five generations within her family. Household size
ranges from a minimum of 2 members to a maximum of 25, with the majority (63
houses) in the 6–10 range, and with a fair proportion (34 houses) in the 11–15
range. Of the total of 136 houses studied, there were 22 houses with between 2 and
5 members, 11 with 16–20 members, and 6 with 21–25 members. Despite the
demographic imbalance between Houses, anything from one to eight houses representing a single matri-house in a particular village, only two cases were found of
marriage within a matri-house.[6]

In terms of those who constitute the inhabitants of a Mẽbengokre household,
what you see is not always what you get. At first glance, on the basis of relative age,
one appears frequently to encounter typical nuclear families made up of adult
couples and their children. When delving deeper, one discovers that a number of
these families are what I have termed 'composite nuclear families', for want of a
better term, constituted by married couples with some of the children being the
mother's by one or more previous marriages and only the younger siblings being
the children of the mother's present husband.[7] Occasionally, men take children by
a previous marriage to live with their present wife, but in all such cases (with only
one exception) the mother of these children was dead. The figures for married
men whose co-resident children are their own is doubtless exaggerated because
every time that I returned to this question I discovered more cases of children
whose apparent father was the pater but not the genitor. Women were sometimes
reluctant to admit this and often did so only because I questioned them about it
explicitly, having obtained the information elsewhere. In various cases, the women
concerned asked me not to reveal this fact in the census that I was elaborating,
requesting me to list the children in question as those of their present husband. I
came across two cases of women having children with a lover whilst remaining
married to their husband. I also discovered at least three cases of men having chil-

TABLE 8.3. *The children Mẽtyktire men live with*

Year	No. of married men whose co-resident WC = their C	No. of married men whose WC are not all their own C	No. of married men with C by a former marriage living with their present W
1978	26	4	1
1979	27	5	1
1982	28	7	1
1987	39	23	6
1994–5	62	21	3 (& 2 grandchildren)

dren outside their marriage whilst remaining married to their wife. One man commented that this practice used to be much more common in the past.

Between 1978 and 1979 various households had one or more adopted adolescents of either sex living with them, mainly Panará. In later censuses these numbers dwindled as they married, the men living uxorilocally and the women living with their adopted family, the husband's family, or neolocally. There was one case of an adopted[8] Machipu from the upper Xingú who had been rejected by its mother, and two cases of one of a pair of twins being adopted out by its parents. Adoption is distinct from fostering. In the latter case, a child is brought up by an elder relative: MM, FM, FZ, etc., with whom it lives during childhood, but it is still regarded as the child of its parents and later returns to live with them if a girl.[9] In the past, during the course of warfare, small children of those attacked were taken captive, whilst men were murdered and women were taken captive if they did not put up great resistance; if they did resist and were difficult to abduct back to a Mēbengokre village, then they were killed and their small children taken captive.

With the demise of warfare, new strategies have evolved to enlarge the population. One was the large-scale adoption of Panará in the late 1970s. Subsequent to this was the incorporation into the village of the small group of Tapayuna who fled from the Suyá village in the 1980s, after the murder of one of their leaders in that village. Apart from the few who had already intermarried with the Mēbengokre, the rest resided in two separate houses within the village of the von Martius waterfall, and in one house at the Kapoto village. Within the new setting of the Xingú Park, created in 1961, individual members of other indigenous groups have gradually intermarried with the Mēbengokre. The number of foreign wives is slightly higher than that of foreign husbands for, when they come to live in a Mēbengokre village, they offer the advantage of acquiring a spouse without simultaneously acquiring parents-in-law with whom the husband is expected to reside.

The few men most closely linked to national society, the *capitão*[10] and FUNAI (National Indian Foundation) wage-earners, appeared to employ one of two strategies to avoid the burden of affines. Either they married a foreign girl (a Trumai or Tapayuna), or a powerless Mēbengokre orphan, with neither parents nor siblings, with whom they lived neolocally either at the Post[11] or within the village, in the space traditionally allocated to the wife's matri-house. Women who bear only male children are doomed, theoretically, to a lonely old age, living on their own or with their aged husband. In the one case of this type, the strategy used to forestall this was for the woman concerned to adopt a Panará who married her son. This enabled the woman to maintain her son in her house from the start of my fieldwork until today. The *capitão* and his wife, and several other families, managed to maintain married sons living with them by similarly marrying them to orphans, though with the one exception, already mentioned, this proved to be a temporary arrangement. Although matri-uxorilocality is predominant, it is no longer a mechanical norm, although it is impossible to tell whether it in fact used to be in the past.

It has been fairly consensual in the anthropological literature (see, for example,

164   *Vanessa Lea*

TABLE 8.4. *Foreign husbands and wives*

Year	Wives	Husbands
1978	Panará 2	Tapirapé 1
	Trumai 1	
1979	Panará 2	Tapirapé 1
	Trumai 1	Panará 2
1981–2	Panará 4	Tapirapé 1
	Trumai 1	Panará 2
	Tapayuna 2	
1987	Panará 4	Tapirapé 1
	Tapayuna 2	Panará 3
		Kayabi 1
1994–5	Panará 4	Tapirapé 1
	Tapayuna 2	Panará 2
	Trumai/Waurá 1	Tapyuna 1
		Kayabi 1

R. Fox 1967 and Gough in Schneider and Gough 1961) that matrilineal societies tend to be disrupted by contact with Western civilization and this doubtless also applies to the Mẽbengokre with their matri-houses.[12] There is a tendency for people who would once have supposedly lived under the one roof to nowadays live next door to one another, and internal divisions have now been constructed in a few houses to separate one or more nuclear families from the rest of the household. One such case involved a dead sister's daughter's family who moved out of the house of her matrilateral parallel cousins to live neolocally with her husband and their children. The introduction of wage earners, linked to the National Indian Foundation (FUNAI), is contributing to this process. One of these wage earners, who moved out of his wife's father's house to the Post (her mother being dead), explained to me that this made it easier to separate out what belonged to him from what belonged to his wife's father. Non-Indian visitors to Mẽbengokre villages automatically refer to the houses as belonging to the eldest male resident as opposed to the female resident; inadvertently this is one of numerous factors contributing to the demise of the matri-houses.

The prominent role played by women within Mẽbengokre society is not merely symbolic, deriving from the fact that matri-houses trace their existence back through a line of uterine ascendants. In practical terms, they play a significant role as household heads, with or without husbands. In 1995 there were three female widowed or divorced heads of households who had occupied this same role since I first knew them in 1978, that is, for seventeen years. Two other women who had also been household heads since 1978 remained unmarried until their death between 1987 and 1994. In 1978, over a quarter of houses (26%) were headed by women (see Table 8.5). There was a small decrease in 1979 and 1981–2, increasing

TABLE 8.5. *Female-headed houses*

Year	Total no. of houses	No. of female-headed households	% of female-headed households
1978	20	7	26
1979	21	6	22
1981–2	23	6	21
1987	31	9	23
1994–5	42	8	16
Total 1978–95	137[a]	36	21

[a] When calculating generations per house I counted 135 houses, omitting two Tapayuna houses for which data were lacking. There was in fact a total of 141 houses, including the Tapayuna ones just mentioned, and a third Tapayuna house (in 1995) for which there are some data. The range of inhabitants per house included 136 houses for which there were data.

again to 23 per cent in 1987, then decreasing to 16 per cent in 1994–5. This shows that it is viable for women to head households without a male partner and that there are insufficient men available to ensure that the oldest women in the community have the chance to remarry.

Previously I had pondered over the fact that no widower remains unmarried for long whereas various widows do. Initially I interpreted this as disinterest on the part of older women to remarry. When I asked one of them about this situation she retorted laughingly: 'And who am I to marry?' I was able to verify from my data that due to the fact that men tend to marry women younger than themselves, there ends up being a contingent of unmarried older women for whom it is impossible to find a new partner. Of the six female household heads that I knew in 1978, none of them later remarried. By 1995 two had died and one was living with her sister and sister's husband.

In Turner's model of the development cycle of Jê and Bororo domestic groups (1979a) it is implied that marriage is 'until death us do part', and the standard pattern is for young sons-in-law to be living with the wife's parents until the parents-in-law become old and weak, leading them to become economically dependent upon their daughters and sons-in-law, whereupon the sons-in-law are themselves attaining the status of father-in-law in their own right, replacing their own father-in-law. It is interesting to compare this model with the statistical results of my own fieldwork concerning who married men were living with in the period studied (1978–95).

Given the high mortality rate and divorce rate, coupled with the fact that divorced men, even if they do have one or more sons-in-law by a deceased or divorced wife, forfeit the right to reside with them when they remarry, as they inevitably do, then it is hardly surprising to find that a very small number of men who become a father-in-law or wife's mother's husband will simultaneously be living with their own wife's father (column V of Table 8.6b). However, even when

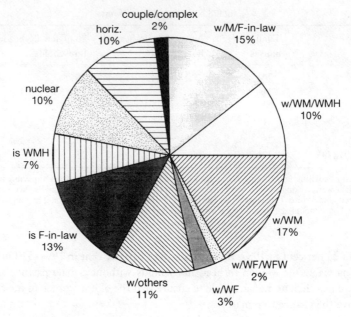

FIG. 8.1. Residence patterns of married men

Key:
The chart summarizes available information for the sum of data between 1978 and 1995.
w/M/F-in-law: with parents-in-law.
w/WM/WMH: with the wife's mother and wife's mother's husband (who is not the wife's father).
w/WM: with the wife's mother.
w/WF/WFW: with the wife's father and wife's father's wife.
w/WF: with just the wife's father.
w/others: with other elder relatives (see Table 8.6a, column VII).
is F-in-law: men who are co-resident fathers-in-law to their daughters' husbands. Married men resid-
    ing with their parents (thus parents-in-law to their wives), their mother, father, father's wife, etc.,
    are listed in Table 8.6a, column VII; it was a temporary arrangement in all but one case.
is WMH: a man who is the husband of the wife's mother, but not father of the wife.
nuclear: nuclear families. There were fourteen simple nuclear families and fourteen composite nuclear
    families. The latter includes families with mutual children of the husband and wife, together with
    children of another father/s, plus two cases of adopted children, and one case of male adolescents
    (who would formerly reside in the men's house) living with a nuclear family at the Post. There were
    also two cases of one child of a couple being fostered out to another house, leaving the child's
    nuclear family incomplete.
horiz.: 'horizontal spreading'. This term refers to families which are not headed by elder relatives or
    affines of married men. Of the thirty cases in this category (and one unclear one), seventeen refer
    to men residing with one or more of the wife's sisters, and in three cases men resided with their own
    sister/s. The remaining 10 cases involve half- or step-sisters, or a wife's half- or step- brother or
    sister, one case of the husbands of Panará cousins, and two cases of classificatory sisters (matrilat-
    eral parallel cousins, of first and second degree).
couple/complex: 2 couples, one of them with several unmarried men (who would have lived in the
    men's house in former times). Four cases were classed as 'complex' in that they involved three
    generational ramifications of composite nuclear families. They are composed of men with and with-
    out children (and children's children) of their own, living with children and daughter's children of
    their wife, with or without mutual children of the couple in question.

TABLE 8.6a. *Mẽtyktire married men living with affines or elder relatives*

I Year	II Lives with M + F- in-law	III Lives with WM + WMH	IV Lives with WM	V Lives with WF + WFW	VI Lives with WF	VII Lives with other elder rels.	VIII Total no. of married men
1978	4	3	10 (incl. 1 WMZ)	0	3	1 (with M)	36
1979[a]	4	4	8	0	4	3 (2 = M; 1 = F)	39
1981–2	5	6	8 (incl. 1 WMZ)	0	0	2 (1 = M + F 1 = M)	40
1987	11	8	14	3	0	12 (2 = M + F 4 = M[b] 1 = MMZ 1 = F + FW 4 = complex[c])	73
1994–5	19	9	11 (incl. 1 WMMZD = 'WM' & 3 WMZs = 'WM')	2	1	17 (incl. 6 F + M[d] 3 M[e] 1 'M' 2 M/MH[f] 1 WFZ/ WFZH 1 FM/FF 2 WMM/ WMF 1 WMF/ WMFW)	99
Total	43	30	51	5	8	33	287

Notes:

    II: Men living with both their mother and father-in-law.
    III: Men living with their wife's mother and wife's mother's husband.
    IV: Men living with just the wife's mother.
    V: Men living with their wife's father and wife's father's wife.
    VI: Men living with just their wife's father.
    VII: Men living with other elder relatives (each particular case is specified within this column).
    VIII: The total number of married men in each census.

[a] There were quite significant changes between 1978 and 1979 in the internal composition of houses.
[b] One man's Panará parents-in-law lived with him and his mother.
[c] This category includes men living with foreign wives, or wives who have lost their mother, along with elder relatives of the wife.
[d] Two cases were temporary, one due to the father's illness, and one husband planning to move to his mother-in-law's in the near future, upon the completion of her new house.
[e] In one case a man's Panará mother-in-law lived with his own mother.
[f] One case was temporary.

TABLE 8.6b. *Men who are co-resident fathers-in-law (or WMH) to daughter's husband, residing with or without elder affines*

I Year	II Total no. of married men	III Is himself a co-resident F-in-law to DH[a]	IV Is a WMH	V Fs-in-law & WMHs living with WF (+ WM or WFW)	VI Fs-in-law & WMHs living with just WM
1978	36	4	3	1	0
1979	39	6	3	1	0
1981–2	40	4	4 (incl. 1 WMZH)	0	0
1987	73	10	5	2 (incl. 1 with WM + WF; 1WF + WFW)	1
1994–5	99	15 (excl. 4 non-co-resident Fs-in-law)	5	1 (with WM + WMH)	3 (incl. 1 WMZ = 'WM')
Total	287	39	20	5	4

Notes:

III: Men who are co-resident fathers-in-law in relation to the daughter's husband.

IV: Men who are the wife's mother's husband (classificatory father-in-law) in relation to daughter's husband.

V: Fathers-in-law, either real or classificatory (alone, or along with the wife's mother or wife's father's wife, as the case may be), who simultaneously still live with their own father-in-law.

VI: Fathers-in-law (real or classificatory) who continue to live with just their own wife's mother. Columns V and VI show the nine instances of people who appear in two categories simultaneously in the various tables.

[a] Fathers-in-law and mothers-in-law to sons' wives can be calculated via column VII of Table 8.6a.

comparing the proportion of fathers-in-law who reside with their sons-in-law with the total number of married men, in any one period, it can be seen that it is very small (columns II and III of Table 8.6b), 4 out of 36 married men in 1978, 10 out of 73 in 1987, and 15 out of 99 in 1994–5. This proportion increases only a little if one includes men who are wife's mother's husband (Table 8.6b, column IV).

When one compares the single most significant category of elder affines or other elder relatives with whom married men reside, the majority, in all but the 1994–5 sample, is the wife's mother (Table 8.6a, column IV). The figures include

TABLE 8.6c. *Summary of Table 8.6a*

I Year	II Men living with WM (cols. II, III, IV of Table 8.6a)	III Men living with WF (cols. II, V, VI of Table 8.6a)	IV Men living with W'F' (= WMH, col. III of Table 8.6a)	V Men living with WF or W'F' cols. III & IV of this table)
1978	17	7	3	10
1979	16	8	4	12
1981–2	19	5	6	11
1987	33	14	8	22
1994–5	39	22	9	31
Total	124	56	30	86

Notes:
II: The total number of men living with the wife's mother.
III: The total number of men living with the wife's father.
IV: The total number of men living with the wife's mother's husband.
V: The total number of men living with either the wife's father or wife's mother's husband.

six cases of classificatory mothers-in-law, that is, five cases of a WMZ and one of a WMMZD. This makes sense in terms of the continuity of the matri-houses. If one compares the number of married men living with their father-in-law or with their mother-in-law (Table 8.6c), the importance of the latter far outweighs the former in all periods examined. Even if wives' fathers are lumped together with wives' mothers' husbands, they are still far outweighed by the wife's mother in terms of who married men live with.[13] It can be seen in Fig. 8.1 that 42 per cent of married men live with their wife's mother (either alone (17%), or along with her daughter's father (15%) or current husband (10%)). Of the men who are either widowed or remarried, only 5 per cent live with their married daughters, and only when the latter have lost their mother.

In the light of the overwhelming importance of the Mẽbengokre mother-in-law, Turner's claim (1979*b*) that men dominate women, who occupy a lower level of the social structure, deserves reconsideration. My research contradicts Turner's image (1979*b*) of the domineering father-in-law as the central figure of the uxorilocal household. He also claims (1979*b*) that society is welded together by male communal institutions, based in the men's house at the village centre, which he opposes to the atomistic nature of the domestic houses on the village 'periphery'. Whilst it is correct that divergent factional interests are played off against one another in the men's house, where all adult males converge to decide the outcome of collective interests, his portrayal of men constituting the superstructure of society, in opposition to women, who constitute the infrastructure, is misleading.

In the last decade or so, gender studies have shown that the old see-saw view of who dominates society, men or women, is anachronistic. Men may dominate in the realm of external affairs and in the establishment of relations with non-Indians, but this does not entail that men dominate women per se. The modern substitute for warfare, hence a male activity, is relations with non-Indians based on negotiation (with the government or NGOs). William and Jean Crocker (1994: 123) may have exaggerated when they talked of the virtual enslavement of Canela sons-in-law by their mothers-in-law, but this claim may at least lend some credence to what has been argued in this chapter concerning the key role of the Mẽbengokre mother-in-law.

Turner argues that: 'the extended-family household is not the primary setting for the realization and expression of the hierarchy of dominance and subordination generated in it' (1979*a*: 167). He claims that it is the trek, organized for accumulating game for the feast that accompanies the closure of naming ceremonies, that allows men to assert their dominance, since the father-in-law takes along his wife, daughters, and their husbands, 'regardless of the collective group affiliation of the sons-in-law' (1979*a*: 178). Nowadays, however, all the men tend to go off on trek together and the women do not necessarily accompany them at all, and so treks do not lead to the temporary breaking up of the household. Turner notes that a man with three sons-in-law does not necessarily have more status than one with no sons-in-law for:

Any man of the age-grade at which he would, other things being equal, be expected to attain the status of 'wife's father' and household head can, as it were, capitalize upon the generalized status and prestige accruing to his age-grade.   (1979*a*: 160)

This is important because one can argue, on the basis of this observation, that what is at stake is in fact a hierarchy of age-grades, while the fact of being a father-in-law or not is of indirect relevance. As I have noted elsewhere (Lea 1986), there is a hierarchy of age based on an empirical conception of knowledge. The older one is the more one has learnt from direct experience and hence the more knowledgeable one is. This is clearly marked in speech by the use of the morpheme *we* which must be appended to all statements which were reported to one by others, thus clearly separating what one has witnessed with one's own eyes from that which has been learnt indirectly through other people. The age hierarchy is still important, although it is gradually being undermined by young men who possess valuable knowledge about the Western world, such as speaking Portuguese, knowing how to drive tractors, motor boats, etc., and being able to earn wages as employees of the national Indian foundation.

In sum, matri-uxorilocality makes sense in terms of being instrumental to the continuity of the matri-houses and does not entail male dominance. When Turner claimed that women 'remain together by simple inertia' (1979*a*: 178), he had entirely overlooked the significance of these matri-houses. Maybury-Lewis makes a similar mistake when he claims that: 'The supposed matriliny of the Northern Gê is thus a misinterpretation based on the cumulative effects of uxorilocality'

(1979*b*: 304). In reality, Mĕbengokre uxorilocality is matrifocal and amounts to far more than a mere residential rule for it is embedded in the institution of the matri-houses, which it serves to perpetuate.

MĚBENGOKRE MATRI-HOUSES (OR HOUSES)

Since (matri-)uxorilocality is taken as one of the defining features of the Jê social structure, occupying pride of place in Terence Turner's model of Jê societies, this led me towards a reinterpretation of the significance of this residential rule. I believe that I have finally understood the discrepancy between my perspective and that of Turner, and that it is a question of the paradigm used. It is not, as some have tried to suggest (see Gordon 1996 for example), that Turner represents the male viewpoint and myself the female viewpoint, fruit of my concentration on the women. He views Mĕbengokre society through the prism of a mixture of Fortes and feminist debates in the 1970s (besides the influences made explicit in his bibliography), which posited the universality of male domination due to the fact that women were constrained to the domestic sphere, whereas the men occupied the public sphere. Fortes's (1969: 89) characterization of the jural domain as relating to rights, duties, and privileges, applies perfectly to Mĕbengokre matri-houses, defined in terms of rights of ownership of jealously guarded and fought over wealth items—personal names, ceremonial roles and prerogatives. Each matri-house (or House) occupies a fixed position in relation to East and West, acts as an exogamic unit, with mythological ascendants and an array of symbolic wealth items. This involves a pie-chart-like model of the universe, in the sense of a Mĕbengokre representation of an ideal total village in which cultural attributes and even some physical ones, like the pupils of the eyes, and biological processes like death, are attributed to the ancestors of present-day Houses.

It is curious that with all the interest in ethnohistory in the last couple of decades there has been so little attention given to genealogies as a source of a society's relationship to its past. The insistence on the categorial aspect of kin terms has overshadowed their genealogical significance. For the Mĕbengokre, genealogies show the paths that names follow, linking the living to dead ascendants, known and unknown, stretching back to mythological times. To deny them their interest in their ancestors is to flatten out their social world as if it were composed only of the living. Stories of the dead, the wars they waged and their vendettas, are recounted by elders in the men's house. They are essential to explain who the Mĕtyktire are as opposed to the Mĕkrãnoti, Gorotire, and Xicrin (other Mĕbengokre subgroups).

There has been much insistence in the anthropological literature on the fact that descent is an imported concept which may distort the reality of lowland South America. However, I can find no other word in the English language to convey what I gloss as 'descent'. For the Mĕbengokre, as for other Jê, genealogies are conceived as upside down (from our point of view). Uterine lines are like plants which sprout upwards and outwards, as descendants multiply. It would be pedantic to designate this as 'ascent'. As Goldman aptly put it: 'descent is a concept of the generative process and of the succession and differentiation of emerging generations' (Goldman 1977: 175).

Mẽbengokre society occupies the interstices of classical typologies, resembling a Venn diagram. Matri-houses are like clans, but emphasis is laid on Houses occupying a specific space, with a heritage of names and prerogatives rather than biological links to a founding ancestor. Uterine relatives in other villages are conceived of as members of the same House rather than as founders of separate lineages.

The Mẽbengokre also have submerged patrilines which do not entail double descent because one has nothing in common with other members of one's line, besides sharing ceremonial obligations to determined others. Patrilines thus act vicariously, defining formal friends, classified as non-relatives, for whom one must perform ceremonial services, and designating ideal marriage partners. As a woman, I preferably marry my daughter to one of my formal friends, inherited patrilineally. To the extent that there is continuity, this process involves patrilines, submerged in relation to the Houses, for the latter are manifest in the position that their members occupy in the village circle. Gregor (1977) described the plaza of a Mehinaku village as a stage. Its layout is similar to that of the Mẽbengokre villages. My contention is that it is as if Turner and others mistook the actors on stage for the scriptwriters, authors of their own lines. When the men occupy the centre of the patio (or plaza), during the performance of the great name confirmation ceremonies, their roles and their adornments are defined by their inherited wealth, rights to which pertain exclusively to the matri-houses. In this sense, the Houses encompass the ceremonial stage, for their heritage dictates who does what. It is the ritual complementarity of the matri-houses, rather than male institutions, which sews society together. The vocabulary of 'domination' and 'control' which forms the basis of Turner's model produces a distorted picture. That women should remain for ever in the household where they are born constitutes doxa from the Mẽbengokre point of view. It is what women have always done as far as can be remembered, bar a few exceptions. Turner's presupposes the validity of Fortes's life cycle model with, in Turner's depiction, dominated sons-in-law eventually substituting their father-in-law as household head. Data collected by me show that men are more likely to end up living with their mother-in-law than with their father-in-law, leading me to conclude that the father-in-law is not the key figure in uxorilocal residence.

Men discuss matters of collective interest in the men's house, but the orchestration of society occurs during ceremonies, when each matri-house contributes its distinctive pieces (roles, songs, and adornments) to the jig-saw of which any particular ceremony is comprised. The living congregate in the plaza in an act of village-wide commensality during the feast that marks the culmination of any major ceremony. The dead occupy the houses which must consequently be avoided by the living. The latter sit or lie down in a circle, and the active celebrants occupy the innermost circles of dancers and singers. This is supremely aesthetic because it produces a totality, like the body of the tapir, whose meat is divided up amongst all the Houses according to hereditary claims to ownership of determined cuts. The tapir provides an apt metaphor for my model of Mẽbengokre society, formed by interlocking parts which produce a whole. In this sense, the symbolic significance of women is eminently collective; their uterine lines attest through myth to all the cultural attributes which define the specificity of Mẽbengokre society: fire from the jaguar, agriculture from Venus, ceremonial leadership from a bat-boy, beautiful names from a man who went to live with the fish, and so forth.

CONCLUSION

Strathern has noted (1988: 68 and *passim*) that the domaining of gender ends up equating women with domesticity per se, in terms of their sociality.[14] Her criticisms of the public/private opposition, as it has been used in Melanesia, apply equally well to the stereotypical and hegemonic view of the Jê and Bororo, with men at the centre of society and the women on the periphery, next but one to nature. Strathern repeats the lesson that should already have been learnt from Dumont (1966), that in the absence of an autonomous economic sphere, separated from the domestic sphere, the latter is not necessarily denigrated as it has tended to be in Euro-American society. Strathern's notion of the partible person[15] helps to elucidate why the theft of names and prerogatives provokes such gut feelings amongst the Mẽbengokre. They constitute partible aspects of the person, metonyms of forebears who impregnate names, roles, and ornaments as they utilize them before passing them down the uterine lines embodied in the matri-houses. Rivière (1980) rightly suspected that the Harvard Central Brazil Project had left certain questions unanswered.

Strathern masterfully demolishes the divide between the public and the private domains, but replaces this with two types of sociality: ' "political" and "domestic", if what is understood is a contrast between collective action (based on shared identities and aims) and particular relations (based on the difference and interdependence between them)' (1988: 97). The dividing line between these contrasting types of sociality is nebulous amongst the Mẽbengokre, but this point cannot be dealt with at length here. I wish to conclude by agreeing with Rivière that the notion of personhood is insufficient as an analytical tool for understanding the Jê. Melatti (1970: 110) noted the exogamy of what he called 'segments', but this question did not receive the attention that it deserved in other Jê ethnographies. It is a fundamental aspect of the Mẽbengokre matri-houses. In sum, it is the ceremonial and matrimonial interdependence of the Houses that makes it necessary and desirable to live in villages, and the larger the better in terms of proximity to the ideal village, composed of all the Houses on either side of the Xingú river which divides the multi-village Mẽbengokre community.

Badinter (1992: 118–19) notes the parallel (that I have also noted 1994: 91) between the segregation and initiation of males into manhood in non-Western societies and British upper-class males, segregated at boarding schools where bullying constitutes a form of initiation. Sexual segregation is weakening to a certain degree in Mẽbengokre society, though it remains strong. Badinter's interpretation of segregation as a mechanism for defeminizing males in order to turn them into men, in other words, as part of the social construction of gender, seems to me to help to understand the significance of the men's house.[16] The matrihouses produce Mẽbengokre, but only men produce men, and they maintain their identity by avoiding over-exposure to femininity in the houses of their mothers and their wives, once they surpass the androgynous phase of early childhood spent in the company of their mother. At the end of life, gender evaporates and it is tolerated that very old men should spend most of their time at home, but few men live to reach this stage.

ACKNOWLEDGEMENTS

Research was carried out between 1978 and 1998 with the support of the CNPq, FINEP, and the Wenner-Gren Foundation. For comments on an earlier version, I wish to thank the Pagu Centre for the study of gender, UNICAMP, and my students in the first term of 1998. I thank the organizer of the festschrift, Laura Rival, and the University of Campinas, for making my participation possible, and the participants for their comments, especially the debater Stephen Hugh-Jones. And I thank Cambridge University Computing Service for assistance with Excel.

NOTES

1. I adopt the standard Brazilian spelling Jê, for it is not usual to translate names, but I maintain the spelling Gê in English quotations.
2. Overing (1981: 151–64) had equally rich insights concerning the Harvard Central Brazil Project, noting that its members had erroneously ignored the significance of alliance and had paid too little attention to genealogical data.
3. Turner supervised a doctoral thesis on the Panará, Southern Kayapó, wherein they are purported to have matri-clans and yet he does not acknowledge that he failed to notice the existence of Mẽbengokre matri-houses. Initially he denied their existence (1987, personal communication) but several years later he recognized that he had been mistaken about this, brushing it aside by claiming that the houses have acquired greater significance since contact, with the demise of warfare and other factors. I disagree entirely, for in my opinion contact with Western society is leading to a demise in the importance of the matri-houses, as W. Crocker (1994) noted with respect to the dominant position of women within Canela households.
4. Turner uses the term matri-uxorilocality in his model of Jê and Bororo societies (1979*a*) but reverts to 'uxorilocality' in his 1979*b* essay on the application of this model to the

Kayapó (Mẽbengokre). Charlotte Seymour-Smith (1986: 185), in the *Macmillan Dictionary of Anthropology*, distinguishes matrilocality and uxorilocality in the following way: 'Matrilocal postmarital residence is residence of the couple with or close to the wife's family, or more specifically the wife's mother. Matrilocality is not necessarily associated with matrilineality, and in order to avoid the confusion of the two concepts many anthropologists prefer to use the term UXORILOCAL which simply refers to residence "in the wife's place" and does not prejudge that the most important element of this residence pattern is coresidence with the wife's mother. The term "matri-uxorilocal" has also been employed to mean residence with the wife's mother or matrilineal kin group.'

5. Only one case was encountered of a sister sleeping occasionally at her brother's house, at the Post, to help out her foreign sister-in-law who often had guests for meals.

6. In one of these cases, the boy who married within his House was the descendant of a Xicrin immigrant, adopted by the matri-house in question.

7. Fig. 8.1 shows that 10% of dwellings housed nuclear families between 1978 and 1995. Of these 28 nuclear families, half were formed by parents and their children; the other half were of the composite type.

8. *Pa jamy*, literally 'arm to clutch', which can be glossed as 'those who have been clutched by the arm'.

9. One girl who was brought up by her MM lived in the same house as her biological mother but slept in the bed of her MM and accompanied the latter and not the mother during the course of daily chores.

10. The Portuguese word *capitão*, literally 'captain', designates the intermediary chief, appointed by non-Indians. The individual referred to ended up eclipsing the traditional leader in terms of prestige.

11. The FUNAI Post is nowadays built beside the village; in it are located the pharmacy, radio, school, and houses of administrative personnel (either non-Indian or Mẽbengokre).

12. Holy (1996: 102–15) considers that the mode of reckoning descent may simply shift in the direction of cognation or patrilineality.

13. The residual category (Table 8.6a, column VII) of other elder relatives with whom married men reside is numerically far less significant than that of the parents-in-law (real or classificatory). It includes the husband's own mother, own father, own parents, own mother's mother's sister, own father and father's wife, a wife's matri-house where her relation to the eldest female member of the house is unknown, and one complex case of a man living in the matri-house of the adoptive father of his Panará wife.

14. Eduardo Viveiros de Castro notes that the Jê and Tukano ethnographies: 'suggest a perspective which emphasizes a balance and a complex tension between the domains of masculinity and femininity, produced by hierarchical encompassments contextually specified, and by a symbolic division of labour where men and women, terms and relations, constantly transmute their values' (1985: 276; my translation).

15. Marilyn Strathern (communication in a seminar at UNICAMP University in October 1998) was inspired by Mauss in formulating this notion.

16. An anonymous reviewer made the following comment: 'The notion of segregation of males being a mechanism for defeminizing males was suggested long ago; most introductory anthropology textbooks mention this idea.' Whilst it is important to note that the idea in question was not new when formulated in Badinter's book, I maintain the

Vanessa Lea

reference to it, for it was that book which I read when considering Strathern's (1988) attempt to de-essentialize gender. In Mẽbengokre, the word 'men' (*mẽmy*) means 'penis people' (literally: prefix for a collectivity (*mẽ-*), and 'penis' (*my*), and the first question asked concerning a newborn child is its sex, therefore gender seems irreducible in the Mẽbengokre case. However, the connotations of biological differences is a complex theme which extends beyond the scope of this chapter.

9

Piercing Distinctions: Making and Remaking the Social Contract in the North-West Amazon

Janet Chernela, *Florida International University*

Anthropologists have long recognized ritual as a vehicle through which the group positions and defines its own identity vis-à-vis others. This chapter examines the role of ritual speech in orchestrating the proximity of social groups in the north-west Amazon of Brazil. It takes as its example the Eastern Tukanoan *bueyoaka*, one form of ritual speaking, in order to consider its role in the shaping of group identities and affinities. In doing so, the essay addresses the way boundary relations are produced and reproduced, established and negotiated through ceremonial speech.

The case of the Eastern Tukanoan-speakers of the north-west Amazon is of particular relevance to questions of group parameters, since there group boundaries are regarded by their memberships as fixed. In spite of these assumptions, this chapter will point to the ways in which reified boundaries, perceived as essential and permanent, are subject to realignment and redefinition through ritual.

TRACING THE ARGUMENT

In an essay written in honour of his mentor, Peter Rivière recalls Evans-Pritchard's definition of Nuer boundaries as the area beyond which feud becomes warfare (Rivière 1971a: 306; Evans-Pritchard 1940). The delineation brings into relief an essential fault line—the limit of moral commitment, beyond which there is no recourse to dispute. Nothing, that is, but warfare itself.

Considering boundary-related behaviour within the context of ceremonial greeting dialogues practised by the Waiwai (Fock 1963), the Trio, and other societies of the northern Amazon basin, Rivière proposed that these forms of stylized greeting speech served as a strategy to prevent disputes in potentially disruptive situations:

In summary, the function of ceremonial dialogue is mediation in situations that are likely to give rise to conflict. Such situations are most likely to arise between those who are unrelated, and this fact is recognized by the increasing formality of the ceremonial dialogue in direct proportion to increasing social and physical distance. The boundary of the ceremonial dialogue is coterminous with Trio territory, and implies that its participants accept certain values and conventions. It is in the coincidence of Trio political and moral boundaries that the similarity between the feud and ceremonial dialogue is most apparent.　(Rivière 1971*a*: 306)

According to Rivière, then, Trio ceremonial dialogue signals diplomacy in cases of potential or perceived conflict. As such it may be regarded as a transformation of the feud, or an alternative to warfare. From this point Rivière proposes a generalized relationship between social distance and speech form, constructing the following heuristic: ceremonial dialogue will be 'used where there is an uncomfortable amount of social distance' (Rivière 1971*a*: 306). The choice of the term 'uncomfortable' as the modifier of distance suggests that the dialogic greeting speech of the northern Amazon is associated with ambiguous social processes such as the formation of new relationships or the resumption of old ones. Ceremonial dialogue, in this sense, then, appears to be an expression of solidarity in contexts of potential fragmentation. To quote Rivière, 'The Trio conception of ceremonial dialogue . . . is . . . a means by which they express . . . their political unity' (1971*a*: 310, n. 21), a 'mediation in situations that are likely to give rise to conflict' (1971*a*: 306).

Today speech style and related structures of participation are recognized for the active role they play in shaping socio-political formations (see, for example, Duranti and Goodwin 1992). However, Rivière's article, preceding by fifteen years a discourse-centred approach to culture (Sherzer and Urban 1986) with its specific treatment of dialogic greeting speech (Urban 1986, 1988*b*), is early in suggesting correlates between greeting speech styles and social phenomena. This chapter builds on the propositions put forth by Rivière linking ritualized speech style to expressions of groupness and group relations. However, unlike other studies of greeting speech in Amazonia, it focuses not on static, but on shifting parameters that delimit distinctions between groups in a social field within which moral commitment may be both extended and withdrawn.

The *bueyoaka* is one of several speech events in the *po'oa*,[1] an exchange ceremony practised by the Wanano and other Eastern Tukanoan speakers in the Uaupés[2] basin of Brazil and Colombia. The term *bueyoaka* may be translated closely as 'the spear thing', since the Wanano term *bueyo* glosses as 'spear'. I refer to it here as 'Piercing Speech' in order to convey what I believe to be its broader semantic range. In this speech event, two agnatic descent groups engage in ceremonial insult and mock warfare. Although the ceremony is practised by speakers of many Eastern Tukanoan languages, my examples derive from ceremonial events in which the participating groups were speakers of the Tukanoan language Wanano. Members of each group consider those of the other to be classificatory brothers, yet the two groups belong to two distinct subgroupings of Wanano. Relations among these subgroupings, the Wamisima and the Wiroa, are ambiguous and strained. The case speaks to Rivière's concern with what he called 'intratribal' relations, particularly ones that may be described as tense or 'uncomfortable'.

LANGUAGE AND IDENTITY IN THE NORTH–WEST AMAZON

The area referred to as the north-west Amazon consists of the drainage basin of the Uaupés river and adjacent areas in Colombia, Venezuela, and Brazil. Groups belonging to the Eastern Tukanoan language family predominate in the area, although nearby Arawakan- and Cariban-speakers participate in the social system. Sorensen (1967, 1973) identifies thirteen languages as members of the Eastern Tukanoan language family, including Tukano, Tuyuka, Tatuyo, Barasana, Piratapuyo, Wanano, Desana, and Kubeo. Despite ongoing contact and a deliberate maintenance of distinct linguistic varieties characterized by separations that exceed those of the Romance group (Sorensen 1967, 1973), models of ethnic pluralism do not accurately describe the Eastern Tukanoan case. A number of factors, including a correspondence between linguistic performance and group membership, loyalty to the language of one's descent group, and marriage across language groups, serve to establish a single speech community in which numerous codes interact according to shared norms and beliefs. Each linguistic variety performs a social function, indexing group membership and kinship within a unified cultural system in which language is a primary icon of identity.[3] Gradations between varieties are backgrounded as each code is considered to be discrete and its speakers members of mutually exclusive groups. Although these relations reflect to some extent genetic proximities between linguistic codes, the named Eastern Tukanoan varieties that are regarded as commensurate with putative descent lines are considered by speakers to be sharply bounded. In this way language is employed to de-problematize group membership.

The recognized linguistic varieties constitute the fundamental social units of the region. Members of each variety conceive of themselves as part of a unilineal kin group, based upon common patrilineal ancestry that is manifest in language. I will call these linguistico-descent groups 'language groups' after Jackson (1974, 1976). Within the language group descent is coterminous with membership and manifest in linguistic performance (see also Goldman 1963, C. Hugh-Jones 1979, and S. Hugh-Jones 1979 for alternative nomenclature of equal validity).[4] The almost universal practice of linguistic exogamy[5] results in a uniquely coherent culture complex, with unilineal descent and cross-cousin marriage major integrating structural principles. In this large regional network, marital and kin ties unite some 14,000 Indians[6] of distinct languages over an area of approximately 150,000 square kilometres.[7]

DESCENT: THE *KOROA*

The Eastern Tukanoan system of classification supposes a nested hierarchy of inclusiveness based upon principles of patrilineal descent where the reference point at each level is a putative, named ancestor. The living reckon affiliation on the basis of descent from one patrilineal totemic ancestor who emblemizes or stands for his descendants. At each level of inclusiveness a different pivotal ancestor becomes relevant, and thus a different calculus of membership is applied. Starting at the lowest level of inclusiveness, an individual is a member of a descent group (also known as a patri-clan or sib), referred to as 'the children of X' where X is the founding ancestor. Residents of the settlements of a single sib are theoretically the children of the founding ancestor of that sib, and all of the sibs of a single language group consider themselves to be descended from a single focal ancestor.

The Wanano term *koroa* refers to an exogamous descent group of any level of magnitude, including language groups and their constituent sibs. Members of a *koroa* are said to be children, or descendants, of a founding ancestor. For the Wanano, the descent group, and its members, take their names from an ancestor's name combined with the suffix *-pona*, meaning 'children of'. By adding *-kûro* (masc.) or *-koro* (fem.), an affix denoting person, a member of the sib Biari Pona, for example, describes himself or herself as a Biari *ponakûro/ponakoro*, a Biari Pona man or woman, literally, a 'child of Biari'. The notion of *koroa* establishes an ingroup based upon the criterion of common descent from a named ancestor. Membership in *koroa* of any level is theoretically fixed and ascribed by birth. As such, membership is non-overlapping and boundaries may be described as 'impermeable'.

The language of kinship reflects the extent of the socio-political unit and defines the area within which familial sentiments and moral commitments prevail. *Koroa* membership is foregrounded, as those within the same *koroa* address one another through kin terms, with the generic *yü korokü/o*, my kinsman/kinswoman. In obvious contrast, members of descent groups other than one's own are referred to and addressed as *paye mahsa*, meaning 'other people'. These terms leave no ambiguity regarding the publicly recognized relatedness of any two interlocutors. A less clear-cut distinction characterizes the subgroups of a single language group.

The sibs of a single language group are thought to be descended from a set of ancestral brothers. The descendants of a first-born ancestral brother are of higher rank than the descendants of a second-born ancestral brother, the latter descendants of higher rank than the descendants of a third-born ancestral brother, and so on, accounting for the idealized ranked placement of all sibs. Forms of address reflect this order of seniority, expressed in metaphors of relative age. The logic an individual uses to calculate rank is simple: if the speaker's father called the father of the addressee 'older brother', then speaker calls addressee 'older brother'. Except in the case of the children of the same man, the use of age in this determination is metaphoric.

Time, space, and seniority are fused in the morphemes that signify sequential order. Thus the root *wa-* in the term *wa'mi*, older brother, is also found in the word *wa'manore*, 'before all else'. Terms indicating relative junior status, such as *bü'u*, 'younger brother', are related to the morphemes found in Wanano words *bü'aro*, meaning 'later', 'after', and 'back'. Exemplifying the linguistic merging of time and space, this morpheme denotes younger in time, lower in rank, and behind in space.

The Wanano report twenty-five sibs (this is likely to be an idealized construction). The first ten of these are known collectively as the Wamisima, literally, 'first', or eldest, brothers. Sibs eleven to fifteen are collectively termed *Tibahana*, 'younger brothers'. The remaining sibs are known as *Wiroa*, considered 'last'. In Brazil Wanano sibs are arranged along the river bank in uninterrupted, continuous territory, a situation that is somewhat unusual since the settlements of language groups are more often discontinuous. The order of seniority as well as the coherence of descent has its basis in cosmology in which Wanano sibs are descended from a set of ancestral brothers who emerged from the body of a primordial anaconda. From the segmented body of the ancestral anaconda, stretched eastward along the Uaupés River, emerged the founding ancestors of each Wanano sib, giving legitimacy to the locations of contemporary sib settlements and the fraternal relations between sibs. Sibs emerging from the head of the anaconda, the Wamisima, furthest downriver, are associated in the ideal with the attributions of the head, including 'leadership'. Sibs emerging from the tail, furthest upriver, are lower in rank. The conceptualization between rank and place holds in a general manner: the Tibahana are, in fact, upriver, and the Wamisima downriver. One outstanding exception to the rule is the downriver location of the Wiroa who reside among the Wamisima. The Wamisima are classified as grandchildren or chiefs, the Wiroa as grandparents or 'slaves'. A conceptualized pairing between grandchildren groups and grandparent groups should account for the relationships between the Wamisima Yahuri and the neighbouring Wiroa, local descent groups who are the exchanging parties in the ritual case discussed here.

In theory, two identifiers, language and common ancestry, conceptualized as transformations of one another, mark group membership. However, the Wiroa/Wamisima relation confounds this equivalence. While Wamisima, Tibahana, and Wiroa all speak Wanano, the origin of the Wiroa is said to be distinct from that of other Wanano. Although Wamisima and Tibahana sibs trace their origins to the bodily substance of the ancestral anaconda, a distinct origin is attributed to the Wiroa, who are said to derive from perching birds created by a powerful Wanano shaman. The separate Wiroa creation is recognized by them as well as all other Wanano, according the Wiroa a difference in substance from other Wanano.

Speculation arises, then, regarding the idealized cladistic nature of Tukanoan group identity and the perceived degrees of relatedness between Wanano constituent entities, the Wamisima, the Tibahana, and the Wiroa. All are speakers of Wanano, yet a difference, exemplified in the different cosmologies, is maintained and perpetuated. The linkages are reproduced, as is the looseness characterizing them and the ambivalences that accompany the intra-group relationship. The ambiguity in the relationship and the loose articulation among constituent units is resonant with Rivière's reference to intra-tribal 'discomfort' described for the Trio.

THE *PO'OA* AND PIERCING SPEECH

The *po'oa* is an exchange cycle carried out among sibs of different settlements, whether kin or in-law. The occasion of the *po'oa* marks life-cycle passages, such as naming, female puberty, male initiation, or marriage. More important than individual transition, however, is group transformation, as each *po'oa* entails a meta-commentary on the relationships of the two participating entities, constructing, and thereby, (re)defining each group's relatedness to the other.

The dramatic centre of the *po'oa* is the gift exchange in which a donor sib presents another with foodstuffs or specialized crafts. Most *po'oa* are returns for previous ones in which the donor/recipient roles were reversed. A *po'oa* is initiated by a male sponsor whom I refer to as the principal donor. Along with the headmen of each sib, he and the principal recipient preside over the event.

The principal donor suggests the ceremony to the headman of the local descent group, who mobilizes the sib members to collect and prepare the offerings. The group decides when to hold the *po'oa* and what to offer, although a receiving group that is owed may specify a preference. As a collective event, each donor sib accumulates goods and presents them in bulk to the receiving sib. Individual contributions are identical in kind, and whatever differences there may be in quantity or quality are ignored; the final product is a group offering. A group *is* what it gives, and its relationship to the receiving group is manifest in the prestation (Chernela 1993). Abundance conveys the generosity and goodwill of the offering group. The act of exchange may establish new relations, repair lapsed ones, or cement existing ones. The gift transfer of any one *po'oa* is part of an ongoing exchange, as the receiving group must reciprocate at a later date. Thus donors and recipients alternate roles ad infinitum so long as the relationship obtains. The language and comportment of the ritual is antagonistic, a reminder of the conditionality of the alliance. The *po'oa*, in this sense, stands for the relationship, and its relative stability.

THE CEREMONIAL ORDER AND TEXT

The texts[8] presented here were derived from field recordings collected during *po'oa* between 1978 and 1981 in Wanano villages along the middle *Uaupés* river in Brazil.[9] One *po'oa*, between a Wamisima and a Wiroa descent group, was selected as an example with which to consider Rivière's point regarding ritual language and intra-tribal relations. The *po'oa* of central concern here was recorded in April 1979, and unless otherwise indicated, all texts are from that ceremony. Three additional excerpts have other origins: one, from a different *po'oa*, and two elicited by me outside of any ceremonial context in order to provide a comparative perspective. These exceptional examples are indicated. Although I utilize the present tense, the specificity of the occasion described here should be kept in mind.

The po'limina: *the 'Giving Ceremony'*

Throughout the course of events several forms of exchange occur, forming an order of sub-prestations within the principal ceremonial. Piercing Speech is one of the modes of exchange known as the language exchanges (*dürüküa kototaro*). The performative frame of the *po'oa* begins at dawn on the specified day and follows an invariant order of seven named speech events that comprise the *po'limina*, the gift exchange portion of the ceremony. Within the prescribed performative score of each event there is substantial room for improvisation, as we will see.

1. *Buhsatise*: Adornment and Preparation

The donor group plans its journey so that it arrives in the village of the recipients shortly after dawn on the day of the *po'oa*. The donors pause in the shelter of the riverbank to paint and adorn themselves before entering the recipient village. Gathering in the large longhouse where the ceremony will take place, the residents too paint themselves. Men place *püsangü*, strands of fragrant vines on their hips and flowers behind their ears. The recipients then sit in ceremonial order along opposite walls of the longhouse to await the visitors. Two benches are left vacant where donors will sit.

2. *Po'osanse*: The Entrance of the Gifts

The gift-giving ceremony begins with the arrival of the visiting donors' convoy of communal canoes at the receiving village. Communal canoes, which are seen as belonging to sibs, may only be used with the approval of sib leaders, and are distinguished from the small canoes used in ordinary chores. Upon arrival donors remove the ritual paraphernalia and offerings from the canoes and place them along the river landing. Men form a procession around the gifts headed by two players of two-metre *toniapuku* flutes, followed by men with panpipes and horizontal flutes. The donors dance in two lines around their offerings in the space between the river and the ceremonial longhouse. From within, the seated recipients are able to hear the music but are unable to see the dancers.

3. *Suaduhpokane*: Exchange of Bad Language

Outside, the wives of the visiting donors join the men in dance. Each donor lifts a heavy offering basket by tump-line onto his or her back, and, thus laden with gifts, dances through the house entrance into the centre of the dance house. There the visitors are greeted with hoots and jeers from the seated recipients. The newly arrived donors reply in kind, and a boisterous, good-natured insult dialogue ensues.

In the April 1979 *po'oa* described here, the playful, mutual insulting took this form:

Recipients: That basket of fruit is too heavy for you—watch out or you'll fall down! [*This jeer simultaneously acknowledges the large size of the gift while teasing the giver for being too weak to carry it.*]

Donors: We're giving you a *po'oa*—it's YOU who will be the ones who fall down—dead drunk!

Recipients: Once you've had our beer, you'll say, 'Come and get me, old lady, I want to lie in the hammock with you, but you'll have to carry me!'

Donors: [calling a recipient by his nickname, Chicken pox]: Sicurure, you'll be chucking it up—vomiting, vomiting, vomiting! That's what we'll do to you. You'll fall on the ground, howling!

Recipients: Yeah, the children of Yahuri [*naming the sib's founding ancestor*] are few, but they drink a lot! When we run out of beer you'll have your heads deep inside the empty bowls, begging and pleading 'Bring us more!'

At a different *po'oa*, recorded in September 1979, the insult exchange took this form:

First Donor: Yeyeyeyeye, with seeds of *patawa* [palm fruit] so numerous we will keep her squatting [defecating]! We only brought the ugliest fruits. These are the leftovers. Bring a basket to carry a chicken [*playing on the nickname of one of the recipient sibs*]! Bring only your smallest baskets to carry these fruits—it wasn't easy to find them so we didn't bring very many!

Recipient: We are going to leave you all collapsed [drunk] in the corners, begging for more!

Recipient: We are going to leave Opossum [*nickname*] in the corner clutching Janet's tape recorder! [*My prominent tape recorder was in the care of the bearer of the nickname Opossum.*]

[*Much back-and-forth shouting*]

Donor: Oh, so you're playing with us? OK [*to sibmates*], put only two seeds in each basket ... [*To recipients*] Here, we searched for these little things because we didn't have anything else to do. Now you can throw them out.

Principal Recipient: We two groups appear to detest each other but we do this so we can live better. Yes, this is a lot of work.

As is clear from the two different examples of *suaduhpokane*, the commonality is ribaldry, manifest in the repeated use of pejorative nicknames and the mention of unflattering behaviour. The joking mocks both the donors, who describe their offerings as meagre, and the recipients, who are portrayed as unable to control their bodily functions. To much laughter, the recipients are described as vomiting and defecating; they cannot hold or keep their gift or drink, discharging these through unseemly bodily functions. Complementarily, the donors cannot give, instead, they 'keep', giving only the smallest or poorest items. The language turns the roles of donors, who should be generous givers, and recipients, who should be 'keepers', on their heads.

4. *Po'ose Nunonawema*: Keeping

In this section, involving the transfer of the gift, speaking is limited to the principal donor and the principal recipient, who ceremoniously occupy the centre. The recipient acknowledges the gifts. Returning to the *po'oa* of 28 April 1979:

Principal Donor: Yes, it's a nasty job to get these things: searching for them in the forest, trekking long distances, lugging them home. When the ancestors were alive, they did these things and enjoyed themselves, sitting in this very place . . . So, we brought these little things [*irony*]. Now, fill your bellies and throw the rest away!
Recipient: Yes. We'll take these little things. We'll take them and keep them.
Donors: Yeyeyeyeye! We are going to throw them at you!'

With the acceptance of the gifts, the donor men begin the anaconda dance, weaving and reversing directions, winding circles around the gifts. The women dance into and out of the circles five times. Their exit leaves the men standing in place around the baskets. The men halt, and, encircling their offering, call out, 'OOO, eee. OOO eee, yeyeyeyeye.' At this shout, the principal recipient and donor enter the centre of the dance house. Spontaneity gives way to conventional and formal statements. Standing on opposite sides of the gifts, the two speak to one another:

Recipient: Eh, *pukami* [father's older (or senior) brother], when our ancestors were still here, alive, making beer, all kinsmen were invited, shouting as they entered the house, taking a bench, placing it in its proper place, and then talking a long time . . . Afterward they drank beer, and talked more; This is how our forefathers lived and sat.[10]

These conventional lines are known by everyone, including the young, and are spoken simultaneously (the relationship terms change depending upon the relationships of the receivers and donors). Invoking the ancestors and the sameness of then-and-now ratifies or authorizes the contract about to take place. The principal recipient now reaches across the gifts to offer a calabash of beer to the principal donor. The wives of the principals, in place behind their foregrounded husbands, now extend reciprocal calabashes of beer to one another. At this point all recipients rise, each carrying a vessel of beer and a calabash ladle. They move along the line of donor men, giving beer to each one in turn.

Asmürë, the wife of the recipient headman enters the centre with a suddenness that breaks through the field of assorted sounds, and sends a long, nasalized, piercing tone throughout the dance house. It is the first phoneme of an utterance she projects across the space of seated spectators. Her pitch is high and frontal. Her phrase is in Tukano, her own language. As the spouse of the donor is also a Tukano speaker, the singer addresses the other as sister:

My sister, I will eat all that you have given me by your hard work. I will take it with me. I will take it, and cook as much as I want. Husband and brothers-in-law will eat; co-wives (*yemenikana*) will eat; we will keep all that you have made with your work.

The role of women, generally backgrounded in matters of the agnatic descent group, is here foregrounded. Asmürë's verse points not just to the men of the receiving descent group but to the in-marrying wives. She emphatically acknow-ledges the women of the donor group and their contribution.

5. *Bueyoaka*:[11] Piercing Speech

Donors and recipients now stand opposite one another, brandishing spears in threatening postures. At once they toss the spears into the ranks of the other. The so-called spears are in fact flexible saplings, without sharp points, and lacking the ability to inflict harm. The feigned tosses are accompanied by 'Piercing Speech', the vigorous and energetic language of accusation and battle. Men briskly pace back and forth, miming warfare by throwing spears haphazardly toward the oppo-site sib. There is some improvisation in these dialogues, allowing the names of groups to change, but the recitation of past wrongdoings against speaker's group is requisite.

In the April 1979 *po'oa* in which the participating sibs were Wamisima Yahuri and Wiroa, individuals shouted these words with punctuated rhythm:

Donor: The Kubeo are over there; these people are over there, and over there, they hate us. Knowing this, we will make puh of them! This Sirio that took my brother away, this Bu, he took my son, and this Wamüpo'nairo, made us suffer, raided us, and left us with noth-ing!

Donor and Recipient in unison: They did this to us, to our grandparents!

Donor: Long ago, before we were pitiable and frightened as we are today, in this place, every-one hated and envied the Wanano. This began long ago, during the time of our fore-fathers. Now we do exactly as our forefathers did. [*The objects of envy are the targets of sorcery.*]

Together the Wiroa headman, sponsor, and shaman, repeat what the donor has said. They wield their spears energetically. The headman of the donor sib speaks:

Donor Headman: This one, that carried off my grandfather, there, in that river, he wanted to end the Wanano. As my grandfathers were here, so am I here—the only Yahuri Ponairo of whom you say, 'Now enters the chief.' But I am not alone. I have my brothers [sibmates]. Seeing what they did to my forefathers, after the deaths of each one of them, I want to say to you: This chief, a Yahuri ponairo, speaks like this. I am here in your midst; you can kill me—I am mortal.

He continues, now joined by the principal donor, and addresses wrongdoings and atrocities committed by other Wanano.

Principal Donor with Headman: When the other came, and my parents were alive, my brother . . . spoke: Biari ponairo, our older [seniormost] brother, he belongs to that place [is the rightful resident of that site] but that Bü'ü nairo [member of lower-ranked sib], and many others captured our grandfathers and forced them out. So they say. Now we are mixed up. They took our grandfathers and kicked them out. They despised our grandfathers. The people who did that had dangerous [sorcerous] thoughts against our grandparents when they were alive.

Eeeeee! Those Tukano did this! This Tukano sib that captured our grandfathers and forced them out! This blasted Tukano! And we who were here before . . . now we are suffering, we, poor, people. And the one that took our grandfathers captives and forced them out—that cruel one too. That terrible Balero that took our grandfathers and forced them out. That vicious one, too. Those that took our grandfathers as captives, and forced them out. These cursed ones! And here we are, bereft and pitiful in this place. While we are here, pitiably, I do this [*demonstrating*]: Puh! for these despicable creatures!

Thinking to elicit a version of the *bueyoaka* removed from a ceremonial context of interested participants, I turned to my elderly friend and frequent source of information, Kündido. I asked him to supply a text of the *bueyoaka* that was not naturally occurring speech, but rather speech-on-request, itself a performative form:

The forefathers did exactly this when they were together. As though they were alive, we are here. And we, while we are alive, we are going to stay in this very place, happy to be together[12] . . . Eh, Eeeeeeeh! These cursed ones who took our grandparents, took them and cast them out! That cruel Patanairo that captured our grandparents, took them as slaves and threw them out! That's what those scoundrels did! These two youngsters [reference to seniority] Patanairo and Balero that captured our grandparents and cast them out with bad thoughts [sorcery]. [We will return to the reference to Patanairo, speakers of *lingua geral*, the trade language based on Amerindian Tupi-Guarani, associated with outsiders.] We got rid of those terrible people! And that other group that helped our forefathers—those terrible Wa'i maküno (Piratapuia) and that blasted Alebu . . . These people captured our grandfathers, these cursed other people captured our grandfathers and kicked them out.

In this recited *bueyoaka*, Kündido refers to the Patanairo and Balero, colonists of European ancestry who entered the Amazon hinterlands during the rubber boom. Balero, a Latinized reference to a rubber collector, was also named in the April 1979 *bueyoaka*. Other groups named in both his recitation and in the *po'oa* of April 1979, the Wa'i maküno (Piratapuia) and Alebu, are members of the fraternal grouping of language groups to which the Wanano belong, and within which they may not marry. These language groups, to whom brotherhood now extends, are said to have formerly practised sorcery against the Wanano. These exemplify the representation of relationships as unchanging, when in fact they are undergoing rearrangement.

6. Uhtuse: *Distribution of the Gifts*

The *bueyoaka* is followed in the *po'oa* sequence by two final events—the gift distribution and the ancestral invocation. The *uhtuse*, the gift distribution, is carried out with as much humour as the opening ceremony, also playing on the opposing notions of 'giving' and 'keeping'. Two donors pick up baskets and pretend to throw them at the recipients. Taunting with their gifts, the donors run toward and away from the seated recipients, alternately offering and withdrawing the gifts as they cry out 'Opa, Opa, Opa!' On the third toss they heave the baskets slightly above the heads of the recipients, provoking shrieks of fun. The donors lift the gifts three more times, dropping them at last with a loud thud before the receiving headman. He rises and accepts the gifts on behalf of his sib. He then distributes one basket to each of his male sib-mates, proceeding in order of seniority.

7. Utamusa: *The Way of our Forefathers*

In this closing portion of the gift exchange, Asmürë, the wife of the headman of the receiving sib chants the welcoming text, 'I came, I came, I am present. I see everything you have done. I will rejoice with you. And you, look at them. Let everyone look upon the others!' Men of the donor sib raise the long *toniapuku* flutes while the principal couples dance the fish-spawning dance, *wa'i turia*. At last the members of the donor sib sit down along the walls of the longhouse. The resident sib members stand and greet each guest individually.

Dancing the *wa'i turia*, a dance of reproduction and rebirth, enacts the alliance, but the mutual recognition inherent in 'looking at one another' affirms it. The act of beholding signals the reach across the boundaries of recognition, of seeing the other. Smoking-chanting finalizes the transformative process and constitutes the contract. As the gifts are removed, ritual and sib leaders pass between them a large ceremonial cigar, held in place by a sacred hardwood holder whose carvings represent the cosmological figure, First Woman. At this point the 'giving ceremony' (*po'limina*) is complete. Sib litanies, dancing, and beer exchanges continue long into the night and over subsequent days.

DISCUSSION

Although an extensive literature (Reichel-Dolmatoff 1971, Goldman 1963, S. Hugh-Jones 1979, Jackson 1983, Chernela 1993 and 1992) on the ceremonies known as *po'oa* exists, little attention has been given to the ritual as a performative event, or to its political implications. This is somewhat surprising, since ritual is one of the loci in which boundary creation, breakdown, and interpenetration are expressed. The occasion of the *po'oa*, when two sib settlements visit one another, carries particular importance, since in it the identities of sibs to one another must be defined and redefined. This is the work of speech in the creation of community.

The ceremonial discourse consists of a score that is at times closely scripted but more often is open, allowing for ample improvisation. Speakers must remain faithful to the intent of the dramatic goals, but may extemporize in order to accomplish them. The result is that each *po'oa* is a unique occurrence depending upon the constituent players and the relations of the moment.

The *po'oa* may be described as a bilateral competitive exchange within an ideology of contestatory sociability. Among the ritualized actions and speeches of the *po'oa* that form interlocking performative bundles of significance is the enacted confrontation with an enemy. The *bueyoaka*, ritual speech accompanied by spear throwing, broadcasts hostility and warfare. In the enactment, each participating sib designates the other as opposite, enemy. Men from descent group A face men from descent group B in postures of violence, brandishing spears and tossing them into one another's ranks. Each enjoins the other into the mock conflict. The theme is displacement and abuse by a group different from one's own.

The texts reproduced here illustrate a diverse array of stated enemies at different levels of relationship and differing degrees of relationship distance. Enemies cited range from those outside the universe of intermarrying language groups, the Patanairo and Balero, to language groups in in-law relation, such as the Tukano; language groups in fraternal (phratric) relation, including the Wa'i maküno (Piratapuia); and, most proximately, sibs within the same language group, such as the Biari Pona and Bü'ünairo. At the extreme of the greatest distance from speaker(s) are Patanairo and Balero. In the north-west Amazon, where you are what you speak, Patanairo refers to a speaker of *lingua geral*, the trade language (based upon Amerindian Tupi-Guarani) spoken by the population of European ancestry who immigrated into the Amazon rainforest following successive waves of demand for *Hevea brasiliensis*, Amazonian rubber. Populations of commercially interested outsiders in pursuit of rubber entered the north-west Amazon from the mid-nineteenth century into the early twentieth, and again in the years 1939 to 1947 when Asian rubber sources were unavailable. In invoking the European Patanairo and Balero, the violence, servitude, and destruction wrought by those populations are inscribed and shaped within memory. The *bueyoaka*, in these tellings, indexes the colonial encounter. It is of interest that Kündido references the European as the enemy when I am the audience. In seeking a *bueyoaka* outside of an actual *po'oa*, I had neglected to consider myself as audience and the possibility that my own presence indexed a political entity with a past history of labour exploitation and atrocities against the peoples of the region. Kündido's text illustrates the way in which the ancestor of the participant group is condemned for past wrongdoings. The naming of ancestral figures associated with my group membership well illustrates the tradition of naming the listener's own group as enemy in one stage in the ritual process. We shall see this again.

Other groups named as enemies in the *po'oa* cited here include in-law groups such as the Tukano, with a recognized history of raiding against the Wanano. Indeed, raiding and marriage were formerly linked through the institution of bride capture (Jackson 1993). Relatedly, many Wanano reported that political alliances were created through marriage with former enemy groups (Chernela 1993). Groups in phratric relation to the Wanano such as the Wa'i Maküno (Piratapuia), are also named in these narratives. The extended brotherhoods of language groups that do not intermarry are currently the loosest social configurations among Eastern Tukanoan language groups. In the Brazilian *Uaupés*, where there is a widespread uncertainty about the membership of phratries, groups in phratric relation may have no contact whatsoever. The phratric level of relationship has been deemed of little relevance in recent times, by both Tukanoan insiders and researching outsiders alike.

The most proximate among the named enemies, and the relationship that corresponds to Rivière's intra-tribal one, is that of the sibs, the intra-linguistic descent groups. In the *po'oa* of April 1979 the participating sibs were both Wanano, one senior Wamisima, one junior Wiroa. Participants addressed one another as 'brother', yet the linkages between them must be characterized as ambiguous. The Wamisima group included in its list of offences the displacement of the Biari Ponairo, a Wamisima chiefly sib, by a low-ranking sib, here called by the generic term for brothers of lesser rank, Bü'ünairo:

Principal Donor with Headman: When the other came, and my parents were alive, my
    brother, for example, came in here, and spoke: 'This cursed other one! Biari Ponairo, our
    older [seniormost] brother, he belongs to the place [is the rightful resident of that site]
    but that Bü'ünairo, and many others that captured our grandfathers and forced them
    out. So they say. Now we are mixed up. They took our grandfathers and kicked them out.
    They despised our grandfathers. The people who did that had dangerous [sorcerous]
    thoughts against our grandparents when they were alive.

The spear-speech laments 'mixing'—the disorder and displacement of Wanano sibs. The spear talk of the Wamisima refers to the displacement of a senior sib, the Biari Pona, by a junior sib. Now, say the Wamisima, 'We are mixed up' (*sü'sari mahsa*), a state regarded as problematic and requiring rectification. In the above narrative the mixing of different Wanano sibs is linked to the displacement of a high-ranking sib by a low-ranking one. The assertion cannot be regarded as neutral since the relations of the two opposing groups parallel those referenced. This discourse of antagonism, although oblique rather than direct, expresses the ambivalences underlying Wiroa/Wamisima relations. It will be recalled that the Wamisima are said to be descended from a primordial anaconda canoe while the Wiroa are accorded a separate, derivative creation. Although the Wiroa are speakers of Wanano, their identity as Wanano is qualified as their ancestors were formed from birds created by a Wamisima ancestral shaman. The Wiroa may therefore be regarded as a Wanano product, not sharing the same original ancestral substance of other Wanano. This is the position held by the Wamisima.

If the criterion for Wanano membership is language, the Wiroa are like, or the same as, the Wamisima. If descent is the criterion for group membership, however, they are other. Sharing the language of brotherhood and exchanging gifts and labour, the Wiroa/Wamisima are qualified kin—mediating between closer kin and total 'other'. 'Made' by a Wanano shaman, the Wiroa are regarded by the Wamisima as *extrinsically*, not *intrinsically*, Wanano. Although they speak Wanano, they are of different descent and therefore the linkage between them and non-Wiroa Wanano is maintained with some degree of distance. The linkage may be fragile, subject to contingency. The references to junior brother groups displacing senior groups references intra-Wanano competition and foregrounds difference. The references to common enemies of other language groups references intra-Wanano solidarity and foregrounds sameness and unity. The possibilities for past, present, and future amalgamations or dissolutions are apparent. As the linkages are reproduced over time, so too are the distinctions. That which is reproduced is the relationship with its contradictions intact and the ambivalences regarding the locations of boundaries that designate inclusion or exclusion.

Through ritual the 'other', a stranger who may be an enemy, is rendered an ally. In the early stages of the April 1979 *po'oa* the named enemies were Wanano. The discourse quickly shifted to reference disputes with distant, and common, enemies. The *po'oa* ceremonial may re-establish or reify ongoing commitments, as it does when the two exchanging groups are of the same language group. Or the ceremony may establish a new, diplomatic proximity, as it might when the two sibs are of different language groups. Through the vocalizations and enactments of antagonistic hostilities the ceremonial moves participants toward a finality in which the two sibs are rendered allies. In the *po'oa* cited here, references to displacement of senior brothers by junior ones gave way to a discourse centred on a common 'other'. By means of the litany of naming and enacting a common enemy (such as the Kubeo, the Tukano, the Sirio, or the European Patanairo) the participant sibs, at first on opposing sides, are eventually brought into common alignment. By the end of the *bueyoaka* the relations of belligerence and bellicosity shift to those of peace, conviviality, and alliance. Each group undergoes a ritual transition from enemy to ally or 'brother'. Obstacles may be overcome; divisions surpassed. The same textual content may be read several ways, depending upon the identities and prior relations of the participating sibs. It may create a new alliance, or cement an existing one. In each case the alliance is created through a re-enactment of hostility. In the one case it would be redundant, with empathies remaining as before; in the other it is novelty; and identifications may be extremely different.

Like the *bueyo* or spear referenced in the name of the speech act, the *bueyoaka* may cut both ways. In 'Piercing Speech' characterized by aggressive language, that which is exchanged is both hostile and contractual. The exchange brings together as it also renders separate. Through the gift and language exchange an alliance is established, albeit a conditional one. Insofar as the proximities between groups are conditional, constructed, and reified through ritual enactment, and based upon the impermanency of diplomacy, they constitute a social contract with contingency. In the diplomatic rhetoric of the *po'oa*, closeness is created as a difference is underscored: it is a closeness with difference. Whatever solidarity is created in a *po'oa* may be as easily broken as it was constructed: through language.

Whereas Rivière's ceremonial dialogue is a formalized distancing mechanism, diplomatic in style but reflecting underlying 'discomfort', the *bueyoaka* is a boisterous and openly aggressive style that signals antagonism and warfare while it produces solidarity. Participating groups are united in opposition to a referenced 'other'. Once allied, the two groups state, in one of the obligatory, memorized portions, 'We two groups appear to detest each other but we do this so we can live better. Yes, this is a lot of work.' The ritual emphatically affirms the new alliance, as expressed in the donor's speech: 'I, your *pukami* (father's older/senior brother), while I am still alive, after our grandfathers all died, recalling, remembering that which our ancestors once did, call our kinsmen, uniting one family, speaking (formally), conversing, drinking, this way. They did this and now we do as they did. Our life is so.'

CONCLUSION

Formal greeting speech among groups self-identified as different, and yet the same, is an appropriate locus from which to examine the symbolic and performative means through which members of a group interpret their own identities to their own constituencies and to others. The ritual speech of the *po'oa* eloquently demonstrates the wide range of linguistic resources drawn upon by participants as they construct closeness and distance, dispute and reconciliation, extending, limiting, and defining the extent of groupness and the degree of relatedness among them. There is a wide range between the total insider (the consanguineal sib-mate), and the outsider (the enemy or captor). Mediating these extremes are several categories of 'other' with varying degrees of closeness. These include in-law groups or fraternally related groups. Apparently fixed, these relations are subject to the vagaries of history. Phrased in terms of timelessness, they are instead, processual. Although the exchanges of goods and words are named *durukua* ('exchange of talk'), and *po'limina* ('exchange of gifts'), the shift which is not named is perhaps the more important: the movement of social alignment, a crossing over.

Group identities and relations are forged in the present through a ritual construction of the past. The *po'oa* is the site where groups establish what they once were, what they will be no longer, and what they wish to become. The *bueyoaka* is a simulation, a pretence in the modality of the vanquished. Neither group claims to be victor. Instead, each group recalls, and perhaps, re-experiences, the pain of former insult and injury. The *po'oa* in general, and the *bueyoaka* in particular, articulate Wanano interpretations of Uaupés historical relations of guesting, feasting, and raiding. The discourse is a trope of history in which the adversaries are neighbours and brothers. It is a reflexive model through which the Wanano locate themselves vis-à-vis others in their social universe. The language of ritual brings groups, formerly distanced, into proximity, as the ritual is a vehicle for reinventing relations. The *po'oa* does so by transforming a past state into an authenticated memory. Speakers use the ritual process, not merely to understand the past, but to create it (and see Hill 1993 for the Wakuenai).

Located between the offering of the gift and its actual transfer, the *bueyoaka* is a transformative moment in the ritual process. Directly preceding the 'closing of the contract' and the culmination of dramaturgical processes leading up to it, the *bueyoaka* is the locus of the shift that situates all parties on the same side. The violent enactment alters and realigns the limits of community, creating a new public order.

Relations between groups may change both by gradual slippage and by abrupt rupture. In ritual, however, relations between groups change through 'authorized revision'. A ritual is collective, anonymous, and non-attributable. It communicates a transindividual reality lying somewhere between authorized history and fiction, presenting events as if they had already occurred. Having a life of its own, it conforms to what Richard Schechner calls 'restored' or 'twice-behaved behaviour' (1985: 36). References to the ancestors render the past and past relations open and close, not closed and distant. In so representing the past, the ritual process names it into existence. By projecting backward to an event-that-was, a future is created by means of a constructed past. The opposition to a previous time is a natural reversal. In the language of the *po'oa*, the past is not restored, it is rectified, like a reconstructed period piece or theme park where the performance aims at a genuine, yet preservable and exhibitable, replica.

Along with a construction of an official memory of the past, the ritual suggests how to interpret it, and how to proceed into a future becoming. If an original source of the behaviour had existed, it is erased, forgotten, concealed, or distorted in the course of the ritual process. For Rivière (1971*a*: 306), one ritual speech form, the Trio *turakane*, known as dialogic greeting speech, functioned to mediate situations where boundary crossing was likely to give rise to conflict. The speech events considered in this essay convey boundaries as created in the act of speaking. In order to avoid conceptual essentialism, the issue of boundaries must be viewed as the result of the communicative processes that shape them. The premises upon which the concept of group boundaries is based, that is, that boundaries are static and groups may be scaled for boundary 'permeability' (Urban 1988*a*), is flawed. Boundaries are conceptualized, subject to context and to vantage point. In order to evaluate the explanatory power of this thesis, it may be useful to draw broader comparisons with other South American societies. For example, the tense dialogical *tankamash* speech of the Ecuadorian Jivaroan Achuar (Descola 1994*a*) or the antagonistic ceremonial feast among Yanomami descent groups may be explored according to the principles and findings established here. The *po'oa*, occurring at the boundaries of groups, illustrates one example of groupness constructed through speech acts. In the *po'oa* we are reminded of the issues raised by Rivière concerning the role of speech in uniting groups in a context of potential divisiveness. Attention to the dilemma of ambiguities and relationship distance elucidates the Wanano/Wiroa case, and the ceremonial speaking style performed by them.

ACKNOWLEDGEMENTS

The author wishes to thank Emilia Trinidade, Pedro de Mello, and Paulo Marquez for their assistance in field tape-recording, and the Center for Latin American Studies at Georgetown University for the facilities in which this chapter was written.

NOTES

1. The Wanano name for this ceremony is *po'oa* or *po'ose*. In this chapter the sign /'/ is used to indicate a voiceless glottal stop.
2. The river name is spelled Vaupés in Spanish-speaking countries and Uaupés in Brazil, where Portuguese is spoken, consistent with pronunciation and orthographic distinctions between Spanish and Portuguese.
3. This phenomenon is discussed in a broader context in Irvine (1982).
4. Besides the 'language group' (Jackson 1974, 1983), this named unit of affiliation has been variously referred to in the literature as a 'tribe' (Goldman 1963), or 'maximal exogamous descent unit' (C. Hugh-Jones 1979).
5. The Kubeo (Cubeo) (Goldman 1963), Makuna (Århem 1981, 1989), and Arapaço (Chernela 1988c, 1989) are exceptions to the pattern of linguistic exogamy.
6. The figure of 14,000 is based upon the 1987 reported census figure of 14,164 compiled by the Centro Ecumenico de Documentação e Informação (CEDI), Museu Nacional, Rio de Janeiro. It exceeds by 5,000 the estimates of Sorensen (1967) and Jackson (1976).
7. The figure of 150,000 square kilometres is the sum of 90,000 km^2 reported by Jackson (1976) for the Colombian Vaupés, and 60,070 km^2 reported by the Centro Ecumenico de Documentação e Informação (CEDI), Museu Nacional, Rio de Janeiro, for the Brazilian Uaupés.
8. Tape recorders were used openly, and are mentioned in the texts. Transcriptions and interlinear translations were prepared in the field with the help of Wanano-speakers Pedro de Mello, a member of the Wamisima Yahuri sib, Emilia Trinidade, a member of the Wiroa sib, and Paulo Marquez, a non-Wanano whose mother's language is Wanano. The versions presented here are verbatim but for the elimination of repetition. While the resulting text is compacted and condensed, lacking the performative impact of the original, it allows for presentation of all portions of the ceremony that the Wanano regard as necessary. Original tape recordings are deposited in the ethnomusicology archives of the University of Indiana. Five texts are published in Chernela (1988a and 1993). The published texts are taken from song and litany exchanges that follow the gift exchange. In this chapter only the gift exchange portion of the ceremony is presented.
9. Orthography: In transcribing Wanano and other Eastern Tukanoan languages, I use the letter *k* to indicate a velar stop as in the English word 'key'; the same sound is represented in written Portuguese and Spanish by the letters *c* or *q*, as in the Portuguese and Spanish *tocar* and *toque*. I use the letter *k* to portray this sound, so that I may follow it with an *h* to indicate an aspiration. I reserve *ch* for the palatalized, voiceless alveolar affricate, in common Wanano usage. This sound is represented in Spanish and English by the same orthography, as shown in the Spanish *coche* and the English 'chilly'. (For a more comprehensive treatment of Wanano phonology and transcription, see Waltz and

Waltz [n.d.).) The following is a key to pronouncing some of the orthographic symbols used in this text:

Transcription Key:

k   unaspirated voiceless velar stop
kh aspirated voiceless velar stop
ch palatalized voiceless alveolar affricate
'   voiceless glottal stop
h   voiceless fricative
ü   high front rounded vowel (as in 'un' Fr., one)
u   high back rounded vowel (as in 'muro', Sp., wall)
a   low central unrounded vowel (as in 'amar' Sp, to love)
i   high front unrounded vowel (as in 'ma fille' Fr., my daughter)
e   mid-high front unrounded vowel (as in 'était' Fr., it was)
o   mid-back high rounded vowel (as in 'todo', Sp., all).

10. For a discussion of 'sitting-and-breathing' see Chernela (1988*a*,*b*).
11. In Tukano, this section is called *Pase wahpase*.
12. This paragraph underscores the importance of invoking the ancestors and linking them to place.

10

Inside and Out: Alterity and the Ceremonial Construction of the Person in the Guianas

Paul Henley, *University of Manchester*

COLORADO VALLEY, 31 MARCH 1976

It is the late dry season and the savannah grass has been reduced to a dusty brown. Although it is only nine o'clock in the morning and still quite cool, the day promises to be stiflingly hot because the sky is clear and already a deep blue. On the horizon, a grey plume of smoke rises where the creoles in the next valley are burning off the grass.

But today the Panare are happy, because today is the culmination of the *katyayïnto´* ceremony, when a group of five boys will be dressed in loincloths for the first time. This will bring to an end a process which began almost four months ago, at the beginning of the dry season. Vast quantities of smoked meat have been assembled, as have many gallons of beer. With charming economy, the Panare refer to this beer as *o´*. Most of it has already been consumed; the smoked meat, on the other hand, known as *kaemo*, has been stashed away in the roof of the longhouse and will be shared out only at the end of the event tomorrow.

There are perhaps two hundred people here now, of all ages, mostly sitting or standing around outside, men on one side of the longhouse, women on the other. Almost everyone is in his or her finest, brightest red loincloth. At this moment, the host women are painting the men with great balls of red onoto (annatto) paste. This red coating will completely smother the intricate, geometric black designs that they painted on themselves the night before with *caruto* juice. But no matter, this is how one should look on the day of the *katyayïnto´*. It is very rare for men and women to touch one another in public, so there is a slight frisson about all this, and much light-hearted banter.

People are feeling tired because they have spent most of the night dancing, chanting, and drinking *o´*. The most common Panare dance consists of moving in two concentric circles around the *no´yan*, the central post of the longhouse. The men form a ring around the outside, each with his right hand on the left shoulder of the man in front and dance forward laterally, with a stamping motion. They are led by a man shaking a maraca, who leads the chanting as well as the dancing. Women form an inner circle, immediately around the *no 'yan*. They not only chant in unison with the men, but strike out a rhythm on the ground with an instrument called *chirijko*, consisting simply of a stick with a bunch of toucan beaks or peccary hoofs attached to the end of it. They dance in the same direction as the men, but backwards.

From time to time, they reverse the direction of the dance and the men then place left hands on right shoulders. They also alternate dancing inside the house with dancing immediately outside, also around a post called *no 'yan*. As they move from inside to outside and vice versa, the men let out a loud modulated scream, the *yikikïet*. They also do this at the end of each dance, and sometimes even just to change direction. When they really get going with the dancing, the stamping of the feet, the rattling of the *chirijko*, and the harmonious chanting of male and female voices set up a series of delicious canons that echo around the savannah.

Last night, the chanting was dedicated to the loincloths and all the other para-phernalia that the initiands will put on. All this stuff is currently hidden away in the roof of the longhouse, next to the *kaemo*. As for the initiands themselves, they are now 'asleep'. They are exhausted because they have had to remain awake night after night, as chants and dances for each of the meats in the *kaemo* have been performed. They have had to observe various dietary restrictions as well as take various bitter-tasting medicinal infusions. At this moment, they are lying on the ground inside the house next to the beer canoe, completely naked, hidden from view beneath a blanket.

Around midday, someone sounds a blast on a cow horn. Manyën, a particular friend of mine, explains that this is to inform the *panakon*, that is, the visitors from another settlement who are camped out at some distance away, that the dancing is about to begin again. 'These *panakon* are really fierce', he explains. 'They like beat-ing people with sticks.' But he smirks as he says so, suggesting that there is more here than meets the eye.

The dancing duly begins, first outside, then moving inside with the customary *yikikïet*. Interestingly, only the men are dancing. The song they are chanting is called *panakon tchan*, literally 'the visitors are coming'. It consists of reiterating, in a strangulated way, the name of a species of small fly, *kochawain*, which is attracted by the smell of the *o '* beer, just as the *panakon* are said to be. Many Panare chants are like this. Based on the repetition of a single name or phrase, they refer in an indirect, metaphorical way to the real subject of the chant.

Then something really rather extraordinary happens. As the men wheel around the interior of the longhouse, the small slits that serve as entrances at each end are blocked up with palm leaf screens lashed to the house frame. Round and round the dancers go, singing the *kochawain* chant. Suddenly, one of the doors is battered down with much violent screaming. This is not the carefully modulated *yikikïet*;

this is an uncontrolled high-pitched bellow. In come about six *panakon*, armed with branches and with their faces painted in a bizarre way. One is dressed like a creole in an old jacket and sandals. They smash the branches over the canoe containing the beer so that leaves and twigs scatter everywhere. The dancers meanwhile have stopped dancing and have retired to the perimeter of the house, chanting continuously. The *panakon* persist in screaming violently, moving right up to the faces of the dancers. But the dancers just go on as if nothing were happening. Finally, having failed to disrupt the proceedings, the *panakon* troop out, whilst the hosts complete their dancing both inside and outside the house.

Once they have finished dancing, some of the hosts begin to harangue the *panakon*. Who are they? What have they come for? If it was for beer, they are wasting their time because there is none for them. It is all finished. They should go home. The *panakon* remain sullenly silent, though from time to time they announce, indignantly, *nakye putapë ana*, 'We are thirsty.' Gradually, the dialogue becomes more conciliatory: the *panakon* are eventually offered generous gourdfuls of beer, one of the hosts even caresses the testicles of a *panakon* whilst simultaneously flaunting his own. Instead of encouraging them to leave, the hosts are now trying to persuade the *panakon* to dress the initiands in their new loincloths.

After an extended show of reluctance, the *panakon* eventually agree. And so, remarkably, the boys are brought out from their seclusion and handed over to these men who, just a few minutes before, had been acting like wild creatures, or violent enemies. To these *panakon*, it seems, will be entrusted the most important ritual moment in the initiands' whole lives.

*

The Panare presently number in the region of some 3,000 people, scattered over 20,000 square kilometres at the western extreme of the Guiana Shield. Their traditional territory straddles the ecological interface between the forested escarpments of the Shield and the flat, sandy littoral savannah of the right bank of the middle Orinoco. Despite regular contact with the local Creole population for over a century, they have retained a very strong sense of their own autonomous identity. Like the Trio, they are a Carib-speaking people and in general social and cultural terms conform to most of the normal characteristics of a Guianese indigenous group.

As Peter Rivière pointed out in his definitive comparative work on the Guianas, one of the central dilemmas of the social life of this area is that although the native ideology may propose the notion that settlements are self-sustaining communities, in reality this is not the case. In fact, not only are inter-settlement links frequent and varied, but they are vital for survival. For whilst it may be generally true that from day to day most Guianese settlements are self-sufficient both economically and politically, their generally small size means that it is simply not possible to provision all the younger members with spouses of an appropriate category. Thus, despite the strong ideological commitment to endogamy, some degree of local exogamy is necessary (Rivière 1984: 72 ff.).

In addition to these inter-settlement relations of the long term, essentially involving the exchange of people, most Guianese groups also engage in more short-term recurrent exchanges with neighbouring groups, of which the most important are trade and ceremonial activities.[1] But whilst trade relations in the Guianas have been the subject of a number of studies (e.g. Coppens 1971, Thomas 1972, Butt Colson 1973), ceremonial exchanges, whilst arguably more significant, have been subject to comparatively few detailed analyses.[2] In most cases, they have been dealt with only in passing, as an aspect of a more general ethnographic study.[3]

In contrast, in recent years, ceremonial events have been the focus of a number of detailed analyses in the anthropological literature concerning other areas of Amazonia, notably the Vaupés, the Xingú, and Central Brazil.[4] By comparing Guianese accounts with these analyses, it is clear that the same themes are found in Guianese ceremonial activities as elsewhere, albeit in a generally more muted form. This tendency for Guianese ethnography to provide a relatively simple, unelaborated version of some pan-Amazonian cultural themes is one that Peter Rivière himself has remarked upon a number of times. Moreover, in his own work, he has used the insights developed in relation to ethnography from these other areas to provide clues about what to look for in the Guianas (1984: 102).

This will also be the strategy that I will adopt in the ensuing analysis of the Panare male initiation ceremonial cycle, the culminating moments of which I described above. My ultimate aim will be to show that, when viewed from this comparative perspective, the extraordinary behaviour of the *panakon* and the allocation of the most important ritual role to them, far from being bizarre, is perfectly congruent with pan-Amazonian principles that govern the ceremonial construction of the person.

Not only from detailed analyses of ceremonial events but also from the general development of anthropological ideas in recent years, a number of important general principles of indigenous Amazonian ceremonial life can now be deduced:

(*a*) Inspired by the seminal paper by Seeger, Da Matta, and Viveiros de Castro (1979), recent analyses have tended to stress that ceremonial events in Amazonia are more concerned with the construction or deconstruction of persons than with the constitution of social groups as such. This suggests an explanation for the well-attested ethnographic fact that rites of passage to do with individual growth, maturation, and eventual dissolution tend to be of greater importance than those to do with changes of social status. Indeed, this may be one of the reasons why marriage is generally subject to such minimal ritual elaboration in Amazonia. However, although the main focus of ritual activity may be on individuals, Amazonian ceremonies usually also involve some sort of celebration of the collectivity.

(*b*) The ceremonial construction/destruction of the person is also often linked with aspects of the natural environment which are either important in subsistence terms or which have a weighty symbolic significance for other reasons. In some cases, this involves fruits and some plant species, but in the majority of instances, it is game animals and the spirits associated with them that are invoked in the course of Amazonian rites of passage. Cultivated plants, on the other hand, usually play a relatively minor role in such events.

(*c*) As Anne-Christine Taylor has argued (1998: 317–18), a diverse range of social actors may contribute to the construction of the individual person in Amazonia: from one may come a name, from another the blood, another the bone, from others again that second skin, body ornaments, whilst the faculties of seeing, hearing, and speech or how to act in a heroic manner may all derive from different sources. One might anticipate therefore that this 'extreme parcellarisation', as she calls it, may also be reflected in the allocation of ceremonial tasks.

(*d*) In this allocation of tasks, it is frequently the case that many of the most important will be assigned to those who fall in some sense into the category of 'other' for the persons who are the focus of the event. These 'others' may be literal outsiders, that is, from other settlements, and/or from other language groups, as in the north-west Amazon, for example, or they may be insiders who partake of some degree of otherness, that is, they may be co-resident affines, or, as in Central Brazil, they may belong to opposed ceremonial moieties. They may even include the animal spirits, enacted or embodied within the performance itself by insiders wearing masks or capes, and/or playing musical instruments supposedly representing their voices.

(*e*) Recent studies have stressed that the treatment of the body in Amazonia is, as Taylor has put it, 'both the principal instrument of indigenous sociology and at the same time its most privileged form of expression' (1998: 317). Thus one should expect that in order to achieve the ceremonial transformation of the person, his or her body will be subject to some degree of intrusive ritual manipulation.

In addition to these general substantive aspects of the ceremonial life of indigenous Amazonians, a number of important theoretical issues have been raised. Recent analyses have tended to underline the importance of indigenous understandings of the instrumental purpose of particular rites, which, it is argued, have sometimes been neglected in previous anthropological analyses.[5] However, whilst it may be true that some analyses have indeed neglected indigenous understandings by overemphasizing the ideological or expressive aspects of the rites in question, these different modes of analysis are not necessarily mutually contradictory. In this contribution, I shall attempt to show that the Panare initiation ceremonies can be analysed from a variety of perspectives, each of which provides a further insight into their significance.

Until the North American Evangelical missionaries arrived in the mid-1970s, the ritual ceremonies surrounding male initiation were one of the most important public events in Panare social life. In contrast, there was no rite of passage for the newly born or the very young. Although girls also went through a ritual event at the time of first menstruation, this was a private affair, only involving the girl and her closest female relatives. As in most Amazonian communities, there was no ceremonial celebration of marriage. Only the funerals of adults, particularly those of senior men with shamanic knowledge, mobilized such great ritual effort on the part of the whole community.

The missionaries did not explicitly oppose initiation rites; in fact, for the first few years of their presence there, they encouraged the Panare to continue with them, albeit with the introduction of certain Christian elements, such as the saying of prayers at crucial moments. But what they were against was the consumption of alcohol of any kind, including the *o´* beer. But for the Panare, the ceremonies were literally synonymous with the beer since the generic term for such ceremonies was also *o´*. They therefore reasoned that if they could not consume *o´*, then it was no longer possible to hold the ceremonies. As a result, in the communities of Western Panare territory where the Evangelical missionaries have been particularly influential, the celebration of major public ceremonies ceased in 1981.

I was fortunate then to arrive just in time to see these events at first hand, and even, in a modest way, to participate in them. In the years 1975–6 and 1980–1 I witnessed a number of male initiation ceremonial cycles, primarily in the community of Colorado, in north-western Panare territory, which was my principal base, but also in a number of neighbouring communities as well. The descriptions contained in this contribution are derived from these experiences. Although initiation ceremonies take place amongst other groups of Panare, continuing in some cases to this day, my impression is that there are significant differences both in the general form and in the detail of these events as one moves from one part of Panare territory to another.

From infanthood, a Panare boy would run about virtually naked except for a hair belt, a monkey-teeth necklace, and bands made of beads or of hair around both arms and legs. But as he reached about 10 years of age, his parents and other immediate relatives would begin to feel that his penis was getting large enough to cause embarrassment and that it should be covered up with a loincloth. They would therefore begin to organize the cycle of ceremonies that would culminate in their son donning a loincloth for the first time. This was the most visible outcome of the male initiation ceremony. Shortly after the ceremony, people would begin to refer to him by an adult name for the first time. But this was merely made possible by the loincloth ceremony, it did not form an integral part of it.[6]

The organization of a cycle of male initiation ceremonies was a major undertaking and it was rare for one family to do it alone. Usually two or three families would pool resources and initiate their sons together. Known as *otijchen*, literally 'owners of the ceremony', the initiands' parents would be responsible for the general direction of the event, including ensuring the orderly conduct of all the ritual processes, persuading a leading singer to chant, supervising the preparation of the *o´* and the assembling of the large quantities of smoked meat to feed all the participants. In order to join in with others, a family might initiate their boys either somewhat later or somewhat earlier than the ideal, so that in practice the range of those being initiated varied from about 7 to 12 years of age. But even the oldest boys were clearly well short of puberty.

The overall course of the ritual process of initiation was structured around three main ceremonies, with a number of minor ones in between, which I shall now briefly describe.

MURANKÏNËTO'

This *o'* opened proceedings and customarily took place in the early dry season at the turn of December and January. Prior to the event, the men would spend three days away from the settlement catching and smoking fish and game whilst the women prepared the *o'*. On their return, the men would establish a camp at some distance from the house and prepare various items of ritual paraphernalia. Amongst these were special baskets, featuring alternately green and yellow palm leaves, which would be used for carrying in the *murajtën*, that is, the smoked meats which they had brought back and from which the name of the ceremony is derived. Other items included palm-leaf cloaks, worn by everyone, and crowns of macaw feathers for the initiands. They also prepared the musical instruments: the *arei-arei*, small panpipes consisting of five bamboo tubes, and the *aramataimë*, twinned pairs of idiophones, about four to five feet long and four inches in diameter, made of the hollow trunks of a large shrub within which a bamboo reed vibrated.

The dance would begin after nightfall as the men approached the longhouse from the bush, wearing their cloaks with the baskets of smoked meat on their backs, and producing a cacophony of sound: the high-pitched descending scale of the panpipes, the sonorous counterpoint of the *aramataimë*, the occasional blast on a shotgun and, as they arrived at the dance arena in front of the house itself, a carillon of *yikikïet* (Fig. 10.1). At this point, the women were supposed to be inside the house waiting for the men to arrive. After a few revolutions around the *no'yan* outside, the men would stop, and the owners of the ceremony would bring out pots of *o'*. 'Drink it all up', they would exhort everyone magnanimously.

After a couple of hours of drinking, *aramataimë* playing, and body painting, dancing would begin around the exterior *no'yan*, headed by a lead chanter marking out the melody with a maraca. The men would still be carrying the baskets of smoked meat and wearing their cloaks, but this time young women would slip out from the house and join in too, forming an inner circle of dancers and playing the *chirijko*. Some minutes later, the male dancers would move inside, to the sound of *yikikïet*. Here, the older women, stationed around the perimeter of the house, would dive into the lines of male dancers and, to general amusement, 'steal' the baskets of meat. Finally, when the men had been divested of all their baskets, the dancing stopped and the women went off to prepare the food.

Following a large collective meal, with men and women eating in separate groups, the remainder of the night and much of the next day would be dedicated to dancing, and to chants referring to the various smoked meats consumed, to the ritual paraphernalia, and body-paint designs. However, the main ritual event of

this *o´* was the piercing of the septums of the initiands' noses, early in the morning, shortly after sunrise. The hole thus created would be ready for the insertion
of the *ëwayeru´*, a nasal ornament which would be put on at the same time as the
initiand's loincloth at the climax of the *katyayïnto´*. The piercing was carried
out by young men who had no precise title, but who acted, as it were, as
'seconds' to the initiands. They escorted them throughout the whole cycle of
events up until the climactic moment of the *katyayïnto´*, ensuring that they
participated in all the dances as they should, observed the correct dietary
constraints, and so forth.

KAEMO YONKONTO´

With the first event successfully completed, the *otijchen* would then organize
collective expeditions to gather together enough meat and fish to feed participants
in the later stages. The meat captured on these expeditions was referred to by a
special term, *kaemo*. Whereas the *murajtën*, the smoked meat for the *murankïnëto´*,
was assembled in a matter of days and consumed immediately during the ensuing
ceremony, the assembling of the *kaemo* took place over several weeks. In fact, most
of the community would simply abandon their longhouses and set up camp in a
distant part of the forest from where the men would set out on daily hunting or
fishing trips. When a sufficient quantity of *kaemo* had been amassed and smoked,
everyone would return to the longhouse and the *kaemo yonkonto´* would be held,
usually in late February or early March. As the name indicated, the principal ritual
event of the ceremony was the raising of the *kaemo* into the roof of the longhouse.
Here it would remain until after the climax of the *katyayïnto´*.

   The general structure of this ceremony was very similar to that of the
murankïnëto´. At nightfall, the men approached the settlement from the bush,
dressed in palm-leaf cloaks, with even larger baskets of smoked meat on their
backs. After dancing inside and out, these were also then 'stolen' by the women.
Thereafter, following a collective meal, there was dancing and chanting until dawn,
with songs dedicated to the smoked meats and ritual paraphenalia. Around about
midday, all the baskets of *kaemo* were assembled into one vast bundle to be raised
into the roof of the longhouse.[7]

KANOWAYANTO´ AND UTOYANTO´

The cycle also involved two other, relatively minor events, which did not always
occur. Early on in the cycle, the men would hollow out a tree trunk and push it
laboriously towards the longhouse as a receptacle for the *o´*.[8] But as they gathered
their forces and, chanting, attempted to push it through the narrow door of the
longhouse, a group of women, stationed inside and armed with manioc tubers,

would attack the *kanowa*, scattering small fragments of manioc all over the long-house floor.

Somewhat later, usually between the *murankïnëto´* and *kaemo yonkonto´*, a minor ceremony would be held in connection with the harvesting of the large quantities of manioc that were necessary to make both the *o´* and the cassava bread that would accompany the *murajtën* and the *kaemo*. For this event, known as *utoyanto´*, liter-ally 'to get manioc', the women would go to the gardens early and dig up large quantities of roots. The men would then arrive later, and having loaded up baskets, would march back to the settlement, chanting as they went. Once everyone arrived back at the longhouse, the manioc would be piled up around the central house-post and there would briefly be some dancing led by two *aramataimë* players.

KATYAYÏNTO´

The name of the third major *o´* in the initiation cycle refers to the putting on of loincloths with which the cycle culminates, described above. But between the *kaemo yonkonto´* and the *katyayïnto´*, a period of about a couple of weeks, there would be nightly chanting in the longhouse. This was the *kaemo warijtëto´*, liter-ally, the singing to the *kaemo*.

On the morning of the event, the initiands would be taken out into the forest by their 'seconds' to take medicines in the forest. Meanwhile, another group of men, even more distantly related to the initiands, would retire to a camp some distance away from the settlement and fabricate the ritual paraphernalia with which they would be dressed. This group of relative outsiders did not have a specific name in Panare, but I shall refer to them as 'thirds'.

In contrast to the previous two *o´*, the *katyayïnto´* did not begin with the arrival of men from the bush. Instead the chanting and dancing simply began around midnight and was dedicated primarily to the initiands' ritual paraphernalia. This then continued, off and on, until around midday the following day when, as described at the beginning of this chapter, the *panakon* arrived to dress the initiands.

Once they had agreed to do the task, the *panakon* lined the boys up on the edge of the dance arena in front of the longhouse. First they dressed the boys in the bark skin belts and loincloths. As they did so, they scolded them, commanding them to look after the paraphernalia carefully because it had taken so much work to make. Then having whipped them lightly, they would lead them into the longhouse. Here, having struck the house poles with clubs given to them specially for the purpose, they were hauled over the beer canoe and returned outside to lean on their sticks.

An interlude in the dressing of the boys then took place, as a group of small children, of both sexes, and ranging from babes in arms to those of 3 or 4 years of age, were gathered around the *no´yan*, the post at the centre of the dance arena, in order to have their ears pierced and to be dressed in various body ornaments. For this purpose, the children were held by women other than their mothers whilst the actual piercing of the ears, carried out with blowgun darts, was performed by unrelated men. These were often the 'seconds', who by this stage had been relieved, at least temporarily, of their obligations to the initiands.

When this had been done, there would be a brief period of dancing, led by the principal chanter, before the dressing of the initiands would begin again. Late in the afternoon, once the initiands had been decked out in all their regalia, there would be yet more dancing, involving virtually everybody in the community, as well as all the visitors.

The next day, the *kaemo* would be taken down from the roof of the house and distributed by the owners of the feast to all the families present. Some would be for taking home, but part was cooked and eaten immediately. It was not regarded as a gourmet occasion: after being stored for several weeks, the meat was very tough and often contained maggots. Whilst the rest of the community ate, the initiands would be taken out into the forest to take more medicines. At nightfall, they would return and eat in the centre of the longhouse but informants went out of their way to stress that on no account should they eat the *kaemo* themselves.

Finally, on the third day, the initiands would go out to take medicines by themselves, returning at midday. After dark, there would be a brief spell of further dancing before the large palm-leaf bundle in which the *kaemo* had been kept would be hung from a nearby tree out on the savannah, along with the cloaks from the earlier *o´*. Here they would be gradually blanched white by the sun, remaining as a fragile testimony to the happy times of the *katyayïnto´* for months, sometimes for years later.

There are several different analytical paths one can trace through these events. In practice, they overlap in many ways with one another, but for the sake of convenience we can consider them under a number of distinct headings.

GENDER

This was, after all, a male initiation ceremony and, as in Panare life generally, it was structured around clear gender divisions: men contributed meat, women contributed the beer, a product of vegetable origin; men arrived at the events from the bush, whilst women waited inside the house; men danced forwards on the outside, women danced backwards on the inside; throughout the event, men and women remained largely separate for collective meals, drinking, socializing. This separation of the genders rendered all the more exciting the few moments when they were directly in contact, as in the onoto body painting, or at certain moments in the dancing, late at night, when young men and women would dare to dance around the longhouse with arms around one another's waist.

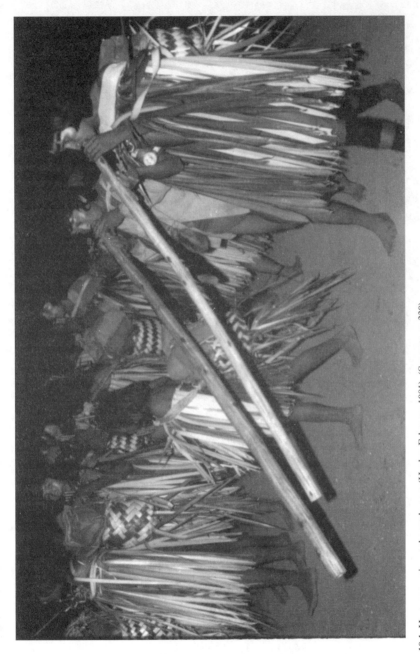

FIG. 10.1. Host men arrive at the settlement (Henley, February 1981). (See note, p. 220)

FIG. 10.2. The initiands are stationed at the edge of the dancing area, with their 'seconds' standing behind them (Henley, February 1981). (See note, p. 220)

FIG. 10.3. The initiands are dressed in their loincloths by the *panakon* (Henley, March 1981). (See note, p. 220)

FIG. 10.4. The grand finale (Henley, March 1981). (See note, p. 220)

More than a mere division, there were also certain moments of apparent antagonism, as when the women attacked the *kanowa* as the men attempted to drag it into
the house. Given the phallic shape of the *kanowa* and the narrow slit of the door-
way in most Panare longhouses, it is difficult to avoid an interpretation in terms of
sexual symbolism here. Given also that the women attack the *kanowa* with lanceolate manioc tubers, one might even be forgiven for interpreting this moment in
terms of the *vagina dentata* theme that Peter Rivière himself has identified as a
characteristic of certain Guianese myths (cf. Rivière 1969*b*). However, the light-
hearted atmosphere in which this moment took place discourages any overempha-
sis on the degree of antagonism involved.

Similarly light-hearted was the 'stealing' of the meat brought in by the men at
the beginning of the first two dances. 'Be careful of your meat', old Achim said to
me, smiling broadly, as I prepared my modest basket of smoked fish, 'the dogs
might get it.' I later learnt that this was a conventional remark to make on these
occasions and that it also appeared to be a sort of euphemism: the 'dogs' in question were actually the women.

It could be argued with some reason that the Panare initiation cycle had an ideological function in the sense that it did not merely express day-to-day gender
differences but served to reinforce male domination, at least of the public sphere.
As a large public event, the initiation of boys contrasted with the small-scale and
entirely private ritual associated with a girl's first menstruation. Although
initiands' mothers were also called *otijchen*, owners of the ceremony, it was the
boys' male relatives who directly managed the events and men of progressive
degrees of non-relation who were responsible for their ritual transformation.

However, gender differences displayed in Panare ceremonial life were relatively
muted compared to those found elsewhere. There was nothing directly comparable to the secret cults of north-west Amazonia or Central Brazil, in which women
are excluded from certain important moments and are expressly forbidden to see
musical instruments or other paraphernalia shown only to male initiates. The closest that the Panare came to this sort of exclusion was the moment when the
initiands, in course of being dressed in their loincloths, had to put their hands over
their eyes, on the grounds that if they did see a woman at this point, they would
die (Fig. 10.3). Indeed, if any exclusion was involved in Panare initiation, it was
men who were excluded from female initiation rather than vice versa.[9]

RELATIONS WITH NATURE

The gendered nature of the Panare initiation cycle was also reflected in the particular form of the relations with nature invoked during the course of the ceremonies.
Although the Panare depend in great measure on horticultural activities, mostly the
domain of women, the chants sung in the initiation cycle primarily celebrate their
predatory activities, exclusively a male domain. Indeed, in the only ceremonial

activity directly related to horticulture, the *utoyanto´*, men could be said to have displaced women because it was they who carried the manioc back to the settlement whereas in everyday life they would never think of doing such a thing. Despite the importance of the manioc beer, which was the women's principal material contribution to the ceremonial cycle, there were no chants dedicated to it.[10]

But if the chants dedicated to the animal species in the *kaemo* are suggestive of a certain respect, this was belied by the comments addressed to them as their charred remains were being stored away in the palm-leaf bundle during the *kaemo yonkonto´*. As each piece of smoked meat was put in, the lead chanter from the night before, and another singer, actually standing inside the bundle, would each chant in turn the song appropriate to the species in question. But immediately afterwards, the second singer would then make some conventional taunting remark, referring to some characteristic trait of the animal in question, such as 'Let's see you nod your head now, guan!', whilst 'Let's see you pull your foreskin back now!' was the comment made to the pathetic remains of a smoked cebus monkey, apparently referring to a common practice amongst these creatures when held in captivity.

Similarly, when all the meats had been stored in the bundle, the men tying it up with lianas would continue to taunt the animals contained within, as in this song to the howler monkey:

> You sat there in your mountain
> Never thinking about my hunger
> Now I want to eat you, that's why I'm tying up your hands
> Once you were free, but now you're all tied up
> You never asked me if I were hungry, did you?

Following the arguments of Philippe Descola (1992) that the management of the symbolic aspects of human–animal relations amongst native Amazonians reflects human–human relations of alterity, one might draw a parallel here between the disrespect shown towards the animals of the *kaemo* and the general distrust of outsiders that characterizes Panare inter-settlement relations. One might also draw a parallel between the animals of the *kaemo* and the *panakon*: both were regarded with a certain hostility, but nevertheless, their wildness had to be tamed and controlled in order to celebrate the initiation of a new generation of boys. However, in contrast to some rites of passage in other areas of Amazonia, whilst the gathering of *kaemo* was essential to male initiation, and a large part of the boys' paraphernalia was made of animal parts, there was no sense in which the animals or any spiritual entities associated with them were considered to play an active role in the ritual transformation of the initiands.

THE DELEGATION OF AUTHORITY

Throughout the cycle, there was a notable defusion of the exercise of authority.

Not only did the owners of the feast delegate ritual tasks to others, but each of these others was supposed to show himself reluctant to take on the task. These tasks included not only those directly related to the initiands, but also leadership of the chanting and dancing. In order for a dance to begin properly, the owner had to persuade the chanter to take the maraca which would be used to lead the chanting. To this end, the pair of them, with further interjections from bystanders, would engage in a prolonged formal dialogue in which it was expected that the chanter would dissimulate about his abilities whilst the owner would intimate that the whole event would have to be abandoned if he refused to take the maraca.

Typical of such dialogues are the following extracts from an exchange recorded in February 1981, between Tëna, owner of the *kaemo yonkonto´* then under way, and Najtë, known as Avila in Spanish, the generally acknowledged leader of the whole Colorado community and, not coincidentally, also the leading chanter.[11] In this *kaemo yonkonto´*, Avila was assisted by another man, also called Najtë, whose Spanish name was Casanova. In fact, in these extracts, Casanova, effectively the understudy, does most of the talking. The initial part of the exchange plays on the fact that the maraca with which the chanter leads the singing is made of the same variety of gourd as the gourds for drinking *o´*:

Tëna: None of us have any idea how to shake the maraca.
Casanova: Well, I don't have any idea how to do it either. Besides, I don't want to get involved in all that work. Why should I say, 'I'll give it a try', when in reality, I don't have any idea? No, put it away!
Tëna: We'll just have to put it away then.
Avila: Now that kind of gourd over there is a different matter!
Casanova: Yes, that's a different matter. I know what to do with those drinking gourds. But the maraca, I've seen it a lot, but I've never actually got hold of one. The type of gourd I intend to get hold of now is that type over there in the pots of beer, the ones that have been cut in half. You can't drink beer with a maraca, so you might as well put it away.
Tëna: That's true, but how are we going to work this?

Although many of the exchanges were entirely conventional, it was also possible to ad lib, and the dialogue could thereby be extended for up to half an hour. But eventually it would arrive at the closing coda in which it was conventional to make a show of lamenting that one had never learnt to chant when one might have had the chance:

Casanova: I didn't want to learn when I was young and now I'm too old.
Avila: I'm the same: too old now.
Casanova: The skill has been lost. But we've got to find someone who knows how our forefathers used to sing.
Tëna: The old people used to say. . .
Casanova: That's right, they used to say, 'What are you going to do when we're dead?' But I never said, 'Give it here'. I never touched the maraca.
Avila: No, he never even touched it. Nor did I.
Casanova: Never even touched it. If I had done, I'd now be saying 'Let's get going', because it's beginning to get light and we don't want to get caught by the dawn.

Tëna: There must be someone who knows how to do it.

Avila: Spontaneous singing during the dancing, that's something that's been lost.

Casanova: That's lost. And yet, even though it's being lost, you can hear it sometimes, even now.

Avila: Even now, you can sometimes hear it. Right here in fact. Somebody clearly knows how to do it.

Tëna: Dawn is approaching

Casanova: It's almost already dawn. If it wasn't for the clouds, it would already be light.

Avila: It's very overcast, there's no light.

Casanova: From now on, it can only get lighter.

Avila: Oh well, let me have a look at that maraca. Give it here. [*In a matter-of-fact way he takes it, glances at it and places it discreetly on the ground beside him, out of sight.*]

Tëna: Let's get going then, come on.

Casanova: Get the baskets of *kaemo* ready.

Avila: That's right, get the *kaemo* ready first.

Lying behind this low-key theatrical performance was a dialogue about power in Panare society. Even by Guianese standards, political authority in Panare society is remarkably diffused. Individuals who have leadership qualities are referred to as *i'yan*, but there is no headship position as such. Just who is, or is not, an *i'yan* is largely a matter of personal opinion: there can be one, several, or no *i'yan* in a given community, depending on whom you talk to. Nor is there any hard and fast list of qualities that have to be fulfilled, though to have the ability to chant is a distinct advantage. But whatever the reason that an individual comes to be regarded as an *i'yan*, the authority which this entails must be exercised indirectly, discreetly, and, when at all visible, with a show of extreme reluctance. The dialogue about the taking of the maraca, when the holder will effectively direct the whole community, perfectly encapsulated this attitude.

RITES OF PASSAGE, THE TRANSFORMATION OF THE BODY AND TRANSGENERATIONAL CONTINUITY

The Panare initiation cycle conformed to many of the characteristics of the canonical rite of passage. The boys were gradually separated from their immediate families and given over to progressively unrelated others who performed ritual acts upon them. Once segregated from their normal lives in this way, they would have to observe special food taboos: they did not eat meat, whilst the vegetable foods which they ate had to be roasted directly on the fire, without the intervention of cooking implements. When they really had to sleep, they were not supposed to use hammocks but to lie directly on the ground. During the *kaemo yonkonto´* and the *katyayïnto´*, they spent large periods of time leaning silently on specially decorated sticks (Fig. 10.2). When they were doing this, they were not meant to be thinking about anything in particular, rather their minds should just be blank. All this points to the fact that at this time, they were in a liminal, asocial condition.

Moreover, at this time, they were thought to be in a very vulnerable condition, and like newborn babies, at the beginning of life, and the very sick and very old, at the end of life, their souls were thought to be only loosely attached to their bodies. When they were taken out to the forest to take strength-inducing medicines, their seconds took great care to sweep the ground where they had lain in order to ensure that no soul-matter would be left behind.

This period of progressive liminality culminated in the moment when they were made to lie on the ground, completely naked, underneath a blanket within the longhouse, immediately prior to their dressing by the *panakon*. But then they were effectively reincorporated into social life and given new identities, by being dressed in public in their ritual gear. Once this was completed, and they had gone out by themselves to take medicines in the forest, they were no longer children, but proto-adults who would soon acquire an adult name.

In this sequence of ritual actions, it is possible to detect a distant but clear echo of the far more elaborate seclusion and symbolic entombment, followed by public decoration and exhibition, that one finds amongst the peoples of Xingú (see Viveiros de Castro 1979). Furthermore, as in the Xingú, the principal stress was more on bringing about a change in the body of the boys rather than in an internal state of mind or soul.[12] In part, this process of transformation entailed strengthening the initiands. This was the principal purpose of the tree-bark infusions that they took in the period leading up the *katyayïnto'*. The barks were taken from particularly resilient hardwood trees and were supposed to have homoeopathic effects on the boys.

But these infusions were but one of a number of interventions intended to strengthen the initiands' bodies or encourage them to grow. Another consisted of dotting their bodies with spots of *ayawa*, a tree resin mixed with charcoal which was believed to have strengthening properties.[13] Yet another means intended to ensure the boys' growth was whipping across the backs of the legs, which occurred at various points in the ceremonial cycle. This whipping was not really very serious: it was carried out with light switches of tree bark and produced no more than a brief stinging effect. After the chants to the dawn had been completed, and people began to emerge from the longhouse, the initiands' seconds would station themselves at the doorways and whip not just the initiands but any young person, male or female, who happened to pass through.

But if the taking of medicines and whipping were means of strengthening the internal bodies of the initiands, the items of ritual paraphernalia in which the boys were dressed in effect transformed their external bodies. Undoubtedly the most intrusive item was the *ëwayëru'* nasal adornment, for which the septums of the boys were pierced during the *kaemo yonkonto'*. But, somewhat curiously, this was worn only on the occasion of *katyayïnto'* and was a relatively unimportant part of the paraphernalia as a whole. In addition to the loincloths themselves, other important items included crowns of macaw feathers, elaborate ear adornments, monkey-teeth necklaces, capes of toucan pelts, bead armbands and human hair leg bands, cotton bandoliers, and, particularly importantly, bark belts painted with snakeskin patterns.

But although the principal focus of ritual attention was on the boys and their bodily transformation, there were also elements of celebration of the Panare collectivity and of transgenerational continuity. For the ritual transformation of the boys' bodies not only ensured their own personal maturation and growth but was also the means by which the reproduction of Panare society as a whole was effected, linking the future with the past. It was very significant in this regard that the dressing of the boys was effectively interrupted in order to allow the ritual transformation of the bodies of younger siblings by having their ears pierced and body ornaments put on.

This association of two cohorts of initiands, actual and potential, was further associated in the minds of adult Panare with ritual procedures laid down in distant times. Again it was my friend Manyën who was quite explicit about this. 'Look,' he said with a beatific smile on his lips as he surveyed the scene of a hundred or more people dancing, their bodies a shimmering red in the late afternoon sun, 'people are very happy now because this is how the ancient people said that things should be done.'[14] (Fig. 10.4)

ALTERITY, THE CONSTRUCTION OF THE PERSON AND SOCIAL ORDER

This is perhaps the analytical path of greatest importance for present purposes given that my ultimate aim is to explain the role of the *panakon* in Panare initiation. We have already noted that the ritual process was conducted by others of progressive alterity vis-à-vis the initiands rather than, say, by their parents, who were the owners of the ceremony, or by an *i´yan* or some other representative of collective authority. In the first stages of the ceremonial cycle, the others to whom the initiands were assigned, that is, those whom I have termed 'seconds', were typically young in-married affines living in the same settlement as the initiand. Often they would be the initiand's sister's husband. But in the period leading up to the *katyayïnto´*, they gave way to the 'thirds', usually even more distantly related to the initiands, and it was the latter who prepared the ritual paraphernalia. However, the thirds then gave way in turn to the *panakon* who effected the actual ritual transformation of the boys' bodies through the act of dressing them.

When I asked the Panare themselves why they delegated ritual roles in this way, they would reply that it was because the boys were often made to suffer physically during the course of the initiation, and no parent could do that to a child. But whilst this may be true, comparison with the ceremonial activities elsewhere in Amazonia suggests that other, less personal factors would also play a part in explaining this pattern.[15]

In the first place, in this progressive delegation of ritual responsibility, it is clearly possible to detect a further example of the 'parcellarisation' of the roles entailed in the construction of the person in Amazonia, as identified by Anne-Christine Taylor. These roles are not elaborated and specified to the degree that one finds in Central Brazil, for example, but the same principle can be discerned here, albeit in a characteristically muted Guianese manner. But more significantly, the role of the Other in the transformation effected in a rite of passage is a theme that reverberates endlessly throughout the ethnography of native Amazonia, linking the Panare initiation ceremony with such diverse ritual institutions as the funeral ceremonies of the Yanomami and the Bororo, the formal friends of Central Brazil, even the cannibal feasts of the ancient Tupi of the Atlantic Coast. In all these cases, the Other, defined in various ways, acts as the agent or catalyst for the construction or deconstruction, as the case may be, of the person who is the focus of the rite.

Even more generally, following the pioneering arguments of Joanna Overing (Kaplan 1981), it has become clear that it is in respect of relationships of alterity, however defined, that one of the most stimulating bases for the general comparison of the indigenous peoples of Amazonia can be established. Whilst all groups would probably recognize that such relationships are essential for reproduction, be it individual or collective, some groups seek to minimize them whilst others aim to develop them. In many regions of Amazonia it would seem that indigenous groups seek systematic relationships with those defined as Other, whilst it is claimed that certain Tupi peoples even aspire to become the Other (cf. Viveiros de Castro 1992). In the Guianas, on the other hand, it is commonly averred that indigenous peoples seek to avoid such relationships whenever possible: hence the widespread preference for endogamy, enhanced to the extent of marriage with a sister's daughter and even a daughter's daughter.[16]

However, even in the Guianas, it is recognized that whilst the inside represents, as Peter Rivière (1969a: 276) once phrased it, harmony and security, it is also potentially sterile. The outside and the beings who inhabit it may be dangerous but they are potentially creative. In this context then, the logic of the progressive delegation of ritual duties to others of increasing alterity in the Panare initiation ceremony comes to make perfect sense. In the early stages of the cycle, the degree of alterity of those involved in the ritual transformation of the boys was relatively modest: the seconds were merely in-married affines, who in a typical Panare settlement were likely to be relatively close consanguines as well. As the cycle proceeded, and the thirds who make the ritual paraphernalia become involved, so too did the degree of alterity of the ritual agents, since these thirds were by definition more distantly related than the seconds to the initiands. But for the moment of greatest transformation, the actual dressing of the boys, it was necessary to engage the most wild and dangerous *panakon*, supposedly from the most distant settlements, since it was their very wildness and dangerousness that imbued them with the power to effect the metamorphosis of the boys.

This was not the ordered harnessing of alterity that one finds in the Bororo funeral or the ceremonial relationships between Gê ritual moieties. Rather it was distinctively Guianese in being somewhat random and anarchic, thereby reflecting the absence of the more elaborate social structural arrangements one finds in Central Brazil. Instead of an Other wearing the precisely defined insignia of his moiety, with a specific set of ritual duties, the Panare *panakon* was a clown, a wild man, a trickster. But what he had in common with these more dignified Others was the power to construct a person.

A concern with the social and cultural ramifications of the distinction between the inside and the outside in Guianese indigenous society has been a recurrent leitmotif of Peter Rivière's work since the very first page of *Marriage among the Trio*, published more than three decades ago. Later, the significance of this distinction would be widely recognized and the insights it generated would be developed, refined, and applied systematically to many other regions of Amazonia. But the perception of the relationship between inside and out as the key to understanding Guianese society is present there in Peter's first major work. This distinction is also, as I have attempted to demonstrate here, the key to understanding the Panare initiation ceremonial cycle. It is therefore with great pleasure that I offer this analysis in honour of Peter Rivière's magnificent contribution to our collective endeavour.

NOTES

1. For some authors in the Lévi-Straussian tradition, warfare is also potentially a form of inter-settlement 'exchange' (cf. Lévi-Strauss 1943*a*, Albert 1985). However, if we follow Peter Rivière's example, and leave the Yanomami out of the general category of Guianese societies, it is fair to say that warfare has not been a particularly marked feature of inter-settlement relationships in this area.

2. A generation ago, the distinction between 'ceremonial' and 'ritual' was the subject of extended debate in the anthropological literature, although like many such definitional discussions, it proved impossible to reach any definitive conclusions. In this contribution, I shall use the term 'ceremonial' to refer in a general way to the whole complex of celebratory activities associated with Panare initiation, including dancing, chanting, and drinking, whilst reserving the term 'ritual' to those aspects of these ceremonies that are specifically concerned with bringing about changes in the condition of the initiands through symbolic means.

3. An interesting exception here is Catherine Howard's study (1993) of the Waiwai ceremonial 'farce', whose principal characters, clown-figures referred to as *pawana*, clearly have certain features in common with the Panare *panakon*, including a probable common etymological origin for the terms themselves. By the time that Peter Rivière arrived amongst the Trio, they had already abandoned their major festivals as a result of the influence of Evangelical missionaries. However, he was able to observe Trio ceremonial dialogues and through a comparative analysis with Fock's material on the Waiwai, show how the strength and intensity of these could be correlated with aspects of political structure (1971*a*).

4. Influential early examples that spring immediately to mind are Stephen Hugh-Jones's analysis of Barasana male initiation (1979), Eduardo Viveiros de Castro (1979) on Yawalpití seclusion, Manuela Carneiro da Cunha on Canela funeral customs (1978), and Sylvia Caiuby Novaes's writings on various aspects of Bororo funerary customs (see Caiuby Novaes 1983).

5. An important contribution to this discussion is Cecilia McCallum's impressive re-analysis of certain Xingú ceremonial events which stress gender differences (1994). One of her central arguments is that the primary ethnographers have tended to overemphasize the ideological character of these events, i.e. as a means of legitimating male dominance of women, at the expense of considering their indigenous rationale as activities intended to bring about changes in the bodies of the participants by symbolic means. In a somewhat similar vein, Graham Townsley (1993) has argued against the tendency to interpret Amazonian shamanic ritual discourses as merely metaphoric statements about the world rather than as highly instrumental attempts to intervene directly in reality and thereby change it for the better, usually in relation to the health of a person who is ill.

6. The Panare have an unusual naming pattern in that they only have six adult male names and four adult female names. Possible confusions of identity are avoided by means of further clarifications based on known kinship relationships, nicknames, Spanish names derived from *compadrazgo* relationships (ritual godparenthood) with local Creoles, or teknonymous constructions based on children's names, of which there are about thirty.

7. About twenty different species were regarded as acceptable as *kaemo* but the most preferred were howler, capuchin, and cebus monkeys; peccary, both the white-lipped and collared species; amongst birds, various species of guan, trumpeter, and curassow; eels and a number of fish species were acceptable but were not as well regarded, so they tended to be consumed during the ceremony itself rather than kept for the *kaemo*. Generally not included were tapir, deer, and alligator, all of which featured commonly in the everyday diet. However, the reasons given for their exclusion were invariably not to do with the symbolism of these animals but rather banally practical, namely that their meat got too tough or tended to rot when kept over several weeks.

8. This container was called a *kanowa*, a term obviously related etymologically to the Carib word that, centuries ago, gave rise to the English term 'canoe'. However, the Panare, who are not a river-going people, would never attempt to use a *kanowa* as a mode of transport.

9. As a man, I was never invited to witness the private rites associated with a girl's first menstruation, which were the closest equivalent to a female initiation ceremony. However, Jana Price, an Evangelical missionary who did witness them described them to me briefly. According to her, shortly after a girl had had her first menses, she would be taken down to the riverside by a small group of her closest female relatives where she would enact the stages of manioc processing, but using sand instead of manioc mash.

10. In relation to the peoples of Peruvian Amazonia, the late Andrew Gray made the inter-esting suggestion that there may be a significant correlation between, on the one hand, societies such as the Ashaninka, Shipibo, and other Panoan groups, for whom plants are very important both in shamanic curing and in subsistence, and who celebrate female puberty rites by linking girls' growth to the maturation of plants, and, on the other hand, groups such as the Arakmbut, whom he himself studied, who lay greater cosmological stress on human–animal relationships and who give greater weight to

male initiation (Gray 1996*a*: 182 n.; 1996*b*: 261). How generalizable this correlation may be is surely worthy of further investigation.

11. Part of this exchange appears in the film, *The Panare: scenes from the frontier* (BBC, 1982), directed by Chris Curling and on which I acted as anthropological consultant.

12. The overwhelming importance of the external body as a marker of identity has been a very common theme of much recent literature on Amazonia and many references could be cited in this context. Amongst many others, the works of Erikson (1985), Taylor (1996), Århem (1996), and, particularly, Viveiros de Castro (1998*a*) have all dealt with this question from a variety of perspectives.

13. It is also believed to have curative properties and will be applied to a sprained or infected part of the body.

14. Although I know of no exact equivalent term in Panare, the sentiment that Manyën evoked seems to be very similar to the feeling described by the Trio word *sasame* (Rivière 1969*a*: 256).

15. Individuals who are relatively 'other' with respect to the person who is the focus of the event, also have important roles to play in Panare funerals. For example, those who dig the grave and actually bury the individual should not be related to the deceased. In this case, the indigenous explanation is that the immediate relatives are too sad to carry out this function.

16. See my arguments on the endogamous possibilities offered by inter-generational marriage strategies in Henley (1983–4).

FIG. 10.1 *Kaemo yonkonto´* (February 1981). Host men arrive at the settlement wearing cloaks of kokorite palm and carrying baskets of smoked meat. The two men in the foreground play a matched pair of *aramataimë* idiophones, the longer and wider one on the left being male and more bass, the one on the right being female. In the background other men and initiands play *are´re´*, bamboo panpipes. However these are not played in time or tune with the *aramataimë* and in combination with the firing of shotguns and *yikïkïet* screams, the overall effect is of cacophony.

Fig. 10.2 *Kaemo yonkonto´* (February 1981). At first light, the initiands are stationed at the edge of the dancing area, with their 'seconds' standing behind them. These young men are typically in-married affines or visitors from very close neighbouring settlements. Although the boys spend long periods in this contemplative stance, their minds are supposed to be entirely blank.

FIG. 10.3 *Katya yïnto´* (March 1981). The culminating moment: the initiands are dressed in their loincloths by the *panakon*. They hide their eyes for fear of seeing a woman which at this moment might cause their deaths. The rectangular designs on their loincloths, painted by the 'thirds', are said to be similar to the patterns of an anaconda's skin, whilst the small circles are referred to as *yoore*, i.e. the stars of the Pleiades.

FIG. 10.4 *Katya yïnto´* (March 1981). The grande finale: in a cloud of dust raised by their feet, and to the rhythm of a staccato chant, all able-bodied adults dance in the late afternoon sun around the external *no´yan* pole, with most women dancing backwards in the centre whilst the men dance forwards around the outside. The initiands, as just visible on the left, dance in the men's line, but flanked by women on either side. Prior to evangelisation, this was the moment when the Panare experienced a sentiment reminiscent of the Trio notion of *sasame*, a sense of collective well-being associated with the successful performance of ancestral dances.

11

Itoto (Kanaima*) as Death and Anti-Structure

Audrey Butt Colson, *University of Oxford*

Audrey Butt Colson, *University of Oxford*

INTRODUCTION

Kanaima, or Itoto, has been described in the literature as 'secret killer' and as 'one who kills suddenly'. They are terms which refer to a complex set of beliefs, constituting a conceptual system within the society and culture of the two Carib-speaking peoples of the circum-Roraima region of the Guiana Highlands, the Kapong (Akawaio and Patamuna) and the Pemong (Arekuna, Kamarakoto, Taurepang, and Makushi), whose lands are the border areas of Brazil, Guyana, and Venezuela.[1] The two terms are co-equivalent. Kanaima is a Pemong word, whilst Itoto (Idodo, Toto, Dodo) is used by the Akawaio. Of the two, Kanaima has a greater extension, being in use amongst neighbouring indigenous peoples, the Lokono (Arawaks) and Kari'na (Caribs), who sometimes attribute deaths to Kanaima action that comes from outside their own communities, often, it is believed, through the hire of Kapong or Pemong Kanaima assassins. Comparative research is still needed on this wider aspect.

Despite all the changes to which the Kapong and Pemong peoples have been subjected during the twentieth century, in particular through the expansion of three nation-states into their territories, there is no indication that the belief in Kanaima or Itoto activities has changed fundamentally. This is despite the introduction of new political and administrative structures, systems of communication, more varied economic pursuits, formal schooling, introduced health services, various forms of Christianity, and a wide variety of cultural innovations and choices. It is also despite the fact that other indigenous institutions, notably shamanism, have dramatically declined. Among both the Pemong on the Gran Sabana and the Akawaio in the upper Mazaruni basin, belief in Kanaima (Itoto) activity remains strong among both traditionalist and progressive (i.e. modern) members of society. As I shall endeavour to show, this durability may be attributed to some of the most fundamental beliefs and structures in their culture and society.[2]

KANAIMA/ITOTO ACTION

Akawaio tell the following story (*bandöɔ*) of the origin of Itoto:

There was once a family living in their house. One night a man came and took off a leaf from the roof, entered the house and killed everyone there. After that there was Itoto.

This brief allegorical statement contains a lot of information. Itoto (Kanaima) is invariably male. Contrary to assertions in the literature concerning a Kanaima spirit, this category of killer is a human being, not a discrete spirit. He attacks people when they can be caught unaware and unprepared, as when asleep at night, and he conceals his identity.

There are two main methods of Itoto (Kanaima) attack. One is when he hides in the forest and assaults his victim from behind, when he or she is alone. The second, as portrayed in the story, is when he hides in the forest by day and at night enters the house of his victim, squeezing in through any small gap. He does not like light and is said not to come when there is moonlight or the house fires are burning. He avoids dogs because they bark and warn their owners. As a consequence, people try never to be alone, especially when outside their settlement, and at night they bar the doors of their houses, keep the fires burning and dogs near by. However, despite such precautions, no one can render this secret killer permanently inactive and most people eventually become his victims.

In the daytime attack in the forest, the victim is waylaid, knocked out with a club or clasped round the neck and thrown to the ground, losing consciousness. The base of the tongue is cut and poison inserted, or the tongue is pierced with snake fangs. This prevents the victim from later speaking of what happened. Itoto (Kanaima) then pinches and bruises the body, dislocates the limbs, breaks the bones, the back, and the neck. He may beat the body with a stick and, making small cuts near the armpits and genital regions, rubs in poisons (*muraɔ*), which spread throughout the body. Then he may insert a forked stick into the rectum, hook out the guts, tie them on the stick so making a tourniquet, and push everything back inside. After a time the victim regains consciousness, gets up and goes home, not knowing what has happened. He, or she, then falls ill and dies in agony within a short time, three days frequently being specified. In the night attack Itoto (Kanaima) creeps into a house and 'blows' (*tareɔ*); that is, he invokes, or casts a spell, at the same time using special powders to send everyone fast asleep, including the dogs. He bruises and breaks the bones of his victim and he blows special poison powders up the victim's nostrils. He may also place special death-dealing substances in a crack in the house wall. In the morning his victim wakes, aching all over, falls ill, and dies within a few days. Apart from these characteristic methods of attack, Itoto (Kanaima) may cause death through daytime 'accidents', such as drowning or burning by pushing his victim into a river or a bonfire. He may attack in the form of an animal or snake. He can impose curses using lethal invocations (*tareɔ*).

As indubitable proof of this form of killing, relatives point to blue-black bruises which may be seen on some corpses, on the limbs and at the joints, and sometimes on the throat, back, and breast. These are believed to result from the man-handling received. People speak of the corpse of the victims of Itoto (Kanaima) as being *ekïloɔ*, 'black' or 'dark'. In contrast, 'people who take a long time to die' and when the corpse is seen as 'white' (*aïmïdïɔ*), are believed to have died of other causes, such as lethal invocation alone or the action of the Mawariton, the category of the vital forces of nature, including ghost spirits, often thought to be manipulated by an enemy shaman.

Although someone who is Itoto (Kanaima), is said to kill in his own person, he is also believed to be able to detach his vital force, or spirit, from his body and to perform his killing whilst disembodied. Akawaio and Pemong say that he can thus be seen as an ordinary person in one place whilst his spirit is a long way away in another place, carrying out the killing that his inherent evil, and 'bad mind' dictates. There are special plant substances (notably of the *kumi* species, which are reeds and coarse grasses) which enable Itoto (Kanaima) to travel many miles within a few minutes.[3] This is consonant with a general belief that all material forms of life consist of a body and an indwelling vital force or spirit (Akawaio, *akwalu*; Pemong, *ekatong*). The vital force leaves its body temporarily during states of unconsciousness: in dreams, when fainting, or in a coma. A shaman deliberately detaches his spirit when hallucinated by tobacco. Itoto (Kanaima) can voluntarily detach his vital force and send it to kill, but he may also send it into another creature, a dog, bird, jaguar, deer, and so forth, using its body as a disguise. This capacity is stressed in the concept of Itoto (Kanaima) as a ghoul.

The substances used by Itoto (Kanaima) to kill are deadly and hot. After killing he is so inflamed that he may be driven to distraction, especially if he is a young, inexperienced killer. He therefore has to cool himself down, and this he does by changing himself so that his indwelling vital force leaves his body and enters an animal. In this guise he goes to his victim's grave and, inserting a hollow tube into it, he sucks up the juices of the decaying corpse. Some maintain that his spirit enters the earth to drink and eat the corpse. At such times he comes with big, glaring eyes, and disappears very quickly if glimpsed. Unless he can cool himself down he will become mad (*sobai*), and in this state he will attack even old graves and ingest the bones, for decaying human remains 'smell sweet' to him. To further cool himself he will go into water and suck an anaconda snake, and if all fails he may drown himself, seeking the coldness of death.[4] Akawaio try to thwart Itoto interference with new graves by burying poisonous substances with the corpse and they keep watch for three nights, lighting a fire near by.

DEATH AND ITOTO (KANAIMA)

Every living body contains radiant light from 'the sun's place' (Akawaio, *akwa*; Pemong, *auka*). This illumination gives 'strength for living' (*merunti*) and conveys

well-being, intelligence, and happiness. It is present throughout the body in countless receptacles (*yewaɔ*). Small fractions of this vital force may be damaged, or
alienated from the body, and then it is the shaman's task to identify the contrary
forces at work, rescue the lost or captured vital force and so restore the patient to
health. It is believed that definitive death of the body occurs when the total vital
force is permanently alienated from it. The body then begins to decay and the
former life force, disembodied, may appear as a shade, when it becomes a Mawari,
which is a vital force of nature including deceased humans.

In their Pemong Dictionary, Cesáreo de Armellada and Mariano Gutiérrez
Salazar (1981: 88), list the Pemong verb *kana-ka-nepui*, meaning to cut or sever
(*cortar*); to terminate, put an end to (*hacer cesar*); to chill, strike dumb, stun
(*pasmar*). The suffix *-imï* is widespread in the Pemong and Kapong languages,
adding the meaning of 'great' and 'powerful', both of size and an intrinsic spiritual
quality and impact. Etymologically therefore, the word Kanaima (Kana-*imï*) may
translate as 'the great—powerful, terminator' (or cleaver, stunner, severer).[5] This
etymology certainly coincides with assertions as to what Kanaima (and Itoto) does
to his victim. His sudden, violent attack frightens the vital force out of its customary body.[6] He then fills the body with poisons, through piercing the tongue and
making cuts where the bones articulate. He blocks up all the body orifices, blowing
poisonous powders into the mouth and up the nostrils, pulling out and knotting the
intestines. Thereby the victim's alienated vital force is prevented from re-entering
its body, which, left poisoned and lifeless, dies rapidly.

The victim is often said to die within three days. The Itoto (Kanaima) ghoul
seeks to consume the fluids of the corpse within three days and concomitantly, a
watch of three days is kept over the grave. As already noted, a living body is a dual-
ity, that is, a vital force bound to a material casing. Itoto (Kanaima) intervenes as a
third factor and, as in the indigenous word for 'three', signifies something different which comes between the complementary, harmonious dual principle (Butt
Colson 1989: 66–70). Shamans in their seances claim to see the vital forces that
affect their patients. They say that when someone 'blows' (invokes) they can see the
vital force of the invoker within the sick person's body together with the vital force
which his, or her, words have summoned. These vital forces either help to restore
health or cause sickness depending on the intent of the invoker. The shaman will
also see the patient's own vital force inside its body. This is the opposite of what a
shaman perceives when Itoto (Kanaima) has attacked. Then, the shaman sees his
patient's body with poisons inside, but empty of its vital force and with the body
openings closed up and preventing its return. At the final stage of disease, shamans
often say that their patient will not recover and is already dead, the vital force, or
spirit, having left, never to return. The non-indigenous observer, on the other
hand, notes that the patient, even if in desperate straits, is still 'alive and breath-
ing'.

Akawaio and Pemong recognize death caused by overt violence as in past war
and raiding, when members of communities in conflict were arrowed and clubbed.

They also recognize open assassination or murder when, through a build-up of personal grievances, a man determines to kill another. In the few instances recalled, this entailed the aggrieved person visiting and shooting his enemy in full view of the latter's family, so creating a blood feud. Despite the almost universal assumption in the literature that Kanaima is a system of vengeance which, in the absence of centralized authority and punishment, is a socially recognized means of retaliation for wrongs done, this is not in fact the case.[7] Itoto (Kanaima) activity is never regarded as legitimate, whatever the context. Nor is it the same as warfare, or the feuding system with personal vendettas that pass down the generations. These are different activities with a different vocabulary to describe them. However, Itoto (Kanaima) accusations often accompany situations of active hostility with 'others' and so reinforce them.

Shamans sometimes diagnose a death as caused by Itoto (Kanaima) and may, through consultation with their spirit helpers (*yachitoɔ*) during seances discover where this Itoto (Kanaima) lives and may name him. However, contrary to what is sometimes asserted, shamans are not qua shamans, Itoto (Kanaima). Shamans, as shamans, characteristically work through the forces of nature, the Mawari, which include vital forces of those, humans and other, whose bodies have died. In shaman diagnoses a death is occasionally attributed to the action of a ghost (who has successfully attracted a beloved relative to him or her). Sometimes too, an individual is said to have died through an act of one of the forces of nature (a Mawari) having been so seriously aggrieved by that person's conduct that death through sickness or a fatal accident was induced. Enemy shamans use their helping spirits to kill their community's enemies.

The deaths which I recorded among the Akawaio as due to 'unseen causes', fall into two main categories. Death through lethal invocation (evil *tareɔ*) is one, and is often used to explain prolonged illness, being described as a gradual poisoning of the victim whose corpse is denoted 'white'. The other is death by Itoto attack, described as sudden and in which the corpse exhibited the characteristic blue-black bruising referred to above. However, in their search for ultimate causation the diagnoses might switch, and an evil invoker might come to be denoted Itoto, who finally finished off his victim after a long illness. Moreover, if, as sometimes happens, a particular person or family gets labelled Itoto, then deaths both past and present come to be attributed to them, even if invocation alone was originally considered the technique used.

There is a fundamental difference between invocations (*tareɔ*) and Itoto (Kanaima). Theoretically at least, any invocation, including lethal ones, can be countered by another invocation, so that when an individual falls ill from what is judged to be *tareɔ*, a search is made for someone who has the right words to effect a cure. By contrast, a full attack by Itoto (Kanaima), which may include the use of special *tareɔ*, is incurable and death is inevitable. This leads us to conclude that according to Akawaio and Pemong beliefs, Itoto (Kanaima) is synonymous with death. This is intrinsic to the word Kanaima, which, as already noted, seems to denote 'the Great Terminator' who severs body from soul, so destroying an individual's material matrix, that is, the embodiment of a life force. If translated into a metaphor, Itoto, or Kanaima, can be understood as depicting death, and might be compared to the notion of 'the Great Reaper' in European culture.[8]

For Akawaio and Pemong, Itoto (Kanaima) is the epitome of evil and, as a universal enemy, is never legitimate. It was thus extremely unfortunate that the Parque Nacional de Canaima y la Gran Sabana, the main Pemong homeland, was given this name.[9] When a group of Venezuelan business men formed an association called 'Fundación Canaima' and held a meeting to explain what they wanted to do, an angry Pemong leader stood up to denounce the plans as endangering and degrading community lands and ignoring their long-standing claim to recognition. He said vehemently that, moreover, in using the word 'Canaima', the Foundation had adopted the nastiest and most ugly word in the Pemong language! As the name, unbeknown to the Fundación Canaima members, depicts the irrevocable moment of death, it suggested that the projected developments spelt certain death for the Pemong as an indigenous society with its own land base and culture. Fundación Canaima threatened to cause a definitive severance of Pemong vital forces from their homeland, which is the matrix in which they, as a distinctive people, live their corporate life, and in which they had been cradled and nurtured from time immemorial.

ITOTO (KANAIMA) AS ENEMY

In Akawaio and Pemong traditional beliefs sickness is not the ultimate cause of death, but attack by Itoto (Kanaima) is. Thus a Kamarang river Akawaio stated: 'Sickness does not kill people. They get up and get better and go to work. With Itoto, people die.' Another informant said: 'People do not believe that sickness alone kills a person: it cannot. But sometimes a bad *piai'chaɔ* (shaman), or someone who cuts himself and rubs in *muraɔ* (charm remedies) as Itoto does, and goes *sobai* (mad), will kill someone. They cause the death, not the sickness. That is why many people have died. These people are at work.'

Akawaio did not ask 'what caused' a particular death, but 'who killed' him or her? So whilst the proponents of scientific medicine (dispensers, hospital staff, doctors) were giving such reasons for death as TB, pneumonia, whooping cough, dysentery, heart attack, stroke, septicaemia, accident, and so forth, the Akawaio were talking of the ultimate, human agents behind these, speculating on identity and motives. Human agency is implicated in the etymology of the Akawaio word *Itoto*, for in several Carib languages in Guiana it means 'human being', ethnic filiation unspecified. Even if it does not mean 'enemy' as such, 'other' humans are invariably ambivalent and potentially dangerous.[10] In making the assumption that irrevocable death from unseen causes is due to evil human agency, the political-social context becomes pre-eminent, for the basic supposition is that individuals and their communities have enemies who want to destroy them.

Akawaio maintained that 'Itoto is everywhere', and they named any country they had heard of, Brazil, Venezuela, and also England and other European countries. For them it was a phenomenon operating universally. However, they also said, 'others have it: not people here', and that 'it comes from the next people, the next place' and, waving a hand about, 'over there'. As I travelled around it became apparent that the identification of more specific locations of Itoto depended on where one was within the network of perceived structures. Akawaio anywhere might accuse other ethnic groups; for example, the Maionggong (Ye'kuana) as long-distance traders of whom they knew little or nothing but who were clearly dangerous and potentially malevolent. Frequently they implicated specific Pemong groups immediately west; for example, one Akawaio leader summed up the Pötsawï-gok (Taurepang Pemong in the Southern Pakaraima area) as 'all bad and all Itoto'! (During his youth a trading visit to them had resulted in violence.) Pemong similarly accused the Akawaio. However, accusations were also made between the Akawaio themselves in the upper Mazaruni, and these were structured according to river group affiliation. The occupants of a river valley are known by the name of the river with the suffix *-gok* (people). Thus the people of the Mazaruni river, the Masalini-gok, accused, and were accused by, the Kamarang river people, Kamalani-gok, and those of the other tributaries, the Kako and Kukui, as being Itoto and responsible for deaths which occurred. The people of each river group considered themselves to be good and blameless but all the other river groups to be either practising Itoto or liable to do so. Although there is a positive side to these intergroup relationships, such as intermarriage and mutual trading, visiting, and feasting, the negative side is underpinned by accusations of Itoto, expressing territorial and organizational separation, conflict of interests, and past conflicts including raiding. Itoto, and Kanaima, accusations are very frequently structured by segmentation, both internal to each ethnic unity and between different ethnicities, and they clearly express the stereotypes, fears, and suspicions, aroused by 'others'.

ITOTO (KANAIMA) MOTIVATION

Although anyone, male, female, young and old, may be attacked and killed by Itoto, he is nevertheless believed to target a particular category of people. These are men of wealth and status, with many followers. I was told that 'He [Itoto] is especially after important people. Itoto has bad in him; he thinks bad, especially of important people. He wants to kill them.' Every Akawaio village leader (*epulu*) complained that Itoto was trying to kill him. So also did many heads of large, extended families and individuals possessing an unusual wealth of trade goods, usually derived from money from selling *balata* (wild rubber bled from the *Manilkara bidentata* tree), or from working in the mining areas of the lower Mazaruni. Followers and relatives of these men (and occasionally women), said that Itoto was trying to kill them individually and even their spouses and babies, and would then proceed to kill their isolated leader, who was the main target.

There is universal agreement on the motivation of Itoto (Kanaima). He kills because he is essentially evil, having learnt the techniques, but he kills out of envy (*ekïnda* in both the Akawaio and Pemong languages). His overwhelming envy fuels a sense of grievance and the desire to destroy. Akawaio and Pemong state that Itoto (Kanaima) is envious of leaders and important men, because of their many relatives and followers; whose eligible daughters bring in a productive workforce of sons-in-law. He is envious because these prominent political and social leaders are men with large gardens and much food and drink, who are generous and givers of hospitality and feasts, who have alliances with other leaders and manipulate exchange systems. He is also envious of those with great knowledge, a reputation for goodness, and who are ritual experts. Beset by envy, Itoto (Kanaima) is profoundly aggrieved at the wealth and success of others—in which he, not being a member of their community, is unable to share. Thus, prosperous Akawaio and Pemong with status fear the distant poor and unesteemed for fear of the envy provoked.[11] So what is new?

It is noteworthy that envy, the deadliest of the seven deadly sins in European, Christian societies with marked differentiations of rank and wealth, should also be found so prominently among the Akawaio and Pemong, generally classified as egalitarian. This suggests that notions of wealth and deprivation are universal and always relative, and that we need to look at the whole concept of egalitarianism, comparatively and in far greater depth than previously. In assuming that the members of their own local community are good people, not Itoto, or Kanaima, Akawaio and Pemong exclude envy and death-dealing activity from within their own local community. Itoto (Kanaima) comes from outside, from other people. The kinship network of a village, traditionally possessed an ethic of giving and sharing, institutionalized through food presentations between households and daily communal meals to which all contributed and in which all shared. Periodic feasting between neighbouring villages and settlements, particularly within the same river area, is also traditional and the Pemong say they promote this so that friendly relations are maintained and suspicion and envy inhibited. Those who accumulate trade goods are subjected to unmerciful begging and forced to give or exchange them. Meanness of any kind is frowned on and, according to shaman pronouncements, angers the environmental spirits, who visit sickness on the culprits. Pride in achievement and possession, shared within the local community, is accompanied by fear of arousing Itoto (Kanaima) envy and attack from an envious outside, leading to death.

DEATH AND SOCIAL DYNAMICS

The death of an important man has far-reaching consequences for a community. As leader he is a key figure in a particular kinship and alliance configuration involving supporting heads of households. The affection and respect accorded him in the address term of *yepotori*, and the authority explicit in the designation *kaipun*[12] well indicate his status. *Epulu*, 'leader', has been assigned two etymologies: 'a central, upright post' (such as holds up the roof of a roundhouse), and 'handle', which is the agent for manipulation of an entity.[13] Remove the central pole, or the handle, and the structure in question starts to fall apart and cease to function. A suitable successor enables a community to persist more or less as previously, but a realignment of the constituent family units inevitably occurs. Some who were previously at the centre of village politics find themselves on the periphery. They tend to reside in their own extended household settlement, attending the central village for feasts, but they may gravitate to another village with closer or more agreeable kin.

Fear of Itoto action and its consequences is well illustrated by the career of Danny, whose reputation was encapsulated in the designation: 'Governor of the Kamarang River'. He headed a large, extended family unit, which constituted a small village and was famous for his hospitality, generosity, and feast-giving. With many daughters, he had several sons-in-law working under his direction, so that he always had abundant food and drink to offer. He was a successful long-distant trader with Pemong partners on the Gran Sabana. He was a great personality. One day Danny went to his garden alone, suffered a dizzy turn and thought he saw figures flitting to one side of him. He managed to get home but was sure he would have been attacked by Itoto had he not had his cutlass in his hand. One of the family said that Itoto planned to kill Danny, Danny's son, and all the sons-in-law. Itoto intended to kill his daughters' husbands so that no children would be born. Itoto would kill first one husband and then another one when a second husband was taken by the widow (this was in explanation of the death of a daughter's two husbands). The group would lose its leader and vigorous males and there would be no future generation. Destruction of this community would thus be complete.

Speculation began on what would happen when Danny died. The son of Danny's deceased elder brother thought the family unit would break up, and he expressed the following worries: 'Will the people whom Danny feasts, be favourable to me? If they continued to live closely together, would some small differences arise—even if I myself did not cause them! These might be magnified.' A few years later Danny died and his community did split up. His son, living uxorilocally with his wife's parents, eventually replaced them as they grew old and died. The most enterprising of Danny's sons-in-law left the Kamarang river and went to live in the upper Cuyuni in Venezuela, returning to his mother's natal area. His wife's sisters, their husbands and families (Danny's daughters and sons-in-law) went with him. Today, some thirty years later, they form a flourishing unit of over one hundred people.

Death is thus a catalyst for profound change in Akawaio and Pemong structures and social relationships. This is because death of an important man, a leader, causes the unravelling of the polity which he upholds and directs. Peter Rivière (1970*a*: 247) wrote of the Trio of Suriname that 'the leader of any village is the symbol of that village's existence, and it is on his ability that its duration depends'.[14] Among the Akawaio and Pemong the traditional leader is likewise the life and soul of a network of kin and allied families which he creates around himself, making a coherent, active unity with internal solidarity, its members free in the main from grievance and envy through the constant sharing which he mediates and directs. Anyone acting to the contrary is pressurized and leaves. This is a unity which defends its integrity from assault by 'others' near and far who may envy its lands, productivity, and well-being. With their leader dead, or isolated through the death of followers, this uniquely constituted unit inevitably changes, and is either replaced by a similar one, but of a different configuration, or it ceases altogether and its leaderless factions enter a long period of reconstitution under new direction and often in a new locality.

The example of Danny's community illustrates very well the vital importance of the parents-in-law/daughter's husband relationship, with its uxorilocal residence and work obligations, in the formation and maintenance of Akawaio and Pemong extended family and village unities. Perhaps it is not surprising, therefore, that Itoto (Kanaima) techniques of killing are believed to be passed down the generations in its structural opposite, from father to son and brother to brother. This is the antithesis of the affinal relationship between parents-in-law and son-in-law and of collaboration between brothers-in-law whose wives are 'sisters' to each other.[15] It is noteworthy that where, through certain sets of circumstances, several brothers live with their father and form an operative group, they tend to attract Itoto/Kanaima accusations. This aspect of Itoto/Kanaima merits detailed treatment. However, so also does the factor of gender. Women are never Itoto, or Kanaima, although having their own envies they may influence husband or sons to target particular individuals. In these societies men are public activators and manipulators. Men are expected to move and to wheel and deal. In contrast, stability and continuity down the generations lie with the solidarity and continuity of the female relationships of mother/daughter and sister/sister. This legitimacy is contradicted when it is replaced by a persisting father/son and brother/brother unity negating the exchange of men and the renewed processes of community creation via affinity and alliance. A patriline may thus be regarded as evidence of subversive political ambitions, fostering the ambitions of Itoto (Kanaima) to kill men of status and wealth who depend on a structural and value-laden opposite.[16]

However, one must not overlook Peter Rivière's finding for the Trio, that 'suspicion of sorcery tends to focus around in-marrying affines and marginal groups' (Rivière 1984: 80). Among the Akawaio, when a marriage breaks down and the son-in-law leaves for his natal family, or is ejected, accusations of Itoto (Kanaima) are very likely to occur between the two communities. It is thus vital to consider the various types of relationships that give rise to accusations of death-dealing activities and to define what, for the communities concerned, constitutes 'the inside' and 'the outside' and whether this dichotomy is the overarching factor.

CONCLUSION

The data I have here presented on Itoto (Kanaima) relate closely to the extremely interesting article by Peter Rivière (1970*a*) entitled 'Factions and Exclusions in Two South American Village Systems'. It deserves to be better known and used comparatively. Referring to the Carib-speaking Trio of the Brazil–Surinam border and the Gê-speaking Âkwe-Shavante of the Central Brazilian plateau, Rivière (1970*a*: 253) describes the Trio village as a 'sorcery-free unit'. It is unable to support serious divisions and enmities within itself, and in cases of serious dispute the weaker faction leaves and becomes liable to open accusations of death-dealing sorcery. This process puts a limit on village size, but the accusations confirm the distinction between the inside and outside, so reinforcing settlement boundaries and, by confirming an internal purity, strengthening its unity (Rivière 1970*a*: 254).

Similarly, in their traditional round and oval houses, lived the Pemong and Akawaio households that constituted an extended family settlement or village. These too were units internally free of the malevolence characteristic of the 'outside' world and exhibiting a strong distinction between 'we ourselves' and 'others'. Pemong say that the house, although a material entity, also has a life, which is the community which inhabits it. When a leader or head of household dies, often resulting in the abandonment of both house and site, the house grows sad, begins to decay, and will itself die. Thus death, in the form of Itoto (Kanaima) has consequences far beyond the individual or nuclear family. Itoto (Kanaima) is synonymous with the death of particular sets of relationships and alliances, and by dissolving these it destroys a corporate unity, a polity. Of course in the longer perspective it also sets the stage for the fabrication of new alignments and unities, but for those individuals in mourning and fearful of the forces of change undermining them, this is no consolation. At this point in time it seems that destructive forces have triumphed. They are those believed to be engendered in a patriline (father to son), or derived from 'other people' (in rival river groups and different ethnic units), who unscrupulously seek their own illegitimate advancement through Itoto (Kanaima) killing.

Thus we arrive at an equation: Itoto (Kanaima) envy = death (of leaders and followers) = death of a polity. This process begins a dynamic of replacement, that is, of a new network of kin and formation of alliances which, although based on similar principles, usher in a new structure for corporate living. However, Itoto (Kanaima) itself and the despair, horror, and anger it arouses, is the essence of destruction. It refers to the moment of dissolution of the unity of a body and soul—not to the later reconstitution of future individuals and their structures for corporate life. 'The Great Terminator, who severs body and soul' (Kanaima), the 'Secret Enemy' (Itoto), is one who, through his inherent evil, effects the termination of social units by eliminating or isolating their key personnel, so leaving the body politic, deprived of its vitality, to wither away. Although today's village is not so fundamentally affected by this death-dealing activity,[17] the integrity of the smaller settlement and extended household unit still is, and individuals in mourning still experience the horror and implications of death by Itoto (Kanaima) as a destroyer of the fabric of life in its variety of facets.

* Over time, and through individual choices, the spelling of 'Kanaima' has greatly varied. At present, there are still several written renderings of the final vowel sound, and these derive from the different religious workers and linguistic experts in the field. The latest symbol to be employed is /ü/, now appearing in printed texts amongst both the Akawaio and the Pemong regional groups in Venezuela. Until a consensus is reached amongst the Amerindians, I have decided to continue to use the form Kanaima (pronounced 'Kanaimï' in the international alphabet phonetic system), as being the rendering most generally encountered and understood in modern literary references in Brazilian Portuguese, Guyanese English, and Venezuelan Spanish.

NOTES

1. Kapong and Pemong are autodenominations representing distinct ethnic unities, although very similar ones. The literature in general has mostly referred to their regional group names (which are attributed nicknames), and has denoted these subdivisions 'tribes' or, in earlier times, 'nations'.
2. Much of the data in this present work derives from my 1950s field research amongst the Akawaio of the Upper Mazaruni District, Guyana. However, during frequent visits to the Gran Sabana Pemong and westernmost settlements of Akawaio in Venezuela, I have accessed more material and continued my inquiries.
3. An instance of this power was related to me by a trilingual and literate Pemong (Taurepang) on the Gran Sabana, as recently as 1998.
4. The complementary oppositions bitter/hot versus cold/sweet operate extensively in Kapong and Pemong remedial practices (see Butt Colson 1976).
5. This was the provisional conclusion that the late RP Cesáreo de Armellada, Capuchin missionary among the Pemong, came to and was hoping to follow up in further linguistic studies in the field.
6. The concept of loss of at least some fractions of vital force from the body owing to the experience of 'fright' is a common diagnosis of 'cold' illness amongst Akawaio, and I assume that this indigenous concept has been at least part of the basis for the Creole concept of *susto* (shock or fright) in Latin American countries (see Butt Colson and Cesáreo de Armellada 1983: 1229, 1234–6, and 1241–2).
7. For example, see im Thurn (1883: 329–32). He divides 'kenai-ma' into two kinds. One is the 'imaginary kenaima' who causes death through sickness. The other is the 'real kenaima' who, in the absence of laws enforced by society, pursues his own vengeance or assumes it as a sacred duty in retaliation for a wrong or death of a near blood relative.
8. I refer to the depiction of death as a very old gaunt man or skeleton, clad in a long cloak, with a scythe, who cuts swaths through the living and harvests them, just as a harvester cuts swaths through his ripened corn.
9. The name 'Canaima' was, I think, derived from the title of the well-known Venezuelan novel *Canaima*, written by Romulo Gallegos. Padre Cesáreo de Armellada always main-

tained that the name of the Park should be changed to 'Parque Nacional de Macunaima', replacing the concept of death which Kanaima (Canaima) represents with the name of the Elder Brother of the twin heroes who are ancestors of the Pemong according to an important saga of origins (see Armellada 1964).

10. See Carlin (forthcoming). It is noteworthy that Akawaio sometimes referred to bone flutes (today made of animal bones) as *wi-toto* ('my enemy'). Early literature describes these peoples as cutting off the arms and legs of enemy war victims and boiling them up to detach the flesh in order to make flutes of them.

11. Interestingly, Walter Little and Antonio Herrera (1995: 21), in their paper entitled *Populism and Reform in Contemporary Venezuela*, write: 'For all the official rhetoric about a nation of constitutionally equal citizens, it seems clear that in Venezuela the poor despise and resent the rich and that the rich fear the poor. This tension is not conducive to the investment that long-term development requires.'

12. *Yepotori* is a word rarely used today. *Kaipun*, which has an authoritative connotation, is the root of *kaipuna*, Akawaio for 'father', but in Pemong it is often used for mother's brother (i.e. father-in-law), who is an even more powerful figure.

13. See Armellada and Gutiérrez Salazar (1981: 59), under *epu*: sostén, mango; and *epuru* (the possessive form), meaning capitán, jefe.

14. Peter Rivière went on to develop in detail his analysis of the nature of leadership and settlements in Guianese societies in his book *Individual and Society in Guiana* (1984: see chaper 6 in particular).

15. In a system of cross-cousin marriage (whether real or classificatory), parents-in-law are also mother's brother and father's sister, and marriage is between the cross-cousins (the children of a brother and sister).

16. This may, in part at least, explain the boasting of the occasional, self-proclaimed Itoto (Kanaima) who, when drunk, confesses to having killed the recently deceased, thereby risking his own future safety. During my field research among the Akawaio there was one notorious family living in their small settlement in the Mazaruni river area. They consisted of six co-resident brothers with, until his death, their aged father. Their occasional drunken boasting of Itoto-killing caused fear and anger throughout the entire population, but when one of the older brothers was challenged on one occasion he assumed an air of contemptuous superiority and appeared to enjoy the notoriety. The brother relationship amongst both Akawaio and Pemong is enshrined in their myth of origin relating to Makunaima and Chikï (Armellada 1964) but it is noticeable that the adventurous comradeship of these heroes changed when one of them took a wife and in-law obligations led to periods of separation. These aspects of Itoto (Kanaima) require special attention.

17. Today, Akawaio and Pemong villages are much larger and more complicated structures than previously. Nor, with a school, health post, elected captains and committees in a national administrative system, can such units be abandoned, as was still feasible in the 1950s at the time of my initial research.

12

Kanaimà: Shamanism and Ritual Death in the Pakaraima Mountains, Guyana

Neil Whitehead, *University of Wisconsin, Madison*

This chapter presents materials on the cultural practice and social consequences of modes of assassination and physical mutilation among the indigenous peoples of the Pakaraima mountains, Guyana, in particular the Patamuna and Makushi. It will be argued that the shamanic death-cult known as Kanaimà illustrates the way in which violence may be used to establish a field of social and cultural power that continuously challenges, and so allows the renegotiation of, the organization of society. The chapter by Butt Colson in this volume also deals with Kanaimà as practised by the northern neighbours of the Patamuna, the Akawaio and Pemon. In that contribution Butt Colson also shows how Kanaimà is a force for 'anti-structure', dissolving both kin and political units through both the actual killing and the fear that such assassination engenders. In this sense both Butt Colson and I are building on Rivière's (1970*a*) earlier insights into the social structural implications of assault sorcery and its associated accusations and recriminations. Research on the Kanaimà has its own special difficulties so that the existing literature is small and uneven but, as Butt Colson notes, 'comparative research is still needed . . .' to understand the prevalence and distribution of Kanaimà. In this chapter I will also argue that distributional and frequency data are not sufficient, and that it is the discursive properties of Kanaimà that need to be more properly integrated into our ethnographic representations. For this reason both Butt Colson and myself reference non-indigenous aspects of Kanaimà and I would go further and suggest that indigenous practice is itself partly inspired by this wider field of significance of the discourse of Kanaimà.

Kanaimà, like Alleluia prophecy to which it is related and which Butt Colson also discusses (Butt Colson 1960), becomes a radical force for reordering society in the face of change. This also helps us understand why there is an ambiguous acceptance of Kanaimà, despite the regular deaths, since it is taken as a mark of an ethnic authenticity and proof of the vitality of tradition, as is also the case with Alleluia. At the same time, the history of conflicts between prophets and death-shamans in highland Guyana parallels that of warrior-chiefs and prophet-shamans in other

parts of South America (see Clastres 1977), reflecting the way in which the physical dismemberment of men and gods is a cipher for the creation and destruction
of human commensality (Viveiros de Castro 1992).

The analysis made here will not be an exercise in the deconstruction of killing,
that that which appears brutal, violent, and fatal is somehow really gentle, pacific,
and creative. But, it will be suggested that killing and mutilation may be
constructed culturally as such—as was the case in Iroquois torture or Tupi anthropophagy. The argument here is that the fatal accident which is the killing of a
person (Lizot 1994) is always more than this; to paraphrase Sahlins's (1983: 88)
remark on cannibalism, the problem is that violence is always symbolic even
though it is real. As such, modalities of violence are neither arbitrary nor purely
instrumental, but are complex acts of expression whose performative qualities tell
us as much, or more, about the meaning of that act as does viewing such acts as
diagnostic of social conflict (Rivière 1970*a*) or individual antagonism (Chagnon
1990).

THE PERFORMANCE OF VIOLENCE IN AMAZONIA

Over the last decade interpretations of war in Amazonia (Taylor *et al.* 1986, Rival
1996*b*, Whitehead 1990) have advanced beyond the ecological-biological-material-
ist paradigm and focus instead on the role of violence in the symbolic reproduction
of group identity. This emphasis on symbolic and discursive form has enabled new
interpretations of a wide range of violent practice, both in Amazonia and beyond,
particularly aggressive shamanism (Stewart and Strathern 1999), as well as the key
symbols and rituals of war, such as head-hunting (Hoskins 1996), mutilation
(Trexler 1995), and cannibalism (Viveiros de Castro 1992). As Arens (1979) says,
cannibalism has been a key conceptual issue for Western anthropology and a part
of a wider colonial discourse on 'the savage' over the last 500 years (Barker *et al.*
1998). As in the case of cannibalism, for example, new approaches escape the usual
theories of psychological or nutritional compulsion and refer instead to an
Amazonian symbolic repertoire in which the trope of anthropophagy is all pervasive (Overing 1986*a*, Conklin 1995). In counter-point to seeing claims as to the
existence of cannibal practice as merely an external projection (which of course it
may be as well), such approaches seek to understand the native trope of violent
hunger and the discourse and discursive practice to which it gives rise. In such a
context the violence of the capture, killing, and consumption of enemies is itself a
ritual form understood by both perpetrator and victim. It is this consensual aspect
that has defied conventional analyses of 'violence' since it is treated as a phenomenon somehow separable from its symbolic meanings. Previous analyses have also
failed to appreciate the reciprocity implied by such acts of violence and so assumed
that acts of violence are necessarily expressive of personal disagreement and/or
diagnostic of political or economic conflicts. In fact they might be seen equally as

expressive of consensus or harmony over the broader questions of socio-cultural reproduction, since both allies and enemies share the cultural quest for human body parts to become killer-gods or man-jaguars. In this way violence and war actually come to represent intercourse, communication, and exchange, which prompts the question as to the semiotics of the combat, capture, and death that are the forms of that communication. By the same token, where cultural consensus as to the forms and modalities of war are lacking, violence becomes a means for the initiation of such a political discourse—just as occurs in colonial and neo-colonial wars or internal 'police actions'.

Of course this issue is deeply political in other ways too since the representation of the violence of others is key in patterning political and more general cultural reactions—evidently enough one person's freedom fighter is another's terrorist, or is the divine warrior really just a savage cannibal? But the analytical issue goes deeper even than this since the hermeneutic key to such behaviour is how it is represented by the perpetrators to themselves and to others. In this auto-representation of violence we must accept that violence appears as both appropriate and valuable, and is not necessarily understood at all as something dysfunctional and pathological. Paralleling this re-conceptualization of the social dynamics of violence then, is a better anthropological appreciation of its discursive and symbolic roles (Basso 1995, Combès 1992, Hendricks 1993, Whitehead 1997).

My own fieldwork in the Guyana Highlands on a series of ritualized killings by death-shamans, Kanaimà, certainly suggests that whatever the moral or criminal meanings such killings may have for outsiders, they are not unambiguously present for either victims or practitioners. Kanaimà is also understood as a culturally 'authentic' act, expressing a hyper-traditionality and resistance to colonizing modernity (Appadurai 1996: 139–57), even as Kanaimà simultaneously involves extreme violence to both individual bodies and the extant body-politic. I therefore disagree with Butt Colson (this volume) that Kanaimà activity is never regarded as legitimate, even if it is always feared and acknowledged as an antisocial force. A Kanaimà practitioner may be informally identified by a refusal to wear coastlander style clothing (shirt and trousers), to use matches or metal cooking-pots, and, most significantly, guns. The refusal to use firearms signals one of the ways in which killing by Kanaimà is to be distinguished from the practice of collective warfare (*weypantaman*) by warriors (*kwayaus*), even though there was a connection in the past, shamanic battle often having been a prelude to physical combat (see Whitehead 1996, 1990).

KANAIMÀ TODAY

The material presented here was collected among the Makushi and Patamuna on the border of Guyana and Brazil. Most previous accounts of Kanaimà (Roth 1915: 354–62) tend to dismiss physical Kanaimà as an immaterial metaphor used to explain death as a result of the malevolence of outsiders. Reference to Kanaimà certainly may work in this way. However, the Patamuna point out that this attitude replicates that of the first Anglican missionaries who, not having an adequate English term, simply dismissed Kanaimà as a spirit, an example of Wittgenstein's observation that '[W]herever our language leads us to believe there is a body, but no body exists, there is a spirit' (1953: I. 36). But the hungry violence of a Kanaimà assassination is charged with the physical and the real.

The Patamuna are certainly entranced by the symbolic force of Kanaimà but I have also made video and sound recordings of detailed descriptions and direct observations of nine recent ritual assassinations, as well as interviewing Kanaimà sorcerers and their shaman enemies (*piyasan*) directly. On the basis of this material, collected on several visits to the Pakaraimas between 1992 and 1997, and although clearly each performance has its special features depending on the characteristics of both victim and assassin, I attempt below to suggest a theory of Kanaimà practice.[1]

The intended victim will first become aware of an impending attack when the Kanaimàs approach his house by night, or on lonely forest trails, making a characteristic whistling noise. As well as being encountered as were-jaguars in the forest, the Kanaimàs can also appear as anteaters in the savannahs. Following these portents a direct physical attack might come at any point, even years thereafter, for during this period of stalking the victim is assessed as to their likely resistance and their suitability as 'food'. This conceptual framework assimilates the victim to the category of prey and so actively 'hunting Kanaimàs' become jaguars tracking, sniffing, and touching the intended victims footprints and spoor. The Kanaimàs literally conceive of themselves as hunting for their food, and so use hunting *beenas* (charms) in just the way a peccary-hunter might. Kanaimà initiation further replicates this notion, since the Kanaimà adept and his initiate are conceived of as a jaguar and his kill. In some attacks the victims may have minor bones broken, especially fingers, and joints dislocated, especially the shoulder, while the neck may also be manipulated to induce spinal injury and back pain. This kind of attack is generally considered to be a preliminary to actual death and mutilation. My data differ from Butt Colson, in the sense that Kanaimà attacks intended initially only to injure the victim have the state of fear in which victim and kin are thus held as the actual objective; fatal attack will certainly follow but, informants stress, many months, or even a year or two, later.

When a fatal physical attack is intended, victims report that they are first confronted by a single Kanaimà from the front, but then they are always struck from behind and physically restrained. A variety of procedures, intended to produce a lingering death, are then enacted. The victim has their tongue pierced with the fangs of a snake, is turned over, and either an iguana or an armadillo tail is inserted into their rectum so that the anal muscles can be stripped out through repeated rubbing. Then, pressing on the victim's stomach, a section of the sphincter muscle is forced out and cut. Finally, the victim's body is rubbed down with astringent plants, usually *koumi* (a ginger), and a thin flexed twig is forced into the rectum, so that it opens the anal tract. Packets of herbs are then rammed in as deeply as possible. This is said to begin a process of auto-digestion, creating the special aroma of Kanaimà enchantment, rotting pineapple (*akaikalak*). The sweet odour of pineapple is therefore a sign of Kanaimà attack for the victims, and the spoor by which their attackers will relocate their bodies after burial.

As a result of the completion of these procedures, the victim is unable to speak or to take any sustenance by mouth. Bowel control is lost and the clinical cause of death becomes acute dehydration through diarrhoea. The interest of the Kanaimàs in their victim does not end here, for they must also make a gift of their prey to the sorcerer who leads them and directs their attacks. In this exchange, the sorcerer becomes identified with the ferocity of *kaikusi-yumu*, Lord Jaguar himself (Whitehead 1990), who will only be assuaged by 'tasting the honey of the dead'. Therefore the Kanaimàs will try and discover the burial place of their victim and await the onset of putrefaction in the corpse that usually occurs within three days. In this time the Kanaimàs are understood to be magically vulnerable and can be intercepted and killed by the dead person's relatives as they try, literally, to smell out these first stages of putrefaction. The missionary William Brett, who encountered just such an individual, wrote (1868: 359):

An Indian, reduced almost to a skeleton, and in a dreadful state of exhaustion, was picked up in the forest by some Arawaks . . . He had lost a portion of his scalp and had his lower lip torn down at each corner. The Acawaios . . . took care of him at first, but afterwards judged, from his refusing certain kinds of food and other signs that he was a devotee and victim of an unappeased Kanaima . . . we had some difficulty in getting him nursed till his strength returned, as they feared lest they should become his future victims.

The need to ward off the Kanaimàs and protect the cadaver from further interference leads to a distinct type of burial of the victim's corpse from that usually practised. This may involve placing the corpse in a rock-niche, covering the grave site with large boulders, or in a sealed ceramic jar, and keeping the location secret.

If the grave site is discovered, a stick is inserted through the ground directly into the cadaver, then the stick is retracted and the *maba* (honey-like) juices sucked off. The juices of putrefaction are said to taste like honey because the grave is 'tasted' with the help of a stick, used in the same way as when eating honey from a hive. The effect of *maba* is both psychotropic and morphic: the satisfied Kanaimà can, like Jaguar, now sleep sated and dream of being Man, but the dream is also a reality since tasting the *maba* thereby transforms Jaguar into Man again. So a Kanaimà will not eat human food after a kill until he has tasted the divine food of the grave, and indeed he must taste the *maba* if the dangerous divine force of Lord Jaguar is to be purged and this return to the domain of the human achieved.

If the corpse is indeed sufficiently 'sweet', it will be partially disinterred in order to recover bone material and, ideally, a section of the anal tract. The use of previous victims' body parts is necessary to facilitate the location and killing of the next victim, since these gifts of death, from the Kanaimà killers to their sorcerer, drive the unending exchanges between divine animals and mundane humans, in the guise of hunter and prey, which it is the aim of the Kanaimà sorcerer to sustain. This key role in the creation and management of the predatory interrelation of humanity, animality, and divinity is why the Kanaimà sorcerer is the source of powerful shamanic techniques, in the same way that the divine gift of tobacco, carried by the *kumalok* (swallow-tailed kite), is the source of shamanic curing and prophecy. As Butt Colson indicates (this volume), the techniques of Kanaimà often may be passed from father to son, so that particular families gain a reputation for Kanaimà. However, a Kanaimà may kill even his consanguineal as well as affinal relations; and he may choose to initiate anyone he pleases. Certain groups, particularly the Akawaio and Makushi, are held to be particularly adept, but the complex is not unique to any one group. In this sense, one may say that Kanaimà is both extra-social (it does not simply mirror the pattern of relations between ethnic collectivities) and anti-social (it is an attack on society itself).

The overall incidence of Kanaimà killings in the village where I worked runs at about one per year. The killing is predominantly of children and adult women. This is because they are the most vulnerable to attack and the most defenceless. 'When one hunts one takes the first prey, the easiest to kill'—was the explanation given by one such killer. The reason for the frequent killing is that Kanaimà is a system of shamanism and in Patamuna conceptions the Lords of Death (Kanaimà) unceasingly battle with the Lords of Life (*piyasan*), the victories of each being expressed through their relative ascent of *karawali* (the spirit-ladder) to the *icheiri* (ancestor stars) who are that critical third term in the disposition of the life and death of humans and animals.

However, it remains possible, if dangerous, to intercede with a Kanaimà sorcerer to ask for the death of a specific enemy, and Kanaimà seems to have accompanied warfare in the past in just this kind of way. These 'revenge' killings have occurred recently as a result of conflicts in the gold and diamond fields but, even where such killings take the idiom of Kanaimà, it is killing, not murder. This distinction between mundane murder and magical death is very clearly drawn by Patamuna. These Kanaimà killings are only partly discussed as a law and order problem for Kanaimà is always more than this since it invokes a whole complex of cosmological ideas. As a result Patamuna attitudes are at best ambiguous, for the existence of Kanaimà also structures outsiders' exchanges with the highland peoples in a way that mediates and resists the socio-cultural cannibalism of the external world (Whitehead 1997). In this context, we may also wish to refer to the literary and symbolic uses of Kanaimà in non-Amerindian thought, as in Romulo Gallegos's seminal novel *Canaima*, as part of the premise of its indigenous practice. The hyper-traditionality of the Kanaimà in matters of dress and domestic habits thus responds to external factors, and may even have been evident from the times of earliest contacts with Europeans (see Whitehead 1998: 30).

THE DISCURSIVE PRACTICE AND POLITICAL MORPHOLOGY OF KANAIMÀ

If the physical existence or non-existence of the Kanaimà has been an ethno-graphic question of the last one hundred years, a 'law and order' problem associated with Kanaimà resulting from the general anarchy of the gold fields and diamond mines is the political–economic context for current practice. Certainly there will have been phases of greater or lesser activity amongst cultists through time and such historical changes may explain varying ethnographic attitudes to the phenomena as being first real, then unreal or metaphorical. In terms relevant to semiotic theory, recent debate on Amazonia has focused on how, by acting on the body, the symbolic construction of persons and the reproduction of society is achieved. It is an obvious corollary that the deconstruction of the person after death is also an aspect of this relation between human bodies and the body politic, that is, the symbolic assemblage that created persons and society must likewise be disassembled at death. This requires that symbolic techniques be carefully performed in order that the various body components reach their appropriate cultural destinations, and this is precisely what Kanaimà mutilation disrupts.

Death is therefore as important for the reproduction of society as other activities more obviously associated with social construction, such as marriage or birth. However, in the context of Kanaimà deaths an important ritual and symbolic discontinuity is initiated by the form of the gift of death. The political economy and its body politic within which that gift, that moment of exchange, takes place, is thereby altered and normal social relations are themselves mutilated. It is therefore necessary to analyse the semiotic properties of the Kanaimà act in terms of both its internal and external meanings, that is, in terms of the endosemiosis of the form of mutilation and the exosemiosis of the possibility of its performance. In the latter case, the suggestion will be that Kanaimà knowingly situates itself as a mediating force between a fierce understanding of traditional Amerindian society (as the appropriate context for the capture and incorporation of a means to shamanic ascendance, i.e. human bodies), and the ferocity of modern society, represented in activities of Creole miners (or *balata* bleeders of a generation ago) and the presence of a colonizing Guyanese and/or Brazilian and/or Venezuelan state. The colonial discourse of cannibalism is thus mimetically linked to the indigenous discourse of Kanaimà.

THE ENDOSEMIOSIS OF KANAIMÀ

Kanaimà mutilation is a form of the gift of death which renders the human hunter as divine prey by inverting the definition of 'person'. A real person is the possessor of an incontinent mouth, to be understood as representing the dangerous capacities for both beautiful words and cannibalism, and a continent anus that stands for the control of those supremely social effluvia of sperm, menstruation, and blood. The flow of these vital substances occurs through the culturally constrained conduct of the socially constituting exchanges of war and marriage. Kanaimà mutilation thus reduces this person to a 'thing', evident from its continent mouth, or lack of speech, achieved through the insertion of snake fangs into the tongue, and incontinent anus, or lack of sociality, since the insertion of the 'magic arrows' of the armadillo tail and flexed sticks renders the victim physically incontinent. By itself, however, such an analysis goes no further than strict Saussurean principles would allow, and so to fulfil the semiotic project described at the start of this chapter, it is necessary to situate these meanings of the gift in the active system of exchanges that show us how such meanings are deployed for wider semiotic purposes.

We can term this system of exchanges a political economy of death. That is, the symbolic configuration of death begins with the idea that human death is always a form of predation by gods or human enemies; as a result, death is understood as a form of external exchange, rather than something which is an internal production of society. Kanaimà may thus be seen as a particular form of the gift of death within a political economy of cosmological exchange which places human killing into a more general idiom of relations between divinities, persons, and things which are conducted either as sexual, or as gastronomic, possession. The semiotics of the ritual symbolism of a Kanaimà death, and most obviously the physical deconstruction of the corpse, may thus be seen as deriving from this political economy of death. The symbolic disruption and discontinuity introduced by a Kanaimà killing is simultaneously an attack on society itself, a means by which the hunter is made prey, just as the Tupian Karai of the old time were subversive of the authority of the ruling elites (Clastres 1977).

Using Bloch's (1992) analysis of ritual, we may say that the attainment of the status of Kanaimà also represents the turning of divine prey (persons) into hunters of humans, seen in the continuous transformation of the adept into jaguars via consumption of the *maba* of their victims. The political contest between warriors and shamans to control the spectacle and rites of such violent ritual was therefore also an important facet of socio-cultural change and innovation, the symbolism of the jaguar permitting a direct connection to violent political behaviour. In Guyana the marginalization of such practices in the last one hundred and fifty years is reflected precisely in the loss of influence of the Kanaimàs and the increase in the influence of the Alleluia cultists. So in the context of the long history of a pervasive native trope of cannibalism, and its persistent physical enactment, the florescence of a 'traditional' mode of killing becomes as much a token of revitalization, as it is of moral decay and social disorder. The Kanaimàs are simultaneously divine cannibal jaguars and mundane criminal assassins, and this is also precisely the attitude of those who are victims, or potential victims.

THE EXOSEMIOSIS OF KANAIMÀ

In discussing ritual violence, and especially cannibalism, anthropologists have been forced into an ideological framework that originates in the sixteenth century's 'discovery of cannibals' (Whitehead 1997). Within this framework, issues as to the external purpose of the ethnographic representation of indigenous performance are to the fore. These may be summarized as the necessity of choice between writing the Patamuna as criminal assassins or cannibal jaguars, that is, interpreting these events as showing either the criminal delinquency of savage tribals, as happened with the Yanomami or Wari (Conklin 1997), or the continuity of culture, the vivacity of indigenous conceptions, and the revitalization of tradition. But this is a false dilemma since we do not have to accept the colonial hermeneutic for cannibalism but rather, in recognition of the processes of mimetic cultural elaboration which that colonial legacy has created, we can say that Kanaimà persists as a mimesis of the continuing colonial consumption of the Amerindians. In the oral history of the Patamuna the cannibal Karinya who raided up the Siparuni river in the nineteenth century were led by a white man who controlled the *balata* bleeders, just as now the highlands are eaten up by miners, anthropologists, and eco-tourists. So as regards ritual and history, we must expect radical discontinuities, signalling transformations in ritual symbolism, not just the 'logical elaborations' of Maurice Bloch (1986), or the 'structural reproductions' of Marshall Sahlins (1985), which appear conceptually incomplete as representations of practice. Undoubtedly Kanaimà killing introduces just such a radical discontinuity, in the manner that the Alleluia prophecy, or the prophecy of the Karai, might be understood as inimical to the extant social order.

This link between Kanaimà and Alleluia as disruptive of the ordering of society may help us understand more subtle links between masculine identities, political success, and radical ritual action. In this light it seems significant that Bichiwung, the first prophet of Alleluia, was repeatedly attacked and finally killed by Kanaimàs. Equally, some of the original prophets, such as Abel and Christ were, until their Alleluia revelation, Kanaimà, and the Kanaimà also appear as obstacles to their shamanic flight to God's heaven in search of that revelation (Butt 1960). A contest for shamanic domination may partly explain why the Kanaimàs are pictured as trying repeatedly to kill Bichiwung and other prophets such as Abel, Christ, and Queen Mulē, and perhaps even the English missionary Thomas Youd (but see Rivière 1995c: 117–18).

Now and in recent times the contest between Kanaimàs and Alleluia prophets continues (see also Butt 1960: 84), with Christianity adding a further layer of spirit armour to the defences of the god-men. This is a clear reason given for a rejection of *piyasan* in favour of Christianity by Amerindian ministers in the Highlands, that is, that whereas the former was weak against Kanaimà, Christianity had proved, like Alleluia, effective against the secret killer. This contest might be deconstructed as no more than a set of 'witchcraft accusations' typical of Amerindian theories of

death as an external exchange, and prompted by vague jealousies of the material benefits of Alleluia prophecy. But given the actuality of physical Kanaimà
and its powerful shamanic dimension, we must also pay attention to the discursive force of such accounts, and take seriously the Amerindian suggestion, still
made, that these outcomes were part of shamanic warfare over access to the
ancestral dead (stars) and their divine sponsors (*makunaima, kaikusi-yumu*). At
this point the discourse on Kanaimà also moves into that on modernity and
tradition and we reach the sources of the cultural ambiguity shown towards the
Kanaimà killers as exponents of a fierce traditionality.

CONCLUSIONS

In the light of these analyses we need to re-conceptualize violence, seeing it not
as inevitably dysfunctional or pathological but rather as a complex socio-
cultural expression of various socio-cultural phenomena. Violence may thus be
intimately connected to the reproduction of society through the affirmation of
a political or cultural group-identity, cultural constructions of manhood, and
the formation of individual psychology. In which case the lack of any unitary
explanation for violence should not surprise us, especially given the pervasiveness of that modality of socio-cultural exchange that we call 'violence and war'.
If this has to date defied adequate anthropological analysis, it is because we
ethnocentrically construct such behaviour as always the outcome of human
imperfection.

Equally, although Rivière's (1970*a*) social structural discussion of sorcery
accusation is an important basis for the interpretation of Kanaimà made here
and in the chapter by Butt Colson, it is evident that Kanaimà also refers to a
wider field of socio-cultural significance that includes both other Amerindian
groups, and the national societies of Guyana, Brazil, and Venezuela. The magic
of the state (Taussig 1996, Coronil 1996) is here complemented and mimetically
validated by reference to the wild savagery of the hinterland, its environment
and peoples.

By the same token, it is not possible to understand properly ritualized
violence, especially where it expresses 'tradition', without reference to the
wider, even globalized, context in which it takes place. In this frame of reference
Kanaimà appears, as with assault sorcery in Papua New Guinea (Stewart and
Strathern 1999) and Africa (Geschiere 1977), or the ethnocide in Rwanda (C.
Taylor 1999) and Bosnia (van de Port 1998), as a profound symptom of the
localization of modernity, where modernity stands for the political and
economic consequences of globalized capitalist relations (Ferguson and
Whitehead 2000). In this way, we may see that Kanaimà violence can be used to
constitute the body politic, even as it destroys the bodies that constitute it.

ACKNOWLEDGEMENTS

I would like to acknowledge the financial support of the Wenner-Gren Foundation and University of Wisconsin–Madison Graduate School for the field projects that enabled this study.

NOTE

1. Although Butt Colson (this volume) is correct that such assassins are 'invariably male', my own ethnographic data include accounts that implicate both women and men as practitioners (see also Whitehead forthcoming).

13

Finding One's Body: Relationships between Cosmology and Work in North-West Amazonia

Thomas Griffiths, *University of Oxford*

In the ethnology of indigenous Amazonian societies the theme of human work has normally been dealt with as part of the ethnographic analysis of the gendered division of labour in the domestic economy.[1] The resulting literature has generated considerable discussion about how gendered work roles determine the relative status of women and men in Amerindian societies.[2] As well as investigating gender issues relating to human labour, Amazonian anthropologists have explored the importance of cultural attitudes towards work in social organization, leadership, and political economy.[3] Numerous studies evaluate the efficiency of labour in providing nutritional and material needs.[4] Some monographs also include indigenous ideas about work as a lexical category encompassing specific types of activity and excluding others.[5]

Together, the various sociological, political, and materialist approaches to work have improved our understanding of native economy and society. We know, for example, that among horticultural groups where women are the main cultivators, the level of production is primarily determined by the cultural construction of work: it is the productive capacity of married women who are culturally defined as the primary gardeners that dictates the amount of food crops produced, and not any shortage of available labour or land resources.[6]

It is clear that particular work patterns and inter-personal and inter-group working relationships define gender, age, and social categories within and between families and settlement groups.[7] Work also confers identity on people in more individual ways. As each producer has the rights over the product of their own labour in accordance with the Amerindian primacy on personal autonomy, so special skills in certain tasks become one important facet of a person's creative self and their identity as a sociable being. In conjunction with circulation and consumption, productive activity is thus a form of personification in Amerindian societies.

The ethnographic record also shows that work in native societies constitutes one primary mode of sociality. Co-operative work is about creating and sustaining cordial social relationships. Above all, work is necessary to meet the needs of spouse and children in order to maintain a harmonious household. Furthermore, autonomous provisioning brought about through work enables a family to give to other co-residents, and to provide hospitality for visitors. Productive tasks therefore embody a strategy of conflict avoidance that aims to foster the social peace that is so essential to the Amerindian sense of well-being.

Another core feature of productive activity shown by the ethnography is that work is an expression of mood and sentiment. The emotive nature of work manifests itself in a number of critical ways. First, the intensity of production in the domestic economy shows a positive correlation with conjugal harmony.[8] Secondly, collective work efforts among members of a settlement group are intensified by positive feelings among the participants. At the same time, such work renews and reinforces the benign sentiments of co-workers. Co-operative labour is consequently a potent form of social bonding in which festive work groups form animated *communitas*.

Following on from these social and cultural values surrounding work, the size and duration of residence groups are partly determined by the maintenance of co-operative work relations between individuals and families. In what Rivière (1984: 90; 1983–4) has termed the 'political economy of people' in native Amazonian societies, labour relations and access to labour are consequently fundamental to leadership.[9] Given all these multiple social and political virtues of productive work, it is perhaps not surprising that unproductive activity and laziness are shunned by most of the Amerindian peoples of lowland South America.

Drawing on my own fieldwork with the Uitoto people in lowland Colombia, I will show that creative and productive activities are not solely valued by Amerindians as a mode of sociality and politic among mortals. Work is also important in the cosmological ideas that instil certain motivations for work and shape material practices. To see human work only as part of an experiential and lived reality in opposition to some abstract and 'imagined' cultural representation about the world, fails fundamentally to recognize the nature of Amerindian ontologies. For this reason, British, French, and Brazilian anthropologists have been asserting for some time that native ideas about supernature and the cosmos cannot be separated from the sociological and visible aspects of material life.[10] I wish to take this key observation as a point of departure in the following brief account outlining why work is so important in Uitoto cosmology and their sense of cultural identity and well-being.

The Uitoto number around six thousand people who live in the eastern lowlands of Colombia and the north-eastern part of Peruvian Amazonia. Settlements are mainly located along the Caquetá, Igaraparaná, Caraparaná, and Putumayo rivers in Colombia, and within the Ampiyacu river basin in Peru. The population is engaged in a mixed economy, participating in swidden horticulture, fishing, and gathering as well as various trade-based and wage-earning activities.

Swidden cultivation remains the mainstay of the indigenous economy, and most families with older children fell and plant a high forest garden each year. As well as subsistence provisioning, surplus garden production is channelled to large cere-monial exchange ceremonies that take place during the dry season.

Like other horticulturist groups in north-west Amazonia, the Uitoto possess a rich and complex body of oral knowledge; and a huge amount of formal discourse relates to the importance of work (e.g. Candre 1996: 142 ff., 185). In particular, all the social and political aspects of work sketched above are highly developed and explicit in Uitoto oral texts, which detail and reflect upon the gendered work roles of spouses, the virtues of hard work for self and others, and the qualities of good leadership.

Elsewhere, I have outlined some key Uitoto ideas about work, and I have argued that they in fact hold an explicit work ethic: laziness is not only shunned, but continuous work is actively advocated and esteemed (Griffiths 1998: 190–209). In some ways, the Uitoto work ethic shows parallels with the Protestant Puritanism described by Weber insofar as both philosophies see continuous work as a means to attain a feeling of inner peace (Weber 1992 [1930]: 108–9). However, the underly-ing logic for achieving emotional calm through work is very different in the two systems of moral value. Whereas the Protestant ethic values labour as a path to other-worldly salvation (Morrison 1995: 253), the Uitoto regard perpetual work as a way to maintain good relations with both people and spirit-beings in daily life.

Fig. 13.1 summarizes the motivations for persistent work effort as explained to me by various Uitoto people over the course of my fieldwork. The figure divides indigenous theories of work into social, cosmological, and political themes for ease of exposition. In reality, the different aspects of human work are closely intercon-nected in native models of livelihood and social reproduction. Notwithstanding such complex interrelatedness in indigenous concepts, it is important to recognize that the cultural values which espouse continuous work are not simply Uitoto ideals: they actually shape material practice, labour effort, and work patterns in the indigenous economy.

Like other native groups in north-west Amazonia, women's work is largely devoted to the time-consuming cultivation and processing of bitter manioc into staple food and drink. Together with feeding, cleaning, and child-care chores, an adult married woman with a family might expend eleven labour hours a day in domestic and subsistence tasks. Women retire to sleep at around eight in the evening, and are normally up by daybreak to bath children and heat the pepper pot for breakfast.

Men are up by about six in the morning—an hour or so after their spouse has risen. Men work in fuel wood gathering, fishing, and the extraction of craft mate-rials with which they fabricate the manioc-processing utensils, tools, and basket-work used by women. Men are also responsible for house building, boat building, and other woodwork. Average daily work effort in these tasks is around five hours.

Also in common with other ethnic groups in the north-west Amazon, the

FIG. 13.1. A summary of Uitoto motivations for persistent labour expenditure

(*a*) SOCIAL

- meet the needs of one's self and one's family (household harmony)
- have enough to share and meet requests of co-residents and guests (no criticism)
- educate children in self-provision

⇓

individual and familial autonomy ⇒ socialize children on how to become moral and capable adults ⇒ conflict avoidance ⇒ attract good spouse for children ⇒ peaceful mind ⇒ health ⇒ well-being

⇓⇑

(*b*) COSMOLOGICAL

- initiate and maintain the support of divinities, spiritual kin, spiritual spouse and ancestor spirits (nurturers, protectors, cosmic-co-workers, teachers, healers)
- sustain the seasonal cycle and the fertility of the garden; and channel 'breath of life' into the individual and familial body
- eliminate and eradicate negative and pathogenic forces in the cosmos affecting the family
- obtain superhuman corporeal senses (eyes, ears, voice)
- acquire ancestral esoteric knowledge needed to care for the family and achieve efficient material practice (invocations, spells, and sacred speech)
- achieve good bodily and mental health: 'find one's body'

⇓

security ⇒ metaphysical preconditions for life and subsistence production ⇒ strong human body and human identity ⇒ capacity to work and meet obligations ⇒ well-being

⇓⇑

(*c*) POLITICAL

- make temporary usufruct claims to a tract of land through garden felling, creating orchard fallows, and extracting and working forest materials
- establish a surplus of food and ritual substances to form a cohesive extended family settlement group
- build a ritual dance house and maintain a permanent *mambeadero* for nocturnal sharing and dialogue with male kin and visitors
- hold ritual dances and publicly confirm the local descent group as an autonomous political and territorial unit

⇓

found a firm base to 'sit down well' ⇒ incorporate ancestral knowledge and souls ⇒ clan demographic growth and reproduction ⇒ human progress ⇒ increased spiritual support of divinities and other spiritual beings who help to sustain the 'good living place'

Uitoto have an important cultural and ritual complex centred on coca and tobacco. Coca powder is normally prepared daily, and an adult man may spend an average of more than five hours a day in the cultivation, harvesting, processing, and ritual consumption of coca. Processing is usually completed by nine in the evening, after which men remain seated and continue to engage in group dialogue or solitary meditation until midnight or so, when they leave the men's circle in the *mambeadero* to bathe before going to 'rest'.[11] As well as its metaphysical virtues which will be discussed below, men say that they value coca powder as their 'work companion' which provides stamina for physical tasks, and clarifies the mind for thoughtful activities like basket-work.

Tobacco is harvested over three or four weeks at the end of the wet season. The work demands a very high investment of labour to produce a fresh stock of thick, pure tobacco paste. During this period, a man may be active for up to eighteen hours a day as cooking pots and fires are tended until the small hours. When a family is preparing large amounts of surplus food, drink, and ritual stimulants for festive work parties or ritual exchange ceremonies, both men and women can work for eighteen hours or more a day for several days or even a week. In the construction of a ritual dance house, the sponsoring 'house-owning group' may follow this intensive work pattern for an entire month to provide guest workers with nourishment, and male workers with plenty of the coca powder that is so essential to the daytime work effort, and to the efficacy of nocturnal dialogue accompanying each stage of the construction (Griffiths 1998: 97–8, 161).

This brief ethnographic sketch intends to show that both women and men in Uitoto society normally engage in prolonged work days, and periodically become involved in intensive work efforts associated with collective work parties and ritual events.[12] The Uitoto case casts doubt on the universality of the idea made popular by Sahlins (1972: 51–69) that 'primitive' people work very little. However, rather than continuing with a description of Uitoto labour expenditure, in this chapter I wish to focus on the cosmological framework in which human work takes place, and show how this relates to the work practices already outlined. By doing this, I will highlight a few basic aspects of Uitoto cosmology which underpin the Uitoto predilection for persistent work.

The Uitoto, as most other Amerindian groups, possess a multi-naturalist cosmology: faunal and floral beings are identified as people who are sentient and wilful persons within the spiritual landscape.[13] Uitoto cosmology is also a dualistic one which opposes the forces of good and evil in the cosmos. A fundamental cosmogonic rupture between humans and animals occurred in the world of creation 'below' which condemned faunal beings to their current bodily forms, their habitats, and their diet.[14]

Particularly evil and treacherous beings who plotted against their creators were destined by creator divinities to be 'the generation to be eaten', and so today exist as game animals. In the reordering of the cosmos, the ancestors and culture heroes of present-day Amerindian humans emerged as the generation who were given the knowledge and tools for swidden gardening, together with 'true' classes of food and ritual crops. The bad feeling caused by the cosmic bifurcation means that certain faunal spirit beings forever hold envy and hatred for humanity, and strive to undermine human progress by causing illness, damage to crops, and the negative sentiments which cause social conflict and the break-up of human settlements.

The human ancestral spirits who marshalled the reorganization of the cosmos are in this-worldly reality embodied in seasonal meteorological phenomena including sunlight, insulation, moderate dry weather, gentle north-east trade winds, rain, and the *friaje*. Ancestral spirit beings are also identified with food and narcotic crops, cultivated medicinal plants, and fertile soils.

Subsistence tools and utensils are similarly animated by sacred ancestral spirits. Communication with these spirit beings is achieved through the processing and consumption of coca and tobacco, which as we have seen demands laborious preparation. As well as communication with a range of ancestral spirits, men assert that such labour is especially necessary to meet the needs of either a spiritual spouse or parental divinity embodied in tobacco and coca. Just as a failure to meet obligations towards mortals causes them to either temporarily cease co-operation or move away, so too a failure to regularly carry out work related to ritual stimulants is certain to cause abandonment by a man's invisible tobacco spouse and kinspeople.

Such spiritual abandonment causes loneliness, fear, anxiety, mental confusion, and lethargy, which leaves a man open to spiritual attack and illness. Crucially, being alert and feeling secure necessitates the ongoing consumption of processed coca and tobacco. The consumption of these ritual stimulants empowers the healing spells and dialogues needed to repel and cure illness, and defend the family and settlement group against spiritual assault. For this reason, men identify the daily round of coca-related tasks and the annual processing of the tobacco harvest as a man's 'proper work' because it seeks to maintain the strength and well-being of a man, his wife, and their children. Male labour associated with the *mambeadero* is also seen as a special form of work activity as the tasks require considerable effort, expertise, and dedication. In fact, Uitoto men often observe that the life of a *mambeador*: 'a coca-consuming man', is a 'tiresome' one because it demands the continual processing of coca on a daily basis. It is precisely this stoical dedication to repetitive work that confers prestige and status on a *mambeador* as a steadfast, serious, and dependable character.[15]

In addition, tasks centred on coca and tobacco are valued because these ritual substances channel the sacred speech, known generically as *rapue*: 'the word of progress', which is essential to the welfare and development of the human generation. Very specific and formalized categories of *rapue* are needed to solicit the help of what I shall term 'cosmic co-workers', who are explicitly recognized as the most potent work companions in the indigenous economy. The work utensil and specific climatic spirits noted above are valued as tireless superhuman workers who are merely guided or assisted by mortal bodies.

Hence, in the case of garden establishment in high forest, formal dialogues call divinities to come to the world 'above' and 'eat'. Texts direct the 'axe mother' to eat her tree food well and hence fell efficiently. The 'Mother of summer' is then called to 'smoke' her wooden and plant 'meat' and so dry the felling thoroughly, after which the 'Mother of fire' is beckoned to come and 'lick clean' her food with her pyric tongue to ensure a good burn and fertile substrate for planting. Felling and burning are believed to eradicate cosmic contamination and evil spirit beings in a process that heals the garden owner and his family.

After a swidden is felled and burnt, dialogues affirm that it was divine beings who truly worked ('touched') the clearing, and not humans who were simply present at the event. The same gardening dialogues underline the fact that in return for the generous provision of woody and faunal food, the maternal ancestor spirit will later show her gratitude to her human offspring by offering her 'hand of plenty' when food crops and ritual crops mature for harvest. The dynamic process of garden establishment and subsequent harvest is thus conceived of as one of reciprocal nurture between humanity and parental spirit beings.

Uitoto gardening lore sets out a multitude of reasons why old growth high-forest gardens must be felled every year without fail. Some Uitoto men stress that high-forest gardens must be felled every year in order to produce the 'force of the community': tobacco paste. They point out that tobacco germinates best on 'cool' ground in gardens felled from old-growth forest whereas the 'hot' ground on gardens cut from bush fallow yields little tobacco. Women say that a 'proper garden' felled from high forest is important because this ground guarantees a durable, long-term source of bitter manioc. They add that women prefer to work this land because it is not colonized so rapidly by pernicious weeds. However, the reasons given for establishing gardens in high forest on an annual basis are not only practical ones.

Another fundamental reason given is that the type of garden felled (old-growth forest as opposed to bush fallow), together with the enthusiasm for work, directly affects the arrival and the length of presence of divinities in the world 'above'. Meagre fellings creating small swiddens, or simple plots cut in young secondary vegetation, do not attract the cosmic kin for any length of time—if at all. Lack of human effort to provide adequate food for the maternal divinity and antipathy towards such work cause only weak dry spells that prevent a good swidden burn.

In years when, to use an indigenous phrase from the middle Caquetá, 'Summer does not arrive', horticultural food supply may be seriously diminished for the following twelve or twenty-four months in geographic areas which have experienced no marked dry season (Griffiths 1998: 97–8). Prior to starting my fieldwork in the middle Caquetá in 1994, poor summers had occurred during the felling and planting seasons in 1992 and 1993. Many people in different villages bemoaned their failure to fell proper high-forest gardens in recent years, which they believed had itself caused the lack of dry weather.

People observed that the decline in garden production meant that they had only a small supply of coca and tobacco, and a limited stock of young manioc stems for transplanting. Furthermore, people complained that what they did have came from old plots and lacked the efficacy of fresh manioc, coca, and tobacco. Some people exclaimed that the failure to fell and plant proper gardens stemming from the reluctance to work hard and their associated neglect of parental divinities, meant that they and their fellow countrymen were through such laziness 'becoming like animals'. Such a strong statement does not simply betray a negative attitude towards certain game animals that sleep during the day and forage by night.

It also highlights a central premise in Uitoto cosmology: behaviour both creates and signifies the identity of living beings. For most Uitoto, *volverse gente*, 'to become (human) people', means to fell and plant gardens; to prepare and consume manioc-based food and drink; to cultivate, process, and consume the 'true' classes of coca and tobacco; to build thatched houses where ritual dances are held, and to search for benevolent ancestral knowledge about the garden and human progress. To adhere to these practices is to express a strong social and ancestral relationship to the parental divinities who showed the human generation how to live well as gardening people. In this sense, horticultural work is seen as a continual affirmation of human identity.

In contrast, to be inactive during the day; to lack cultivated resources; to secretly take food from the gardens and orchards of others; to spend time becoming envious of those with plentiful food and ritual stimulants; to spend a lot of time in the forest; to search for forest herbs and knowledge, or to consistently engage in night-time wandering without torch light is to *volverse animal*, 'to become an animal' (see also Pineda 1990: 163; Espinosa 1995: 79, 84). Such behaviour is a negation of a relation with the gardening divinities and is disrespectful of other human ancestral beings. Crucially, lack of horticultural work also causes the neglect of plant children in the garden, and the spiritual tobacco woman spouse in the home.

At this juncture, it is important to clarify that work is not viewed as the exclusive practice of Amerindian humans. For example, termites, honey bees, and nest-building birds are all admired by the Uitoto for their industry. Indeed, such energetic and co-operative beings are invoked in sacred speech to speed human work tasks. The association between indolence and animality refers primarily to game species, who are mostly inactive during the day and move by night. It is these game animals and other nocturnal forest species who embody the beings that hindered human development in the mythic past. Native people in the middle Caquetá normally use the Spanish gloss 'animal' in relation to these species who are grouped under the Uitoto category *riyyeniaɨ*, 'the community to be eaten', as outlined above.

It is such cosmogonic and cosmological convictions that cause ongoing unproductive and antisocial behaviour to bring into question the true identity of an individual. A woman who does not wish to carry out her conjugal chores and does little work is suspected of being possessed by the 'false woman', who is one spirit mother of forest animals. Although outward appearance is that of a woman, the 'true' identity may be that of a non-human being who has temporarily infiltrated the human settlement.[16] Likewise, male identity can become ambiguous where behaviour is persistently directed towards unproductive and solitary occupations, or the pursuit of uncultivated magical herbs and knowledge belonging to faunal spirit beings of the forest. Over time, moral putrefaction is thought to cause bodily degeneration.

Bodily deterioration together with the associated slippage in human identity can be remedied by a definitive change in behaviour.[17] In particular, it is through renewed and dedicated effort in productive tasks and the acquisition of benign knowledge that a person may activate a process of self-healing and self-reform which may ultimately lead him or her to the 'good living place'. Persistent physical work is believed to make the body so resilient that it can 'reflect back illness'. With perseverance, a person will obtain a 'healthy' and 'beautiful' body.

For the Uitoto then, human bodily identity is not given, but achieved. Even after the critical formative stages of the *couvade*, infancy, and childhood, the body is always, as it were, 'work in progress'. If simply taken for granted, the body will degenerate, rapid ageing will occur, and ill health prevail. Persistent work is necessary to repeatedly recharge the body with vital life juice and cosmic 'breath' stemming from new garden crops.

Such forces for bodily regeneration are only available through prolonged work during the labour peaks in the Uitoto calendar; and in the daily grind of food preparation by women, and through the processing of coca and tobacco by men. What emerges as central to indigenous ideas about social reproduction, is a logic of working to enable the replenishment and renewal of vital life forces. With no ailments, the body feels pleasantly light and agile, and the mind is alert and calm. In such good form, a person can meet all work obligations, and thereby forestall any criticism by his or her spouse, kin, and co-residents. At this stage, the person is said to have 'found their body'. Such a person acquires a youthful, shiny, and muscular body with an agreeable odour. With the bodily perfection achieved through work comes moral virtue. Uitoto formal dialogues thus stress that a man and a woman may, through garden work and the production of plenty, approach the identity of ideal moral beings.

A hard-working man may come to embody the figure of the culture hero *monípue jitdóg*, 'the son of abundance', while his spouse may adopt the identity of *monípue ríngo*, 'the woman of plenty'. Striving to obtain good health and success in productive tasks in order to take on the identity of these culture heroes is a primary cultural project for couples who wish to commence a ritual career. In Uitoto theories of well-being, ancestral divinities and spiritual helpers are essential for this cultural project. As we have seen, the only way that such superhuman help can be assured is through consistent work in the gardening economy, the continual processing of coca, and the annual preparation of tobacco paste. Further and more encompassing support can be achieved through ongoing ritual dances.

The specific dialogues involved in hosting ritual events, and the preceding intense garden production bolster the degree of seasonality in the local and regional territory. Regular ritual dances intensify the length of the dry season, and ensure that all the families enjoy a good swidden burn and can look forward to a good food supply the coming year. At the same time, the rituals function to purify garden and wild fruits over a large territory by eliminating potent and potentially harmful substances originating from the depths of creation. They also seek to eradicate especially evasive malignant beings causing illness and social conflict over a wide area. There is no space here to explain how these goals are achieved through ritual. The essential point is that ritual events, and the huge amount of human work that they entail, are geared towards recreating the proper conditions for human life and subsistence production.

The heightened social atmosphere and extraordinary vibrant collective songs sung by guest groups provide a sacred space in which name souls can be reborn in members of the host family and house-owning group. This rebirth of clan souls is seen as the renewal of the ancestral intelligence and power essential for the reproduction of society. Work dedicated to ritual exchange ceremonies is therefore partly directed towards imparting the definitive identity and personhood which differentiates patrilineal descent groups. In sum, human work associated with ritual strives to drive the process of social reproduction by reproducing the life-giving components of the cosmos and repelling the debilitating forces which continually threaten humanity.

CONCLUSION

All the linkages between human work, personhood, bodily well-being, and social reproduction are laid out in detail in different categories of Uitoto dialogues about work and human morality. Given the lack of space, further discussion of Uitoto ideas about work and well-being must be curtailed at this point. But I think there is now sufficient evidence to make a few concluding observations.

In the first place, the Uitoto seem to differ from some other groups in lowland South America, who have a preference for moderate work expenditure, and do not possess a work ethic (e.g. Descola 1994*a*: 298; 1994*b*: 220; Thomas 1982: 44). Amazonian ethnology shows how work practices and work patterns can vary considerably between different ethnic groups. Consequently, any application of general laws such as the 'least effort principle' to explain indigenous practices in this culture area must be treated with caution (cf. Colchester 1981: 60).

Uitoto attitudes towards work and their heavy work investment in complex architecture and ritual ceremonies remind us that it is problematic to treat lowland South American Indians as a homogeneous cultural category. The Uitoto, Tukanoan, and Xinguano preference for relatively permanent settlements, large dance houses, and the production of large garden surpluses for ritual events differs markedly from the nomadic, seminomadic, and relaxed lifestyles of the Huaorani,

Araweté, and Panare, for example (Rival, personal communication 1998; Viveiros de Castro 1992: 92 ff.; Henley 1982: 61–3).

Yet even among those groups who lead a carefree lifestyle and exhibit only a limited daily labour expenditure, application in productive activity may still be positively valued. Even if the Huaorani reportedly do not condemn inactivity, Huaorani chants in initiation rites encourage youths and girls to 'work hard, hunt and gather diligently' (Rival 1993: 640). Although by objective measures of time allocation, indigenous peoples can be characterized as enjoying the benefits of an 'original affluent society', it would be interesting to consider the opinion of indigenous people themselves.

It is clear that in a Uitoto cosmos charged with destructive forces, the goals of 'finding one's body' and 'the good living place' are ideals that are difficult to achieve and even more difficult to sustain. Even if achieved, complete peace and happiness are only transitory states of being. Hence, Uitoto dialogues stress that one must work hard to move closer toward a lived approximation of the good life, and by so doing maintain an acceptable level of health and well-being in the family and settlement group. We may therefore ask ourselves to what extent the portrayal of native societies living with limited needs in simple contentment is the product of anthropological constructions of South American Indians as different from ourselves.

It is possible that the preoccupation with negative and pathogenic forces which results in a cultural emphasis on the need to continually recreate a healthy space for human life is markedly accentuated in Uitoto culture.[18] But leaving aside particular concepts of well-being, I think in other ways Uitoto cosmological concepts relating to work and material practice strike a chord with many indigenous peoples in the tropical lowlands of South America. The fundamental concept which joins bodily form and habitual conduct with identity has been pinpointed in cosmologies across the region by Rivière (1994a: 257) and by Viveiros de Castro (1996a, 1998a). As Peter Rivière (1994a: 261) observes, in judging the identity of a being, for most native Amazonians: 'behaviour is a better guide than appearances'. Furthermore, in what Rivière has characterized as the 'highly transformational world' of indigenous Amazonian ontologies, bodily states are not rigidly fixed, but ephemeral and at times transient (Rivière 1994a: 259).[19]

The Uitoto example shows how continual work and a particular set of practices are seen to guarantee the retention of the human body and affirm human identity. It is a specific type of ongoing activity and pattern of behaviour that determines identity and the network of social and spiritual relations in which a person is embedded. Moreover, these spiritual relations are themselves social. Through garden work and the execution of rituals, Uitoto people live within a web of relations with both mortal and spiritual persons: Uitoto people engage in a 'cosmic economy of people' which Viveiros de Castro in this volume has identified as a key feature of Amerindian cosmologies and theories of social reproduction throughout Amazonia.

Uitoto theories of work provide another example that shows how the indigenous economy in the Amazonian lowlands is primarily directed towards the production of people rather than material goods. This is not to say that material production is unimportant in indigenous theories of social reproduction, but to recognize that such material items and processes are a means to an end. Amazonian ethnology shows how indigenous cosmologies and concepts surrounding social reproduction are dominated by themes of corporeality which focus on the creation of human persons through circulation, consumption, specific dietary and behavioural patterns, periodic ritual transformations, and the continual acquisition of cultural knowledge.[20]

The role of human work in maintaining and reproducing the essential metaphysical and environmental conditions for human existence is perhaps made more explicit in Uitoto cosmology than has been recorded for other ethnic groups in the region. None the less, it is common for indigenous peoples in the region to see a marked seasonality in the subsistence calendar as a product of their own ritual cycle.[21] It is therefore also plausible to observe that in many indigenous Amazonian societies human work is not only about the production of people, but also the reproduction of the world and the cosmos.

If the role of work in the native cultures of lowland South America is to be fully understood, we cannot ignore native work concepts that do not relate to the supposedly 'real' issues of gender conflict, local politics, prestige, and power. Uitoto men's assertion that the tasks relating to the ritual economy of coca and tobacco are 'proper work' do not constitute false or irrelevant ideologies that obscure true social realities.

Anthropologists must be prepared to treat such declarations as literal statements which reflect indigenous concepts and priorities regarding social reproduction, welfare, and well-being. In doing so, the anthropology of work in Amazonia can start to move beyond the potentially parochial Western concerns with gender equality, energy efficiency, power, and prestige. I do not deny that these are crucial forces at play in native Amazonian societies and in indigenous theories of economy and society as Fig. 13.1 has indicated. I only suggest that the study of work in relation to native cosmologies can broaden still further the understanding of the cultural values shaping labour patterns and attitudes to work in some indigenous communities.

ACKNOWLEDGEMENTS

Sincere gratitude is extended to the host Uitoto families with whom I lived and worked throughout fieldwork. I am especially grateful to the Uitoto elders Vicente Makuritdope, Bartolomé Castro, José Vicente Suárez, Oscar Román, Misael Morales, and Manuel Ranoke, who became my teachers and mentors during my time in the middle Caquetá. Every effort has been made to present accurate information in this chapter. However, if there are any incorrect observations or flawed interpretations in this account of Uitoto work and cosmology they are entirely my own errors.

Ethnographic fieldwork with the Colombian Uitoto of the middle Caquetá region was funded by the UK Economic and Social Research Council (ESRC). Funds for field equipment were also secured from the Latin American Centre of St Antony's College Oxford. Support from the Radcliffe-Brown Memorial Fund administered by the Royal Anthropological Institute is also gratefully acknowledged. I wish to thank Peter Rivière, Paul Henley, Audrey Butt Colson, Andrew Gray, and Laura Rival for comments on earlier versions of this chapter given during a seminar at Linacre College Oxford in November 1998. I am especially grateful to Stephen Hugh-Jones, who made comments on the draft chapter before submission to the editors.

NOTES

1. See, for example, Siskind (1973: 54, 68–9, 117–18), Whitten (1976: 82–101), Dumont (1976: 62–5), Gregor (1977: 23–4), Turner (1979*a*: 154–6), C. Hugh-Jones (1979: 170–3), Henley (1982: 60–8), Journet (1981), Brown (1985: 126–8), and Kensinger (1995: 36–41).

2. The gender debate is centred on whether or not native ideologies of the complementary gender work roles obscure a fundamental inequality between men and women (cf. Rivière 1983–4: 352; 1984: 92–3; 1987*a*; 1989*a*; Mentore 1987; McCallum 1989*a*; Seymour-Smith 1991; Lorrain 1994 and this volume).

3. Rivière (1983–4), Overing (1989*b*, 1992, 1993*b*), Gow (1989, 1991: 122 ff.), McCallum (1989*b*, 1990), and Lorrain this volume.

4. Detailed time allocation studies in native communities include Johnson (1975), Bergman (1980: 212), Dufour (1983), Lizot (1984), Hames (1989), and Descola (1994*a*: 286–95, 1994*b*: 217–19).

5. Amerindian horticulturist peoples primarily associate 'work' with physical effort in forest clearance and horticultural activity, whilst extractive tasks are not classified as 'work', but as the practice of searching or looking for different resources (e.g. Descola 1994*a*: 296 ff.; Gow 1991: 101 ff.). In the same way, Uitoto people especially associate '*daɨɨe*, 'work' with clearing vegetation and cultivation. 'Work' includes other arduous tasks like grating manioc, twisting a manioc press, woodwork, and the portage of heavy items. The term also relates to less strenuous but productive activities like basket making that require careful thought either sitting upright or standing. Craft activity lying in a hammock is more usually seen as a relaxing and restful activity that is not 'work'. Indeed, the verb *jaɨrónaitde*, 'to be resting', normally refers to reposing in a hammock. Like many groups in Amazonia, the Uitoto commonly use the Spanish noun *trabajo* in a specific way to mean 'paid work' in the cash economy. Itinerant and varied trade-based occupations which may be remunerated in kind or cash, are generally referred to as 'searching for sundries' or 'searching for money' (see Griffiths 1998: 243).

6. See, for example, Goldman (1963: 52), Henley (1982: 83), Gros (1991: 62), Descola (1994*a*: 310).

7. On the way specific work relations mark different social categories and inter-personal ties, see especially Siskind (1973: 67 ff., 1978), Da Matta (1979), Rosengren (1987: 106 ff.), Gow (1989), and Viveiros de Castro (1992: 101).

8. See Goldman (1963: 73), Gregor (1977: 203), Rivière (1987a: 193), Gow (1989: 573), and Descola (1994a: 149, 313).
9. To become a leader, a headman must talk and behave well. But he and his spouse must also work consistently to meet both their own needs, and to retain a surplus of food, drink, and ritual substances within their settlement. Such a surplus is needed to (a) continually share with co-residents to prevent any bad feeling that might eventually lead to settlement fission, and (b) periodically sponsor festive work parties and ceremonial events that reaffirm a leader's status as a giver to the community, and reproduce the positive sentiments necessary for continued social co-operation and conviviality, e.g. Goldman (1963: 57, 155), Rivière (1969a: 49, 216; 1984: 73), Kracke (1978: 175), Chernela (1985; 1993: 133), McCallum (1990: 418–19), and Gow (1991: 209, 228). Alongside the goal of creating a multifamily residence group, an above average work effort by a headman and his wife may also be tied to their desire for political status within a local system of prestige (e.g. Descola 1994a: 312).
10. Overing (1985b: 170), Rivière (1987b; 1993: 514; 1995a: 48–9; n.d.), Viveiros de Castro (1992: 255; 1993: 184), Albert (1985), Descola and Taylor (1993: 21), Descola (1994a: 3, 191, 208), Gray (1996a, 1996b).
11. The name *mambeadero* derives from the vernacular Spanish noun *mambe* (coca powder) and the colloquial verb *mambear*, which means 'to masticate', 'to imbibe coca powder'.
12. Long work days among Uitoto women were recorded by Thomas Whiffen on his journey through Uitoto territory during 1908 and 1909 (Whiffen 1915: 50). A more or less continuous work day from dawn until dusk is also reported for the Búe Uitoto (Calle 1986: 88–90). Calle and Crooke (1969: 92) highlight the very long and intensive work days leading up to Uitoto ritual exchange ceremonies.
13. On the concept of a multi-naturalist cosmology, see Viveiros de Castro (1998a).
14. When referring to cosmology, the word *ána*, 'below' relates to temporal distance from an ancient mythic time of 'first generations', and does not clearly relate spatially to a subterrestrial world. Likewise, the word *árɨ*, 'above', relates to relatively recent cosmogonic events and to the contemporary reality of present-day life forms.
15. It is noteworthy that some Uitoto men point out that their own work toasting, pounding, and sieving coca leaves is *liviano*: 'light' when compared to women's arduous and heavy daily work transforming bitter manioc into food and drink.
16. Uitoto mythology is replete with episodes in which a person's body or its image are taken over by malicious spirits, and stories in which human bodily appearance masks the true identity of deceitful intruders who visit a house or settlement to do harm.
17. Using the same behavioural logic, the Uitoto say that to live entirely from purchased foods, to eat only rice, pasta, beans, beef, and chicken; and to drink sugar-cane alcohol and coffee is to *volverse blanco*, 'become a whiteman'. Yet these states are not rigidly fixed: by consistently working in the Amerindian subsistence and ritual economy, and by consuming Amerindian foods, coca, and tobacco and thereby acquiring Amerindian practical and esoteric knowledge, an indigenous person who has been away living among whites for many years, can again gradually *volverse indígena*, 'become an indigenous person'.
18. The strong dualistic character of Uitoto cosmology, which opposes good and evil, may partly stem from a destructive colonial encounter and relatively recent historical engagement with an aggressive form of merchant capitalism, which brought disease, death, and conflict to Uitoto territory (see Taussig 1987 and Echeverri 1997).

19. Despite the fact that bodies may be transitory and sometimes illusory covers for true identities within, it is clear Uitoto theories of the person hold a concrete notion of the ideal human body whose appearance and smell can reveal something about the inner qualities of a person.

20. Rivière (1974*a*), Seeger, Da Matta, and Viveiros de Castro (1979), Da Matta (1979: 105), Melatti (1979: 65–8), C. Hugh-Jones (1979: 107 ff.), Seeger (1981: 148–72), Roe (1982: 136 ff.), Crocker (1985: 50–63), Gregor (1985: 150, 194–5), Sullivan (1988: 303 ff.), Turner (1986; 1995), Gow (1989), Erikson (1996*a*), McCallum (1996), Viveiros de Castro (1996*a*: 130).

21. See, for example, Viveiros de Castro (1992: 76, 116), Hill (1989: 19), Reichel-Dolmatoff (1989: 127), Seeger (1987: 70), Van der Hammen (1992: 85), S. Hugh-Jones (1979: 207).

14

The Hierarchy Bias and the Equality Bias: Epistemological Considerations on the Analysis of Gender

Claire Lorrain, *McGill University*

INTRODUCTION

It has been argued that some analyses of Amazonian gender politics involve a hierarchy bias stemming from Western political philosophy (McCallum 1994; Overing 1986*b*: 138, 142; 1989*b*: 160; 1989*a*: 97). Interpretations of symbolic violence in myths and rituals as the pure and simple expression of 'male dominance' or a 'battle of the sexes' (Bamberger 1974; Gregor 1985; Nadelson 1981) would seem a clear example of such a bias (McCallum 1994), given that Amazonian gender symbolism has complex, multi-layered meanings which are clearly not reducible to any simple interpretation (S. Hugh-Jones 1996*b*: 8; Jackson 1992; Lorrain 1994, 1997, 2000; McCallum 1994).

There remains, however, the question of a potential equality bias: indeed, contemporary obsessions with hierarchy and equality are by definition inextricably bound to one another in Western libertarian and egalitarian ideology. This chapter starts with a reflection on some of the epistemological questions raised by such biases; it then shows how a given set of data can give rise to opposed interpretations, depending on the analytic perspectives on which they are predicated.

THE HIERARCHY BIAS AND THE EQUALITY BIAS

There is probably a general agreement, at least in theory, on the fact that Amazonian gender politics cannot be considered 'extremely simple and transparent', as in Marx's presumed vision of gender in the so-called 'primitive tribal community' (1906: 91). On the other hand, there is no general agreement as to precisely what is or is not transparent; namely, what is or is not straightforwardly egalitarian or inegalitarian. Therefore in the same way as a hierarchy bias can lead to a mistakenly transparent view of non-Western political forms as inegalitarian, it may also be argued that an equality bias can lead to an erroneously transparent view of these same political forms as egalitarian. If indeed all we can expect from anthropology is 'the intersection of two subjectivities', where anthropologists cannot pretend to do more than apply themselves to others (Lévi-Strauss 1973: 16–17; see also Hastrup 1992: 119; Leach 1984: 22; Okely and Callaway 1992; Pocock 1973 in Hastrup 1978: 129), it is unlikely that any discussion of Amazonian politics is entirely free of either an equality bias or a hierarchy bias.

This brings us to the oft-recurring theme of the 'hall of mirrors' (Sax 1998), with its unsettling implication that wherever anthropologists turn, they can only see the multiple reverberations of their own, culturally specific paradigm. To that extent anthropology is a form of ideology, with its own 'internal constraints' (Dumont 1985: 19, 132, 203), and areas of 'transparency' and 'opacity' (Lefebvre 1966: 50). The positive Western valuation of equality would seem to act as an 'internal moral constraint' (Dumont 1985: 203), in the form of equality and hierarchy biases. Anthropology may thus be regarded as a form of 'moral science' (Dumont 1985: 132, 203; Marx 1964: 150; Myrdal 1954; 1967: 44), insofar as it expresses Western forms of morality through the analysis of imagined others (Overing 1992: 197; 1993*b*).

The anthropology of gender has been suspected of having an ethnocentric, ideological, and moral perspective that is equality-blind, and poses negative moral judgements about gender relations that are mistakenly considered inegalitarian (Overing 1986*b*). In this same hall of mirrors, however, egalitarian perspectives on the same social relations may also appear biased, this time by hierarchy-blind, positive moral judgements stemming from the same ideological background. Both egalitarian and hierarchical perspectives may thus equally be seen as indulging in the 'illusions of epistemological privilege' (Whitaker 1996: 9) or 'anthropological authority' (Clifford and Marcus 1986) to substantiate their culturally specific views and 'decide, on behalf of [other] peoples whether men or women "have" power' (Strathern 1987: 6), thereby distorting the 'true nature' of indigenous societies.

At a proximal analytic level, this quandary may seem to boil down to the perennial problem of how to get through to the 'authentic indigenous point of view', above and beyond the thick maze of ethnocentric biases. This, however, opens yet another can of worms: even the attempt at a straightforward descriptive analysis of how indigenous populations 'make it known to themselves that this or that category is powerful, that these persons are unequal, and so on' (Strathern 1987: 6) is, in itself, fraught with difficulties that are far from devoid of either anthropological, or indigenous ideological opacity.

According to the 'axiom of direct experience' (Kaplan 1984: 33), which seems rather pervasive in this poststructuralist and postmodern era, the direct experience that indigenous populations have of their own culture is a necessary and sufficient condition for the acquisition of all knowledge pertaining to that culture. By extension, anthropologists are presumed to gain access to this knowledge by means of participant observation, that should ideally provide them with an untainted indigenous perception of sorts; or namely, a perception that is uncontaminated, as it were, by the cross-cultural and inter-subjective nature of the fieldwork encounter.

However, the attempt at immersion in indigenous representations, although it is indispensable to any anthropological project, brings to the fore the eminently problematic question of 'how to go about poking into another people's turn of mind' (Geertz 1983: 59) in a unbiased manner. For instance, hierarchical points of view on indigenous societies may be considered immersed in cultural decontextualization by means of 'experience-distant' (Geertz 1983: 57–8) concepts deemed inaccurate because they are alien to the authentic indigenous point of view. Conversely, egalitarian perspectives may also be seen as immersed in decontextualization by means of equally ethnocentric concepts, or else submerged in 'experience-near' concepts (ibid.) whereby indigenous social norms or normative behaviour are conflated with actual social relations.

Furthermore, the attempt to focus on the authentic indigenous point of view does not remove the necessity to make choices regarding what should be considered relevant data. To that extent, it can be argued that whatever anthropologists find out depends in the end on what they are or are not ready to perceive in the first place. In other words, as many others have stressed before me, perception is intrinsically biased, and therefore observation and description in themselves can only be interpretative, and hence distorting (Hastrup 1978: 129; Leach 1984: 21; Myrdal 1967; Sperber 1981). Any consensus, if only transitory, as to what constitutes anything close to an anthropological truth, can thus reasonably be regarded as resulting primarily from a culturally mediated 'agreement to agree about new things' (Collins and Pinch 1993: 42; Sperber 1981: 86; Ziman in Carrithers 1990: 265–6) within a 'community of knowers' (Carrithers: ibid.), rather than from the authenticity of anthropological findings per se. In other words, even though some representations are undoubtedly false (Quigley 1999: 21), and some are certainly truer than others, it is none the less probable that no anthropologist can claim the seal of untainted indigenous authenticity without engaging, even with the best, politically correct intentions, in a form of epistemological authority.

Even supposing that anthropologists could actually access the authentic native point of view, there still would remain the *traduttore traditore* conundrum. In a Geertzian or Wittgensteinian perspective, this can be formulated as a dilemma between, on the one hand, a translation of indigenous representations by means of anthropological meta-representation and its inbuilt biases, and, on the other hand, a complete identification with indigenous representations (insofar as this is at all possible), in which case one remains submerged in empiricist immediacies and there is no anthropological theory proper (Geertz 1983: 57–9; Hastrup 1993*a*: 174–7; 1993*b*: 152–5; Wittgenstein 1958*a*: 8; 1958*b* in Whitaker 1996: 8).

It thus seems to me that if anthropology has any pertinence at all it does not lie in an illusory, empiricist quest for identification with an authentic indigenous point of view, whereby raw data are somehow 'out there' to be collected by the unprejudiced observer (Hastrup 1978: 129; Leach 1984: 21). It would rather seem to lie in

theoretical research that remains permanently aware of the culturally specific paradigms that it stems from.

POLITICAL PERSPECTIVES, ANALYTIC LEVELS, AND CULTURAL FILIATION

This section briefly examines how different perspectives on Amazonian equality
and hierarchy are largely a function of the analytic levels regarded most pertinent,
and how these relate in part to different, culturally related anthropological traditions. Rivière explains that the political aspect of kinship relations in Guiana
should be understood according to a multiple standard depending on both gender
and age:

Broadly speaking, the relationship between those of the same sex is egalitarian, whereas that
between those of the opposite sex is asymmetrical, with women in the subordinate position.
However, in both cases the nature of the relationship is modified by age difference. Thus
the equality of the same-sex, same-age relationship becomes modified and more unequal
with increasing age difference.   (Rivière 1984: 56)

The combination of age and sex variables thus produces gradients of equality
(Kent 1999) and inequality, whereby Guianan societies can be considered both
egalitarian and inegalitarian to variable degrees depending on the specific sets and
subsets of social relations involved.

   Similarly, Overing and Santos Granero observe the coexistence of equality and
hierarchy in lowland South American populations, but contrarily to Rivière they
consider these primarily egalitarian. In their view, what differentiates the egalitarian and hierarchical aspects of these societies is not the specific set of social relations they are associated with, but rather their structural relation to one another.
According to Overing, 'for the Amazonian groups, hierarchy must be understood
through the more encompassing institutions of equality, and not vice versa' (1989*b*:
161–2). By contrast, Santos Granero argues that the Amuesha are an example of
'equality within hierarchy' (1986: 111–12), and that therefore hierarchy is structurally encompassing. None the less, he reaches the same conclusion as Overing
with regard to the primacy of egalitarianism, in that 'it is the encompassed egalitarian values, rather than the encompassing hierarchical ones, which are socially
enacted' (1986: 129). These enacted values are strikingly 'angelic' (Taylor 1996:
206), however, which raises the question as to whether they correspond to the full
gamut of enacted relations, or to their normative aspect.

   This distinction of analytic levels points to a central contrast in the complex
web of affinities and differences between British and French Durkheimian lines of
descent. I am referring here to a certain British focus on 'eunomia', namely on the
harmonious working together of an 'orderly arrangement of social relations'
(Radcliffe-Brown 1952: 154, 182–3), where a normative, moral system of affect
(Fortes 1969; Radcliffe-Brown 1952: 160; 1967) is considered a focal source of

social equilibrium. In Amazonianist anthropology, this eunomia is analysed on an intimacy mode, at the level of inter-personal relations rather than social structure, by anthropologists who are either British (Gow 1989; 1991; McCallum 1989*b*; Overing 1983–4; 1986*a*; 1986*b*; 1988; 1989*a*; 1989*b*; 1992; 1993*a*; 1993*b*), or of British intellectual filiation (Belaunde 1992, 1994; Santos Granero 1986, 1991). Taylor contrasts this 'angelic', or 'irenic' point of view (1996: 206, 213), which focuses on normative indigenous models and practices, with the perspective of most Amazonianists who are either French (such as Albert 1985; Clastres 1972; Combès and Saignes 1991; Erikson 1986), or of French intellectual filiation (such as Carneiro da Cunha and Viveiros de Castro 1985), and who focus on the inbuilt, contradictory and conflictual aspects of social relations as rich and informative dimensions of social structure.

This distinction between culturally related Amazonianist schools is undeniably far from simple and clear-cut, however. For example, Rivière's monograph on the Trio shows an explicit preoccupation with differentiating and analysing both social norms and actual social practices (Rivière 1969*a*: 171, 227, *passim*). Furthermore, most of his work also highlights the inbuilt 'tension lines' of Amazonian social structure that pertain between different social categories (Rivière 1969*a*; 1970*a*; 1971*a*; 1974*a*; 1983; 1983–4; 1984; 1987*a*), and thus challenges fundamental aspects of egalitarian theories. As regards gender, Rivière argues similarly to Meillassoux (1960; 1980), that Amazonian populations are political economies of people (1983–4; 1984: 93–4; 1987*a*: 182) where men control the labour of their sons-in-law by means of the control they have over their daughters.

The focus on normative indigenous models is in part correlated, in irenic Amazonianist accounts, with the aforementioned preoccupation with the authentic native point of view, which has become especially prominent with the advent of a new, post-colonial Western awareness in the form of Geertzian actor-centred perspectives, and of poststructuralist and postmodern critical analyses of anthropological representation. This has brought about new ways of writing Amazonianist anthropology, which among other things attempt to give the reader a 'truer', emotional grasp of indigenous perspectives, and whose style may be coined a 'moral economy of intimacy' (Viveiros de Castro 1996*b*: 189), or a moral political philosophy of equality.

Belaunde, Gow, McCallum, Overing, and Santos Granero successfully give a vivid feeling of 'being there' among Amazonian populations, and thus contribute to the myth of the anthropologist turned native whose knowledge is legitimized by the axiom of direct experience. However this feeling, although it can undeniably give the impression of experiencing indigenous 'authenticity', can only be an illusion: writer and reader alike inescapably remain, as in all anthropological accounts, in the anthropologist's mind. The feeling of 'being there' is perhaps especially treacherous, in that it may be more difficult for the reader to keep a critical distance from such appealing portraits of the anthropologist's point of view on the native point of view, than it is from a more distant style of writing (Keesing 1989 in

Carrithers 1990: 275), such as that of Rivière. Indeed Rivière obviously does take into account the indigenous point of view, as all anthropologists do; but rather than putting it at the forefront in support of his analysis, he explicitly acknowledges that what he is putting forward is his own, anthropological perspective (1969*a*: 263).

THE DIVISION OF LABOUR IN THE AMAZON: EGALITARIAN AND
HIERARCHICAL INTERPRETATIONS

As Viveiros de Castro pointed out in the context of the conference on which this volume is based, we do not know as yet to what extent anthropological accounts of differences between Amazonian populations may stem from actual ethnological differences, or from the analytic perspectives themselves. To that extent, it is interesting to examine how any given set of data may give rise to different interpretations, depending on the culturally related intellectual background of anthropologists, and the analytic levels they consider most pertinent. I shall base my argument on the division of labour among the Kulina, an Arawá-speaking horticultural population of south-west Amazonia in Brazil. Given that egalitarian interpretations of similar labour divisions in the Amazon have been abundantly discussed elsewhere (McCallum 1989*b*; 1990: 417–18; Overing 1983–4: 331; and Santos Granero 1986: 125), much of what follows focuses on my own, hierarchical perspective.

Among the Kulina, women replant sweet manioc as they harvest it, collect forest fruit, fish and hunt on occasion, help men clear and plant gardens and thatch houses, do most of the weeding, carve cotton looms, spin and weave cotton, do the sewing and washing, weave baskets and fire fans, twist hammock ropes, fetch water, sweep houses, do most of the cooking, and are responsible for most child-care. Women's contribution to the productive system is considered indispensable, and is highly valued by all; but it is men who are considered primary providers. This is because men are the primary providers of cleared and planted gardens, raw fish and meat, houses, canoes, and market goods; they are also important providers of forest fruit.

Above and beyond those normative values, however, both men and women acknowledge that in practice some men are incompetent or lazy, and persistently provide relatively less fish, meat, or market goods to their dependants. It is also common knowledge that even good providers cannot always produce fish or meat, because on occasion they may be unsuccessful at fishing or hunting, involved in other pursuits, away on trading expeditions, or drunk. Such variations have a direct effect on dependants, because fish and meat are by far the main and most appreciated sources of protein, and productive insufficiencies are only partly compensated for by the generalized food-sharing system. Finally, the Kulina openly speak about the generalized hunger that strikes on occasion, when male strife impedes the yearly, collective garden-making, and forces an entire village to undertake serial migrations to other villages until the following year.

One may look at this division of labour from a normative point of view, namely as a functional system predicated on social harmony, and hence dismiss such flaws as mostly irrelevant anomalies. Alternately, one may also regard these flaws as indicative of significant social tensions and contradictions, and therefore as a means of probing into deeper analytic levels. From a normative point of view, given that women transform the animal and plant products that men provide them with, and each gender goes about its daily tasks with little or no direct interference from the opposite gender, this typically Amazonian division of labour might be seen as predicated on egalitarian complementarity and interdependence, as argued by Belaunde (1992: 145; 1994: 106, 108), McCallum (1989*b*; 1990: 417–18), Overing (1983–4: 331), and Santos Granero (1986: 125) for other populations.

This, however, does not account for the fact that in this economic system where men are the main providers, differential fish and meat consumption between households in everyday life, as well as episodes of village hunger and migration, are both overwhelmingly associated with flaws in male, rather than female productive activities. To that extent, women are much more dependent on men than men are on women. Furthermore, if one looks at gender-specific tasks as part of the productive system seen as an organic whole, rather than as two parallel and inter-dependent processes, it becomes clear that male tasks encompass female tasks: by contrast with male tasks, none of which requires previous female input, all female tasks require previous male input, which is why flaws in male productive tasks can have such an important impact. According to Dumont's definition of hierarchy as a relation between encompassing and encompassed categories (Dumont 1966: VIII, 105), this division of labour is therefore both complementary and hierarchical (the use I make of Dumont's concept of hierarchy is limited to this notion of encom-passment). Its hierarchical character is also apparent in the Kulina's own view of their political system, where leadership is male and explicitly associated with generous providing of gardens, fish, and meat.

From a Western perspective the concept of hierarchy tends to be associated with violence and direct coercion, and conversely the absence of such coercion and violence tends to be associated with equality. For example, in Overing's view the absence of physical violence and coercion among the Piaroa indicates social harmony (1985*a*: 270; 1986*a*: 87–8; 1988: 172; 1989*a*: 79, 96), which she associates with equality (1989*a*: 169; 1989*b*). The questions thus arise as to whether or not the Kulina division of labour is enforced by means of coercion and physical violence, and what relationship this has with gender politics.

The Kulina ethic strongly emphasizes the importance of being *bica*, which can mean a variety of positive attributes such as 'beautiful', 'nice', 'gentle', 'good', and 'generous'. In contrast, the antonym *huaidira* can mean a variety of negative attributes such as 'bad', 'evil', or 'stingy'. Being *boque*, that is 'angry', 'violent', or 'fierce', is the most reprehensible way of being *huaidira*: in this population that used to be one of fierce warriors (Rivet and Tastevin 1938: 73–5), and where most deaths are attributed to shamanism, any form of anger can be associated with extremely negative and wide-ranging consequences. However, although the ideal Kulina is *bica*, there is in actual fact an explicit disillusion with such reprehensible behaviours as stealing, wickedness, jealousy, selfishness, aggressiveness, and physical violence, which are fairly recurrent even though they do not usually dominate the social scene. Being *bica* is therefore an ideal that is constantly striven for with much effort, and is often attained, but is also constantly defeated by what is seen as the fundamentally *huaidira* and *boque* character of all human beings—women, men, and children. In short, one may say that the Kulina have an irenic, somewhat Rousseauist moral philosophy; but that they none the less also have a somewhat Hobbesian, pragmatic view of themselves that differs significantly from their normative values. Most importantly, these diametrically opposed views of themselves coexist on a constant basis in the discourses and practices of everyday life.

An example of this is that although physical violence is strongly disapproved of, except in ritual contexts, in practice wife-beating does happen on occasion and is not usually sanctioned in any way. When a man beats his wife, this is often because he finds her a lazy or uncooperative producer; and to that extent the division of labour is enforced to some degree by physical violence. However, female productive activities are not otherwise directly constrained except for the fact that women are forbidden the use of hunting snuff, that is made of tobacco pounded with ashes and the toasted hair of game animals, and represents an important means of enhancing hunting skills. Therefore gender hierarchy in the division of labour seems to be enforced primarily by means of a soft, indirect form of violence, namely the symbolic violence (Bourdieu 1977; 1980) expressed in rituals, myths, implicit mythology, shamanic practices, and the discourses of everyday life.

This does not imply, however, that the cosmology of gender can be reduced to this violence, which is at the nexus of the cosmic cycle of reproduction and as such does many more things than legitimate gender hierarchy. None the less, the power of this symbolic violence in enforcing the division of labour is apparent in the fact that by contrast with men, who occasionally perform a wide variety of female tasks, no amount of hunger will normally induce women to make gardens, or provide more than the usual, minimal amounts of fish or meat.

When women feel hungry because men do not provide enough fish or meat, they may endure their lot while complaining to a third party, or refraining from saying or doing anything. With variable degrees of success they may also complain to their husbands, or even order them to fish or hunt. However, they can do nothing to improve their situation when men are unsuccessful, drunk, or engaged in other productive activities.

The Kulina do not relate this division of labour to sexual dimorphism, female reproductive functions, or the impossibility for any individual to be competent in all productive tasks. In contrast with the anthropologist, they mostly seem to find it does not need any explaining. Interestingly, however, some men say that women cannot hunt big game because they are too afraid of jaguars. This, however, does not explain why women do not hunt small game with shotguns in village surroundings, as men often do, why women collect fruit deep into the forest without the protection of a shotgun unless they are accompanied by men, and why it seems to be mostly men, rather than women, who speak of their own fear of jaguars. Finally, when asked why women do not carry shotguns when they travel in the forest, given their presumed greater fear of jaguars, men offer the circular argument that women do not know how to use them. The explicit indigenous point of view on the division of labour as offered by these men thus involves a great deal of ideological opacity.

The implicit indigenous point of view, however, as inferred from rituals, mythology, and implicit mythology, is considerably more elaborate. Its logic rests in a typically Amazonian symbolic association of male genitals with hunting and fishing projectiles. The opacity of this association contributes to its symbolic power, and to the matter-of-fact character of a division of labour that is taken for granted. For example, women may bitterly complain about men who do not bring them enough fish or meat; but given the very close association of labour division with gender identity, questioning this division is none the less quite literally unthinkable for both genders. Notwithstanding the undeniably biased character of anthropological constructs, the axiom of direct experience thus has a somewhat limited heuristic value.

It might seem untenable, from a Western libertarian, voluntarist perspective and in keeping with the axiom of direct experience, that any amount of social hierarchy would not stick out a mile from the indigenous point of view, and that members of encompassed social categories might complain about their situation without actually questioning it. It is in fact quite understandable, however, if one considers the ideological effectiveness of symbolism, which transmutes social differentiations into natural distinctions that are part of an intrinsically unquestionable 'doxa', and hence are not an object of discourse: as such, these differentiations are commonsensical, in that they arise from a 'habitus' associated with a culturally specific cosmology and praxis (Bourdieu: 1972; 1977; 1980). What pertains here is therefore a form of hierarchy that needs not involve much physical violence or direct coercion, by Western standards.

The fact that gender relations are hierarchical does not mean, however, that hierarchy is encompassing in Kulina society. As in Guianan populations portrayed by Rivière, social relations involve both equality and hierarchy, neither of which is encompassing: relations between members of a same gender and age category are overall strikingly egalitarian, whereas relations between members of different categories generally have hierarchical dimensions.

CONCLUSION

In this brief exploration of the meanders of equality and hierarchy biases, I have initially attempted to provide a glimpse of how they are intrinsically related to one another. I have then looked at how opposed conclusions can be reached on the nature of gender politics, and by extension the political structure of society, depending on the analytic levels considered most pertinent such as the specific sets and subsets of relations examined, normative values and social relations versus pragmatic indigenous values and actual social relations, physical versus symbolic violence, and direct coercion versus habitus.

Such analytic choices are associated in part with culturally related ideological paradigms that have specific internal, moral constraints and areas of opacity and transparency. This hall of mirrors is perhaps not a major epistemological problem if one considers anthropology an art (Leach 1982: 52–3) or 'soft science' (Geertz 1973: 16) whose aim should be to interpret (Evans-Pritchard 1951: 62) and 'gain insight' (Leach 1982: 52–3; Taylor 1996: 211), rather than attain objectivity; all the more so if it is considered that the natural sciences themselves are also distorted by cultural paradigms (Carrithers 1990; Collins and Pinch 1993). It none the less points yet again to the importance of a constant awareness of the intrinsically partial, culturally biased character of anthropological analyses.

ACKNOWLEDGEMENTS

I thank the participants of the conference organized to honour Peter Rivière's work for their comments on the paper on which this chapter is based, especially Catherine Alès, Audrey Butt Colson, Philippe Erikson, Dieter Heinen, Stephen Hugh-Jones, David Maybury-Lewis, Fernando Santos Granero, and Eduardo Viveiros de Castro. I also owe special thanks to Laura Rival, Peter Rivière, and Jérôme Rousseau for their most useful comments on a first version of this chapter. I remain, however, solely responsible for the ideas developed here. Funding for fieldwork-based research was generously provided by the Fonds FCAR (Gouvernement du Québec), the Social Sciences and Humanities Research Council of Canada, the Wenner-Gren Foundation for Anthropological Research Inc. (Grant 5137), the Wyse Fund (Trinity College, University of Cambridge), King's College (University of Cambridge), the Richards Fund and the Ling Roth Fund (Department of Social Anthropology, University of Cambridge), the Sir Ernest Cassel Educational Trust, and the Radcliffe-Brown Memorial Fund (Royal Anthropological Institute). I also thank the Fonds FCAR and McGill University for providing the funds to participate in the conference on which this book is based.

REFERENCES

AIGLE, D. *et al.* (eds.) (2000), *La politique des esprits: Chamanismes et religions Universalistes* (Nanterre: Société d'Ethnologie).

AIJMER, G. (1997), *Ritual Dramas in the Duke of York Islands: An Exploration of Cultural Imagery* (Göteborg: IASSA).

ALBERT, B. (1985), 'Temps du sang, temps des cendres: représentation de la maladie, système rituel et espace politique chez les Yanomami du sud-est (Amazonie brésilienne)', unpub. doctoral thesis (Nanterre: University of Paris X).

ALVARD, M. (1995), 'Intraspecific Prey Choice by Amazonian Hunters', *Current Anthropology*, 36: 789–818.

APPADURAI, A. (1996), *Modernity at Large: Cultural Dimensions of Globalization* (Minneapolis: University of Minnesota Press).

ARENS, W. (1979), *The Man-Eating Myth: Anthropology and Anthropophagy* (New York: Oxford University Press).

ÅRHEM, K. (1981), *Makuna Social Organization* (Uppsala Studies in Cultural Anthropology; Stockholm: Almqvist and Wiksell International).

—— (1987), 'Wives for Sisters: The Management of Marriage Exchange in Northwest Amazonia', in H. Skar and F. Salomon (eds.), *Natives and Neighbours in South America* (Göteborg: Ethnographic Museum), 130–77.

—— (1989), 'The Makú, the Makuna and the Guiana System: Transformations of Social Structure in Northern Lowland South America', *Ethnos*, 54(I–II): 5–22.

—— (1996), 'The Cosmic Food Web: Human-Nature Relatedness in the Northwest Amazon', in P. Descola and G. Pálsson (eds.), *Nature and Society: Anthropological Perspectives* (London: Routledge), 185–204.

—— (1998a), 'Powers of Place: Landscape, Territory and Local Belonging in Northwest Amazonia', in N. Lovell (ed.), *Locality and Belonging* (London: Routledge), 78–102.

—— (1998b), *Makuna: Portrait of An Amazonian People* (Washington, DC: Smithsonian Institution Press).

—— (2000), *Ethnographic Puzzles: Essays on Social Organisation, Symbolism and Change* (London: Athlone).

ARMELLADA, C. DE (1964), *Taurón Pantón: cuentos y leyendas de los indios Pemón* (Caracas: Ediciones del Ministerio de Educación).

—— and GUTIÉRREZ SALAZAR, M. (1981), *Diccionario Pemón* (Caracas: Universidad Católica Andrés Bello).

BADINTER, E. (1992), *De l'identité masculine* (Paris: Odile Jacob).

BAER, G. (n.d.), 'Masques, esprits, femmes et yurupari. Réflexions sur un thème sud-améri- cain (Pérou oriental, Brésil Central, Nord-Ouest Amazonien)', paper presented at the Séminaire Inter-Américanistes (Paris, 12 March 1999).

BALANDIER, G. (1969), *Anthropologie politique* (Paris: Presses Universitaires de France).

BAMBERGER, J. (1974), 'The Myth of Matriarchy: Why Men rule in Primitive Society', in M. Zimbalist Rosaldo and L. Lamphere (eds.), *Women, Culture and Society* (Stanford: Stanford University Press), 263–80.

BARKER, F. *et al.* (1998), *Cannibalism and the Colonial World* (Cambridge: Cambridge University Press).

BASSO, E. (1973), *The Kalapalo Indians of Central Brazil* (New York: Holt, Rinehart and Winston).

—— (1995), *The Last Cannibals: A South American Oral History* (Austin: University of Texas Press).

BAUDRILLARD, J. (1989), *For a Critique of the Political Economy of the Sign*, trans. Ch. Levin (Saint Louis: Telos Press).

BAUMAN, R., and SHERZER, J. (1974), *Explorations in the Ethnography of Speaking* (Cambridge: Cambridge University Press).

BECKERMAN, S. (1994), 'Hunting and Fishing in Amazonia: Hold the Answers, what are the Questions', in A. Roosevelt (ed.), Amazonian Indians from Prehistory to the Present (Tucson: University of Arizona Press), 177–200.

BELAUNDE, L. E. (1992), 'Gender, Commensality and Community among the Airo-Pai of Western Amazonia (Secoya, Western Tukanoan speaking)', unpub. Ph.D. diss. (London School of Economics, University of London).

—— (1994), 'Parrots and Oropendolas: The Aesthetics of Gender Relations among the Airo-Pai of the Peruvian Amazon', *Journal de la Société des Américanistes*, 80: 95–111.

BERGMAN, R. (1980), *Amazon Economics: The Simplicity of Shipibo Wealth* (Syracuse: Syracuse University Press).

BERTRAND-RICOVER, P. (1994), 'Vision blanche/vision indienne. Traversée anthropologique d'une culture amazonienne: les Shipibo de l'Ucayali', 4 vols., unpub. doctoral thesis (Université Paris V-Sorbonne).

BLOCH, M. (1986), *From Blessing to Violence: History and Ideology in the Circumcision Ritual of the Merina of Madagascar* (Cambridge: Cambridge University Press).

—— (1992), *Prey into Hunter: The Politics of Religious Experience* (Cambridge: Cambridge University Press).

—— (1993), 'Domain Specificity, Living Kinds and Symbolism', in P. Bayer (ed.), *Cognitive Aspects of Religious Symbolism* (Cambridge: Cambridge University Press).

BOGLÁR, L. (1950), 'Some More Data on the Spreading of the Blowgun in South-America', *Acta Ethnographica*, 1(1–4): 121–37.

BOSTER, J. S. (1985), 'Selection for Perceptual Distinctiveness: Evidence from Aguaruna Cultivars of Manihot esculenta', *Economic Botany*, 39: 310–25.

BOURDIEU, P. (1972) *Esquisse d'une théorie de la pratique* (Geneva: Librairie Droz).

—— (1977), 'Sur le pouvoir symbolique', *Annales ESC*, 3: 405–11.

—— (1980), *Le Sens pratique* (Paris: Les Éditions de Minuit).

BRETT, W. H. (1868), *The Indian Tribes of Guiana* (London: Bell and Daldy).

BROWN, M. (1985), *Tsewa's Gift: Magic and Meaning in an Amazonian Society* (Washington, DC: Smithsonian Institution Press).

BUTT, A. J. (1960), 'The Birth of a Religion', *Journal of the Royal Anthropological Society*, 90: 66–106.

BUTT COLSON, A. J. (1973), 'Inter-Tribal Trading in the Guiana Highlands', *Antropológica*, 34: 1–70.

—— (1976), 'Binary Oppositions and the Treament of Sickness among the Akawaio', in J. Loudon (ed.), *Social Anthropology and Medicine* (London: Academic Press), 422–99.

—— (1989), 'La Naturaleza del Ser. Conceptos Fundamentales de los Kapón y Pemón', in

J. Bottasso (ed.), *Las Religiones Amerindias 500 Años Después*, vol. iv (Quito: Abya-Yala), 53–90.

—— and DE ARMELLADA, C. (1983), 'An Amerindian Derivation for Latin American Creole Illnesses and their Treatment', *Social Science and Medicine*, 17(17): 1229–48.

CAIUBY NOVAES, S. (1983), 'Tranas, cabaas e couros no funeral Bororo—a propósito de um processo de constituiçao de identidade', in José de Souza Martins (ed.), *A morte e os mortos na sociedade brasileira* (São Paulo: Hucitec), 303–14.

CALAVIA SAEZ, O. (1994), 'O nome e o tempo dos Yaminawa: Etnologiae história dos Yaminawa do rio Acre', unpub. doctoral thesis (USP, São Paulo).

CALIXTO MÉNDEZ, L. (1987), 'La organización social matses y su sistema de valores y creencias: Aspectos Socio-Culturales del uso de la tierra en el grupo etnico matses', manuscript at the Instituto de Investigaciones de la Amazonia Peruana, 3 vols. (Iquitos).

CALLE, H. (1986), 'Medicina tradicional y occidental en una comunidad Indígena del Amazonas', *Informes Antropológicos* (Bogotá: ICAN), 2: 75–104.

—— and CROOKE, I. (1969), 'Los Huitotos—notas sobre sus bailes y sobre su situación actual', *Revista de la Dirección Cultural*, 3 (Apr.–Aug.): 80–95.

CANDRE, H. (1996 [1993]), *Cool Tobacco, Sweet Coca: Teachings of an Indian Sage from the Colombian Amazon* (Totnes: Themis Books).

CARLIN, E. (forthcoming), 'WYSIWYG in Trio: The Grammaticalised Expression of Truth and Knowledge', *JASO*.

CARNEIRO, R. (1983), 'The Cultivation of Cassava among the Kuikuru of the Upper Xingu', in R. B. Hames and W. T. Vickers (eds.), *Adaptive Responses of Native Amazonians* (New York: Academic Press), 65–111.

CARNEIRO DA CUNHA, M. (1978), *Os mortos e os outros: Uma análise do sistema funerário e da noção de pessoa entre os Índios Krahó* (São Paulo: Hucitec).

—— and VIVEIROS DE CASTRO, E. (1985), 'Vinganza e temporalidade: os Tupinambas', *Journal de la Société des Américanistes*, 71: 195–208.

CARRITHERS, M. (1990), 'Is Anthropology Art or Science?', *Current Anthropology*, 31(3): 263–82.

CARSTEN, J., and HUGH-JONES, S. (eds.) (1995), *About the House. Lévi-Strauss and Beyond* (Cambridge: Cambridge University Press).

CASTELNAU, F. DE (1850–9), *Expédition dans les parties centrales de l'Amérique du Sud, de Rio de Janeiro à Lima, et de Lima au Para; éxécutée par ordre du gouvernement français pendant les années 1843 à 1847*, 14 vols. (Paris).

CHAGNON, N. (1990), Reproductive and Somatic Conflicts of Interest in the Genesis of Violence and Warfare among Tribesmen, in J. Haas (ed.), *The Anthropology of War* (Cambridge: Cambridge University Press), 77–104.

CHAUMEIL, B., and CHAUMEIL, J. P. (1992), 'L'Oncle et le neveu: La parenté du vivant chez les Yagua', *Journal de la Société des Américanistes*, 78(2): 25–37.

CHAUMEIL, J. P. (1983), *Voir, savoir, pouvoir* (Paris: EHESS).

—— (1984), 'Canto del pijuayo: En torno al Bactris gasipaes y su importancia entre los Yagua', *Amazonia Indígena*, 8: 12–14.

—— (1987), *Los Yagua del Nor-oriente peruano* (Lima: CAAAP).

—— (1994), 'Los Yagua', in F. Santos and F. Barclay (eds.), *Guía Etnográfica de la Alta Amazonia*, vol. i (Quito: FLACSO/IFEA), 181–307.

—— (1997), 'Les os, les flûtes, les morts: Mémoire et traitement funéraire en Amazonie', *Journal de la Société des Américanistes*, 83: 83–110.

CHAUMEIL, J. P. *et al.* (2000), *La Politique des esprits: Chamanismes et religions Universalistes* (Nanterre: Société d'Ethnologie).

CHERNELA, J. (1985), 'Why One Culture Stays Put', in J. Hemming (ed.), *Change in the Amazon Basin*, vol. i (Manchester: Manchester University Press), 228–36.

—— (1987), 'Os cultivares de mandioca na área do Uaupés (Tukano)', in Bertha Ribeiro (ed.), *SUMA: Etnológica Brasileira*, 1 (Petropolis: FINEP/VOZES), 151–8.

—— (1988*a*), 'Gender, Language and "Placement" in Uanano Songs and Litanies', *Journal of Latin American Lore*, 14(2): 193–206.

—— (1988*b*), 'Some Considerations of Myth and Gender', in R. Randolph and D. Schneider (eds.), Dialectics and Gender: Anthropological Approaches (Boulder, Colo.: Westview Press), 67–79.

—— (1988*c*), 'Righting History in the Northwest Amazon', in Jonathan Hill (ed.), *Rethinking History and Myth* (Urbana: University of Illinois Press), 35–49.

—— (1989), 'Marriage, Language, and History among Eastern Speaking Peoples of the Northwest Amazon', *Latin American Anthropology Review*, 1(2): 36–42.

—— (1992), 'Social Meaning and Material Transaction: The Wanano-Tukano of Brazil and Colombia', *Journal of Anthropological Archaeology*, 11: 111–24.

—— (1993), *The Wanano Indians of the Brazilian Amazon: A Sense of Space* (Austin: University of Texas Press).

CHIARA, V. (1987), 'Armas: bases para uma classificação', in Bertha Ribeiro (ed.), *SUMA: Etnologica Brasileira*, (Petropolis: FINEP/VOZES), 27–93.

CIR (1993), *Os indios no futuro de Roráima* (Boa Vista: Conselho Indigena de Roráima).

CLASTRES, H. (1975), *La Terre Sans Mal: Le Prophétisme Tupi-Guarani* (Paris: Seuil).

CLASTRES, P. (1972), *Chronique des Indiens Guyaki* (Paris: Plon).

—— (1977), *Society Against the State: The Leader as Servant and the Human Uses of Power among the Indians of the Americas*, trans. R. Hurley (Oxford: Basil Blackwell).

CLIFFORD, J., and MARCUS, G. E. (eds.) (1986), *Writing Culture: The Poetics and Politics of Ethnography* (Berkeley: University of California Press).

COLCHESTER, M. (1981), 'Ecological Modeling of Indigenous Systems of Resource Use: Some Examples from the Amazon of South Venezuela', *Antropológica*, 55: 56–72.

COLLIER, J., and ROSALDO, M. (1981), 'Politics and Gender in Simple Societies', in S. Ortner and H. Whitehead (eds.), *Sexual Meanings* (Cambridge: Cambridge University Press).

COLLINS, H., and PINCH, T. (1993), *The Golem: What Everyone should Know about Science* (Cambridge: Cambridge University Press).

COLOMBO, C. (1997), 'Étude de la diversité génétique des maniocs américains (Manihot esculenta Crantz) par les marqueurs moléculaires (RAPD et AFLP)', unpub. Ph.D. diss. (ENSAM, Montpellier).

COMAROFF, J. (1984), 'The Closed Society and its Critics: Historical Transformations in African Ethnography', *American Ethnologist*, 11(3): 571–83.

COMBÈS, I. (1992), *La Tragédie cannibale chez les anciens Tupi-Guarani* (Paris: Presses Universitaires de France).

—— and SAIGNES, T. (1991), *Alter ego: naissance de l'identité chiriguano* (Paris: Éditions de l'École des Hautes Études en Sciences Sociales).

CONKLIN, B. (1995), ' "Thus are our bodies, thus was our custom": Mortuary Cannibalism in an Amazonian Society', *American Ethnologist*, 22(1): 75–101.

—— (1997), 'Consuming Images: Representations of Cannibalism on the Amazonian Frontier', *Anthropological Quarterly*, 70(2): 68–78.

COPPENS, W. (1971), 'Las relaciones comerciales de los Yekuana del Caura-Paragua', *Antropológica*, 30: 28–59.

CORONIL, F. (1996), *The Magical State: Nature, Money, and Modernity in Venezuela* (Chicago: University of Chicago Press).

CORREA, F. (1996), *Por el camino de la anaconda remedio: dinámica de la organización social entre los Taiwano del Vaupès* (Bogotá: Universidad Nacional).

CROCKER, C. (1985), *Vital Souls: Bororo Cosmology, Natural Symbolism and Shamanism* (Tucson: University of Arizona Press.

CROCKER, J., and CROCKER, W. (1994), *The Canela: Bonding through Kinship, Ritual, and Sex* (Fort Worth: Harcourt Brace College Publishers).

DA MATTA, R. (1979), 'The Apinayé Relationship System: Terminology and Ideology', in D. Maybury-Lewis (ed.), *Dialectical Societies: The Gê and Bororo of Central Brazil* (Cambridge, Mass.: Harvard University Press), 83–127.

DEBOER, W. (1990), 'Interaction, Imitation, and Communication as Expressed in Style: The Ucayali Experience', in M. W. Conkey and Ch. A. Hastorf (eds.), *The Uses of Style in Archaeology* (Cambridge: Cambridge University Press), 82–104.

DESCOLA, P. (1981), 'From Scattered to Nucleated Settlement: A Process of Socio-Economic Change among the Achuar', in N. Whitten (ed.), *Cultural Transformations and Ethnicity in Modern Ecuador* (Urbana: University of Illinois Press), 614–46.

—— (1986), *La Nature domestique, symbolisme et praxis dans l'écologie des Achuar* (Paris: Éditions de la Maison des Sciences de l'Homme).

—— (1992), 'Societies of Nature and the Nature of Society', in A. Kuper (ed.), *Conceptualizing Society* (London and New York: Routledge), 107–26.

—— (1993), *Les Lances du crépuscule: Relations Jivaros, Haute-Amazonie* (Paris: Plon).

—— (1994a), *In the Society of Nature: A Native Ecology in Amazonia* (Cambridge: Cambridge University Press).

—— (1994b), 'Homeostasis as Cultural System: The Jivaro Case', in A. Roosevelt (ed.), *Amazonian Indians from Prehistory to the Present: Anthropological Perspectives* (Tucson: University of Arizona Press), 203–24.

—— (1999), 'Des proies bienveillantes', in F. Héritier (ed.), *De la violence*, vol. ii (Collection Opus 88; Paris: Odile Jacob), 19–44.

—— and TAYLOR, A.-C. (1993), 'Introduction', in P. Descola and A.-C. Taylor (eds.), *La Remontée de l'Amazone: anthropologie et histoire des sociétés amazoniennes* (Special Edition of *L'Homme*, 126–8; Paris: École des Hautes Études en Sciences Sociales), 13–24.

DINIZ, E. S. (1966), 'O perfil de uma situação interétnica', *Antropologia: Boletím do Museu Paraense Emilio Goeldi*, 31: 1–31.

DUFOUR, D. (1983), 'Nutrition in the Northwest Amazon: Household Dietary Intake and Time Energy Expenditure', in R. Hames and W. Vickers (eds.), *Adaptive Responses of Native Amazonians* (New York: Academic Press), 329–55.

DUMONT, J. P. (1976), *Under the Rainbow: Nature and Supernature among the Panare Indians* (Austin: University of Texas Press).

DUMONT, L. (1966), *Homo hierarchicus: Le système des castes et ses implications* (Paris: Gallimard).

—— (1971), *Introduction à Deux Théories d'anthropologie* (Paris: Mouton).

—— (1983a), 'Stocktaking 1981: Affinity as Value', in *Affinity as a Value: Marriage Alliance in South India with Comparative Essays on Australia* (Chicago and London: University of Chicago Press).

DUMONT, L. (1983*b* [1978]), 'La Communauté anthropologique et l'idéologie', in *Essais sur l'individualisme: une perspective anthropologique sur l'idéologie moderne* (Paris: Seuil), 187–221.

—— (1985), *Homo aequalis*, vol. i: *Genèse et épanouissement de l'idéologie moderne* (Paris: Gallimard).

DURANTI, A., and GOODWIN, C. (1992), *Rethinking Context: Language as an Interactive Phenomenon* (Studies in the Social and Cultural Foundations of Language 11; Cambridge: Cambridge University Press).

DUVERNAY, J. (1973), 'Les Voies du chamane'. *L'Homme*, 13(3): 82–92.

ECHEVERRI, J. (1997), 'The People of the Centre of the World: A Study in Culture, History and Orality in the Colombian Amazon', unpub. doctoral thesis (New School for Social Research, New York).

ELIAS, M. (2000), 'Traditional Cultivation of Cassava among Makushi Amerindians in Guyana', unpub. doctoral thesis (University of Montpellier, France).

—— RIVAL, L., and McKEY, D. (2001), 'The Interaction between Genetic Selection and Human Selection: Makushi Management of Varietal Diversity in Manihot esculenta Crantz', *Journal of Ethnobiology*.

EMPERAIRE, L., PINTON, F., and SECOND, G. (1998), 'Une gestion dynamique de la diversité variétale du manioc en Amazonie du Nord-Ouest', *Nature, Science et Société*, 6(2): 27–42.

ERIKSON, P. (1986), 'Altérité, tatouage et anthropophagie chez les Pano: la belliqueuse quête du soi', *Journal de la Société des Américanistes*, 72: 185–210.

—— (1988), 'Choix des proies, choix des armes, et gestion du gibier chez les Matis et d'autres Amérindiens d'Amazonie', in L. Bodson (ed.), *L'Animal dans l'alimentation humaine, les critères de choix* (Anthropozoologica, 2nd Special No., Liège), 211–20.

—— (1990), 'How crude is Mayoruna Pottery?', *Journal of Latin American Lore*, 16(1): 47–68.

—— (1995), 'Los Matses/Matis', in F. Santos and F. Barclay (eds.), *Guía Etnográfica de la Alta Amazonía*, vol. ii (Quito: FLACSO/IFEA), 1–127.

—— (1996*a*), *La Griffe des Aïeux: marquage du corps et démarquages ethniques chez les Matis d'Amazonie brésilienne* (Paris: Editions Peeters and Centre National de la Recherche Scientifique).

—— (1996*b*), 'Le Masque matis: matière à réflexion, réflexion sur la matière', paper presented at the symposium 'Iconologie de l'objet: réflexion anthropologique' (30, 31 May, 1 June 1996), organized by Danielle Geirnaert, Michèle Coquet, and Claude-François Baudez (to be published in *L'Homme*).

—— and MONOD BECQUELIN, A. (2000), *Les Dialogues du rituel: Promenades ethnolinguistiques en terres amérindiennes* (Nanterre: Société d'Ethnologie).

ESPINOSA, M. (1995), *Convivencia y poder político entre los andogues* (Santafé de Bogotá: Editorial Universidad Nacional (eun)).

EVANS-PRITCHARD, E. E. (1940), *The Nuer* (Oxford: Clarendon Press).

—— (1951), *Social Anthropology* (London: Routledge and Kegan Paul).

EWART, E. (2000), 'Living with Each Other: Selves and Alters amongst the Panará of Central Brazil', unpub. Ph.D. thesis (London School of Economics).

FARABEE, W. C. (1917), 'The Amazon Expedition of the University Museum', *Museum Journal*, 8(1): 61–82.

—— (1918), *The Central Arawaks* (Anthropological publications 9; Philadelphia: University Museum).

—— (1924), *The Central Caribs* (Museum of Anthropology Publications 10; Philadelphia: University of Pennsylviana).

FARAGE, N. (1991), *As muralhas dos sertões. Os povos indígenas no Río Branco e a colonização* (São Paulo: Paz e Terra).

FAUSTO, C. (1997), 'A dialética da predação e familiarização entre os Parakanã da Amazônia Oriental. Por uma teoria da guerra amerindia', unpub. doctoral thesis (PPGAS, Museu Nacional, UFRJ).

FEJOS, P. (1943), *Ethnography of the Yagua* (Publications in Anthropology 1; New-York: Viking Fund).

FERGUSON, R. B., and Whitehead, N. L. (2000), *War in the Tribal Zone: Expanding States and Indigenous Warfare* (2nd edn.; Santa Fe: School of American Research Press).

FIGUEROA, Fr. DE (1986), *Informe de las misiones en el Marañón, Gran Para o rio de las Amazonas por el P. Francisco de Figueroa, 1661* (Informe de Jesuitas en el Amazonas; Monumenta Amazónica; Iquitos: IIAP/CETA).

FOCK, N. (1963), *Waiwai: Religion and Society of an Amazonian Tribe* (Ethnographic Series (ed. A. Duranti and C. Goodwin), No. 8; Copenhagen: Danish National Museum).

FORTE, J. (1999), *Makusipe Komanto Iseru (Sustaining Makushi Way of Life)* (Georgetown: ARU).

FORTES, M. (1958), 'Introduction', in J. Goody (ed.), *The Development Cycle in Domestic Groups* (Cambridge: Cambridge University Press), 1–14.

—— (1969), *Kinship and the Social Order* (Chicago: Aldine Publishing Company).

FOX, J. (1971 [1967]), 'Sister's Child as Plant: Metaphors in an Idiom of Consanguinity', in R. Needham (ed.), *Rethinking Kinship and Marriage* (London: Tavistock), 219–52.

FOX, R. (1974 [1967]), *Kinship and Marriage* (London: Pelican).

GASCHÉ, J. (1972), 'L'Habitat Witoto: progrès et tradition', *Journal de la Société des Américanistes*, 61.

GEERTZ, C. (1973), *The Interpretation of Cultures* (New York: Basic Books).

—— (1983), *Local Knowledge: Further Essays in Interpretive Anthropology* (New York: Basic Books).

GESCHIERE, P. (1997), *The Modernity of Witchcraft: Politics and the Occult in Postcolonial Africa* (University Press of Virginia).

GIDDENS, A. (1994), 'Living in a Post-Traditional Society', in U. Beck, A. Giddens, and S. Lash (eds.), *Reflexive Modernization: Politics, Tradition and Aesthetics in the Modern Social Order* (Oxford: Polity Press).

GODELIER, M. (1982), *La Production des grands hommes* (Paris: Fayard).

GOLDMAN, I. (1963), *The Cubeo: Indians of the Northwest Amazon* (Urbana: University of Illinois Press).

—— (1977), 'Time, Space and Descent: The Cubeo Example', in J. Overing (ed.), *Social Time and Social Space in Lowland South American Societies*, Actes du xlii Congrès International des Américanistes, 2 vols. (Paris), 175–83.

GORDON, C. (1996), 'Aspectos da Organizão Social Jê: De Nimuendajú a Década de 1990', Masters thesis (Museu Nacional, Federal University of Rio de Janeiro).

GOULARD, J. P. (1998), 'Les Genres du corps: Conceptions de la personne chez les Ticuna de la haute Amazonie', unpub. doctoral thesis (EHESS, Paris).

GOVOROFF, N. (1993), 'The Hunter and his Gun in Haute-Provence', in P. Lemonnier (ed.), *Technological Choices: Transformation in Material Cultures since the Neolithic* (London and New York: Routledge), 227–37.

Gow, P. (1989), 'The Perverse Child: Desire in a Native Amazonian Subsistence Economy', *Man*, 24(4): 567–82.

—— (1991), *Of Mixed Blood: Kinship and History in Peruvian Amazonia* (Oxford: Clarendon Press).

—— (1997), 'O parentesco como consciência humana: o caso dos Piro', *Mana*, 3(2): 39–65.

Gray, A. (1996*a*), *The Arakmbut: Mythology, Spirituality and History* (Oxford: Berghahn Books).

—— (1996*b*), *The Last Shaman: Change in an Amazonian Community* (Oxford: Berghahn Books).

Gregor, T. (1977), *Mehinaku: The Drama of Daily Life in a Brazilian Indian Village* (Chicago: University of Chicago Press).

—— (1985), *Anxious Pleasures: The Sexual Lives of Amazonian People* (Chicago: University of Chicago Press).

Gregory, C. (1982), *Gifts and Commodities* (London: Academic Press).

Grenand, P. (1993), 'Fruits, Animals and People: Hunting and Fishing Strategies of the Wayãpi of Amazonia', in C. M. Hladik *et al.* (eds.), *Tropical Forests, People and Food: Biocultural Interactions and Applications to Development* (Paris: Unesco), 425–34.

—— (1994), 'De l'arc au fusil, un changement technologique chez les Wayãpi de Guyane', in F. Grenand and V. Randa (eds.), *Transitions plurielles: exemples dans quelques sociétés des Amériques* (Paris: Peeters), 23–53.

Griffiths, T. F. W. (1998), 'Ethnoeconomics and Native Amazonian Livelihood: A Study of Culture and Economy among the Nípode Uitoto of the Middle Caquetá Basin in Colombia', unpub. D.Phil. thesis (St Antony's College, University of Oxford).

Gros, C. (1991), *Colombia Indígena: Identidad cultural y cambio social* (Bogotá: CEREC).

Gumperz, J. J. (1971), *Language in Social Groups* (Stanford: Stanford University Press).

—— (1982), *Language and Social Identity* (Cambridge: Cambridge University Press).

Guss, D. (1989), *To Weave and to Sing: Art, Symbol, and Narrative in the South American Rain Forest* (Berkeley: University of California Press).

Hage, P. (1999), 'Marking Universals and the Structure and Evolution of Kinship Terminologies: Evidence from Salish', *Journal of the Royal Anthropological Institute*, 5(3): 423–41.

Hames, R. B. (1980), 'Game Depletion and Hunting Zone Rotation among the Yekwana and Yanomamo of Amazonas, Venezuela', in R. Hames (ed.), *Studies in Hunting and Fishing in the Neotropics* (Bennington College, Vermont: Working Papers on South American Indians, 2), 31–64.

—— (1989), 'Time, Efficiency, and Fitness in the Amazonian Protein Quest', *Research in Economic Anthropology*, 11: 43–85.

Hastrup, K. (1978), 'The Post-Structuralist Position in Social Anthropology', in E. Schwimmer (ed.), *The Yearbook of Symbolic Anthropology*, i (Montreal: McGill-Queens University Press), 123–47.

—— (1992), 'Writing Ethnography; State of the Art', in J. Okely and H. Callaway (eds.), *Anthropology and Autobiography* (London: Routledge), 116–33.

—— (1993*a*), 'The Native Voice and the Anthropological Vision', *Social Anthropology*, 1(2): 173–86.

—— (1993*b*), 'Native Anthropology? A Contradiction in Terms?', *Folk*, 35: 147–61.

Heinen, D. (forthcoming), 'The Relationship System of the Kamarata Pemon', *JASO*.

HENDRICKS, J. (1993), *To Drink of Death: The Narrative of a Shuar Warrior* (Tucson: University of Arizona Press).

HENLEY, P. (1982), *The Panare: Tradition and Change on the Amazon Frontier* (London: Yale University Press).

—— (1983–4), 'Intergenerational Marriage amongst the Carib-Speaking Peoples of the Guianas: A Preliminary Survey', in A. Butt Colson and H. D. Heinen (eds.), *Themes in Political Organization: The Caribs and their Neighbours* (Antropológica, 59–62), 155–82.

—— (1996), *South Indian Models in the Amazonian Lowlands* (Manchester Papers in Social Anthropology 1; Manchester).

HILL, J. (1989), 'Ritual Production of Environmental History among the Arawakan Wakuénai of Venezuela', *Human Ecology*, 17(1): 1–25.

—— (1993), *Keepers of the Sacred Chants: The Poetics of Ritual and Power in an Amazonian Society* (Tucson: University of Arizona Press).

HOLY, L. (1996), *Anthropological Perspectives on Kinship* (London: Pluto Press).

HORNBORG, A. (1988), *Dualism and Hierarchy in Lowland South America: Trajectories of Indigenous Social Organization* (Uppsala Studies in Cultural Anthropology 9; Stockholm: Almqvist and Wiksell International).

HOSKINS, J. (ed.) (1996), *Headhunting and the Social Imagination in Southeast Asia* (Stanford: Stanford University Press).

HOUSEMAN, M. (1984), 'La Relation hiérarchique: idéologie particulière ou modèle général?', in J.-C. Galey (ed.), *Différences, valeurs, hiérarchie: textes offerts à Louis Dumont* (Paris: École des Hautes Études en Sciences Sociales), 299–318.

—— (1988), 'Toward a Complex Model of Parenthood: Two African Tales', *American Ethnologist*, 15: 658–77.

HOWARD, C. V. (1993), 'Pawana: a farsa dos "visitantes" entre os Waiwai da Amazónia setentrional', in E. Viveiros de Castro and M. Carneiro da Cunha (eds.), *Amazónia: etnologia e história indígena* (São Paulo: NHII–USP and FAPESP), 229–64.

HUGH-JONES, C. (1979), *From the Milk River: Spatial and Temporal Processes in Northwest Amazonia* (Cambridge: Cambridge University Press).

HUGH-JONES, S. (1979), *The Palm and the Pleiades: Initiation and Cosmology in Northwest Amazonia* (Cambridge: Cambridge University Press).

—— (1981), 'Historia del Vaupès', *Revista Maguaré*, 1(1): 29–51.

—— (1988), 'The Gun and the Bow: Myths of White Men and Indians', *L'Homme*, 106–7: 138–55.

—— (1992), 'Yesterday's Luxuries, Tomorrow's Necessities: Business and Barter in Northwest Amazonia', in C. Humphrey and S. Hugh-Jones (eds.), *Barter, Exchange and Value: An Anthropological Approach* (Cambridge: Cambridge University Press), 42–74.

—— (1993), 'Clear Descent or Ambiguous Houses? A Re-examination of Tukanoan Social Organization' (Special Editon of *L'Homme*, 126–8, vol. XXXIII; Paris: École des Hautes Études en Sciences Sociales), 95–120.

—— (1995), 'Inside-Out and Back-to-Front: The Androgynous House in Northwest Amazonia', in *About the House: Lévi-Strauss and beyond* (Cambridge: Cambridge University Press), 226–52.

—— (1996a), 'De bonnes raisons ou de la mauvaise conscience? Ou de l'ambivalence de certains Amazoniens envers la consommation de viande', *Terrains*, 26: 123–48.

—— (1996b), 'The gender of some Amazonian Gifts: An Experiment with an Experiment',

Wenner-Gren Symposium No. 121: 'Amazonian and Melanesia: Gender and Anthropological Comparison' (Mijas, Spain, 7–15 September).

HYMES, D. (1962), 'The Ethnography of Speaking', in T. Gladwin and W. Sturtevant (eds.), *Anthropology and Human Behavior* (Washington, DC: Anthropological Society), 113–53.

—— (1972), 'Models of the Interaction of Language and Social Life,' in J. Gumperz and D. Hymes (eds.), *Directions in Sociolinguistics: The Ethnography of Communication* (New York: Holt, Rinehart and Winston), 35–71.

—— (1981), *In Vain I Tried to Tell You: Essays in Native American Ethnopetics* (Philadelphia: University of Pennsylvania Press).

IM THURN, Sir EVERARD E. (1883), *Among the Indians of Guiana, being Sketches Chiefly Anthropologic from the Interior of British Guiana* (London: Kegan Paul, Trench and Co.).

INGOLD, T. (1992), 'Culture and the Perception of the Environment', in E. Croll and D. Parkin (eds.), *Bush Base: Forest Farm. Culture, Environment and Development* (London: Routledge), 39–75.

IRVINE, J. (1982), 'Language and Affect: Some Cross-Cultural Issues', in H. Byrnes (ed.), *Contemporary Perceptions of Language: Interdisciplinary Dimensions* (Washington, DC: Georgetown University Press), 31–47.

JACKSON, J. E. (1974), 'Language Identity of the Colombia Vaupés Indians', in R. Bauman and J. Sherzer (eds.), *Explorations in the Ethnography of Speaking* (Cambridge: Cambridge University Press), 50–64.

—— (1976), 'Vaupés Marriage: A Network System in an Undifferentiated Lowland Area of South America', in C. Smith (ed.), *Regional Analysis*, ii: *Social Systems* (New York: Academic Press), 65–93.

—— (1983), *The Fish People: Linguistic Exogamy and Tukanoan Identity in Northwest Amazonia* (New York: Cambridge University Press).

—— (1993), 'The Meaning and Message of Symbolic Sexual Violence in Tukanoan Ritual', *Anthropological Quarterly*, 65(1): 1–18.

JAMESON, F. (1988), 'Post-Modernism and Consumer Society', in E. A. Kaplan (ed.), *Post-Modernism and its Discontents* (London: Verso), 13–29.

JAMOUS, R. (1991), *La Relation frère–sœur: parentés et rites chez les Meo de l'Inde du Nord* (Paris: EHESS).

JOHNSON, A. (1975), 'Time Allocation in a Machiguenga Community', *Ethnology*, 14(3): 301–10.

JOSEPHIDES, L. (1985), *The Production of Inequality: Gender and Exchange among the Kewa* (London: Tavistock).

JOURNET N. (1981), 'Los Curripacos del Rio Isana: economía y sociedad', *Revista Colombiana de Antropología*, 23: 125–82.

—— (1995), *La Paix des jardins: Structures sociales des indiens curripaco du haut Río Negro (Colombie)* (Paris: Musée de l'Homme).

KAPLAN, A. (1984), 'Philosophy of Science in Anthropology', *Annual Review of Anthropology*, 13: 25–39.

KAPLAN, J. OVERING (1975), *The Piaroa* (Oxford: Clarendon Press).

—— (1981), 'Amazonian Anthropology', review article, *Journal of Latin American Studies*, 13(1): 151–65.

KARADIMAS, D. (1997), 'Le Corps sauvage: Idéologie du corps et représentations de l'environnement chez les Miraóa d'Amazonie colombienne', 2 vols., unpub. doctoral thesis (Paris X-Nanterre).

KEESING, R. M. (1989), 'Exotic Readings of Cultural Texts', *Current Anthropology*, 30: 459–77.

KEIFENHEIM, B. (1992), 'Identité et alterité chez les indiens Pano', *Journal de la Société des Américanistes*, 78: 79–93.

KELLY, J. A. (1999), 'Fractality and the Exchange of Perspectives', (Cambridge: manuscript).

KENSINGER, K. (1975), *The Cashinahua of Eastern Peru* (Brown University: The Haffenreffer Museum of Anthropology).

—— (1995), *How Real People Ought to Live: The Cashinahua of Eastern Peru* (Prospect Heights: Waveland Press).

KENT, S. (1999), 'How Egalitarian are Highly Egalitarian Societies? Variation among Kalahari Foragers', unpub. manuscript.

KHAN, F. (1997), *Les Palmiers de l'Eldorado* (Paris: Orstom).

KOCH-GRÜNBERG, T. (1909), *Zwei jahre unter den indianern: Reisen im Nordwest Brasilien, 1903–1905* (2 vols.) (Berlin: E. Wasmuth).

KRACKE, W. H. (1978), *Force and Persuasion: Leadership in an Amazonian Society* (Chicago: University of Chicago Press).

LAKOFF, G. (1984), *Classifiers as a Reflection of Mind* (Cognitive Science Report 19, Institute of Cognitive Studies; Berkeley: University of California).

—— (1987), *Women, Fire and Dangerous Things: What Categories Reveal about the Mind* (Chicago: University of Chicago Press).

LANGE, A. (1912), *In the Amazon Jungle: Adventures in Remote Parts of the Upper Amazon River, including a Sojourn among Cannibal Indians* (New York and London: G. P. Putnam's Sons, the Knickerbocker Press).

LEA, V. (1984), 'Brazil's Kayapó, cursed by gold', *National Geographic*, 165(5): 674–94.

—— (1986), 'Nomes e nekrets Kayapó: uma concepção de riqueza', Ph.D. thesis (Museu Nacional, Federal University of Rio de Janeiro).

—— (1994), 'Género Feminino Mẽbengokre (Kayapó): Desvelando Representaões Desgastadas. Núcleo de Estudos de Género', *Cadernos Pagu* (Campinas: Unicamp), 3: 85–116.

—— (1995), 'The Houses of the Mẽbengokre (Kayapó) of Central Brazil—A New Door to their Social Organization', in J. Carsten and S. Hugh-Jones (eds.), *About the House: Lévi-Strauss and beyond* (Cambridge: Cambridge University Press), 206–25.

LEACH, E. R. (1964 [1954]), *Political Systems in Highland Burma* (London: Bell).

—— (1982), *Social Anthropology* (Glasgow: Fontana Paperbacks).

—— (1984), 'Glimpses of the Unmentionable in the History of British Social Anthropology', *Annual Review of Anthropology*, 13: 1–23.

LEENHARDT, M. (1979 [1947]), *Do Kamo: Person and Myth in the Melanesian World*, trans. Basia Miller Gulati (Chicago: University of Chicago Press).

LEFEBVRE, H. (1966), *La Sociologie de Marx* (Paris: Presses Universitaires de France).

LEFÈVRE, F. (1989), 'Ressources génétiques et amélioration du manioc, Manihot esculenta Crantz, en Afrique', unpub. thesis (Paris: INAPG).

LÉVI-STRAUSS, C. (1943a), 'Guerre et commerce chez les Indiens d'Amérique du Sud', *Renaissance*, 1: 122–39.

—— (1943b), 'The Social Use of Kinship Terms among Brazilian Indians', *American Anthropologist*, 45: 398–409.

LÉVI-STRAUSS, C. (1958 [1956]), 'Les Organisations dualistes existent-elles?', in *Anthropologie structurale*, vol. i (Paris: Plon), 147–80.

—— (1966), *Mythologiques*, vol. ii: *Du miel aux cendres* (Paris: Plon).

—— (1967 [1949]), *Les Structures élémentaires de la parenté* (Paris: Mouton).

—— (1973), *Anthropologie structurale*, vol. ii (Paris: Plon).

—— (1984), *Paroles données* (Paris: Plon).

—— (1985), *La Potière jalouse* (Paris: Plon).

—— (1987), *Anthropology and Myth: Lectures 1951–1982* (Oxford: Blackwell).

—— (1991), *Histoire de Lynx* (Paris: Plon).

LITTLE, W., and HERRERA, A. (1995), *Populism and Reform in Contemporary Venezuela* (Institute of Latin American Studies, University of London, Occasional Papers 11).

LIZOT, J. (1984), *Les Yanômami Centraux* (Cahiers de l'Homme 22; Paris: EHESS).

—— (1994), 'Words in the Night: The Ceremonial Dialogue', in L. Sponsel and T. Gregor (eds.), *The Anthropology of Peace and Nonviolence* (Boulder: Lynne Rienner), 213–40.

LORIOT, J., LAURIAULT, E., and DAY, D. (1993), *Diccionario Shipibo–castellano* (Pucallpa: ILV).

LORRAIN, C. (1994), 'Making Ancestors: The Symbolism, Economics and Politics of Gender among the Kulina of Southwest Amazonia', unpub. doctoral thesis (King's College, University of Cambridge).

—— (1997), 'Symbolic Sexual Violence in Lowland South America: Is 'Male Dominance' a Western Construct?', paper presented at the 1st International Conference 'Beyond Boundaries: Sexuality Across Cultures' (Workshop: Sexuality and the Meaning of Violence; Amsterdam, 28 July–1 August).

—— (2000), 'Cosmic Reproduction, Economics and Politics among the Kulina of Southwest Amazonia', *Journal of the Royal Anthropological Institute*, 6(2): 293–310.

LYON, P. (1987), 'Language and Style in the Peruvian Montaña', in R. Auger *et al.* (eds.), *Ethnicity and Culture* (Calgary: University of Calgary Archaeological Association), 101–14.

MCCALLUM C. (1989*a*), 'The Ventriloquist's Dummy?', *Man*, 23(4): 560–1.

—— (1989*b*), 'Gender, Personhood and Social Organization among the Cashinahua of Western Amazonia', unpub. doctoral thesis (London School of Economics, University of London).

—— (1990), 'Language, Kinship and Politics in Amazonia', *Man*, 25(3): 412–33.

—— (1994), 'Ritual and the Origin of Sexuality in the Alto Xingu', in P. Harvey and P. Gow (eds.), *Sex and Violence: Issues in Representation and Experience* (London: Routledge), 90–114.

—— (1996), 'The Body that Knows: From Cashinahua Epistemology to a Medical Anthropology of Lowland South America', *Medical Anthropology Quarterly*, 10(3): 1–26.

MALINOWSKI, B. (1944), *A Scientific Theory of Culture and Other Essays* (Chapel Hill: University of North Carolina Press).

MANSUTTI, R. (1986), 'Hierro, barro cocido, curare y cerbetanas: el comercio intra e interét-nico entre los Uwotjuja', *Antropológica*, 65: 3–75.

MARX, K. (1906 [1867]), *Capital: A Critique of Political Economy* (New York: The Modern Library/Random House).

—— (1964 [1844]), *Economic and Philosophic Manuscripts of 1844* (New York: International Publishers).

MAYBURY-LEWIS, D. (1967), *Akwe Shavante Society* (New York and London: Oxford University Press).

—— (ed.) (1979*a*), *Dialectical Societies: The Gê and Bororo of Central Brazil* (Cambridge, Mass.: Harvard University Press).

—— (1979*b*), 'Introduction' and 'Conclusion', in Maybury-Lewis (1979*a*).

MEILLASSOUX, C. (1960), 'Essai d'interprétation du phénomène économique dans les sociétés traditionnelles d'auto-subsistance', *Cahiers d'Études Africaines*, 4: 38–67.

—— 1980 [1975]), *Femmes, greniers et capitaux* (Paris: Maspero).

MELATTI, J. C. (1970), 'O Sistema Social Krahó', unpub. doctoral diss. (University of Brasilia).

—— (1979), 'The Relationship System of the Krahó', in D. Maybury-Lewis (ed.), *Dialectical Societies: The Gê and Bororo of Central Brazil* (Cambridge, Mass.: Harvard University Press), 46–79.

—— (1981), *Povos Indígenas no Brasil, vol. 5* (São Paulo: Javari, CEDI).

MENGET, P. (1982 [1979]), 'Time of Birth, Time of Being: The Couvade', in M. Izard and P. Smith (eds.), *Between Belief and Transgression: Structuralist Essays in Religion, History and Myth* (Chicago: Chicago University Press), 193–209.

MENTORE, G. (1987), 'Waiwai Women: The Basis of Wealth and Power', *Man*, 22: 511–27.

MÉTRAUX, A. (1949), 'Weapons', *Handbook of South American Indians* vol. v (Washington, D.C.: Smithsonian), 229–63.

MILTON, K. (1994), 'No Pain, no Game', *Natural History*, 9: 44–51.

MOORE, S. F. (1987), 'Explaining the Present: Theoretical Dilemmas in Processual Ethnography', *American Ethnologist*, 149(4): 727–36.

—— (1994), 'The Ethnography of the Present and the Analysis of Process', in R. Borofsky (ed.), *Assessing Cultural Anthropology* (New York: McGraw-Hill), 362–74.

MORRISON, K. (1995), *Marx, Durkheim, Weber: Formations of Modern Social Thought* (London: Sage Publications).

MURPHY, R., and Murphy, Y. (1974), *Women of the Forest* (New York: Columbia University Press).

MYRDAL, G. (1954), *The Political Element in the Development of Economic Theory* (Cambridge, Mass.: Harvard University Press).

—— (1967), *Objectivity in Social Research* (New York: Pantheon Books).

NADELSON, L. (1981), 'Pigs, Women, and the Men's House in Amazonia: An Analysis of Mundurucú Myths', in S. B. Ortner and H. Whitehead (eds.), *Sexual Meanings: The Cultural Construction of Gender and Sexuality* (Cambridge: Cambridge University Press), 240–72.

NEEDHAM, R. (ed.) (1973), *Right and Left: Essays on Dual Symbolic Classification* (Chicago: University of Chicago Press).

OHNUKI-TIERNEY, E. (1990), 'Introduction: The Historicization of Anthropology', in E. Ohnuki-Tierney (ed.), *Culture Through Time: Anthropological Approaches* (Stanford: Stanford University Press), 1–25.

OKELY, J., and CALLAWAY, H. (eds.) (1992), *Anthropology and Autobiography* (London: Routledge).

OLSSEN, K. M., and SCHAAL, B. A. (1999), 'Evidence on the Origin of Cassava: Phylogeography of Manihot esculenta', *Proceedings of the National Academy of Science*, 96: 5586–91.

ORDINAIRE, O. (1887), 'Les Sauvages du Pérou', *Revue d'Ethnographie*, 6: 266–322.

OVERING, J. (1981), 'Amazonian Anthropology', review article, *Journal of Latin American Studies*, 13(1): 151–65.

OVERING, J. (1983–4), 'Elementary Structures of Reciprocity: A Comparative Note on Guianese, Central Brazilian, and North-West Amazon Socio-Political Thought', *Antropológica*, 59–62: 331–48.

—— (1985*a*), 'There is no End to Evil: The Guilty Innocents and their Fallible God', in D. Parkin (ed.), *The Anthropology of Evil* (Oxford: Basil Blackwell), 244–78.

—— (1985*b*), 'Today I shall call him Mummy: Multiple Words and Classificatory Confusion', in J. Overing (ed.), *Reason and Morality* (ASA Monograph No. 24; London: Tavistock Publications).

—— (1986*a*), 'Images of Cannibalism, Death and Domination in a "Non-Violent" Society', in D. Riches (ed.), *The Anthropology of Violence* (Oxford: Basil Blackwell), 86–102.

—— (1986*b*), 'Men Control Women? The "Catch 22" in the Analysis of Gender', *International Journal of Moral and Social Studies*, 1(2): 135–56.

—— (1988), 'Personal Autonomy and the Domestication of the Self in Piaroa Society', in I. M. Lewis and G. Jahoda (eds.), *Acquiring Culture: Cross-Cultural Studies in Child Development* (London: Croom Helm), 169–92.

—— (1989*a*), 'Styles of Manhood: An Amazonian Contrast in Tranquillity and Violence', in S. Howell and R. Willis (eds.), *Societies at Peace: Anthropological Perspectives* (London: Routledge), 79–99.

—— (1989*b*), 'The Aesthetics of Production: The Sense of Community among the Cubeo and Piaroa', *Dialectical Anthropology*, 14: 159–75.

—— (1992), 'Wandering in the Market and the Forest: An Amazonian Theory of Production and Exchange', in R. Dilley (ed.), *Contesting Markets* (Edinburgh: Edinburgh University Press), 180–200.

—— (1993*a*), 'Death and Loss of Civilised Predation among the Piaroa of the Orinoco Basin', in P. Descola and A.-C. Taylor (eds.), *La Remontée de l'Amazone: anthropologie et histoire des sociétés amazoniennes* (Special Edition of *L'Homme*, 126–8; Paris: Éditions des Hautes Études en Sciences Sociales), 191–211.

—— (1993*b*), 'The Anarchy and Collectivism of the "Primitive Other": Marx and Sahlins in the Amazon', in C. Hann (ed.), *The Anthropology of Socialism* (ASA Monograph Series; London: Routledge), 43–58.

PATIÑO, V. M. (1958), 'El cachipay o pijibay (Guilielma gasipaes bailey), y su papel en la cultura y en la economia de los pueblos indígenas de América tropical', *América Indígena*, 18(3): 177–204; (4): 299–332.

PINEDA, R. (1990), 'Convivir con las dantas', in F. Correa (ed.), *In La selva humanizada: ecología alternativa en el trópico húmedo colombiano* (Bogotá: ICAN), 147–65.

PINZÓN SANCHEZ, A. (1979), *Monopolios, misioneros y destrucción de indígenas* (Bogotá: Ediciones Armadillo).

POCOCK, D. (1973), 'The Ideal of a Personal Anthropology', paper read at ASA Decennial Conference (Oxford).

POWLISON, P. (1993), *La mitologia Yagua: Tendencias épicas en una Mitologia del Nuevo Mundo* (Comunidades y Culturas Peruanas 25; Yarinacocha: ILV).

—— (ed.) (1995), *Diccionario Yagua–Castellano* (Serie Linguistica Peruana 35; Yarinacocha: ILV).

QUIGLEY, D. (1999), 'What is Truth?', *Anthropology Today*, 15(4): 21.

RADCLIFFE-BROWN, A. R. (1952), *Structure and Function in Primitive Society* (New York: The Free Press).

—— (1967), *The Andaman Islanders* (New York: Free Press).

REICHEL-DOLMATOFF, G. (1971), *Amazonian Cosmos: The Sexual and Religious Symbolism of the Tukano Indians* (Chicago: University of Chicago Press).

—— (1989), 'Biological and Social Aspects of the Yuruparí Complex of the Colombian Vaupès Territory', *Journal of Latin American Lore*, 15(1): 95–135.

—— (1997), *Chamanes de la Selva Pluvial: Ensayos sobre los Indios Tukano del Noroeste Amazónico* (Dartington: Themis Books).

RENVOIZE, B. S. (1972), 'The Area of Origin of Manihot esculenta as a Crop Plant—a Review of the Evidence', *Economic Botany*, 26: 352–60.

RIVAL, L. (1993), 'The Growth of Family Trees: Understanding Huaorani Perceptions of the Forest', *Man*, 28(4): 635–52.

—— (1996a), 'Blowpipes and Spears: The Social Significance of Huaorani Technological Choices', in P. Descola and Gísli Pàlsson (eds.), *Nature and Society, Anthropological Perspectives* (London: Routledge), 145–64.

—— (1996b), *Hijos del sol, padres del jaguar: los Huaorani de ayer y hoy* (Quito: Abya-Yala).

—— (1998a), *El Niño Crisis in the North Rupununi Savannas of Guyana* (APFT Briefing Note 18; European Union, DG VIII, Brussels).

—— (1998b), 'Androgynous Parents and Guest Children: The Huaraoni Couvade', *Journal of the Royal Anthropological Institute*, 4(4): 619–42.

—— SLATER, D., and MILLER, D. (1998), *Sex and Sociality: Comparative Ethnographies of Sexual Objectification (Theory, Culture and Society*, Special issue on Love, Eroticism and Sexuality, 15(3–4)), 294–321.

RIVET, P., and TASTEVIN, C. (1938), 'Les Langues arawak du Purus et du Juru (Groupe arauá)', *Journal de la Société des Américanistes,* 30: 71–114, 235–88.

RIVIÈRE, P. (1963), 'An Ethnographic Survey of the Indians on the Divide of the Guianese and Amazonian River Systems', unpub. B.Litt. (University of Oxford).

—— (1965), 'The Social Organisation of the Trio Indians of Surinam', unpub. doctoral diss. (University of Oxford).

—— (1966a), 'A Note on Marriage with the Sister's Daughter', *Man* (NS), 1(4): 550–6.

—— (1966b), 'Age: A Determinant of Social Classification', *Southwestern Journal of Anthropology* 22(1): 43–60.

—— (1966c), 'Oblique Discontinuous Exchange: A New Formal Type of Prescriptive Alliance', *American Anthropologist*, 68(3): 738–40.

—— (1966d), 'A Policy for the Trio Indians of Surinam', *Nieuwe West-Indische Gids*, 45(2–3): 95–120 (incl. 6 photographs).

—— (1967a), 'The Caboclo and Brazilian Attitudes', *Bulletin of the Society for Latin American Studies*, 8: 18–21.

—— (1967b), 'The Honour of Sanchez', *Man* (NS), 2(4): 569–83.

—— (1969a), *Marriage among the Trio: A Principle of Social Organization* (Oxford: Clarendon Press).

—— (1969b), 'Myth and Material Culture: Some Symbolic Interrelations', in R. F. Spencer (ed.), *Forms of Symbolic Action* (Seattle: University of Washington Press), 151–66.

—— (1970a), 'Factions and Exclusions in Two South American Village Systems', in M. Douglas (ed.), *Witchcraft, Confessions and Accusations* (ASA Monographs 9; London: Tavistock), 245–56.

—— (1970b), *Primitive Marriage by J. F. McLennan* [1865] Classics in Anthropology; (Chicago: University of Chicago Press).

—— (1971a), 'The Political Structure of the Trio Indians as Manifested in a System of

Ceremonial Dialogue', in T. O. Beidelman (ed.), *The Translation of Culture* (London: Tavistock), 293–311.

RIVIÈRE, P. (1971*b*), 'Marriage: A Reassessment', in R. Needham (ed.), *Rethinking Kinship and Marriage* (ASA 11; London: Tavistock), 57–74.

—— (1972a), *The Forgotten Frontier: Ranchers of North Brazil* (New York: Holt, Rinehart and Winston).

—— (1972*b*), *Lucien Lévy-Bruhl by Jean Cazeneuve* (Explanations in Interpretative Sociology, gen eds. Philip Rieff and Bryan R. Wilson; Oxford: Basil Blackwell).

—— (1973), 'The lowland South American Culture Area: Towards a Structural Definition', paper presented at the 72nd American Anthropological Association meetings (New Orleans).

—— (1974*a*), 'The Couvade: A Problem Rreborn', *Man*, 9(3): 423–35.

—— (1974*b*), 'Some Problems in the Comparative Study of Carib Societies', *Atti de XL Congresso Internazionale degli Americanisti*, vol. ii (Genoa: Tilgher), 639–43.

—— (1975), *The Notebook on Primitive Mentality of Lucien Lévy-Bruhl* (Oxford: Basil Blackwell).

—— (1977), 'Some Problems in the Comparative Study of Carib Societies', in Ellen B. Basso (ed.), *Carib-Speaking Indians: Culture, Society and Language* (Anthropological Papers of the University of Arizona No. 28; Tucson: Arizona University Press), 39–41.

—— (1978*a*), *The Origin of Civilisation by John Lubbock* [1870] (Classics in Anthropology; Chicago: University of Chicago Press).

—— (1978*b*), book review of *Mehinahu: The Drama of Daily Life in a Brazilian Indian Village* by Thomas Gregor, *Man*, 13(2): 329–30.

—— (1980), 'Dialectical Societies', review article, *Man*, 15 (3): 533–40.

—— (1981), 'The Wages of Sin is Death: Some Aspects of Evangelisation among the Trio Indians', *Journal of the Anthropological Society of Oxford*, 12(1): 1–13.

—— (1983–4), 'Aspects of Carib Political Economy', in A. Butt Colson and H. D. Heinen (eds.), *Themes in Political Organization: The Caribs and their Neighbours* (*Antropológica*, 59–62), 349–58.

—— (1984), *Individual and Society in Guiana: A Comparative Study of Amerindian Social Organisation* (Cambridge: Cambridge University Press).

—— (1985), 'Unscrambling Parenthood: The Warnock Report', *Anthropology Today*, 1(4): 2–7.

—— (1987*a*), 'Of Women, Men and Manioc', in H. Skar and F. Salomon (eds.), *Natives and Neighbours in South America* (Gothenburg: Ethnographic Museum), 178–201.

—— (1987*b*), 'South American Indians: Indians of the Tropical Forest', in M. Eliade (ed.), *The Encyclopaedia of Religion* (New York: Macmillan), 472–82.

—— (1989*a*), 'Men and Women in Lowland South America', *Man*, 24(3): 570.

—— (1989*b*), 'New Trends in British Social Anthropology', *Cadernos do Noroeste*, 2(2–3): 7–23.

—— (1992), 'Baskets and Basketmakers of the Amazon', in L. Mowat, H. Morphy, and P. Dransart (eds.), *Basketmakers: Meaning and Form in Native American Baskets* (Pitt Rivers Museum: Monograph 5; Oxford), 147–58.

—— (1993), 'The Amerindianization of Descent and Affinity' (Special Edition of *L'Homme*, 126–8, vol. XXXIII (2–4): Paris; École des Hautes Études en Sciences Sociales), 507–16.

—— (1994*a* [1996]), 'WYSINWYG in Amazonia', *Journal of the Anthropological Society of Oxford*, 25(3): 255–62.

—— (1994*b*), 'Four Letters to Radcliffe-Brown from Durkheim and Mauss', *Journal of the Anthropological Society of Oxford*, 25(2): 169–78 (trans. and comm.).

—— (1995*a*), 'Ambiguous Environments', in M. Marner and M. Rosendahl (eds.), *Threatened peoples and Environments in the Americas*, Proceedings of the 48th International Congress of Americanists (Stockholm: Institute of Latin American Studies), 39–49.

—— (1995*b*), 'Houses, Places and People: Community and Continuity in Guiana', in J. Carsten and S. Hugh-Jones (eds.), *About the House: Lévi-Strauss and Beyond*, (Cambridge: Cambridge University Press), 189–205.

—— (1995*c*), *Absent-Minded Imperialism: Britain and the Expansion of Empire in Nineteenth-Century Brazil* (London: Tauris).

—— (1995*d*), 'William Robertson Smith and John Ferguson McLennan: The Aberdeen Roots of British Social Anthropology', in William Johnstone (ed.), *William Robertson Smith: Essays in Reassessment* (Journal for the Study of the Old Testament, Suppl. Ser. 189; Sheffield: Sheffield Academic Press), 292–302.

—— (1997), 'Carib Soul Matters—Since Fock', *Journal of the Anthropological Society of Oxford*, 28(2): 139–48.

—— (1998*a*), *Christopher Columbus* (Stroud, Glos.: Sutton Publishing).

—— (1998*b*), 'From Science to Imperialism: Robert Schomburgk's Humanitarianism', *Archives of Natural History*, 25 (1): 1–8.

—— (1999), 'Shamanism and the Unconfined Soul', in M. James and C. Crabbe (eds.), *From Soul to Self* (London and New York: Routledge), 70–88.

—— (2000*a*), 'Indians and Cow-Boys: Two Fields of Experience', in P. Dresch and D. Parkin (eds.), *Anthropologists in a Wider World* (New York and Oxford: Bergahn Books), 27–43.

—— (2000*b*), 'The more we are together . . .', in J. Overing and A. Passes (eds.), *The Anthropology of Love and Anger: The Aesthetics of Conviviality in Native Amazonia* (London: Routledge), 252–67.

—— (n.d.), 'The Native Amazonian Environment and Idioms of Knowledge', unpub. manuscript.

—— Lynch, C. M., and Bennett Dyle, I. (1983), 'Estimating Vital Rates from Incomplete Pedigrees', *Human Biology*, 55(1): 63–72.

—— Gaye, T. B., and Dyke, B. (1984*a*), 'Estimating Mortality from Two Censuses: An Application to the Trio of Surinam', *Human Biology*, 56(3): 489–501.

—— —— —— (1984*b*), 'The Population Dynamics and Fertility of the Trio of Surinam: An Application of a Two Census Method', *Human Biology*, 56(4): 691–701.

—— and Koelewijn, Cees (1987), *Oral Literature of the Trio Indians of Surinam* (Koninklijk Instituut voor Taal-, Land, en Volkenkunde, Caribbéan Studies 6; Dordrecht and Providence: Foris Publications).

Roe, P. G. (1982), *The Cosmic Zygote: Cosmology in the Amazon Basin* (New Brunswick: Rutgers University Press).

Romanoff, S. (1984), 'Matses Adaptations in the Peruvian Amazon', unpub. doctoral diss. (New York: Columbia University).

Rosengren, D. (1987), *In the Eyes of the Beholder: Leadership and the Social Construction of Power and Dominance among the Matsigenka of the Peruvian Amazon* (Etnologiska Studier 39; Göteborg: Ethnographic Museum).

ROTH, W. R. (1915), *An Inquiry into the Animism and Folklore of the Guiana Indians*, 30th Annual Report of the US Bureau of American Ethnology (Washington, DC: Smithsonian Institution).

SAHLINS, M. (1972), *Stone Age Economics* (London: Routledge).

—— (1981), *Historical Metaphors and Mythical Realities: Structure in the Early History of the Sandwich Islands Kingdom* (ASAO Special Public. 1; Ann-Arbor: University of Michigan Press).

—— (1983), 'Raw Women, Cooked Men, and Other "Great Things" of the Fiji Islands', in P. Brown and D. Tuzin (eds.), *The Ethnography of Cannibalism* (Washington, DC: Society for Psychological Anthropology), 72–93.

—— (1985), *Islands of History* (Chicago: University of Chicago Press).

—— (1994), 'Goodbye to Tristes Tropes: Ethnography in the Context of Modern World History', in R. Borofsky (ed.), *Assessing Cultural Anthropology* (New York: McGraw-Hill), 377–93.

SALICK, J., CELLINESE, N., and KNAPP, S. (1997), 'Indigenous Diversity of Cassava: Generation, Maintenance, Use and Loss among the Amuesha, Peruvian Upper Amazon', *Economic Botany*, 51(1): 6–19.

SANTILLI, P. (ed.) (1994), *As fronteiras da república: Historia e política entre o Macuxi no vale do río Branco* (NHU-USP, FAPESP, São Paulo).

SANTOS GRANERO, F. (1986), 'The Moral and Social Aspects of Equality amongst the Amuesha of Central Peru', *Journal de la Société des Américanistes*, 72: 107–31.

—— (1991), *The Power of Love: The Moral Use of Knowledge amongst the Amuesha of Central Peru* (London School of Economics Monographs in Social Anthropology 62; London: The Athlone Press).

SAX, W. S. (1998), 'The Hall of Mirrors: Orientalism, Anthropology, and the Other', *American Anthropologist*, 100(2): 292–301.

SCAZZOCCHIO, F. (1979), 'Curare Kills, Cures and Binds: Change and Persistence of Indian Trade in Response to the Contact Situation in North-Western Montaña', *Cambridge Anthropology*, 4(3): 30–57.

SCHECHNER, R. (1985), *Between Theater and Anthropology* (Philadelphia: University of Pennsylvania Press).

SCHEFFLER, H. (1984), 'Markedness and Extension: The Tamil Case', *Man*, 19: 557–74.

SCHNEIDER, D., and GOUGH, K. (1961), *Matrilineal Kinship* (Berkeley: University of California Press).

SCHOEPF, D. (1994), 'Une étrange massue pour affronter les Wayãpi ou les avatars de la technologie chez les Wayana de la région Brésil-Guyane', *Bulletin de la Société Suisse des Américanistes*, 57–8 (1993–4): 69–88.

SCHREMPP, G. (1992), *Magical Arrows: The Maori, the Greeks, and the Folklore of the Universe* (Madison: University of Wisconsin Press).

SEEGER, A. (1981), *Nature and Society in Central Brazil: The Suya Indians of Mato Grosso* (Cambridge, Mass.: Harvard University Press).

—— (1987), *Why Suyá Sing: A Musical Anthropology of an Amazonian People* (Cambridge: Cambridge University Press).

—— DA MATTA, R., and VIVEIROS DE CASTRO, E. (1979), 'A construáo da pessoa nas sociedades indígenas brasileiras', *Boletim do Museu Nacional—Antropología*, 32: 1–20.

SEYMOUR-SMITH, C. (1986), *Macmillan Dictionary of Anthropology* (London: Macmillan).

—— (1991), 'Women have no Affines and Men no Kin: The Politics of the Jivaroan Gender Relations', *Man*, 26(4): 629–49.

SHAPIRO, W. (1971), book review of *Marriage among the Trio* by Peter Rivière, *American Anthropologist*, 73(4): 851–2.

SHERZER, J. (1982), 'Poetic Structuring of Kuna Discourse: The Line', *Language in Society* 11: 371–90.

—— (1983), *Kuna Ways of Speaking* (Austin: University of Texas Press).

—— and URBAN, G. (1986), *Native South American Discourse* (New York: Mouton de Gruyter).

SILVESTRE, P., and ARRAUDEAU, M. (1983), *Le Cassava* (ACCT, collection techniques agricoles et productions tropicales; Maisonneuve et Larousse).

SISKIND, J. (1973), *To Hunt in the Morning* (Oxford: Oxford University Press).

—— (1978), 'Kinship and Mode of Production', *American Anthropologist*, 80(4): 860–72.

SORENSEN, A. P., Jr. (1967), 'Multilingualism in the Northwest Amazon', *American Anthropologist*, 69: 670–84.

—— (1969), 'The Morphology of Tukano', unpub. doctoral diss. (New York: Columbia University).

—— (1973), 'South American Indian Linguistics at the Turn of the Century', in Daniel Gross (ed.), *Peoples and Cultures of Native South America* (New York: Doubleday), 312–41.

SPERBER, D. (1981), 'L'Interprétation en anthropologie', *L'Homme*, 21(1): 69–92.

STEWARD, J. (ed.) (1948–56), *The Handbook of South American Indians* (Washington, DC: Smithsonian Institution Press).

STEWART, P., and STRATHERN, A. (1999), 'Feasting on My Enemy: Images of Violence and Change in the New Guinea Highlands', *Ethnohistory* 46(4): 645–70.

STRATHERN, M. (1987), 'Introduction', in M. Strathern (ed.), *Dealing with Inequality: Analysing Gender Relations in Melanesia and Beyond* (Cambridge: Cambridge University Press), 1–32.

—— (1988), *The Gender of the Gift: Problems with Women and Problems with Society in Melanesia* (Berkeley: University of California Press).

—— (1992), 'Parts and Wholes: Refiguring Relationships in a Post-Plural World', in *Reproducing the Future: Anthropology, Kinship, and the New Reproductive Technologies* (New York: Routledge), 90–116.

STRAUSS, C., and QUINN, N. (1997), *A Cognitive Theory of Cultural Meaning* (Cambridge: Cambridge University Press).

SULLIVAN, L. E. (1988), *Incanchu's Drum: An Orientation to Meaning in South American Religions* (New York: Macmillan).

SURALLÈS, A. (1998), 'Au cœur du sens: Objectivation et subjectivation chez les Candoshi de l'Amazonie péruvienne', unpub. doctoral thesis (Paris, EHESS).

TAUSSIG, M. (1987), *Shamanism, Colonialism and the Wildman: A Study of Terror and Healing* (Chicago: University of Chicago Press).

—— (1996), *The Magic of the State* (New York: Routledge).

TAYLOR, A-C. (1981), 'God-Wealth: The Achuar and the Missions', in N. Whitten (ed.), *Cultural Transformations and Ethnicity in Modern Ecuador* (Urbana: University of Illinois Press), 647–76.

—— (1983), 'The Marriage Alliance and its Structural Variations in Jivaroan Societies', *Social Science Information*, 22: 331–53.

—— (1985), 'L'Art de la réduction', *Journal de la Société des Américanistes*, 71: 159–73.

TAYLOR, A-C. (1993), 'Remembering to Forget: Identity, Mourning and Memory among the Jivaro', *Man* (NS), 28(4): 653–78.

—— (1994), 'Les Bons Ennemis et les mauvais parents: le traitement symbolique de l'alliance dans les rituels de chasse aux têtes des Jivaros de l'Equateur', in E. Copet and F. Héritier-Augé (eds.), *Les Complexités de l'alliance*, iv: *Économie, politique et fondements symboliques de l'alliance* (Paris: Éditions des Archives Contemporaines), 73–105.

—— (1996), 'The Soul's Body and its States: An Amazonian Perspective on the Nature of being Human', *Journal of the Royal Anthropological Institute*, 2(2): 201–15.

—— (1998), 'Corps immortels, devoir d'oubli: formes humaines et trajectoires de vie chez les Achuar', in M. Godelier and M. Panoff (eds.), *La Production du corps: approches anthropologiques et historiques* (Amsterdam: Éditions des archives contemporaines), 317–38.

—— (2000), 'Le Sexe de la proie. Représentations jivaro du lien de parenté', *L'Homme*, 154–5: 309–34.

—— and CHAU, E. (1983), 'Jivaroan Magical Songs: Achuar anent of Connubial Love', *Amerindia*, 8.

—— et al. (1986), 'Guerre et les visions du monde' (Special Issue), *Journal de la Société des Américanistes*, 72: 133–56.

TAYLOR, C. (1999), *Sacrifice as Terror: The Rwandan Genocide of 1994*, (Oxford: Berg).

TEDLOCK, D. (1977), 'Toward Oral Poetics', *New Oral/Literary History*, 8(3): 507–19.

—— (1983), *The Spoken Word and the Work of Interpretation* (Philadelphia: University of Pennsylvania Press).

TESSMANN, G. (1930), *Die Indianer Nordost-Perus* (Hamburg: Friederichsen, de Gruyter).

THOMAS, D. J. (1972), 'The Indigenous Trade System of Southeast Estado Bolívar, Venezuela', *Antropológica*, 30: 3–37.

—— (1982), *Order without Government: The Society of the Pemon Indians of Venezuela* (Urbana: University of Illinois Press).

TOWNSLEY, G. (1993), 'Song Paths: The Ways and Means of Yaminahua Shamanic Knowledge', in P. Descola and A.-C. Taylor (eds.), *La Remontée de l'Amazone: anthropologie et histoire des sociétés amazoniennes* (Special Edition of *L'Homme*, 126–8; Paris: Éditions des Hautes Études en Sciences Sociales), 449–68.

TREXLER, R. (1995), *Sex and Conquest: Gendered Violence, Political Order, and the European Conquest of the Americas* (Ithaca: Cornell University Press).

TURNER, T. (1966), 'Social Structure and Political Organization among the Northern Kayapó', Ph.D. thesis (Harvard University).

—— (1979a), 'The Gê and Bororo Societies as Dialectical Systems', in D. Maybury-Lewis (ed.), *Dialectical Societies: The Gê and Bororo of Central Brazil* (Cambridge, Mass.: Harvard University Press), 147–78.

—— (1979b), 'Kinship, Household and Community Structure among the Kayapó', in D. Maybury-Lewis (ed.), *Dialectical Societies: The Gê and Bororo of Central Brazil* (Cambridge, Mass.: Harvard University Press), 179–217.

—— (1980), 'The Social Skin', in J. Cherfas and R. Lewin (eds.), *Not Work Alone* (Beverly Hills: Sage), 112–40.

—— (1984), 'Dual Opposition, Hierarchy, and Value: Moyety Structure and Symbolic Polarity in Central Brazil and Elsewhere', in J. C. Galey (ed.), *Différences, valeurs, hiérarchie: textes offerts à Louis Dumont* (Paris: Éditions de l'EHESS), 335–70.

—— (1986), 'Production, exploitation and social consciousness in the peripheral situation', *Social Analysis*, 19: 91–5.